The Expositor's Bible
The Book Of Deuteronomy

by

Andrew Harper

Double 9
BOOKS

The Expositor's Bible
The Book Of Deuteronomy
by Andrew Harper

Copyright © 2024

All Rights reserved.

ISBN: 978-93-61159-83-1

Published by

DOUBLE 9 BOOKS

2/13-B, Ansari Road
Daryaganj, New Delhi – 110002
info@double9books.com
www.double9books.com
Tel. 011-40042856

ABOUT THE AUTHOR

Andrew Harper was a Scottish-Australian biblical scholar, educator, and school and university college principal. Harper was born at 167 Main Street in Glasgow's Gorbals, Scotland, as the son of grocer Robert Harper and his wife Elizabeth, née Calderwood. After some basic studies at The Glasgow Academy, he relocated to Australia and enrolled at Scotch College in Melbourne. Harper joined the civil service, passed the University of Melbourne's matriculation examination in 1864, and graduated with a BA in 1868. Harper then attended the University of Edinburgh, where he earned a BD in 1872 and received the Cunningham fellowship. Harper was an excellent speaker and debater who wielded considerable power in the Presbyterian Church of Australia, particularly among ministerial candidates who studied under him. He had firm convictions but understood the hardships of others. Personally, he was modest and completely sincere, devoted to the Christian faith while believing in scientific investigation, a wise and empathetic mentor during a time of transition and reshaping, when many previously held ideas were being challenged. Harper retired as Principal of St Andrew's College in 1921 and as Professor in May 1924, when he was 80 years old. He retired to Edinburgh and died on November 25, 1936, twelve days after his 92nd birthday.

CONTENTS

PREFACE

An adequate exposition of Deuteronomy requires the discussion of many topics. The author has endeavoured to keep these various claims in view: at the same time the limits of the volume have dictated selection and compression. In particular, a chapter on miracle in the Old Testament has been wholly omitted. That topic cannot be said to have a peculiar or exclusive relation to Deuteronomy. Yet the writer would have wished to include in the volume a reasoned statement of the grounds on which he owns and asserts the supernatural in Old Testament history; all the more because he admits critical views which have sometimes been associated, and still oftener supposed to be associated, with rationalistic views generally. For the present this discussion is postponed. In some instances, also, the writer has been obliged to content himself with statements on critical questions more brief than he could have desired; but it is hoped that enough has been said to explain the position assumed, and to make clear the main lines of argument.

The task of adjusting the matter to the space would have been easier if it had seemed legitimate to omit the critical and archæological questions on the one hand, or, on the other, to leave untouched the bearing of the thoughts and Laws of Deuteronomy on the religious history of the race, and on the dangers and duties of our own age. But an exposition of Deuteronomy must endeavour to open the appropriate outlooks in all these directions.

Owing to the author's distance from London the work of passing the book through the press has necessarily been left wholly to others. It is hoped that oversights which may have arisen from this cause will be pardoned.

CHAPTER I
THE AUTHORSHIP AND AGE
OF DEUTERONOMY

In approaching a book so spiritually great as Deuteronomy, it might seem superfluous to allude to the critical questions which have been raised concerning it. On any supposition as to origin and authorship, its spiritual elevation and the moral impulse it gives are always there; and it might consequently seem sufficient to expound and illustrate the text as we have it. Minute and vexatious inquiry into details, such as any adequate treatment of the critical question demands, tends to draw away the mind, in a disastrous way, from the spiritual and moral purpose of the book. That however is precisely what the expositor has to elucidate and apply; and so it might seem to be an error in method to enter upon extraneous matters such as those with which criticism has mainly to do.

On the other hand, this has to be taken into account. The truth about the composition of a book, about the authorities it is founded on, about the times in which and the circumstances under which it was composed, if it be attainable, often throws a very welcome light upon the meaning. It clears up obscurities, removes chances of error, and often, when two or three possible paths have opened before us, it shuts us up to the right one. But if that is the case when no special conflict of opinion has arisen, it is much more so when a revolution of opinion concerning the whole religious life of a nation has been caused by the critical view of a book adopted by able men. Now that is plainly the case here. Deuteronomy has been the key of the position, the centre of the conflict, in the battle which has been waged so hotly as to the growth of religion in Israel. The attack upon the views hitherto generally held within the Church in regard to that matter has rested more upon the character and date of Deuteronomy than upon anything else. Consequently every part of the book has been the object of intense and microscopic scrutiny, and there is scarcely a cardinal point in it which must not be regarded differently, according as we accept or reject the strictly Mosaic origin of the book as a whole, or even of the legal portions. The difference is probably never absolutely fundamental. On either supposition, as we have said, the spiritual and moral teaching remains the same; but the mind is apt to be clouded with harassing doubt as to many important points, until clear views on the critical question have been attained. This is felt more or less acutely by all readers of the Old Testament who are touched by recent debates, and they expect that any new exposition shall help them to a clearer view. Many will even demand that some effort in that direction should be made; and, as we think, they rightly demand it.

But there is still another reason for dealing with the questions gathering round the authorship and age of our book, and it is decisive. The debate concerning the critical views of the Old Testament has reached a stage at which it is no longer confined to the professed teachers and students of the Old Testament. It has filtered down, through magazines first, and then through newspapers, into the public mind, and opinions are becoming current concerning the results of criticism which are so partial and ill-informed that they cannot but produce evil results of a formidable kind in the near future. By those who are sceptically inclined, as well as by those who cling most closely to the teaching of the Churches, it is loudly proclaimed that the acceptance of the critical view—viz. that the Levitical law, as a written code, came into existence after the Exile, and that Deuteronomy, written in the royal period of Israelite history, occupies a middle position between the first legislation (Exod. xx.-xxiii.) and this latest—destroys the character of the Old Testament as a record of Revelation, and undermines Christianity itself. The former class rejoice that this should be so, and think their scepticism is thereby justified. The latter, on the contrary, reject the critical conclusions with vehemence. They have found God through the Scripture, and, resting upon this experience, they turn away from theories which they believe to be in direct conflict with it. To write an exposition of Deuteronomy therefore, without correcting the false impression that the critical view as to its age, etc., is incompatible with faith in a Divine revelation, would be to miss one of the great opportunities which fall to writers on the Old Testament in our day. Questions regarding the age, authorship, and literary form of the books of Scripture cannot ultimately be so decided as to nullify the testimony borne to them by the experience of so many generations of Christian men and women. Whatever makes itself ultimately credible to the human mind in regard to such matters, will always be capable of being held along with a belief in the manifestation of Himself which God has given in the history and literature of Israel. But nothing will make that fact so readily apprehensible, nothing will make it stand out so clearly, as an exposition of a book like Deuteronomy, which takes account of all that seems established in the critical view. Even the most extreme critical positions, when separated from the totally irrelevant assumption (which too often accompanies them) that miracle is unhistorical, are compatible with a real faith in Revelation and Inspiration. It is not the fact of Revelation, but the common conception of its method, which is challenged by the critical theories. We shall therefore only try to meet a clamant need of our time, if we take with us into the explanation of the Deuteronomic teaching a definite conclusion as to the authorship, age, and literary character of the book.

As regards authorship, the ordinary opinion still is that Deuteronomy was written by Moses. This was the view handed over to Christianity in pre-critical ages by the Jews, and accepted as the natural one. But if the Mosaic authorship of the whole contents of the other books of the Pentateuch is now given up, much more should it be given up in the case of Deuteronomy. For Deuteronomy does not even claim to be written by Moses. It is not merely that in it Moses is often spoken of in the third person; that, if it were carried out consistently, as it is, for instance, in Cæsar's Commentaries, would be compatible with Mosaic authorship. But what we find is that the author, "whenever he speaks himself, purports to give a description in the third person of what Moses did or said,"[1] while Moses, when he speaks, always uses the first person. The book, consequently, falls naturally into two portions: the subsidiary, introductory framework of statement, in which Moses is always spoken of in the third person, together with the historical portions; and the utterances of Moses himself, which these introduce and hold together, and in which Moses always uses the first person.[2] Again, wherever the expression "beyond Jordan" is used in the portions where the author speaks for himself, it signifies the land of Moab.[3] Wherever, on the contrary, Moses is introduced speaking in the first person, "beyond Jordan" denotes the land of Israel.[4] The only exception is iii. 8, where at the beginning of a long archæological note, which cannot have originally formed part of the speech of Moses, and consequently must be a comment of the writer, or of a later editor of Deuteronomy, "beyond Jordan" signifies the land of Moab. If, consequently, the book be taken at its word, there can be no doubt that it professes to be an account of what Moses did and said on a certain day in the land of Moab, before his death, written by another person, who lived to the west of the Jordan. The author must consequently have lived after Moses' day; and he has taken pains by his use of language to distinguish himself from Moses in a most unmistakable way. It is no doubt possible, though not probable, that Moses might have written of himself in the third person in the connecting passages, and in the first person in the remainder of his book: but that he should have made the anxious distinction we have seen as to the phrase "beyond Jordan" does not seem possible.

But if our book, as we have it, is not by Moses, but is an account by another person of what Moses did and said on a certain occasion, that fact has a very important bearing upon the speeches reported as Mosaic. For the style of the whole book up to the end of the twenty-eighth chapter is, for all practical purposes, one. The parts where the author speaks, and the parts where Moses speaks, are all alike in style, and that style is in all respects different from the style of the speeches attributed to Moses in other parts of the Pentateuch. Consequently we cannot accept the speeches and laws as being in the very words of Moses. They may contain the exact ideas of Moses, but these have manifestly passed through the mind and clothed themselves in the vocabulary of the author of Deuteronomy. Even Delitzsch is quite decisive on this point.[5] In the tenth of his *Pentateuch Kritische Studien*, after distinguishing the Deuteronomist from Moses, he continues thus: "The addresses are freely reproduced, and he who reproduces them is the same who also contributed the historical framework and the historical details between the addresses. The same colouring, though in a less degree, may also be remarked in the repetition of the law in chapters xii.-xxvi. to which the book owes its name. All the component parts of Deuteronomy, not excepting the legal prescriptions, are woven through and through with the favourite phrases of the Deuteronomist."

Under these circumstances, the question immediately suggests itself to what degree this representation of Moses' legislation can be regarded as purely and unmixedly Mosaic. Was this legislation given in the main or entirely by Moses, and, if it was so given, may there not be mingled with what he gave inferences drawn by the author in whose style the book is written, and adaptations demanded by the exigencies of his later times? A full discussion of this point would, of course, be out of the question here, and it would, moreover, be superfluous. In Dr. Driver's article on "Deuteronomy" in Smith's *Dictionary of the Bible*, and in his *Introduction to Hebrew Literature*, detailed discussions will be found. All that is necessary here is that one or two large and salient aspects of the question should be looked at.

In the first place, it is important to know whether the author of Deuteronomy can have been a contemporary of Moses, or a younger contemporary of his contemporaries. If he were, the relation between the speeches and legislation in his book and that which Moses actually uttered would be similar to that between the speeches of Christ reported by St. John in his Gospel and the actual words of our Lord. They might, in fact, be taken to be in all respects a reliable, though not a verbal, representation of what Moses actually said or commanded. If, on the contrary, it should be proved, either from the character of the legislation itself, or from the evidence we have as to the date of the authorities whom the Deuteronomist quotes, and upon whom he relies, that he must have lived centuries later, then any such confidence would be materially weakened. Now there can be no doubt, to take the last point first, that Deuteronomy, taken as a legal code, though not wanting in laws which have been first formulated by its author, is mainly intended to be a repetition and a reinforcement of what we find in the Book of the Covenant (Exod. xx.-xxiii.). The result of Driver's careful tabulation of the subjects dealt with in the two codes is "that the laws in JE,[6] viz. Exod. xx.-xxiii. (repeated partially in xxxiv. 10-26) and the kindred section xiii. 3-16, *form the foundations of the Deuteronomic legislation.* This is evident as well from the numerous verbal coincidences as from the fact that nearly the whole ground covered by Exod. xx.-xxiii. is included in it; almost the only exception being the special compensations to be paid for various injuries (Exod. xxi. 18, xxii. 15), which would be less necessary in a manual intended for the people." This is also the conclusion of other scholars, and indeed is plainly demanded by the facts. It is, moreover, what may be called the Biblical hypothesis, for Moses is supposed to have been renewing the covenant made at Horeb, and repeating its conditions.

But in the present condition of our knowledge, the fact of Deuteronomy's dependence upon the Book of the Covenant brings into view unexpected consequences. It is true, certainly, that the laws of the latter code existed before they were incorporated in the text where we now find them. Consequently no verbal coincidences would give us the assurance that the Deuteronomist had before him the actual book in which these laws have come down to us. But a conclusion may be reached in another way. A comparison of the historical portions of Deuteronomy with the corresponding narrative in the previous four books of our Bible shows that for his history also the author of Deuteronomy relies upon these earlier narratives, and that he must have had portions at least of them before him in the same text as we have now. The verbal coincidences tabulated in Driver, pp. 75 f., as well as the general and exact agreement in the events recorded in Deuteronomy with those recorded in the earlier books, show that the author has not only drawn his information from the same sources as those of the earlier books, but that he must have had before him at least that section which contains the laws.

Now, as it happens, in the course of the analysis of the Pentateuch it has come to be all but universally acknowledged that Exod. xx.-xxiii. form part of a document which can be traced, dovetailed into others, from Genesis to Joshua, and perhaps beyond it. This document has been called by Wellhausen the Jehovist document, and in all critical books it is referred to as JE, as being made up of two sections, one of which uses Yahweh for the Divine name, and the other Elohim. The only generally known scholar who denies the existence of JE is Professor Green, of Princeton in America, who, rightly enough, sees that the Mosaic authorship of the Pentateuch cannot be held, if these separate component documents are acknowledged. But the separate existence and character of JE may be regarded as demonstrated, and also that it has been interwoven with another narrative, largely parallel, but which deals of preference with priestly matters, and has consequently been called the Priest codex, or P. Together these make up the first four books of the Pentateuch; and the remarkable thing is that, both as regards law and history, Deuteronomy is dependent upon JE. "Throughout the parallels just tabulated," says Driver,[7] "(as well as in the others occurring in the book), not the allusions only, but the words cited, will be found, all but uniformly, to be in JE, not in P. An important conclusion follows from this fact. Inasmuch as, in our existing Pentateuch, JE and P repeatedly cross one another, the constant absence of any reference to P can only be reasonably explained by one supposition, viz. that when Deuteronomy was composed JE and P were not yet united into a single work, and JE alone formed the basis of Deuteronomy." And this is not Driver's conclusion only. Dillmann, who argues with splendid ability against Wellhausen for the dating of P in the ninth century B.C. instead of after the Exile, and consequently considers that it was in existence before Deuteronomy, still holds that in general JE is the Deuteronomist's authority both for law and history, contenting himself with affirming that D shows undoubted acquaintance with laws, etc., known *to us* only in P. Clearly, therefore, Deuteronomy must have been written after JE had been made public, or at least after J and E had been written.

The question therefore arises, what is their date? An answer can be gradually approached in this way. As JE reappear as an element in the Book of Joshua,[8] and contribute to it an account of Joshua's death and burial, they cannot have been written by him, nor before his death. That is the first fixed point. Then we may proceed a step further. In various parts of JE there occur phrases which cannot all be later glosses, and which imply that the land, when the writer lived, had long ceased to be in possession of the Canaanites, if some of them do not even presuppose a time when the original inhabitants had been absorbed into Israel, as Solomon attempted to absorb them by making them slaves of the State. Such passages are Gen. xii. 6, "And the Canaanite was then in the land"; Gen. xiii. 7, "Moreover the Canaanites and the Perizzites dwelled then in the land"; Gen. xl. 15, in which Joseph says of himself, "I was stolen away out of the land of the Hebrews," a name which the country could not have acquired till some little time at least after the conquest. Further, in Numbers xxxii. 41, which belongs to J or E, probably the latter, we have an account of the rise of the name Hawwoth Jair. Now in Judges x. 3-5 we are informed that the Jair from whom the Hawwoth Jair had their name was a judge in Israel after the time of Abimelech, who made new conquests for his tribe east of the Jordan. Unless, therefore, the unlikely hypothesis be accepted that both the district bearing this name in Judges and its conqueror are other than those mentioned in Numbers, the verse brings down JE at least to the period of Abimelech, which Kautzsch in his *View of the History of the Israelites*, appended to his translation of the Old Testament, states as about 1120 B.C., *i.e.* two hundred years after the Exodus.

The next step is suggested by Gen. xxxvi. 31-39, a passage from JE in which a list of Edomite kings is given with this heading: "These are the kings that reigned in the land of Edom before there reigned any king over the children of Israel." That sentence clearly cannot have been written before kings arose in Israel; consequently JE must be later than the days of Saul, and probably than David, since the Israelite kingship appears to the author's mind here as a firmly established institution. The author of Deuteronomy must have lived and written at a still later date, and we are thus gradually brought down to the time of Solomon, or perhaps even later.

And the literary indications of date confirm this conclusion. For instance, two books are quoted occasionally in JE as authorities, which must consequently have existed before that work—the Book of the Wars of Yahweh (Numb. xxi. 14, 15), and the Book of Yashar (Josh. x. 12 f.). The former has indeed been declared by Geiger to be the product of false punctuation; but soberer critics have accepted it and date it in Solomon's day. However that may be, there can be no doubt that the latter actually existed, and was probably a collection of songs, since from it the verses describing the standing still of the sun and moon are quoted. But we learn from 2 Sam. i. 18 that David's beautiful lament for Saul and Jonathan was contained in this book, and was quoted from it by the sacred historian. The book must therefore have been compiled, or at least completed, after David's lament. As it was manifestly a compilation, and the poems it contained may have been of very various ages, much stress in our search for dates cannot be laid upon it. It is still of some weight, however, that this post-Davidic book is quoted by JE; so far as it goes, that fact confirms the conclusion arrived at from other indications.

In the same way, the linguistic indications, though not of themselves conclusive, point towards the same period. It is, of course, true that we are as yet far from having a general agreement as to the history of the Hebrew language. That can only be established along with the history of the Hebrew literature and the Hebrew people; and perhaps we never shall be able to fix any definite stages in the growth and decay of the language. Nevertheless no careful reader of JE will deny what Professor Driver says regarding them: "Both belong to the golden period of Hebrew literature. They resemble the best parts of Judges and Samuel (much of which cannot be greatly later than David's own time); but whether they are actually earlier or later than these, the language and style do not enable us to say. There is at least no *archaic* flavour perceptible in the style of JE."[9] That is an admirably balanced judgment, and we may rely upon the indication it gives as an additional confirmation of what we have already seen to be probable.

It is impossible that these various lines of inquiry should converge, as they have done, towards the early centuries of the kingship as the date of JE, if Moses had written Deuteronomy, in which JE is drawn upon at every moment. We may consequently dismiss that view finally, and admit that the author of Deuteronomy cannot well have written before the middle of the kingly period. But we have still to inquire what the character of the Mosaic speeches and the Mosaic writings given in Deuteronomy is in that case. Had the author lived and written near the time of Moses, we might, as has been said, have accepted them as the Church generally accepts the Johannine speeches of Christ. But if the Deuteronomist wrote four, or five, or six centuries after Moses, what are we to say? In one view it must be granted that his account may be as accurate as if it had been written within fifty years of Moses' death. For an author of our own day, by keeping close to original written authorities, and strenuously endeavouring to keep out of his mind any information he may have as to later times, may reproduce with marvellous correctness the actual state of things, as regards law and other departments of public life, which existed in England, say, five hundred years ago. Similarly the author of Deuteronomy *may* have handed on to us, without flaw or defect, the information as to Moses' sayings and doings in the plains of Moab which he had received from the written accounts of Moses' contemporaries. He may have done so; but when we consider that his authorities may have been in part not much earlier than his own time, that the critical sifting of history was then unknown, and finally and most important of all, that the Deuteronomist has hortatory much more than purely historical aims, we cannot evade the question whether a good deal that is here set down to Moses may not turn out to be additions to and deductions from the original Mosaic germs of law, made by inspired law-givers and prophets who took up and carried on Moses' work. Many assert that this is so, and we must face and try to settle the question they raise.

The theory held by those who most strenuously deny this assertion is that all the laws in the Pentateuch are Mosaic in the strict sense, that the codes were given by Moses in the order in which they now stand in the Pentateuch, and that they were enacted with all their modifications in a period of not more than forty years, all of which was spent in the desert. In order to ascertain whether this view is tenable, we shall take one or two of the more important matters, such as the place of worship, the agents of worship, and the support of the cultus; and we shall compare the provisions of the various codes in order to see whether they can be supposed to belong to so short a period, or to have been all enacted by one man.

Let us take first the place of worship. The three codes—that called the Book of the Covenant (Exod. xx.-xxiii.), that contained in Leviticus and Numbers and called the Levitical code, and that in Deuteronomy—all contain directions about this. In the first the prescriptions are (Exod. xx. 24): "An altar of earth shalt thou make to Me, and thou shalt sacrifice upon it thy burnt offerings and thy peace offerings, thy sheep and thy oxen. In every place where I cause My name to be remembered I will come unto and bless thee." In the Levitical law "the altar" is to be of Shittim or acacia wood overlaid with copper, and the place for it is to be in the court of the Tabernacle. There all sacrifices are to be offered, and thither every slaughtered animal is to be brought (Lev. xvii. 1 ff.), and this is to be a statute for ever unto them throughout their generations. In Deuteronomy again (chap. xii.) it is enacted that all sacrifices are to be brought "unto the place which Yahweh your God shall choose out of all your tribes to put His name there," and ver. 21, "If the place which Yahweh thy God hath chosen to put His name there be too far from thee, then thou shalt kill of thy herd and of thy flock" and eat them as game was eaten without bringing it to the Sanctuary. But Moses is not represented as ordering this law to be introduced immediately. It is only when they go over Jordan and dwell in the land which Yahweh their God giveth them, and when He giveth them rest from all their enemies round about so that they dwell in safety, that they are to do this. Nay, according to ver. 20 the new order is to be fully introduced only when Yahweh their God shall enlarge their border as He had promised, *i.e.* when their boundaries should be (xi. 24) the wilderness on the south and Lebanon on the north, the Euphrates on the east and the Mediterranean on the west. Now these boundaries were attained only in David's day, and the rest from all their enemies round about was, as Dillmann says, given as a matter of fact only in the times of David and Solomon (cf. 2 Sam. vii. 11 and 1 Kings v. 18), notwithstanding Josh. xxi. 42. Consequently the Temple at Jerusalem must have been the place referred to. This is distinctly the view of 1 Kings iii. 3 and viii. 16. The latter passage is peculiarly emphatic. Solomon says, at the dedication of the Temple, "Since the day that I brought forth My people Israel out of Egypt, I chose no city out of all the tribes of Israel to build an house that My name might be therein." The Deuteronomic view consequently is that the law requiring sacrifice at *one* sole altar was intended by Moses to be enforced only after the Temple at Jerusalem had been built.

These are the provisions of the three codes. Can they have been the successive ordinances of a man legislating under the influence of Divine inspiration within a period of less than forty years? Let us see. The first legislation was given at Sinai, in the third month after the Exodus: the Levitical legislation on the matter was given about nine months later when the Tabernacle was finished, and during that time they had not removed from Sinai: thirty-eight years afterwards the Deuteronomic code was given in the plains of Moab. Let us look at the character of the legislation given first of all at Sinai. The meaning of the decisive phrase, "In every place where I cause My name to be remembered I will come unto thee and bless thee," has been much discussed; yet taken as it stands, without reference to laws which on any supposition are later, it cannot mean that sacrifices were to be offered only at one central shrine. It specially provides for sacrifices being offered at different places, but restricts them to places which Yahweh Himself has chosen. At every such place He promises to come to them and bless them. So much, men of all schools admit; difference of opinion arises only as to whether these places are meant to be successive, or whether they may be simultaneous. The view of those who accept all the legislation of the Pentateuch as Mosaic in the strict sense is that the places could only be successive, since otherwise the words would imply that originally worship at one altar was not prescribed. Delitzsch, for example, maintains that these words imply necessarily only this, that the place of sacrifice would, in the course of time, be altered by Divine appointment, and he declares that to be their meaning. Others, again, suppose that the command was meant only to justify worship at the various places where the Tabernacle was called to halt on the people's journeyings, whether in the wilderness or in Palestine. Now it cannot be denied that only on some such interpretation can Exodus be brought into harmony with Leviticus, and that undoubtedly has influenced, and rightly so, the scholars who take this view. If it were tenable it would be by far the most satisfactory interpretation. But it can hardly be considered tenable if we look at the time at which this law was given. There was as yet no other law, and this was given as soon as the people came to Mount Sinai. The law in Leviticus was not on any supposition given till nine months later. Now, if Exod. xx. 24 was meant for immediate use only, and was superseded by the Levitical law after so short a time, it is difficult to understand why it was given, and still more difficult to conceive why it was preserved. In any case it cannot have been understood to command worship at only one place. It could have no other sense than that the people, so long as they were at Sinai, were to sacrifice only at Sinai where Yahweh had revealed Himself, or at other places in the neighbourhood which He should sanctify, or had sanctified, by revealing His presence at them. At any such place, if there He had once revealed Himself, He would continue to meet them. Without the colour thrown upon them by succeeding laws, that is surely the only meaning that *could* be put upon the words, and so understood they undoubtedly authorise sacrifice at two or more places simultaneously. If, on the other hand, this law was meant more for the future than the present, as some of the laws in the Book of the Covenant undoubtedly were, it must have been intended to be in force concurrently with Lev. i. f. But if so, the "places" it refers to cannot be the mere halting-places on the wilderness journey. No doubt these were determined by Yahweh, and the tabernacle was set up at places He may be said to have chosen, but the places themselves were of no consequence at all. The Divine presence is declared to be always in the Tabernacle. That was certainly a place where Yahweh caused His name to be remembered, and without further inquiry about place, the men of Israel knew that He would always meet them and bless them in sacrifice there. The different character of the altar in the Book of the Covenant too, a mere heap of earth or unhewn stone, and that in the Tabernacle, made of acacia wood overlaid with copper, corroborates the view that the altar aimed at in Exod. xxiv. is not the Tabernacle altar. The only coherent view, on the supposition of the concurrence of the two laws, is therefore that while, as a rule, sacrifice was to be offered at the Tabernacle, yet if the people came to any place where Yahweh had caused His name to be remembered, sacrifice might be offered there on an altar of earth or unhewn stone, as well as at the Tabernacle. Either way therefore there is permission to worship at more than one place. But then the difficulty is that Leviticus appears to denounce upon pain of being "cut off from the people" absolutely every sacrifice not offered at the Tabernacle.

Now if so far matters have been far from clear on the traditional supposition of the date and order of these codes, a glance at Deuteronomy will produce absolute confusion in every mind. As we have seen, Deuteronomy represents Moses as restricting sacrifice most rigorously to one altar after the building of the Temple at Jerusalem, but virtually declaring that worship at various shrines was to be blameless until that time. We have also seen that that is the view taken by the author of the Book of Kings. Now this might be regarded as a temporary relaxation of the law, intended to meet the difficult circumstances of a period of war and conquest, were it not for one thing. That is, that Moses in Deut. xii. 8, after prescribing worship at one altar, adds, "Ye shall not do after all that *we* do here this day, every man whatsoever is right in his own eyes," and as if to render mistake as to the meaning impossible, in ver. 13 he explains ver. 8 thus: "Take heed to thyself that thou offer not thy burnt offerings in every place that thou seest." Notwithstanding the efforts of conservative scholars like Keil and Bredenkamp to explain ver. 8 as a reference to the intermissions in, *e.g.*, the daily sacrifice, brought about by the desert wanderings, or to the arbitrariness and illegality of the generation which had brought judgment upon themselves by refusal to obey Yahweh in attacking Canaan, it still seems impossible to accept that view. Of course if we knew that Moses was the giver of all these laws, these words would have to be explained away in some such fashion. But if they are approached by an inquirer seeking to discover whether they all are Mosaic, sound exegesis demands that they should be taken as Dillmann and others take them. In the plain sense of words Moses here admits that, up till the time at which he is speaking, sacrifices were offered wherever men chose, and that he had participated in the practice. And observe, he does not refer to the Levitical law. He does not say this conduct of ours is a sin which we must repent of and turn from at once. He calmly permits this state of things to continue after Israel is in Canaan, and looks forward with equanimity to its continuance till the Temple shall be erected in Jerusalem. With this passage before us we ask, Can this be the same inspired legislator who thirty-eight years before compelled sacrifice at one central altar on pain of death?

The traditional hypothesis being thus encompassed with difficulties, students of the Old Testament have sought another which would correspond better with all the data. Relying upon the fact that the author of Deuteronomy founds his book almost entirely on JE, and that if he knows some of the laws and some of the facts mentioned in P only, there are no proofs that he knew that book as we have it, they put it aside in this matter also. Immediately, when that is done, light breaks in upon our problem. If we take Exod. xxiv. 20 in the natural sense given to it above, sacrifice at various altars was permitted from Sinai onwards, the only limitation being that there should have been, at the place chosen, authentic proof of a theophany or some other manifestation of the Divine presence. That is the state of things out of which Moses speaks in Deuteronomy. It will be noticed, however, that there is a slight contradiction of Exod. xx. 24. The Moses of Deuteronomy speaks as if every man's arbitrary choice had been his only guide. Probably, however, with his mind full of the stringent unity he desires to see, he speaks hyperbolically of the looseness of the former law, and means nothing else than the practice prescribed by it. In all ways this view is supported by the history. From the patriarchs till the time of Samuel, the practice was to sacrifice at various altars.[10] Consequently, according to both the Book of the Covenant and Deuteronomy, and according to the history, the worship of Yahweh at sacred places throughout the land was legal, until the Temple was erected at Jerusalem. The centralisation of worship was, consequently, a new thing when the division of the kingdoms took place, and was not an express law till Deuteronomy. If that book was not written till perhaps Hezekiah's day, the fact will account as nothing else will do for Elijah's words (1 Kings xix. 10), "The children of Israel have forsaken Thy covenant, thrown down Thine altars, and slain Thy prophets with the sword." Even in the presence of Yahweh he, without rebuke, calls the altars in the Northern Kingdom His.

The first attempt we know of to centralise worship was made by Hezekiah; a second and more strenuous attempt was made under Josiah, but the work was not actually accomplished till after the Return from the Captivity. All the facts taken together suggest that the movement towards centralisation was an age-long development. At first all holy places might be sacrificed at, though a certain primacy belonged to a central sanctuary, and this may have been stamped by Moses with approval. When the Solomonic Temple was built the primacy began to take the form of a claim for exclusive validity. The experiences in both kingdoms strengthened that claim, by showing that if Yahwism was to be kept pure the worship at the High Places must be abolished. The inspired writer of Deuteronomy then completed Moses' work by embodying that which had been always a tendency of the Mosaic system, and had now become a necessity, in his revisal of the Mosaic legislation. This was adopted by the nation under Josiah, and the Priest Codex must in that case represent a later stage of the development, when the centralisation was neither a tendency nor a demand, but a realised fact. Such a process accounts much better for the facts than the traditional belief; and though it is not free from difficulties it at least releases us from the confusion of mind which the ordinary supposition forces upon us.

The inquiry as to the agents of the cultus need not detain us so long. In the Book of the Covenant no priests are mentioned at all. The person addressed, the "thou" of these chapters, which is either the individual Israelite or the whole community, has been held by some to indicate that the individual offerer was the only agent in sacrifice. But that is to press the word too far. Even in Leviticus, while the whole people are addressed, the actions enjoined or prohibited are such as are done by "any man of them," and in Deut. xii. 13 we have precisely the same expression, "Take heed to thyself that thou offer not thy burnt offerings in every place that thou seest," used at a time when there was undeniably a priestly tribe and even the High Places had a regular priesthood. But while in Exod. xx.-xxiii. there is no evidence to show whether a priesthood existed, in the previous chapter (xix. 22, 24) priests who "come near to Yahweh" are twice mentioned. This would be a fact of the first importance were it not that the words occur in a passage which is admitted to be in its present shape the work of the later editor. Dillmann maintains, and with good reason, that he has inserted and adapted here a fragment of J. If so then J may have held the view that there were priests before Sinai was reached, but under the circumstances we cannot be certain that the mention of them may not be an anachronism introduced by the later hand. In favour of the view that it is so is the fact that in the account given by JE of the ratification of the Covenant between Yahweh and the people (Exod. xxiv. 1 ff.), Moses erected an altar and then "sent the young men of the children of Israel which offered burnt offerings and sacrificed peace offerings of oxen unto Yahweh." He himself however performed the specially priestly act of sprinkling the blood upon the altar. Had there been priests or Levites accustomed to perform priestly functions, we should have expected them to act, instead of "the young men of the children of Israel." But, on the other hand, we must not omit to notice that the Levites occupy in all these transactions, as narrated by JE, a very prominent position. Dillmann,[11] as we have seen, separating J and E, considers that the passages in which priests before the Sinaitic legislation are spoken of belong to J, and adds: "Indeed, it appears from Exod. iv. 14, 'Is not Aaron the Levite thy brother?' and xxiv. 1, 9, that for him even then the Levites were the priestly persons." To these passages Driver adds Exod. xviii. 12: "And Jethro, Moses' father-in-law, took a burnt offering and sacrifices for God; and Aaron came, and all the elders of Israel, to eat bread with Moses' father-in-law before God." Further, Nadab and Abihu are Levites, nay, sons of Aaron, and in Exod. xxiv. 1 and 9 they go with Moses, Aaron, and the seventy elders as the complete representation of the people, and Moses, himself a Levite, performs all the greater priestly acts. [12] Moreover JE knows of the ark, and speaks frequently of the "tent of meeting" (Exod. xxxiii. 7 ff.; Numb. xi. 24 f., xii. 4 ff. and Deut. xxxi. 14 ff.). But a very notable thing in connection with the inquiry as to the performers of priestly duties appears in Exod. xxxiii. 7 ff., where E's account of the "tent of meeting" is given. When Moses turned again into the camp "his minister (*mesharetho*) Joshua, the son of Nun, a young man, departed not out of the tent," yet Joshua was an Ephraimite (1 Chron. vii. 22-27). In Exod. xxxii. 29, however, the same authority describes the consecration of the Levites to the priesthood, after the apostasy of the golden calf.

In Deuteronomy, on the contrary, the priests are very prominent; they are called, however, the Levitical priests, or priests simply, but never sons of Aaron. The whole tribe of Levi is regarded as priestly in some sense. They constitute, in fact, a clerical order, though there are clear indications of ranks, of men being assigned to special duties. Curiously enough, the tribe thus highly honoured is spoken of as being notoriously and all but universally poor. No sacrifice can legitimately be offered without them; and, though the question of the place of sacrifice has not yet been finally settled, the position of the Levitical priests as sacrificers is so entirely established that it is regarded as needing neither assertion nor justification. Nay, in one passage, Deut. x. 6—which there is no valid reason, except the wish to get rid of its contents, for supposing to belong to another authority than D[13]—the hereditary succession to the chief place among the priesthood is assigned to the family of Aaron. In xviii. 5 also the hereditary character of the priesthood is asserted in the words, "For Yahweh thy God hath chosen him—*i.e.* the priest—out of all thy tribes, to stand to minister in the name of Yahweh, *him and his sons for ever.*" As for the body of the Levites, their position is somewhat ill-defined. On the authority of xviii. 6 ff. many claim that at the date of Deuteronomy every Levite was, at least potentially, a priest, that in fact Levite and priest were synonymous. But, as will appear in the exposition of the verses referred to, that is a very questionable proposition. Nevertheless it cannot be denied that in Deuteronomy the line between priests and Levites is a very indistinct one; there is *prima facie* reason to believe that it could be passed, and the gap between the two is certainly not nearly so wide as it appears to be in the undeniably post-exilic literature.

In the Priest Codex again, the priesthood is confined exclusively to the house of Aaron, with the high priest at their head. The Levites have no possible way of entrance into the priesthood. They are Yahweh's gift to the priests, and are confined most strictly to the duty of waiting upon these in the ministration of the Sanctuary. They have none but the most subordinate share in the sacrifices; they are shut out from the holy places of the Tabernacle; and they have assigned to them cities in which they may dwell together when they are not on duty at the Sanctuary. There is no word there of Levites being poor, and altogether the position of the tribe is, through the priests, much more dignified and prosperous in a worldly sense than we found it to be in Deuteronomy.

Now, taking all these data together, we find here, just as we did in the previous section, that the Levitical law is a disturbing element between Exodus and Deuteronomy. If we take it out of the way, J, E, and D harmonise well enough. The main difference is that the latter shows the same fundamental conditions as we find in the former, only consolidated and developed by time, but by a longer time than forty years. In fact D makes explicit that importance of the Levites which is only hinted at and foreshadowed in JE. They have come to be the only authorised agents of sacrifice; they have a hereditary headship in the house of Aaron; various orders and degrees must be held to exist (cf. Deut. xviii. 1 ff.). Compared with this state of things, the Levitical arrangements of P, supposed to have been given thirty-eight years before, are very different. In every respect they are more definite, more detailed, and show a much more differentiated organisation than those sketched in Deuteronomy. These latter indicate a state of matters which would suit admirably as an embryonic stage of the full-grown Levitical system, and which can hardly be fitted into their place otherwise.

It is suggested, in reply, that allusions in Deuteronomy *imply* the existence of a system of a much more elaborate kind than any that we could construct from the explicit statements of the book, and that is certainly true. But no reasonable interpretation of these allusions can lead us to a system identical with that in P. Nor can Deuteronomy's use of the name Levites (though undoubtedly it has been pressed by some too far) be held to be consistent with the public recognition of the "great gulf fixed" in P between the Aaronic priests and the Levites as a body. Nor will the fact that Deuteronomy is the people's book, and is consequently not called upon to go into technical details, cover the difference. Indeed nothing will, short of recognising the fact that, as publicly acknowledged organisations, the tribe of Levi in P and the tribe of Levi in D are different, and that the state of things in D's day is earlier than that in P. If this is not so, then the Levitical legislation, conceived as given by Moses, must be held to have proved impracticable, and Deuteronomy must then be regarded as an abrogation of it for the time.

And the same conclusions suggest themselves if we look more closely into the curious fact that Deuteronomy always speaks of the Levites as poor. Some have supposed that this poverty is the result of the centralisation of the cultus which the author demands, and that the constant insistence that the Levite shall be invited to all sacrificial feasts, along with the widow and the orphan, and other helpless classes, is a provision against the poverty to be brought upon them by the abolition of the High Places. But that is not so. We know the manner of the Deuteronomist when he is providing for contingencies arising from the new state of things he wishes to bring about, and it is quite different from his manner here. Clearly, the Levites were poor before the suppression of the High Places, and were so, as Deuteronomy tells us, from the fact that they had no inheritance in the land. But that poverty is not consistent with their whole position as sketched in the Levitical legislation. There we have the Levites launched as a regularly organised priestly corporation, endowed with ample revenues, and ruled and represented by a high priest of the family of Aaron, clothed with powers almost royal, surrounded by a priestly nobility of his own family and by a bodyguard of tribesmen entirely at his disposal. Such a body never has remained chronically and notoriously poor. In the wilderness they would not be so in contrast with others, for all were poor, and there was nothing to hinder the Levites having cattle as the other tribes had, and being on the same level as they. In the promised land, instead of becoming poor, they would at once enter upon the enjoyment of their various tithes and dues, and would moreover have such a share in the booty of Canaan as would more than make up at first for their want of a heritage. The priests were to receive one five-hundredth part of the army's half, and the Levites the fiftieth share of the people's half (Numb. xxxi. 28 ff.). Gradually, too, they would be put in possession of the priestly cities. Evidently, therefore, if the Levites were ever poor, it cannot have been till some time after Israel had been settled in the land, and then only if P's laws and organisations of the tribe were not enforced.

Deuteronomy supports the same argument. Since want of a heritage was the cause of the Levites' poverty, they cannot have been *exceptionally* poor in the wilderness. Nor can they have been poor during the time of the conquest; for even if the Levitical law was in force and the tribe was then wholly organised for the priesthood, they must have shared in the fighting and the spoil. But if the order of legislation, as we maintain, was (1) Exodus xx.-xxiii., (2) Deuteronomy, (3) the Priest Codex, then as the booty from war ceased to be a source of income, the Levites as a body remaining nomads, while the other tribes became agricultural, would necessarily become poor in comparison with their fellow-countrymen. It is out of that state of things the Deuteronomist speaks.[14]

The same conclusions follow when the regulations are examined which bear upon the support of the priestly tribe. The outstanding matters in this department are tithes and firstlings. Space will not admit of a full discussion of these topics; but if the reader will compare, in regard to tithes, Numb. xviii. 21-24 and Lev. xxvii. 30, 32, with Deut. xii. 17, and in regard to firstlings Numb. xviii. 18 with Deut. xii. 6, 17 f., and xv. 19 f., he will see that the application of tithes and of firstlings according to Deuteronomy is quite different from that in the Levitical legislation. The difference is such as will not comport with the hypothesis of a single legislator and a consistent legislation. Expedients with a view to solve the difficulty have been suggested by Keil and others; but each of those expedients is burdened with specific difficulties of its own.

The inevitable conclusion from all this would seem to be that in the Deuteronomic as in the Levitical laws we have not the legislation of Moses or of his age alone. The roots of all the legislative codes are Mosaic, but in all save perhaps the Book of the Covenant the trunk and branches are of much later growth. The authors of them are not careful to distinguish what came from Moses himself from that which had been developed out of it under the influence of the same inspiration. In both D and P there were Mosaic elements, and in both there are laws not given by him. To disentangle these completely now is impossible, and it is probably best for expository purposes to take the codes as giving what the Mosaic legislation had become at the time of the writer. What we have in Deuteronomy therefore cannot be better described than in Driver's words (*Introduction*), as "the prophetic re-formulation and adaptation to new needs of an older legislation." Its relations to the other codes are as the same critic states: "It is an *expansion* of that in JE (Exod. xx.-xxiii.); it is, in several features, *parallel* to that in Lev. xvii.-xxvi.; it contains *allusions* to laws such as those codified in some parts of P, while from those contained in other parts of P it differs widely." And the state of things in which these various codes originated is more and more coming to be conceived in the manner stated by Dr. A. B. Davidson.[15] "It is evident," he says, "that two streams of thought, both issuing from a fountain as high up as the very origin of the nation, ran side by side down the whole history of the people, the prophetic and the priestly. In the one Jehovah is a moral ruler, a righteous king and judge, who punishes iniquity judicially or forgives sins freely of His mercy. In the other He is a Person dwelling among His people in a house, a Holy Being or Nature, sensitive to every uncleanness in all that is near Him, and requiring its removal by lustrations and atonement. Those cherishing the latter circle of conceptions might be as zealous for the Lord of Hosts as the prophets. And the developments of the national history would extend their conceptions and lead to the amplification of practices embodying them, just as they extended the conceptions of the prophets. A growth of priestly ideas is quite as probable as a growth of prophetic ideas. That the streams ran apart is no evidence that they were not equally ancient and always contemporaneous, for we see Jeremiah and Ezekiel both flourishing in one age. At one point in the history the prophetic stream was swelled by an inflow from the priestly, as is seen in Deuteronomy, and from the Restoration downwards both streams appear to coalesce."

The actual date of Deuteronomy still remains to be settled. Already it has been brought down to post-Solomonic days. How much later must it probably be put? The book must have been written before the eighteenth year of Josiah, 621 B.C., for the Book of the Law which was then found in the Temple was undoubtedly not the whole Pentateuch, but approximately Deut. i.-xxvi. But it can hardly have been produced in Josiah's reign, because it would never have been permitted to drop out of sight had it been known to that pious king and the reforming high priest Hilkiah. On the other hand, it can hardly have been written or known before Hezekiah's reforms, for otherwise it would have been made the basis of them, as it was made the basis of Josiah's. Probably, therefore, we may date it between Hezekiah and Josiah. Indeed we may with great likelihood affirm, as Robertson Smith suggests, that it was the need of guidance caused by Hezekiah's reforms which suggested and called out this book.[16]

But, say some, if the body of the book is not Mosaic, then this is nothing else but forgery, and no forged or even pseudonymous book can be inspired!

Others again, most gratuitously, suppose that Hilkiah found the book only because he had forged it and put it where it was found. But there is neither need nor room for such suppositions; and our effort must be to conceive to ourselves the means by which such a book could come into existence, and be found as it was, without fraud on the part of any one.

To modern, and especially Western notions, it seems difficult to conceive any legitimate process by which a book of comparatively modern date could be attributed, so far as its main part is concerned, to Moses, and published as Mosaic. But if we take into account the character of Deuteronomy as only an extension and adaptation of the Book of the Covenant set in a framework of affectionate exhortation, and that all men then believed that the Book of the Covenant was Mosaic, we can see better how such action might be considered legitimate. Even on modern and Western principles we can see that; but at that early time and in the East, literary methods and literary ideas were so different from ours that there may have been customs which made the publication of a book in this way not only natural but right. An example from modern India will make this clear. Among the sacred books of the Hindus one of the most famous is the *Laws of Manu*. This is a collection of religious, moral, and ceremonial laws much like the Book of Leviticus. It is generally admitted that it was not the work of any one man, but of a school of legal writers and lawgivers who lived at very various times, each of whom, with a clear conscience and as a matter of course, adapted the works of his predecessors to the need of his own day. And this practice, together with the belief in its legitimacy, survives to this day. In his *Early Law and Custom* (p. 161) Sir Henry Maine tells us that "A gentleman in a high official position in India has a native friend who has devoted his life to preparing a new Book of Manu. He does not, however, expect or care that it should be put in force by any agency so ignoble as a British-Indian Legislature, deriving its powers from an Act of Parliament not a century old. He waits till there arises a king in India who will serve God and take the law from the new 'Manu' when he sits in his Court of Justice." There is here no question of fraud. This Indian gentleman considers that his book *is* the Book of Manu, and would be amazed if any one should question its identity because he had edited it; and he supposes that the king he looks for, if he should come in his day, would accept and act upon it as a Divine authority. So strangely different are Eastern notions from those of the West. It is legitimate to suppose that *this* Eastern book originated in something of the same fashion. In the evil days of persecution, when all the prophetic spokesmen were cut off, and when the priests were occupying the chief position among the supporters of pure religion, some pious man, inspired, but not with the prophetic inspiration, set himself, like this modern Hindu, to re-write and adapt the legislation which he believed to be Mosaic to the needs of his own day. Altering the fundamental points as little as might be, he developed it to meet the evils which were threatening the Mosaic religion; and he inspired it with the passion for righteousness and the love of God which had already thrilled the hearts of faithful men in Israel through the ministry of the great prophets. Hoping for the coming of a king who should serve God and judge Israel out of this new Book of Moses, but while the darkness still clouded the future, he died, committing his book to some temple chamber where he might hope that it would be discovered when God's set time should come. In such a supposition there is perhaps something to shock the conventional theories of our time. But, so far as can be seen, there is nothing to shock any open-minded man who knows how widely ancient and Eastern thought differs from modern and Western thought. It is certain that at this day Eastern men of the highest character and of the most burning zeal for religion would act in this manner without a qualm of conscience. We may well believe, therefore, that in ancient days it was the same. If so, this was a literary method which inspiration might well use; and the supposition that Deuteronomy was so produced is certainly more consistent with its history and character than any other. It explains how it so exactly met the needs of the time and summed up all its aspirations; and it gives to its claim of inspiration a new support by laying bare the circumstances of its birth and its psychological presuppositions.

But it may still be asked, what are we to think of the Mosaic speeches, which, as has been seen, contain, to say the least, much non-Mosaic matter? The answer probably is that in these, as in the laws, the author relies upon earlier documents. From the appearance in the codes of laws which would have little or no meaning if originated in the time of the Deuteronomist, it has rightly been concluded that there are very ancient and Mosaic elements in them. So, in the speeches there are references and allusions that suggest an ancient tradition of a final address of Moses, and perhaps a written account of its general purport, in which even a hope that the worship might be centralised may have been contained.[17] This the author has adapted to his purpose of inciting his contemporaries to be faithful to the Mosaic teaching, and has woven into it all that later experience could suggest as effective ground of exhortation. So much as that all ancient historians would have done, and some moderns would do, without the faintest intention to deceive, or any feeling of guilt; and so much may probably have been done here. Delitzsch,[18] Robertson Smith,[19] and Driver[20] are all at one as to this, and in the proofs they produce of the necessity of accepting this view. In the words of Driver, "It is the uniform practice of the Biblical historians in both the Old and New Testaments to represent their characters as speaking in words and phrases which cannot have been those actually used, but which they themselves select and frame for them." The speeches of David in Samuel and Chronicles serve for examples. In Samuel he speaks in the language of Samuel, in Chronicles in the language of Chronicles. "In some of these cases," Driver continues, "the authors no doubt had information as to what was actually said on the occasions in question, which they recast in their own words, only preserving, perhaps, a few characteristic expressions; in other cases, they merely gave articulate expression to the thoughts and feelings which it was presumed that the persons in question would have entertained. In the Deuteronomic speeches both these characteristic methods have probably been employed, and we must just accept the inspired record for what it reveals itself to be, setting aside, with the inevitable sighs, our own *à priori* assumptions of what it ought to be."

These then are the conclusions regarding Deuteronomy on which the exposition offered here will rest. They have been reached after a careful consideration of the evidence on both sides, and are stated here not altogether without regret. For, as Robertson Smith has well said,[21] "to the ordinary believer the Bible is precious as the practical rule of faith and life in which God still speaks directly to his heart. No criticism can be otherwise than hurtful to faith if it shakes the confidence with which the simple Christian turns to his Bible, assured that he can receive every message which it brings to his soul as a message from God Himself." Now, though it can be demonstrated that the view of Scripture which permits of such conclusions as those stated above is quite compatible with this believing confidence, there can be little doubt that Christian people will for a time find great difficulty in accepting this assurance. The transition from the old view of inspiration, so complete, comprehensible, and effective as it is, to the newer and less definite doctrine, cannot fail to be trying, and the introduction of it here cannot but be a disturbing influence which it would have been greatly preferable to avoid.

It is not to be wondered at, therefore, that to the minds of the working ministry and of their earnest fellow-labourers, who come into constant contact with the actual needs of men, the change should be unwelcome. But it cannot now, in my judgment, be avoided. Even the best and most scholarly work of those who still hold the traditional view does not convince. Rather it is their writings, more even than those on the modern side, which make it clear that the traditional view can no longer be held. These writers admit the facts upon which their opponents' case rests, and then explain them all away, harmonising everything by a crowd of hypotheses, often scholarly, generally acute, but almost always such as can be accepted only if we know beforehand that the view they support is true. But far too many hypotheses are needed. Each case has to be set right by a special effort of the imagination; while the new view has this great advantage, that it makes room for all the facts, by a hypothesis, suggested not by one difficulty, but by almost all the discrepancies and difficulties which are encountered. And, after all, this view does not move men away from the central truth of inspiration, even as it was conceived by the last generation. Apart from any care for averting errors in detail which can be ascribed to Divine wisdom according to the old view or the new, the central thing in both surely is the revelation of God Himself. It was always God that was held to be revealed, and this the advocates of the newer view insist upon most strenuously. They hold that chosen men, the wisest, best, most truthful of their respective generations, those who travailed most in thought, received exceptional impressions of the Divine nature. They saw God, and their whole being bore the impress henceforth of this illumination. In every word and act the light they had received found expression for itself. They did not receive this revelation in mere propositions about God, which had to be carefully repeated with minute verbal accuracy. They saw, and their natures were in their degree uplifted, changed, and harmonised with the Divine. They could no more be false in speaking of what they had thus experienced, than a sincere and tender nature can be false in speech or thought about death, when it once has found its love frustrated and overborne by that dread messenger of God. The impression in both cases is true as it is final, and it will triumphantly convey itself to others with substantial and effective truth, whatever the man's knowledge or ignorance otherwise may be. When a man has received an impression, or a sight of God which has shaken his very soul, will it be lost in its essential parts because in the speech in which he utters it he shows ignorance of science, or accepts as simply true the historic knowledge of his day? The thing is impossible. The light that is within him must shine out, even though the medium through which it shines be here and there blackened by imperfection. In the fundamental point, therefore, the old school of critics and the new are entirely at one. On the basis of this essential harmony it should be possible for each to speak to the other for edification. This is what has been attempted here; and if those who hold by the Mosaic authorship of Deuteronomy will tolerate the opposite view, they will find that in dealing with the Scriptures as a revelation of God, and as an infallible guide in all that concerns religious and moral truth, there is no difference. To make the sacred word living and powerful as an instrument of spiritual regeneration is our common effort; and our common hope must be that, if in anything we have been led into error, the mistake may be discovered and removed, before it has wrought evil in the Church of God.

CHAPTER II
THE HISTORIC SETTING OF DEUTERONOMY

Whatever may be the date of the first publication of Deuteronomy, there can be no doubt that it was accepted by Josiah and the people of his time with an energy and thoroughness of which we find no previous example. Its main lessons were learnt and put into practice by them, and from that period the religious conceptions of Deuteronomy dominated and formed the Hebrew mind in a manner of which we have no earlier trace. For practical purposes, therefore, we may say that this was the Deuteronomic period. The book gathered up and embodied the higher strivings of that time; and to understand it thoroughly we need to know the history of which it was, in part at least, the outcome. Indeed, on any supposition as to age and authorship, a study of the history of Judah from the end of the eighth century B.C. to the end of the seventh is indispensable if we would adequately understand our book, for that was the time when the book is seen entering as a living force into the history of Israel.

Unfortunately, however, there are few periods of Israelite history as to which we have less of reliable information. During much of the period the main currents of the national life ran contrary to all better influences, and in such epochs the compilers of the Book of Kings took no interest. For the most part they were content to "look and pass," gathering up the results of such times of declension in a few condemnatory words. It is only when the nation is on the upward slope that they enter into details. They wrote at a time when the purpose of God in their national life was becoming clear, and the splendour of it possessed them so that nothing else but the increase of this purpose seemed worthy of any intenser contemplation. Victories and defeats, successes and failures, and last of all the tremendous catastrophe of the Exile, had taught them this discernment; and they pressed forward so eagerly to record the deeds and thoughts of those who had learned the secret of Yahweh that they had eyes for nothing else. Consequently the eighty years after the fall of Samaria, which for our purpose would be so extremely instructive, are passed over in all our sources, almost without mention. But there are some facts and events of which we can be entirely sure; and from these it is possible to conceive in outline the way in which things must have shaped themselves in these eventful years.

Brought about as it had been by the appeal of Ahaz to the king of Assyria for help against the continual aggressions of Syria and Israel, the fall of Samaria must have come to the king and people of Judah as a relief. Their enemy had fallen, and they would henceforth be free from the anxiety and harassment which Israel's enmity had caused. But those must have been blind indeed with whom this feeling was permanent. Very soon it must have become apparent to all thoughtful men in Judah that, if they had been freed from the worrying and exasperating enmity of their kindred, their very success had brought them into the presence of a much more serious foe. With Assyria on their immediate frontier, settled in the lands both of Damascus and Samaria, they must have felt themselves exposed to chances and dangers they had never hitherto had to face. Under the old conditions, except during comparatively short periods when there was actual war between the two kingdoms, Israel had stood between Judah and any danger from the North. But now the people of the Southern Kingdom were summoned from "the safe glad rear to the dreadful van." Henceforth no patriot could fail to be haunted by fear of that ambitious and conquering Assyrian nation. The whole of Hezekiah's reign was filled with more or less convulsive efforts to maintain the independence of Judah. These were giving but faint promise of success, when the great deliverance of Jerusalem foretold by Isaiah gave the king a breathing space, and raised the highest hopes in the minds of his people. It seemed for a little quite possible that the ancient independence of Israel might be restored. To many it seemed that the Messianic times were at hand; faith in Yahweh carried all before it. But Hezekiah died not long after; and in the succeeding reigns of Manasseh and Amon the whole temper and policy of Israel underwent a most serious and reactionary change.

The causes of this are not far to seek. During the greater part of Hezekiah's reign Isaiah had received only moderate support. According to his own vision of his future work, he was to preach without success; he was to say, "Hear ye indeed, but understand not; and see ye, but perceive not"; and, so far as the mass of the people were concerned, that prevision was justified. Only the astounding success with which his opposition to the Assyrians had been crowned had turned the tide of popular opinion in his favour. It was probably, therefore, only then that Hezekiah's reforms were instituted. They had been too short a time in force at his death to have sent out their roots into the national life. But that was not all. One of the most characteristic points in all prophecy was that the *time* when the full Messianic Kingdom should appear was never clearly defined. Neither the Prophet nor his hearers knew when it would be. It loomed always as a bright but vague background to the deliverance which lay immediately before them; and in almost every case neither speaker nor hearers had any conception of the long and weary way which divided those sunlit mountain peaks from the dark and threatening pass which they were approaching. Now the literal interpretation of Isaiah's prophecies with regard to the deliverance from Assyria had inevitably led the mass of the people to believe that the raising of the siege of Jerusalem would mean the immediate destruction of Assyria, and the advent of the Messianic day of peace and glory for Israel. But the facts completely falsified that expectation. Instead of being destroyed Assyria only grew more powerful, and instead of the Messianic time there was only the old position of vassalage to Assyria. So men grew weary, and said then as they have said so often since, "All things are as they have been from the beginning, and where is the promise of His coming?" The true-hearted said it with sadness; and the false-hearted, saying it in mockery and unbelief, fell back upon the old heathenish test, and said, "The gods of Assyria are stronger than Yahweh, and we must give them a place in our adoration." With the bulk of the people this required no really great change in their point of view. They had believed in Yahweh and agreed to purify His worship, because He had proved Himself stronger than Sennacherib and his gods; and now when, in the long run, Assyria was triumphing, they must have seemed to themselves only to be following the teachings of experience in giving the host of heaven equal honour with their own ancestral God. The reaction, therefore, was more in the outward expression than in principle, and we can easily understand how it was so swift and so universal. Manasseh, Hezekiah's son, had probably opposed his father's policy, as the heir-apparent has so often opposed the policy of the reigning monarch; and if, as many suppose, Hezekiah lived for sixteen years after the destruction of Sennacherib's host, Manasseh came to the throne just when men's minds were most weary with hope deferred, and when the Assyrian success was about to reach its highest point before its final fall.

Accordingly Manasseh would seem to have undone at once all that his father and Isaiah had accomplished. Nay, he went further in the introduction of idolatry than any even of the idolatrous kings who had preceded him. In the Book of Kings the charges made against him are three:—1st, that he introduced the worship of the host of heaven according to the Assyrian ritual; 2nd, that he took part in the Moloch-worship; and 3rd, that he restored the old semi-Canaanite worship which it had been Isaiah's most strenuous effort to root out. And this policy, evil as it was in the eyes of all who cared for the higher destinies of Israel, had at once great and striking external success. For it meant complete submission to Assyria, a willing vassalage from which even the wish for independence had disappeared. The heart of the old Israelite independence had been faith in Yahweh and confidence in

Israel's calling as His people. Even so late as Isaiah's day it had been faith in Yahweh which had kept Hezekiah steady in his opposition to apparently overwhelming force. But now Manasseh and the people who supported him exalted the gods of Assyria as an even surer refuge than Yahweh had been. Having made that admission, there was nothing left for them but to humble themselves under the mighty hand of the great king and his great gods. And this Israel under Manasseh did most thoroughly. As Stade has strikingly said, "The Temple of the one God of Israel became a Pantheon." The feeble attempts which Ahaz had made in the same direction were utterly swept out of men's memory by the completeness of Manasseh's apostasy. With this degradation of the religious faith there also came, naturally, an intellectual degradation. Superstition, baser even than idolatry, seized upon the minds of men, and illegitimate efforts to pry into the future or to influence the destinies of men by magic and incantations became part of the popular fashion of the day. The old religion of Israel had sternly set itself against all such debasing practices. Alone amid the religions of the ancient world, it had relentlessly refused the help of necromancy and magic generally. But the barrier the religion of Yahweh had erected fell at once when its purity and uniqueness had been sacrificed, and Manasseh gave himself up to "practise augury and to use enchantments, and to deal with them that had familiar spirits and with wizards." And to superstition he also added cruelty. Not content with his signal victory over all the best impulses of the past, not content with the applause of the multitude who gladly followed him to do evil, he endeavoured to force those whose work he had destroyed to bow before the gods they both hated and despised. We know too little of the circumstances of the time to be sure of his motives, but his action may have been founded upon a craven fear that if he did not suppress the voices of those who spoke for freedom, he might be visited with the anger of the Assyrian king. Or it may have been that feeling, so powerfully expressed in Browning's poem "Instans Tyrannus," which makes a tyrant feel that all his life is made bitter to him if there remain within his power one free man whom he cannot bend to his will. In any case it is certain that he attacked the prophetic party with sanguinary fury. Though he had the gods of the great battalions on his side, he was dimly afraid of the power of ideas; and, so far as faithful men were concerned, he instituted a "reign of terror." According to the graphic statement of the historian, "he filled Jerusalem with innocent blood from lip to lip," and for the time at least was able to silence righteousness so far as public utterance was concerned. There is a tradition that even Isaiah fell a victim to his fury, being sawn asunder between two planks at his command. It is perhaps not likely that Isaiah had survived so long. But, beyond all doubt, many suffered for their faithfulness to God; and it seems probable that the wonderful picture of the Suffering

Servant in the Deutero-Isaiah owes much of its colour to the pathetic and painful memories of this evil time.

All this apostasy brought with it worldly success. Manasseh reigned long, and under him the land had peace. Assyria *could* have no quarrel with a people and a king who anticipated its very desire by eager submission. Peace brought material prosperity. The land was so naturally fertile that it always grew rich when war was kept from its borders. We may surmise, too, that a kind of bastard culture became popular when the Jewish mind had opened to it, for good and evil, a world of myth and song and legend which, if known before, had until now been barred from complete and triumphant entrance by faith in a living God. Once only would Manasseh appear to have asserted himself, and, according to the Book of Chronicles, he was taken prisoner in Jerusalem by the master he had served so well, and learned to know in the bitterness of a Babylonian prison that sycophancy does not always lead to safety. And the wisdom he learned went further even than that. At the end of his life he appears to have wished to undo, at least in some measure, the evil he had laboured throughout his reign to establish and make strong. But he found that to be impossible; and if his repentance was deep and sincere he must have learned how severely the heavenly powers can punish, by opening a man's eyes to the evil he has done when it cannot be undone. Nor did his late repentance affect his son, for under Amon all things continued in their previous evil course. Indeed the prevailing idolatry had rooted itself so firmly that even in the early years of Josiah, when the prophetic influence was beginning to reappear, it still retained its hold with unshaken power.

But what of the prophetic party during those evil days? Precipitated from power in an instant at Hezekiah's death, it had at once become feeble and obscure. Its leading supporters, we may well believe, had to seek safety in hiding or in flight; and after some of its chief speakers had been cut off, the once dominant party had to take the position of persecuted remnants for whom all public work was impossible. Under such circumstances what could these faithful men do? They could only wait and pray, and prepare for that better day of whose return their faith in Yahweh would not suffer them to despair.

From the position afterwards taken up by the high priest, it would seem probable that the Temple clergy were in full sympathy with the prophetic movement. We need not suppose that that sympathy arose wholly from the tendency of prophetic thought and effort towards the suppression of the High Places. We should probably do the better spirits among the priesthood grievous wrong if we thought that their personal interest was their main motive in supporting even that reform. Notwithstanding the earlier prophets' denunciation of the priests as a class, there can be little doubt that they had advanced, with the better classes of their nation generally, in their appreciation of spiritual religion. And we may well believe that the sight of the havoc which the now degraded worship at the High Places was working in the popular mind made them earnest in their endeavours to restore the true faith. Privileged as they were, they would naturally be sheltered from the full fury of the persecution. Consequently, when the time came for the supporters of true religion to take their place in public life again, it was natural and inevitable that the priests should be at their head. The fact, too, that Josiah at his accession was a child, for whose guardian no fitter person could be found than the chief priest, gave the future into their hands. But they did not move prematurely. So long as Josiah was a minor they contented themselves with instilling their principles into the mind of the king. In outward political life, so far as we can ascertain, they did not interfere at all, and the ground was moved away from beneath the feet of the idolatrous party, while they thought themselves firmly established. In Josiah's eighteenth year the results of this quiet preparation appeared. In that year Hilkiah, the high priest, told Shaphan the scribe that he had found "the Book of the Law" in the Temple. That this was Deuteronomy, if not altogether, yet practically, as we have it now, there can be but little doubt; and it immediately became the text-book of religion for all that remained of Israel.

Now it is obvious that the whole hopes of the religious party would naturally be fixed upon it. They would turn to it as eagerly as the Reformers turned to the Bible, after it had been rediscovered by Luther at Erfurt. For obviously, if the people could be got to acknowledge the law, the axe would be laid at the root of every evil which they deplored. The High Places would be destroyed; the primacy of the Temple at Jerusalem would be secured; and the prophetic teaching, with its insistence upon judgment and the love of God as the essentials of true worship, would, for the first time, become the dominant influence in civil and religious life. Never since Israel was a nation had the condition of the people called so loudly for the enforcement of such a law, and now for the first time was there hope that it might be actually enforced. The character of the evils that afflicted the nation, the history of the last half-century, and the teachings of the great canonical prophets had all converged, as it were, to this one point, and we can understand how all who strove for the higher life of Israel would strive that Deuteronomy, whether ancient or modern, should be neglected no longer. The result was that the whole power of the State was thrown into the struggle against idolatry and the half-heathen Bamoth-worship. The prophets and the priests joined hands to spread the principles of the true religion, as voiced by Deuteronomy. Professor Cheyne, in his *Jeremiah*, conjectures, with considerable likelihood, that the break in that prophet's activity which occurred at this time is to be accounted for by the zeal with which he devoted himself to Deuteronomic propaganda throughout the land. In any case, for the moment the purer worship obtained a completer victory than ever before. Unfortunately it came too late and proved too evanescent. But in the inward sphere, the Deuteronomic view of religion as having its centre in love to God, the tender, thoughtful evangelical spirit which distinguishes the whole outlook of its author, laid hold upon all the higher minds that came after it. To Jeremiah and to St. Paul alike, it, *par excellence*, represented the law of God. Produced, or at any rate first prized, at a time when Israel had fallen very low, when evil was triumphant and good persecuted, it recommended and exemplified a cheerful courage, born of faith in the high destiny of Israel and the truth of God. That, more than anything else, helped to bear the ark of the Church over the tumultuous centuries which separated those two great servants of God, and when Christ appeared it was seen that this book, more than any in the Old Testament save perhaps the Psalms, had anticipated His cardinal teachings regarding the attitude of man to God and of man to man. The conflicts and needs of the seventh century B.C., which are so clearly reflected in it, gave inspiration the opportunity it needed to reveal that inner secret of God's Kingdom. Out of defeat and disaster this revelation came, and through times of defeat and backsliding it proved its Divine origin by keeping steadfast and calm those who specially waited for the coming of the Messiah.

CHAPTER III
THE DIVINE GOVERNMENT

Deut. i.-iii

After these preliminary discussions we now enter upon the exposition. With the exception of the first two verses of chapter i., concerning which there is a doubt whether they do not belong to Numbers, these three chapters stand out as the first section of our book. Examination shows that they form a separate and distinct whole, not continued in chapter iv.; but there has been a great diversity of opinion as to their authorship and the intention with which they have been placed here. The vocabulary and the style so resemble those of the main parts of the book, that they cannot be entirely separated from them; yet, at the same time, it seems unlikely that the original author of the main trunk of Deuteronomy can have begun his book with this introductory speech from Moses, followed it up with another Mosaic speech, still introductory, in chapter iv., and in chapter v. begun yet another introductory speech running through seven chapters, before he comes to the statutes and judgments which are announced at the very beginning. The current supposition about these chapters, therefore, is that they are the work of a Deuteronomist, a man formed under the influence of Deuteronomy and filled with its spirit, but not the author of the book. This seems to account for the resemblances, and would also explain to some extent the existence of such a superfluous prologue. But the hypothesis is, nevertheless, not entirely satisfactory. The resemblances are closer than we should expect in the work of different authors; and one feels that the supposed Deuteronomist must have been less sensitive in a literary sense than we have any right to suppose him if he did not feel the incongruity of such a speech in this place. Professor Dillmann has made a very acute suggestion, which meets the whole difficulty in a more natural way. Feeling that the style and language were in all essentials one with those of the central Deuteronomy, he seeks for some explanation which would permit him to assign this section to the author of the book himself. He suggests that as originally written this was a historical introduction leading up to the central code of laws; a historical preface, in fact, which the author of

Deuteronomy naturally prefixed to his book. *Ex hypothesi* he had not the previous books, Exodus, Leviticus, and Numbers, before him as we have them. These now form a historical introduction to Deuteronomy of a very minute and elaborate kind; but he had to embody in his own book all of the past history of his people that he wished to emphasise. But when the editor who arranged the Pentateuch as we now have it inserted Deuteronomy in its present place, he found that he had a double historical preface, that in the previous books and this in Deuteronomy itself. As reverence forbade the rejection of these chapters, he took refuge in the expedient of turning the originally impersonal narrative into a speech of Moses; which he could all the more blamelessly do as the probability is that the whole book was regarded in his time as the work of Moses. This hypothesis, if it can be accepted, certainly accounts for all the phenomena presented by these chapters—the similarity of language, the archæological notes in the speech, and the historic colour in the statements regarding Edom, for example, which corresponds to early feeling, not to post-exilic thought at all. It has besides the merit of reducing the number of anonymous writers to be taken account of in the Pentateuch, a most desirable thing in itself. Lastly, it gives us in Deuteronomy a compact whole more complete in all its parts than almost any other portion of the Old Testament, certainly more so than any of the books containing legislation.

Moreover, that the Deuteronomic reinforcement and expansion of the Mosaic legislation, as contained in the Book of the Covenant, should begin with such a history of Yahweh's dealings with His people, is entirely characteristic of Old Testament Revelation. In the main and primarily, what the Old Testament writers give us is a history of how God wrought, how He dealt with the people He had chosen. In the view of the Hebrew writers, God's first and main revelation of Himself is always in conduct. He showed Himself good and merciful and gentle to His people, and then, having so shown Himself, He has an acknowledged right to claim their obedience. As St. Paul has so powerfully pointed out, the law was secondary, not primary. Grace, the free love and choice of God, was always the beginning of true relations with Him, and only after that had been known and accepted does He look for the true life which His law is to regulate. Naturally, therefore, when the author of Deuteronomy is about to press upon Israel the law in its expanded form, to call them back from many aberrations, to summon them to a reformation and new establishment of the whole framework of their lives, he turns back to remind them of what their past had been. Law, therefore, is only a secondary deposit of Revelation. If we are true to the Biblical point of view we shall not look for the Divine voice only, or even chiefly, in the legal portions of the Scripture. God's full revelation of Himself will be seen in the process and the completion of that age-long movement, which was begun when Israel first became a nation by receiving Yahweh as their God, and which ended with the life and death of Him who summed up in Himself all that Israel was called, but failed, to be.

That is the ruling thought in Scripture about Revelation. God reveals Himself in history; and by the persistent thoroughness with which the Scriptural writers grasp this thought, the unique and effective character of the Biblical Revelation is largely accounted for. Other nations, no doubt, looked back at times upon what their gods had done for them, and those who spoke for these gods may often have claimed obedience and service from their people on the ground of past favour and under threats of its withdrawal. But earlier than any other people which has affected the higher races of mankind, Israel conceived of God as a moral power with a will and purpose which embraced mankind. Further, in the belief which appears in their earliest records, that through them the nations were to be blessed, and that in the future One was coming who would in Himself bring about the realisation of Israel's destiny, they were provided with a philosophy of history, with a conception which was fitted to draw into organic connection with itself all the various fortunes of Israel and of the nations.

Of course, at first much that was involved in their view was not present to any mind. It was the very merit of the germinal revelation made through Moses that it had in it powers of growth and expansion. In no other way could it be a true revelation of God, a revelation which should have in it the fulness, the flexibility, the aloofness from mere local and temporary peculiarities, which would secure its fitness for universal mankind. Any revelation that consists only of words, of ideas even, must, to be received, have some kind of relation to the minds that are to receive it. If the words and ideas are revealed, as they must be, at a given place and a given time, they must be in such a relation to that place and time that at some period of the world's history they will be found inadequate, needing expansion, which does not come naturally, and then they have to be laid aside as insufficient. But a revelation which consists in acts, which reveals God in intimate, age-long, constant dealings with mankind, is so many-sided, so varied, so closely moulded to the actual and universal needs of man, that it embraces all the fundamental exigencies of human life, and must always continue to cover human experience. From it men may draw off systems of doctrines, which may concentrate the revelation for a particular generation, or for a series of generations, and make it more potently active in these circumstances. But unless the system be kept constantly in touch with the revelation as given in the history, it must become inadequate, false in part, and must one day vanish away.

The revelation then in life is the only possible form for a real revelation of God; and that the writers of the Old Testament in their circumstances and in their time felt and asserted this, is in itself so very great a merit, that it is almost of itself sufficient to justify any claims they may make to special inspiration. The greatest of them saw God at work in the world, and had experience of His influence in themselves, so that they had their eyes opened to His actions as other men had not. The least of them, again, had been placed at the true point of view for estimating aright the significance of the ordinary action of the Divine Providence, and for tracing the lines of Divine action where they were to other men invisible, or at least obscure. And in the records they have left us they have been entirely true to that supremely important point of view. All they deal with in the history is the moral and spiritual effects of God's dealing; and the great interests, as the world reckons them, of war and conquest, of commerce and art, are referred to only briefly and often only in the way of allusion. To many moderns this is an offence, which they avenge by speaking contemptuously of the mental endowment of the Biblical writers as historians. On the contrary, that these should have kept their eyes fixed only upon that which concerned the religious life of their people, that they should have kept firm hold of the truth that it was there the central importance of the people lay, and that they have given us the material for the formation of that great conception of supernatural revelation by history in which God Himself moves as a factor, is a merit so great that even if it were only a brilliant fancy they might surely be pardoned for ignoring other things. But if, as is the truth, they were tracing the central stream of God's redemptive action in the world, were laying open to our view the steps by which the unapproachably lofty conception of God was built up, which their nation alone has won for the human race, then it can hardly seem a fault that nothing else appealed to them. They have given God to those who were blindly groping for Him, and they have established the standard by which all historic estimates of even modern life are ultimately to be measured.

For though there were in the history of that particular nation, and in the line of preparation for Christ, special miraculous manifestations of God's power and love, which do not now occur, yet no judgment of the course of history is worth anything, even to-day, which does not occupy essentially the Biblical position. Ultimately the thing to be considered is, what hath God wrought? If that be ignored, then the stable and instructive element in history has been kept out of sight, and the mind loses itself hopelessly amid the weltering chaos of second causes. Froude, in his *History of England*, has noted this, and declares that in the period he deals with it was the religious men who alone had any true insight into the tendency of things.

They measured all things, almost too crudely, by the Biblical standard; but so essentially true and fundamental does that show itself to be, that their judgment so formed has proved to be the only sound one. This is what we should expect if God's power and righteousness are the great factors in the drama which the history of man and of the world unfolds to us. That being so, the suicidal folly of the policy of any Church or party which shuts the Bible away from popular use is manifest. It is nothing short of a blinding of the people's eyes, and a shutting of their ears to warning voices which the providential government of the world, when viewed on a large scale, never fails to utter. It renders sound political judgment the prerogative only of the few, and sets them among a people who will turn to any charlatans rather than believe their voice.

It was natural and it was inevitable, therefore, that the author of Deuteronomy, standing, as he did, on the threshold of a great crisis in the history of Israel, should turn the thoughts of his people back to the history of the past. To him the great figure in the history of Israel in those trying and eventful years during which they wandered between Horeb, Kadesh-Barnea, and the country of the Arnon, is Yahweh their God. He is behind all their movements, impelling and inciting them to go on and enjoy the good land He had promised to their fathers. He went before them and fought for them. He bare them in the wilderness, as a man doth bear his son. He watched over them and guided their footsteps in cloud and fire by day and night. Moreover all the nations by whom they passed had been led by Him and assigned their places, and only those nations whom Yahweh chose had been given into Israel's hand. In the internal affairs of the community, too, He had asserted Himself. They were Yahweh's people, and all their national action was to be according to His righteous character. Especially was the administration of justice to be pure and impartial, yielding to neither fear nor favour because the "judgment is God's." And how had they responded to all this loving favour on the part of God? At the first hint of serious conflict they shrank back in fear. Notwithstanding that the land which God had given them was a good and fruitful country, and notwithstanding the promises of Divine help, they refused to incur the necessary toils and risks of the conquest. Every difficulty they might encounter was exaggerated by them; their very deliverance from Egypt, which they had been wont to consider "their crowning mercy," became to their faithless cowardice an evidence of hatred for them on the part of God.

To men in such a state of mind conquest was impossible; and though, in a spasmodic revulsion from their abject cowardice, they made an attack upon the people they were to dispossess, it ended, as it could not but end, in their defeat and rout. They were condemned to forty years of wandering, and it was only after all that generation was dead that Israel was again permitted to approach the land of promise. But Yahweh had been faithful to them, and when the time was come He opened the way for their advance and gave them the victory and the land. For His love was patient, and always made a way to bless them, even through their sins.

That was the picture the Deuteronomist spread out before the eyes of his countrymen, to the intent that they might know the love of God, and might see that safety lay for them in a willing yielding of themselves to that love. The disastrous results of their wayward and faint-hearted shrinking from this Divine calling is the only direct threat he uses but in the passage there is another warning, all the more impressive that it is vague and shadowy. God is to the Deuteronomist the universal ruler of the world. The nations are raised up and cast down according to His will, and until He wills it they cannot be dispossessed. But He had willed that fate for many, and at every step of Israel's progress they come upon traces of vanished peoples whom for their sins He had suffered others to destroy. The Emim in Moab, the Zamzummim in Ammon, the Horites in Seir, and the Avvims in Philistia, had all been destroyed before the people who now occupied these lands, and the whole background of the narrative is one of judgment, where mercy had been of no avail. The sword of the Lord is dimly seen in the archæological notes which are so frequent in this section of our book and thus the final touch is given to the picture of the past which is here drawn to be an impulse for the future. While all the foreground represents only God's love and patience overcoming man's rebellion, the background is, like the path of the great pilgrim caravans which year by year make their slow and toilsome way to Mohammedan holy places, strewn with the remains of predecessors in the same path. With stern, menacing finger this great teacher of Israel points to these evidences that the Divine love and patience may be, and have been, outworn, and seems to re-echo in an even more impressive way the language of Isaiah: "The anger of Yahweh was kindled (against these peoples), and He stretched forth His hand (against them) and smote (them); and the hills did tremble, and (their) carcases were as refuse in the midst of the streets. For all this His anger is not turned away, but His hand is stretched out still." Without a word of direct rebuke he opens his people's eyes to see that shadowy outstretched hand. Behind all the turmoil of the world there is a presence and a power which supports all who seek good, but which is sternly set against all evil, ready, when the moment comes, "to strike once and strike no more."

Yet another glimpse is given us in these chapters of God's manner of dealing with men. We have seen how He guides and rules His chosen ones. We have seen how He punishes those who have set themselves against the

Divine law. And in chapter ii. 30 we are told how men become hardened in their sin, so as to render destruction inevitable. Of Sihon, king of Heshbon, who would not let the Israelites pass by him, the writer says: "Yahweh thy God hardened his spirit, and made his heart obstinate, that He might deliver him into thy hand, as appeareth this day." But he does not mean by these expressions to lay upon God the causation of Sihon's obstinacy, so as to make the man a mere helpless victim. His thought rather is, that as God rules all, so to Him must be ultimately traced all that happens in the world. In some sense all acts, whether good or bad, all agencies, whether beneficent or destructive, have their source in and their power from Him. But nevertheless men have moral responsibility for their acts, and are fully and justly conscious of ill desert. Consequently that hardening of spirit or of heart, which at one moment may be attributed solely to God, may at another be ascribed solely to the evil determination of man. The most instructive instance of this is to be found in the history of Pharaoh, when he was commanded to let Israel go. In that narrative, from Exodus iv. to xi., there is repeated interchange of expression. Now it is Yahweh hardened Pharaoh's heart; now, as in viii. 15 and 32, Pharaoh hardened his own heart; and, again, Pharaoh's heart was hardened. In each case the same thing is meant, and the varying expressions correspond only to a difference of standpoint. When Yahweh foretells that the signs He authorises Moses to show will fail of their effect, it is always "Yahweh will harden Pharaoh's heart," since the main point in contemplation is His government of the world. If, on the other hand, it is the sinful obstinacy of Pharaoh which is prominent in the passage, we have the self-determination of Pharaoh alone set before us. But it is to be noted, and this is indeed the cardinal fact, that Yahweh never is said to harden the heart of a good man, or a man set mainly upon righteousness. It is always those who are guilty of palpable wrongs and acts of evil-doing upon whom God thus works.

Now we know that the author of Deuteronomy had two at least of the ancient historical narratives before him which are combined in Exod. iv.-xi., and he takes up their thinking. Expressed in modern language, the thought is this. When men are found following their own will in defiance of all law and all the restraints of righteousness, that is manifestly not the first stage in their moral declension. This obstinacy in evil is the result and the wages of former evil deeds, beginning perhaps only with careless laxity, but gathering strength and virulence with every wilful sin. Until near the end of a completed growth in wickedness no man deliberately says, "Evil, be thou my good." Nevertheless each act of sin involves a step towards that, and the sinner in this manner hardens himself against all warning. Like the sins which work this obduracy, this hardening is the sinner's own act. The ruin which falls upon his moral nature is his own work. That is the inexorable result of the moral order of the universe, and from it no exception is possible. But if so, God too has been active in all such catastrophes. He has so framed and ordered the world that indulgence in evil must harden in evil. This it was which the Israelite religious mind saw and dwelt upon, as well as upon man's share in the dread process of moral decay. We also do well to take heed to this aspect of the truth. When we do, we have solved the Scriptural difficulty regarding the Divine hardening of man's heart. It is simply the ancient formula for what every mind that is ethically trained recognises in the world to-day. Those who recognise themselves as children of God, and acknowledge the obligations of His law, are dealt with in the way of discipline with infinite love and patience. Those who definitely set themselves against the moral order of the world which God has established are broken in pieces and destroyed. Between these two classes there are the morally undetermined, who ultimately turn either to the right hand or to the left. The process by which these pass on to be numbered among the rebellious is pictured in Scripture with extraordinary moral insight. The only difference from a present-day description of it is, that here God is kept constantly present to the mind as the chief factor in the development of the soul. To-day, even those who believe in God are apt to forget Him in tracing His laws of action. But that is an error of the first magnitude. It darkens the hope of man; for without a sure promise of Divine help there is no certainty of moral victory either for the race or the individual. It narrows our view of the awful sweep of sin; for unless we see that sin affects even the Ruler of the universe, and defies His unchanging law, its results are limited to the evil that we do our fellow-men, which, as we see it, is of little importance. Further, it degrades moral law to a mere arbitrary dictum of power, or to an opinion founded upon man's purblind experience. The acknowledgment of God, on the contrary, makes morality the very essence of the Divine nature, and the unchangeable rule for the life of man.

CHAPTER IV
THE DECALOGUE—ITS FORM

Deut. v. 1-21

As the fourth chapter belongs to the speech which concludes the legislative portion of Deuteronomy both in contents and language (see Chapter XXIII.), we shall pass on now to the fifth chapter, which begins with a recital of the Decalogue. As has already been pointed out, the main trunk of the Book of Deuteronomy is a repetition and expansion of the Law of the Covenant contained in Exod. xx.-xxiii.[22] Now, both in Exodus and Deuteronomy, before the more general and detailed legislation, we have the Decalogue, or the Ten Words, as it is called, in substantially the same form; and the question immediately arises as to the age at which this beautifully systematised and organised code of fundamental laws came into existence. Whatever its origin, it is an exceedingly remarkable document. It touches the fundamental principles of religious and moral life with so sure a hand that at this hour, for even the most civilised nations, it sums up the moral code, and that so effectively that no change or extension of it has ever been proposed. That being its character, it becomes a question of exceeding interest to decide whether it can justly be referred to so early a time as the days of Moses. In both the passages where it occurs it is represented as having been given to the people at Horeb by Yahweh Himself, and it is made the earliest and most fundamental part of the covenant between Him and Israel. It would accordingly seem as if a claim were made for it as a specially early and specially sacred law. Now, much as critics have denied, there have been found very few who deny that in the main some such law as this must have been given to Israel in Moses' day. Even Kuenen admits as much as that in his *History of the Religion of Israel*. The only commandment of the ten he has difficulty in accepting is the second, which forbids the making of any graven image for worship. That, he thinks, cannot have been in the original Decalogue, not because of any peculiarity of language, or because of any incoherency in composition, but simply because he cannot believe that at that early day the religion of Yahweh could have been so spiritual as to demand the prohibition of images. But his reasons are extremely inadequate; more especially as he admits that the Ark was the Mosaic Sanctuary, and that in it there was no image, as there was none in the Temple at Jerusalem. That Yahweh was worshipped under the form of a calf at Horeb, and afterwards in Northern Israel at Bethel and elsewhere, proves nothing. A law does not forthwith extinguish that against which it is directed, for idolatry continued even after Deuteronomy was accepted as the law. Moreover, if, as Kuenen thinks, calf-worship had existed in Israel before Moses, it was not unnatural that it took centuries before the higher view superseded the lower. Even by Christianity the ancient superstitions and religious practices of heathenism were not thoroughly overcome for centuries. Indeed in many places they have not yet been entirely suppressed. Nor does Wellhausen[23] make a better case for a late Decalogue. His hesitation about it is most remarkable, and the reasons he gives for tending to think it may be late are singularly unsatisfactory. His first reason is that "according to Exodus xxxiv. the commandments which stood upon the two tables were quite different." He relies on the words in ver. 28 of that chapter—"And he (Moses) was there with the Lord forty days and forty nights; he did neither eat bread nor drink water. And he wrote upon the tables the words of the covenant, the ten words"—taking them to imply that the immediately preceding commandments, which are of the same ritual character with those which follow the Decalogue in Exodus xx., are here called the ten words. But it is not necessary to take the passage so. According to ver. 1 it was Yahweh who was to write the words on the tables, and we cannot suppose that so flagrant a contradiction should occur in a single chapter as that here it should be said that Moses wrote the tables. Yahweh, who is mentioned in the previous verse, must therefore be the subject of *wayyikhtobh* (ver. 28), and the ten words consequently are different from the words (up to ver. 27) which Yahweh commanded Moses to write, somewhere, but not on the tables. Besides, every one who attempts to make ten words of the commands before ver. 27 brings out a different result, and that of itself, as Dillmann says, is sufficient to show that the second Decalogue in chapter xxxiv. is entirely fanciful. Wellhausen's second reason is this: "The prohibition of images was quite unknown during the other period: Moses himself is said to have made a brazen serpent, which down to Hezekiah's time continued to be worshipped as an image of Jehovah." But the Decalogue does not prohibit the making of every image; it prohibits the making of images for worship. Therefore Moses might quite well have made a figure of a serpent, even though he wrote the Decalogue, if it was not meant for worship. But there is nothing said to lead us to believe that the serpent was regarded as an image of Yahweh. Indeed the very contrary is asserted; and if Israel in later times made a bad use of this ancient relic of a great deliverance, Moses can hardly be held responsible for that. In the third place, Wellhausen says: "The essentially and necessarily national character of the older phases of the religion of Yahweh completely disappears in the quite universal code of morals which is given in the Decalogue as the fundamental law of Israel; but the entire series of religious personalities throughout the period of the Judges and Kings—from Deborah, who praised Jael's treacherous act of murder, to David, who treated his prisoners of war with the utmost cruelty—make it very difficult to believe that the religion of Israel was from the outset one of a specifically moral character." Surely this is very feeble criticism. On the same grounds we might declare, because of the Massacre of St. Bartholomew, or on account of Napoleon's reported poisoning of his own wounded at Acre, that Christianity was not a religion of a "specifically moral character" at this present moment. Surely the facts that people never live at the level of their ideals, and that the lifting of a nation's life is a process which is as slow as the raising of the level of the delta of the Nile, should be too familiar to permit any one to be misled by difficulties of this kind. Nor is his last ground in any degree more convincing. "It is extremely doubtful," he says, "whether the actual monotheism which is undoubtedly presupposed in the universal moral precepts of the Decalogue could have formed the foundation of a national religion. It was first developed out of the national religion at the downfall of the nation." The obvious reply is that this is a *petitio principii*. The whole debate in regard to this question is whether Moses was a monotheist, or at least the founder of a religion which was implicitly monotheistic from the beginning; and the date of the Decalogue is interesting mainly because of the light it would throw upon that question. To decide this date therefore by the assertion that, being monotheistic, the Decalogue cannot be Mosaic, is to assume the very thing in dispute. Wellhausen himself, elsewhere, seems to favour the opposite view. In speaking of what Moses did for Israel he says that through "the Torah," in the sense of decisions given by lot from the Ark, "he gave a definite positive expression to their sense of nationality and their idea of God. Yahweh was not merely the God of Israel; as such He was the God at once of Law and of Justice, the basis, the informing principle, and the implied postulate of their national consciousness"; and again, "As God of the nation Yahweh became the God of Justice and of Right; as God of Justice and Right, He came to be thought of as the highest, and at last as the only power in heaven and earth." In the Mosaic conception of God, therefore, Wellhausen himself being witness, there lay implicitly, perhaps even explicitly, the conception of Yahweh as "the only power in heaven and earth." In that case, is it reasonable to put the Decalogue late, because being moral it is universal, and so implies monotheism?

But there is still other, and perhaps stronger evidence, that the universality of the Decalogue is no indication of a late date. On the contrary it would seem, from Professor Muirhead's account of the Roman *fas*, that universality in legal precept may be a mark of very primitive laws. Speaking of Rome in its earliest stages of growth, when the circumstances of the people in very many respects resembled those of the Hebrews in Mosaic times,[24] he says: "We look in vain for, and it would be absurd to expect, any definite system of law in those early times. What passed for it was a composite of *fas*, *jus*, and *boni mores*, whose several limits and characteristics it is extremely difficult to define." He then proceeds to describe *fas*: "By *fas* was understood the will of the gods, the laws given by Heaven for men on earth, much of it regulative of ceremonial, but a by no means insignificant part embodying rules of conduct. It appears to have had a wider range than *jus*. There were few of its commands, prohibitions, or precepts that were addressed to men as citizens of any particular state; *all mankind came within its scope*. It forbade that a war should be undertaken without the prescribed fetial ceremonial, and required that faith should be kept with even an enemy—when a promise had been made to him under sanction of an oath. It enjoined hospitality to foreigners, because the stranger guest was presumed, equally with his entertainer, to be an object of solicitude to a higher power. It punished murder, for it was the taking of a God-given life; the sale of a wife by her husband, for she had become his partner in all things human and Divine; the lifting of a hand against a parent, for it was subversive of the first bond of society and religion, the reverence due by a child to those to whom he owed his existence; incestuous connections, for they defiled the altar; the false oath, and the broken vow, for they were an insult to the divinities invoked," etc. In fact, the Roman *fas* had much the same character as the Decalogue and the legislation of the first code (Exod. xx.-xxiii.). Consequently those who have thought that all early legislation must be concrete, narrow, particularistic, bounded at widest by the direct needs of the men making up the clan, tribe, or petty nationality, are wrong. The early history of law shows that, along with that, there is also a demand for some expression of the laws of life seen from the point of view of man's relation to God. That fact greatly strengthens the case for the early date of the Decalogue. For practically it is the Hebrew *fas*. If it has a higher tone and a wider sweep, if it provides a framework into which human duty can, even now, without undue stretching of it, be securely fitted, that is only what we should expect, if God was working in the history and development of this nation as nowhere else in the world. In short, the history of primitive Roman law shows that, without inspiration, a feeble wavering step would have been taken to the development of a code of moral duty, within the scope of which all mankind should come. With inspiration, surely this effort would also be made, and made with a success not elsewhere attained.

In none of the reasons which have been advanced, therefore, is there anything to set against the Biblical statement that the ten words were older and more sacred than any other portion of the Israelite legislation, and that they were Mosaic in origin. The universal hesitation shown by the greater among the most advanced critics in definitely removing the Decalogue from the foundations of Israel's history, although its presence there is so great an embarrassment to them, lets us see how strong the case for the Mosaic origin is, and assures us that the evidence is all in favour of this view.

But if it be Mosaic, at first sight the conclusion would seem to be that the form of the Decalogue given in Exodus is the more ancient, and that the text in Deuteronomy is a later and somewhat extended version of that. Closer examination, however, tends to suggest that the original ten words, in their Mosaic form, differed from any of the texts we have, and that of these the Exodus text in its present form is later than that in Deuteronomy. The great difference in length between the two halves of the Decalogue suggests the probability that originally all the commandments were short, and much the same in style and character as the last half, "Thou shalt not steal," and so on. Further, when the reasons and inducements given for the observance of the longer commands are set aside, just such short commands are left to us as we find in the second table. Lastly, differences between the versions in Exodus and Deuteronomy occur in almost every case in those parts of the text which may be regarded as appendices. In fact there are only two variations in the proper text of the commands. In the fourth, we have in Exodus "Remember the Sabbath day," while in Deuteronomy we have "Observe the Sabbath day"; but the meaning is the same in both cases. In the tenth, in Exodus the command is "Thou shalt not covet thy neighbour's house"; and the "house" is explained by the succeeding clause, "Thou shalt not covet thy neighbour's wife, nor his manservant," etc., to mean "household" in its widest sense. In Deuteronomy the old meaning of "house" as household and goods has fallen out of use, and the component parts of the neighbour's household possessions are named, beginning with his wife. Then follows the "house" in its narrow meaning, as the mere dwelling, grouped along with the slaves and cattle, and with *tithawweh* substituted in Hebrew for *tachmodh*. Fundamentally therefore the two recensions are the same. Even in the reasons and explanations there is only one really important variation. In Exod. xx. 11 the reason for the observance of the fourth commandment is stated thus: "For in six days Yahweh made heaven and earth, the sea and all that in them is, and rested the seventh day; therefore Yahweh blessed the Sabbath day, and hallowed it." In Deuteronomy, on the other hand, that reason is omitted, and in its place we find this: "And thou shalt remember that thou wast a servant in the land of Egypt, and Yahweh thy

God brought thee out thence by a mighty hand, and by a stretched out arm; therefore Yahweh thy God commanded thee to keep the Sabbath." Now if the reference to the creation had formed part of the original text of the Decalogue in the days of the author of Deuteronomy, if he had that before him as actually spoken by Yahweh, it is difficult to believe that he would have left it out and substituted another reason in its stead. He would have no object in doing so, for he could have added his own reason after that given in Exodus, had he so desired. It is likely, therefore, that in the original text no reason appeared; that Deuteronomy first added a reason; while ver. 11 in Exod. xx. was probably inserted there from a combination of Exod. xxxi. 17 *b* and Gen. ii. 2 *b*, — "For in six days Yahweh made heaven and earth, and on the seventh day He rested and was refreshed"; "and He rested on the seventh day from all His work which He had made." Both these texts belong to P and differ in style altogether from JE, with whose language all the rest of the setting of the Decalogue corresponds. On these suppositions Exod. xx. 11 would necessarily be the latest part of the two texts. Originally, therefore, the Mosaic commands probably ran thus:—

> "I am Yahweh thy God, which brought thee out of the land of Egypt, out of the house of bondage.
>
> "I. Thou shalt not have any other gods before Me.
>
> "II. Thou shalt not make unto thee any graven image.
>
> "III. Thou shalt not take the name of Yahweh thy God in vain.
>
> "IV. Remember (*or* Keep) the day of rest to sanctify it.
>
> "V. Honour thy father and thy mother.
>
> "VI. Thou shalt not kill.
>
> "VII. Thou shalt not commit adultery.
>
> "VIII. Thou shalt not steal.
>
> "IX. Thou shalt not bear false witness against thy neighbour.
>
> "X. Thou shalt not covet thy neighbour's house."

In that shape they contain everything that is fundamentally important, and exhibit the foundations of the Mosaic religion and polity in an entirely satisfactory and credible form.

But, before passing on to consider the substance of the Decalogue, it will be worth our while to consider what the full significance of these differing recensions of the Decalogue is. In both places the words are quoted directly as having been spoken by Yahweh to the people, and they are introduced by the quoting word "saying." Now if we do not wish to square what we read with any theory, the slight divergences between the two recensions need not trouble us, for we have the substance of what was said, and in the main the very words, and that is really all we need to be assured of. But if, on the contrary, we are going to insist that, this being part of an inspired book, every word must be pressed with the accuracy of a masoretic scribe, then we are brought into inextricable difficulties. It cannot be true that at Horeb Yahweh said two different things on this special occasion. One or both of these accounts must be inaccurate, in the pedantic sense of accuracy, and yet both have the same claim to be inspired. In fact both *are* inspired; it is the theory of inspiration which demands for revelation this kind of accuracy that must go to the wall.

It will be seen that this instance is very instructive as to the method of the ancient Hebrews in dealing with legislation which was firmly held to be Mosaic, or even directly Divine. If we are right in holding that originally the ten words were, as we have supposed, limited to definite short commands, this example teaches us that where there could be no question of deceit, or even an object for deceiving, additions calculated to meet the needs and defects of the particular period at which the laws are written down, are inserted without any hint that they did not form part of the original document. If this has been done, even to the extent we have seen reason to infer, in a small, carefully ordered, and specially ancient and sacred code, how much more freely may we expect the same thing to have been done in the looser and more fluid regulations of the large political and ceremonial codes, which on any supposition were posterior, and much less fundamental and sacred. That there is for *us* something disappointing, and even slightly questionable, in such action is really nothing to the purpose. We have to learn from the actual facts of revelation how revelation may be, or perhaps even must be, conveyed; and we cannot too soon learn the lesson that to a singular degree, and in many other directions than their notions of accuracy, the ancient mind differs from the modern mind, and that at any period there is a great gulf to be crossed before a Western mind can get into any intimate and sure *rapport* with an Eastern mind.

One other thing is noteworthy. Wellhausen has already been quoted as to the quite universal and moral character of the Decalogue; and his view, that a code so free from merely local and ceremonial provisions can hardly be Mosaic, has been discussed. But, while rejecting his conclusion, we must adhere to his premises. By emphasising the universal nature of the ten commandments, and by showing that they preceded the ceremonial law by many centuries, the critical school have cut away the ground from under the semi-antinomian views once so prevalent, and always so popular, with those who call themselves advanced thinkers. It is now no longer possible to maintain that the Decalogue was part of a purely Jewish law, binding only upon Jews and passing away at the advent of Christianity as the ceremonial law did. Of course this view was never really taken seriously in reference to murder or theft; but it has always been a strong point with those who have wished to secularise the Sunday. Now if the advanced critical position be in any degree true, then the ten commandments stand quite separate from the ceremonial law, have nothing in common with it, and are handed down to us in a document written before the conception even of a binding ceremonial law had dawned upon the mind of any man in Israel. Nor is there anything ceremonial or Jewish in the command, Remember *or* Observe the rest-day to keep it holy. In the reasons given in Exodus and Deuteronomy we have the two principles which make this a moral and universal command — the necessity for rest, and the necessity of an opportunity to cultivate the spiritual nature. Nothing indeed is said about worship; but it lies in the nature of the case that if secular work was rigorously forbidden, mere slothful abstinence from activity cannot have been all that was meant. Worship, and instruction in the things of the higher life, must certainly have been practised in such a nation as Israel on such a day; and we may therefore say that they were intended by this commandment. Understood in that way, the fourth commandment shows a delicate perception of the conditions of the higher life, which surpasses even the prohibition of covetousness in the tenth. In the words of a working man who was advocating its observance, "It gives God a chance"; that is, it gives man the leisure to attend to God. But the moral point of view which it implies is so high, and so difficult of attainment, that it is only now that the nations of Europe are awaking to the inestimable moral benefits of the Sabbath they have despised. Because of this difficulty too, many who think themselves to be leaders in the path of improvement, and are esteemed by others to be so, are never weary of trying to weaken the moral consciousness of the people, until they can steal this benefit away, on the ground that Sabbath-keeping is a mere ceremonial observance. So far from being that, it is a moral duty of the highest type; and the danger in which it seems at times to stand is due mainly to the fact that to appreciate it needs a far more trained and sincere conscience than most of us can bring to the consideration of it.

CHAPTER V
THE DECALOGUE—ITS SUBSTANCE

That the Decalogue in any of its forms must have been the work of one mind, and that a very great and powerful mind, will be evident on the most cursory inspection. We have not here, as we have in other parts of Scripture, fragments of legislation supplementary to a large body of customary law, fragments which, because of their intrinsic importance or the necessities of a particular time, have been written down. We have here an extraordinarily successful attempt to bring within a definite small compass the fundamental laws of social and individual life. The wonder of it does not lie in the individual precepts. All of them, or almost all of them, can be paralleled in the legislation of other peoples, as indeed could not fail to be the case if the *fundamental* laws of society and of individual conduct were aimed at. These must be obeyed, more or less, in every society that survives. It is the wisdom with which the selection has been made; it is the sureness of hand which has picked out just those things which were central, and has laid aside as irrelevant everything local, temporary, and purely ceremonial; it is the relation in which the whole is placed to God,—these give this small code its distinction. In these respects it is like the Lord's Prayer. It is vain for men to point out this petition of that unique prayer as occurring here, that other as occurring there, and a third as found in yet another place. Even if every single petition contained in it could be unearthed somewhere, it would still remain as unique as ever; for where can you find a prayer which, like it, groups the fundamental cries of humanity to God in such short space and with so sure a touch, and brings them all into such deep connection with the Fatherhood of God? In both cases, in the prayer and in the Decalogue alike, we must recognise that the grouping is the work of one mind; and in both we must recognise also that, whatever were the natural and human powers of the mind that wrought the code and prayer respectively, the main element in the success that has attended their work is the extraordinary degree in which they were illumined by the Divine Spirit. But where, between the time of Moses and the time when Deuteronomy first laid hold upon the life of the nation, are we to look for a legislator of this pre-eminence? So far as we know the history, there is no name that would occur to us. So far as can be seen, Moses alone has been marked out for us in the history of his people as equal to, and likely to undertake, such a task. Everything, therefore, concurs to the conclusion that in the Decalogue we have the first, the most sacred, and the fundamental law in Israel. Here Moses spoke for God; and whatever additions to his original ten words later times may have made, they have not obscured or overlaid what must be ascribed to him. He may not have been the author of much that bears his name, for unquestionably there were developments later than his time which were called Mosaic because they were a continuation and adaptation of his work; but we are justified in believing that here we have the first law he gave to Israel; and in it we should be able to see the really germinal principles of the religion he taught.

Now, manifestly, a religion which spoke its first word in the ten commandments, even in their simplest form, must have been in its very heart and core moral. It must always have been a heresy therefore, a denial of the fundamental Mosaic conception, to place ritual observance *per se* above moral and religious conduct, as a means of approach to Yahweh. On any reading of the commandments only the third and fourth (two out of ten) refer to matters of mere worship; and even these may more correctly be taken to refer primarily to the moral aspects of the cultus. All the rest deal with fundamental relations to God and man. Consequently the prophets who, after the manner of Amos and Hosea, denounce the prevailing belief that Yahweh's help could be secured for Israel, whatever its moral state, by offerings and sacrifices, were not teaching a new doctrine, first discovered by themselves. They were simply reasserting the fundamental principles of the Mosaic religion. Reverence and righteousness—these from the first were the twin pillars upon which it rested. Before ever the ceremonial law, even in its most rudimentary form, had been given, these were emphasised in the strongest way as the requirements of Yahweh; and the people whom the prophets reproved, instead of being the representatives of the ancient Yahwistic faith, had rejected it. Whether the popular view was a falling away from a truer view which had once been popular, or whether it represented a heathen tendency which remained in Israel from pre-Mosaic times and had not even in the days of Amos been overcome, it seems undeniable that it was entirely contrary to the fundamental principles of Yahwism as given by Moses. Even by the latest narrators, those who brought our Pentateuch into its present shape, and who were, it is supposed, completely under the influence of ceremonial Judaism, the primarily moral character of Yahweh's religion was acknowledged by the place they gave to the ten commandments. They alone are handed down as spoken by Yahweh Himself, and as having preceded all other commands; and the terrors of Sinai, the thunder and the earthquake, are made more intimately the accompaniments of this law than of any other. Unquestionably the mind of Israel always was, that here, and not in the ceremonial law, was the centre of gravity of Yahwism. In the view of that fact it is somewhat hard to understand how so many writers of our times, who admit the Decalogue to have been Mosaic, or at any rate pre-prophetic, yet deny the prevailingly moral character of the early religion of Israel. When this law was once promulgated, the old naturalism in which Israel, like other ancient races, had been entangled was repudiated, and the relation between Yahweh and His people was declared to be one which rested upon moral conduct in the widest sense of that term. And the ground of this fact is plainly declared here to be the character of Yahweh: "I am the Lord thy God, that brought thee out of the land of Egypt, out of the house of bondage." He was their deliverer, He had a right to command them, and His commands revealed His nature to His people.

The first four commandments show that Yahweh was already conceived as a spiritual being, removed by a whole heaven from the gods of the Canaanite nations by whom Israel was surrounded. These were mere representatives of the powers of nature. As such they were regarded as existing in pairs, each god having his female counterpart; and their acts had all the indifference to moral considerations which nature in its processes shows. They dwelt in mountain tops, in trees, in rude stones, or in obelisks, and they were worshipped by rites so sanguinary and licentious that Canaanite worship bore everywhere a darker stain than even nature-worship elsewhere had disclosed. In contrast to all this the Yahweh of the Decalogue is "alone," in solitary and unapproachable separation. Amid all the unbridled speculation that has been let loose on this subject, no one, I think, has ever ventured to join with Him any name of a goddess, and He sternly repudiates the worship of any other god besides Him. Now, though there is nothing said of monotheism here, *i.e.* of the doctrine that no god but one exists, yet, in contrast to the hospitality which distinguished and distinguishes nature-worship in all its forms, Yahweh here claims from His people worship of the most exclusive kind. Besides Him they were to have no object of worship. He, in His unapproachable separateness, had alone a claim upon their reverence. Further, in contrast to the gods who dwelt in trees and stones and pillars, and who could be represented by symbols of that kind, Yahweh sternly forbade the making of any image to represent Him. Thereby He declared Himself spiritual, in so far as He claimed that no visible thing could adequately represent Him. In contrast to the ethnic religions in general, even that of Zarathushtra, the noblest of all, where only the natural element of fire was taken to be the god or his symbol, this fundamental command asserts the supersensuous nature of the Deity, thereby rising at one step clear above all naturalism.

So great is the step indeed, that Kuenen and others, who cannot escape the evidence for the antiquity of the other commandments, insist that this at least cannot be pre-prophetic, since we have such numerous proofs of the worship of Yahweh by images, down at least to the time of Josiah's reform. But, by all but Stade, it is admitted that there was at Shiloh under Eli, and at Jerusalem under David and Solomon, no visible representation of Deity. Now the same writers who tell us this everywhere represent the worship of Yahweh by images as existing among the people. According to their view, the nation had a continual and hereditary tendency to slip into image-worship, or to maintain it as pre-Mosaic custom. And it is quite certain that up even to the Captivity, and after, when, according to even the very boldest negative view, this command had been long known, image-worship, not only of Yahweh, but also of false gods and of the host of heaven, was largely prevalent. Only the Captivity, with its hardships and trials, brought Israel to see that image-worship was incompatible with any true belief in Yahweh. Undeniably, therefore, the existence of an authoritative prohibition does not necessarily produce obedience; and the Biblical view that the Decalogue is Israel's earliest law proves to be the more reasonable, as well as the better authenticated of the two. If, after the command beyond all doubt existed in Israel, it needed the calamities of Israel's last days, and the hardships and griefs of the Exile, to get it completely observed, and if in Jerusalem and at Shiloh in the pre-prophetic time Yahweh was worshipped without images, there can hardly be a doubt that this command must have existed in the earliest period. For no religion is to be judged by the actual practice of the multitude. The true criterion is its highest point; and the imageless worship of Jerusalem is much more difficult to understand if the second commandment was not acknowledged previously in Israel, than it would be if the Decalogue, essentially as we now have it, was acknowledged in the days before the kingship at least.[25]

The arguments advanced by Kuenen and Wellhausen for a contrary view, beyond those we have just been considering, rest on an undue extension of the prohibition to make any likeness of anything. They adduce the brazen serpent of Moses, and the Cherubim, and the brazen bulls that bore the brazen laver in the court of the Temple at Jerusalem, and the ornaments of that building, as a proof that even in Jerusalem this commandment cannot have been known. But, as we have seen, the original command prohibited only the making of a *pesel*, i.e. of an image for worship. The making of likenesses of men and animals for mere purposes of art and adornment was never included; and the whole objection falls to the ground unless it be asserted that the bulls under the basin were actually worshipped by those who came into the Temple!

The supersensuous nature of Yahweh must, therefore, be taken to be a fundamental part of the Mosaic religion. But besides being solitary and supersensuous, Yahweh was declared by Moses, perhaps by His very name, to be not only mighty, but helpful. The preface to the whole series of commandments is, "I am Yahweh thy God, who brought thee forth out of the land of Egypt." Now of all the derivations of Yahweh, that which most nearly commands universal acceptance is its derivation from *hayah*, to be. And the probabilities are all in favour of the view that it does not imply mere timeless existence, as the translation of the explanation in Exodus[26] has led many to believe. That is a purely philosophical idea entirely outside of morality, and it can hardly be that the introduction to this moral code, which announces the author of it, should contain no moral reference. If the name be from Qal, and be connected with *ehyeh*, then it means, as Dillmann says (*Exodus and Leviticus*, p. 35), that He will be what He has been, and the name involves a reference to all that the God of Israel has been in the past. Such He will be in the future, for He is what He is, without variableness or shadow of turning. If, on the other hand, it be from Hiphil, it will mean "He who causes to be," the creator. In either case there is a clear rise above the ordinary Semitic names for God, Baal, Molech, Milkom, which all express mere lordship. No doubt Yahweh was also called Baal, or Lord, just as we find Him in the Psalms addressed as "my King and my God"; but the specially Mosaic name, the personal name of the God of Israel, does undoubtedly imply quite another quality in God. It is the Helper who has revealed Himself to Israel who here speaks. Hence the addition, "who brought thee out of the land of Egypt." It is as a Saviour that Yahweh addresses His people. By His very name He lifts all the commands He gives out of the region of mere might, or the still lower region of gratification at offerings and precious things bestowed, into the region of gratitude and love.

Further, by issuing this code under the name of Yahweh Moses claimed for Him a moral character. Whether the Hebrew word for holy, *qādhōsh*, implied more in those days than mere separateness, may be doubted; but it is impossible that the idea which we now connect with the word "holy" should not have been held to be congruous to, and expressive of, the nature of Yahweh. Here morality in its initial and fundamental stages is set forth as an expression of His will. And similarly, righteousness must also be an attribute of His, for justice between man and man is made to be His demand upon men. He Himself, therefore, must be faithful as well as holy, and His emancipation from the clinging chain of mere naturalism was thereby completed. The Yahweh of the Decalogue is therefore absolutely alone. He is supersensuous. He is the Helper and Saviour, and He is holy and true.

These are His fundamental qualities. Such qualities may be supposed to be present only in their elements, even to the mind of Moses himself: yet the fundamental germinal point was there: and all that has grown out of it may be justly put to the credit of this first revelation.

A moment's thought will show how the teaching that Yahweh alone was to be worshipped broke away from the main stream of Semitic belief, and prepared the way for the ultimate prevalence of the belief that God was one. That He was supersensuous, so that He could not rightly or adequately be represented by any likeness of anything in heaven or earth or sea, left no possible outlet for thought about Him, save in the direction that He was a Spirit. In essence consequently the spirituality of God was thereby secured. Still more important perhaps was the conception of Yahweh as the Helper and Deliverer, the Saviour of His people; for this at once suggested the thought that the true bond between God and man was not mere necessity, nor mere dependence upon resistless power, but love—love to a Divine Helper who revealed Himself in gracious acts and providences, and who longed after and cared for His people with a perfectly undeserved affection. Lastly, His holiness and faithfulness, His righteousness in fact, held implicit in it His supremacy and universality. As Wellhausen has said, "As God of justice and right, Yahweh came to be thought of as the highest, and at last as the only power in heaven and earth." Whether that last stage was present to the mind of Moses, or of any who received the commandments in the first place, is of merely secondary importance. At the very least, the way which must necessarily lead to that stage was opened here, and the mind of man entered upon the path to a pure monotheism, a monotheism which separated God from the world, and referred to His will all that happened in the world of created things. God is One, God is a Spirit, God is Love, and God rules over all—these are the attributes of Yahweh as the Decalogue sets them forth; and in principle the whole higher life of humanity was secured by the great synthesis.

Like all beginnings, this was an achievement of the highest kind. Nowhere but in the soul of one Divinely enlightened man could such a revelation have made itself known; and the solitude of a lonely shepherd's life, following upon the stir and training of a high place in the cultured society of Egypt, gave precisely the kind of environment which would prepare the soul to hear the voice by which God spoke. For we are not to suppose that this revelation came to Moses without any effort or preparation on his part. God does not reveal His highest to the slothful or the debased. Even when He speaks from Sinai in thunder and in flame, it is only the man who has been exercising himself in these great matters who can understand and remember. All the people had been terrified by the Divine Presence, but they forgot the law immediately and fell back into idolatry. It was Moses who retained it and brought it back to them again. His personality was the organ of the Divine will; and in this law which he promulgated Moses laid the foundation of all that now forms the most cherished heritage of men. The central thing in religion is the character of God. Contrary to the prevailing feeling, which makes many say that they know nothing of God, but are sure of their duty to man, history teaches that, in the end, man's thought of God is the decisive thing. Everything else shapes itself according to that; and by taking the first great steps, which broke through the limits of mere naturalism, Moses laid the foundation of all that was to come. There was here the promise and the potency of all higher life: love and holiness had their way prepared, so that they should one day become supreme in man's conception of the highest life: the confused halting between the material and the spiritual, which can be traced in the very highest conceptions of merely natural religions, was in principle done away. And what was here gained was never lost again. Even though the multitude never really grasped all that Moses had proclaimed Yahweh to be; and though it should be proved, which is as yet by no means the case, that even David thought of Him as limited in power and claims by the extent of the land which Israel inhabited; and though, as a matter of fact, the full-orbed universality which the ten commandments implicitly held in them was not attained under the old covenant at all; yet these ten words remained always an incitement to higher thoughts. No advance made in religion or morals by the chosen people ever superseded them. Even when Christ came, He came not to destroy but to fulfil. The highest reach of even His thoughts as regards God could be brought easily and naturally under the terms of this fundamental revelation to Israel.

The remaining commands, those which deal with the relations of men to each other, are naturally introduced by the fifth commandment, which, while it deals with human relations, deals with those which most nearly resemble the relations between God and man. Reverence for God, the deliverer and forgiver of men, is the sum of the commandments which precede; and here we have inculcated reverence for those who are, under God, the source of life, upon whose love and care all, at their entrance into life, are so absolutely dependent. Love is not commanded; because in such relations it is natural, and moreover it cannot be produced at will. But reverence is; and from the place of the command, manifestly what is required is something of that same awful respect which is due to Yahweh Himself. The power which parents had over their children in Israel was extensive, though much less so than that possessed, for example, by Roman parents. A father could sell his daughters to be espoused as subordinate wives;[27] he could disallow any vows a daughter might wish to take upon her;[28] and both parents could bring an incorrigibly rebellious son to the elders of the city[29] and have him stoned publicly to death. But, according to Moses, the main restraining forces in the home should be love and reverence, guarded only by the solemn sanction of death to the openly irreverent, just as reverence for Yahweh was guarded.

There was here nothing of the sordid view, repudiated so energetically by Jewish scholars like Kalisch,[30] that we ought "to weigh and measure filial affection after the degree of enjoyed benefits." No; to this law "the relation between parents and children is holy, religious, godly, not of a purely human character"; and it is a mere profanation to regard it as we in modern times too often do. In our mad pursuit after complete individual liberty we have fallen back into a moral region which it was the almost universal merit of the ancient civilisations to have left behind them. It is true, certainly, that there were reasons for this advance then which we could not now recognise without falling back from our own attainments in other directions; but it was the saving salt of the ancient civilisations that the parents in a household were surrounded with an atmosphere of reverence, which made transgressions against them as rare as they were considered horrible. The modern freedom may in favourable circumstances produce more intimate and sympathetic intercourse between parents and children; but in the average household it has lowered the whole tone of family life; and it threatens sooner or later, if the ancient feeling cannot be restored, to destroy the family, the very keystone of our religion and civilisation. This commandment is not conditioned on the question whether parents have been more or less successful in giving their children what they desire, or whether they have been wise and unselfish in their dealing with their children. As parents they have a claim upon their respect, their tenderness, their observance, which can be neglected only at the children's peril. Even the average parent gives quite endless thought and care to his children, and almost unconsciously falls into the habit of living for them. That brings with it for the children an indelible obligation; and along with the new and wiser freedom which is permitted in the modern home, this reverence should grow, just as the love and reverence for God on the part of those who have been made the free children of God through Christ ought far to exceed that to which the best of the Old Testament saints could attain.

Want of reverence for parents is, in the Decalogue, made almost one with want of reverence toward God, and, in the case of this human duty alone, there is a promise annexed to its observance. The duty runs so deep into the very core of human life, that its fulfilment brings wholesomeness to the moral nature; this health spreads into the merely physical constitution, and long life becomes the reward. But apart from the quietude of heart and the power of self-restraint which so great a duty rightly fulfilled brings with it, we must also suppose that in a special manner the blessing of God does rest upon dutiful children. Even in the modern world, amid all its complexity, and though in numberless instances it may seem to have been falsified, this promise verifies itself on the large scale. In the less complex life of early Israel we may well believe that its verification was even more strikingly seen. In both ancient and modern times, moreover, the human conscience has leaped up to justify the belief that of all the sins committed without the body this is the most heinous, and that there does rest upon it in a peculiar manner the wrath of Almighty God. It is a blasphemy against love in its earliest manifestations to the soul, and only by answering love with love and reverence can there be any fulfilling of the law.

After the fifth, the commandments deal with the purely human relations; but in coming down from the duties which men owe to God, this law escapes the sordidness which seems to creep over the laws of other nations, when they have to deal with the rights and duties of men. The human rights are taken up rather into their relation to God, and cease to be mere matters of bargain and arrangement. They are viewed entirely from the religious and moral standpoint. For example, the destruction of human life, which in most cases was in ancient times dealt with by private law, and was punished by fines or money payments, is here regarded solely as a sin, an act forbidden by God. The will of a holy God is the source of these prohibitions, however much the idea of property may extend in them beyond the limits which to us now seem fitting. They begin with the protection of a man's life, the highest of his possessions. Next, they prohibit any injury to him through his wife, who next to his life is most dear to him. Then property in our modern sense is protected; and lastly, rising out of the merely physical region, the ninth commandment prohibits any attack upon a man's civil standing or honour by false witness concerning him in the courts of justice. To that crime Easterns are prone to a degree which Westerns, whom Rome has trained to reverence for law, can hardly realise. In India, at this hour, false witnesses can be purchased in the open market at a trifling price; and under native government the whole forces of civil justice become instruments of the most remediless and exasperating tyranny. So long as the law has not spoken its last word *against* the innocent, there is hope of remedy; justice may at last assert itself. But when, either by corrupt witnesses or by a corrupt judge, the law itself inflicts the wrong, then redress is impossible, and we have the oppression which drives a wise man mad. Both murder and robbery, moreover, may be perpetrated by false swearing; and the trust, the confidence that social life demands, is utterly destroyed by it.

But it is in the tenth commandment especially that this code soars most completely away beyond others. In four short words the whole region of neighbourly duty, so far as acts are concerned, has been covered, and with that other codes have been content. But the laws of Yahweh must cover more than that. Out of the heart proceed all these acts which have been forbidden, and Yahweh takes knowledge of its thoughts and intents. The covetous desire, the grasping after that which we cannot lawfully have, that, too, is absolutely forbidden. It has been pointed out that the first commandment also deals with the thoughts. "Thou shalt have no other gods before Me," separated from the prohibition of idol-worship, can refer only to the inward adoration or submission of the heart. And in this last commandment also it is the evil desire, the lust which "bringeth forth sin," which is condemned. In its beginning and ending, therefore, this code transcends the limits ordinarily fixed for law; it leads the mind to a view of the depth and breadth of the evil that has to be coped with, which the other precepts, taken by themselves and understood in their merely literal sense, would scarcely suggest.

This fact should guard us against the common fallacy that Moses and the people of his day could not have understood these commandments in any sense except the barely literal one. In the first and tenth commandments there is involved the whole teaching of our Lord that he that hateth his brother is a murderer. The evil thought that first stirs the evil desire is here placed on the same interdicted level as the evil deed; and though until our Lord had spoken none had seen all that was implied, yet here too He was only fulfilling, bringing to perfection, that which the law as given by Moses had first outlined. With this in view, it seems difficult to justify that interpretation of the commandments which refuses all depth of meaning to them. The initial and final references to the inner thoughts of men, the delicate moral perception which puts so unerring a finger on the sources of sin, show that such literalism is out of place. No interpretation can do this law justice which treats it superficially; and instead of feeling safest when we find least in these commandments, we should welcome from them all the correction and reproof which a reasonable exegesis will sustain.

Some of those who adopt the other view do so in the interests of the authenticity of the commandments. They say, We must be careful not to put into them any idea which transcends what was possible in the days of Moses; otherwise we must agree with those who bring down the date of these marvellous ten words to the middle of the seventh century B.C. But there is much ground for distrusting modern judgments as to what men can have thought and felt in earlier and ruder stages of society. So long as the *naïve* interpretation of the state of man before the fall prevailed, which Milton has made so widely popular, the tendency was to exaggerate the early man's moral and spiritual attainments. Now, when the most degraded savages are taken as the truest representatives of primitive man, the temptation is to minimise both unduly. How often have we been told, for example, that the Australian is the lowest of mankind, and that he has no other idea of a spiritual world than that when he dies he will "jump up" a white man! Yet Mr. A. W. Howitt,[31] an unexceptionable authority, as having himself been "initiated" among the Australian blacks, tells us that they give religious and moral instruction to their boys when they receive the privileges of manhood. His words are: "The teachings of the initiation are in a series of 'moral lessons,' pantomimically displayed in a manner intended to be so impressive as to be indelible. There is clearly a belief in a Great Spirit, or rather an anthropomorphic Supernatural Being, the 'Master of all,' whose abode is above the sky, and to whom are attributed powers of omnipotence and omnipresence, or, at any rate, the power 'to do anything and to go anywhere.' The exhibition of his image to the novices, and the magic dances round it, approach very near to idol-worship. The wizards who profess to communicate with him, and to be the mediums of communication between him and his tribe, are not far removed from an organised priesthood. To his direct ordinance are attributed the spiritual and moral laws of the community. Although there is no worship of Daramülun, as, for instance, by prayer, yet there is clearly an invocation of him by name, and a belief that certain acts please while others displease him." To most it would have seemed absurd to attribute religious ideas of such a kind to a people in the social and moral condition of the Australian aborigines. Yet here we have the testimony of a perfectly competent and reliable witness, who, moreover, has no personal bias in favour of theologic notions, to prove that even in their present state their theology is of this comparatively advanced kind.

Many critics like Stade, and even Kuenen, would deny to Israel in the days of Moses any conception of Yahweh which would equal the Australian conception of Daramülun! Not to speak of the "regrettable vivacities" of Renan in regard to Yahweh, Kuenen would deny to the Mosaic Yahweh the title of Lord of all; he would deny to Him the power "to go anywhere and to do anything," binding Him strictly to His tribe and His land; he would make His priests little more than the Australian wizards; and purely moral laws like the Decalogue Wellhausen would remove to a late date mainly because such laws transcend the limits of the thought and knowledge of the Mosaic time. But can any one believe that Israel in the Mosaic time had lower beliefs than those of the Australian aborigines? In every other respect they had left far behind them the social state and the merely embryonic culture of the Australian tribes. Moses himself is an irrefragable proof of that. No such man as he could have arisen among a people in the state of the Australians. Even the fact that the Hebrews had lived in Egypt, and had been compelled to do forced labour for a long series of years, would of itself have raised them to a higher stage of culture. Moreover they built houses, and owned sheep and cattle, and must have known at least the rudiments of agriculture. Indeed Deut. xi. 10 asserts this, and the testimony of travellers as to the habits of the tribes in the wilderness of the wanderings now confirms it. Further, they had been in contact with Egyptian religion, and they had been surrounded by cults having more or less relation to the ancient civilisations of Mesopotamia. Under such circumstances, even apart from all revelation, it could not be assumed that their religious ideas must needs correspond to modern notions of the low type of primitive religions. On the contrary, nothing but the clearest proof that their religious conceptions were so surprisingly low should induce us to believe it. On any supposition, they had in the Mosaic time the first germs of what is now universally admitted to be the highest form of religion. Can we believe that only 1300 years B.C., in the full light of history, coming out of a land where the religion of the people had been systematised and elaborated, not for centuries, but for millenniums, and only 600 years before the monotheistic prophets, a people at such a stage of civilisation as the Hebrews can have had cruder notions of Deity than the Wiraijuri and Wolgal tribes of New South Wales![32] It may have been so; but before we take it to have been so, we have a right to demand evidence of a stringent kind, evidence which leaves us no way of escape from a conclusion so improbable.

Moreover the acceptance of the view now opposed does not get rid of the necessity for supernatural enlightenment in Israel. It only transfers it from an earlier to a later time. For if the knowledge of Israel in Moses' day was below the Wolgal standard, then it would seem inexplicable that the ethical monotheism of the prophets should have grown out of it by any merely natural process. If there were no inspiration before the prophets, though they believed and asserted there was, then their own inspiration only becomes the more marvellous. It is not needful to deny that the Hebrew tribes may at some time have passed through the low stage of religious belief of which these writers speak. But they err conspicuously in regarding every trace of animistic and fetichistic worship which can be unearthed in the language, the ceremonies, and the habits of the Hebrews at the Exodus, as evidence of the highest beliefs of the people at that time. As a matter of fact, these were probably mere survivals of a state of thought and feeling then either superseded or in the process of being so. Besides, the mass of any people always lag far behind the thoughts and aspirations of the highest thinkers of their nation; and if we admit inspiration at all as a factor in the religious development of Israel, the distance between what Moses taught and believed himself, and what he could get the mass of the people to believe and practise, must have been still greater. If he gave the people the ten commandments, he must have been far above them, and dogmatic assertions as to what he can have thought and believed ought to be abandoned.

Granting, however, that all we have found in the Decalogue's conception of Yahweh was present to the mind of Moses, and granting that the commands which deal with the relations of men to each other are not mere isolated prohibitions, but are founded upon moral principles which were understood even then to have much wider implications, there still remains a gap between the widest meaning that early time could put into them, and that which Luther's Catechism, or the Catechism of the Westminster Divines, for example, asserts. The question therefore arises whether these wider and more detailed explanations, which make the Decalogue cover the whole field of the moral and religious life, are legitimate, and if so, on what principle can they be justified? The reply would seem to be that they are legitimate, and that the ten words did contain much more than Moses or any of his nation for many centuries after him understood. For any fruitful thought, any thought which really penetrates the heart of things, must have in it wider implications than the first thinker of it can have conceived. If by any means a man has had insight to see the central fact of any domain of thought and life, its applications will not be limited to the comparatively few cases to which he may apply it. He will generally be content to deduce from his discovery just those conclusions which in his circumstances and in his day are practically useful and are most clamorously demanded. But those who come after, pressed by new needs, challenged by new experiences, and enlightened by new thoughts in related regions, will assuredly find that more was involved in that first step than any one had seen. The scope of the fruitful principle will thus inevitably widen with the course of things, and inferences undreamed of by those who first enunciated the principle will be securely drawn from it by later generations. Now if that be true in regard to truths discovered by the unassisted intellect of man, how much more true will it be of thoughts which have first been revealed to man under the influence of inspiration? Behind the human mind which received them and applied them to the circumstances which then had to be dealt with, there is always the infinite mind which sees that

"Far-off Divine event
To which the whole creation moves."

The Divine purpose of the revelation must be the true measure of the thoughts revealed, and the Divine purpose can best be learned by studying the results as they have actually evolved themselves in the course of ages. Consequently, while the fundamental point in sound interpretation of a book such as the Bible is to ascertain *first* what the statements made therein signified to those who heard them first, the second point is not to shut the mind to the wider and more extensive applications of them which the thought and experience of men, taught by the course of history, have been induced, or even compelled, to make. Both the narrower and the wider meanings are there, and were meant to be found there. No exposition which ignores either can be adequate.

That all works of God are to be dealt with in this way is beautifully demonstrated by Ruskin (*Fors Clavigera*, Vol. I., Letter V.). In criticising the statement of a botanist that "there is no such thing as a flower," after admitting that in a certain sense the lecturer was right, he goes on to say: "But in the deepest sense of all, he was to the extremity of wrongness wrong; for leaf and root and fruit exist, all of them, only—that there may be flowers. He disregarded the life and passion of the creature, which were its essence. Had he looked for these, he would have recognised that in the thought of nature herself, there is, in a plant, nothing else but flowers." That means, of course, that the final perfection of a development is the real and final meaning of it all. Now any thought given by God in this special manner which we call "inspiration" has in it a manifold and varied life, and an end in view, which God alone foresees. It works like leaven, it grows like a seed. It is supremely living and powerful; and though it may have begun its life, like the mustard seed, in a small and lowly sphere, it casts out branches on all sides till its entire allotted space is filled. So in the Decalogue; the central chord in all the matters dealt with has been touched with Divine skill, and all that has further to be revealed or learned on that matter must lie in the line of the first announcement.

It is not, therefore, an illegitimate extension of the meaning of the first commandment to say that it teaches monotheism, nor of the second that it teaches the spirituality of God, nor of the seventh that it forbids all sensuality in thought or word or deed. It is true that probably only the separateness of God was originally seen to be asserted in the first, and the words may possibly have been understood to mean that the "other gods" referred to had some kind of actual life. The second, too, may have seemed to be fulfilled when no earthly thing that was made by man was taken to represent Yahweh. Lastly, those who say that nothing is forbidden in the seventh commandment but literal adultery have much to say for themselves. In a polygamous society concubinage always exists. The absence of the more flagrant of what in monogamous societies are called social evils does not in the least imply the superior morality, such as many who wish to disparage our Christian civilisation have ascribed, for instance, to Mohammedans. The degraded class of women who are the reproach and the despair of our large towns are not so frequent in those societies, because all women are degraded to nearer their level than in monogamous lands. Both lust and vice are more prevalent: and they are so because the whole level of thought and feeling in regard to such matters is much lower than with us.

Now, undoubtedly, ancient Israel was no exception to this rule. In it, as a polygamous nation, there was a licence in regard to sexual relations with women who were neither married nor betrothed which would be impossible now in any Christian community. It may be, therefore, that only the married woman was specially protected by this law. But in none of these cases did the more rudimentary conception of the scope of the commandments last. By imperceptible steps the sweep of them widened, until finally the last consequences were deduced from them, and they were seen to cover the whole sphere of human duty. It may have been a long step from the prohibition to put other gods along with Yahweh to St. Paul's decisive word "An idol is nothing in the world," but the one was from the first involved in the other. Between "Thou shalt not make unto thee a graven image" and our Lord's declaration "God is a Spirit, and must be worshipped in spirit and in truth," there lies a long and toilsome upward movement; but the first was the gate into the path which must end in the second. Similarly, the commandment which affirmed so strongly the sacredness of the family, by hedging round the house-mother with this special defence held implicit in it all that rare and lovely purity which the best type of Christian women exhibit. The principles upon which the initial prohibitions were founded were true to fact and to the nature both of God and man. They were, therefore, never found at fault in the advancing stages of human experience; and the meaning which a modern congregation of Christians finds in these solemn "words," when they are read before them, is as truly and justly their meaning as the more meagre interpretation which alone ancient Israel could put upon them.

How gradually, and how naturally, the advancing thoughts and changed circumstances of Israel affected the Decalogue may be seen most clearly in the differences between its form as originally given, and as it is set forth in Exodus and in Deuteronomy. If the original form of these commandments was what we have indicated (p. 69), they corresponded entirely to the circumstances of the wilderness. There is no reference in them which presupposes any other social background than that of a people dwelling together according to families, possessing property, and worshipping Yahweh. None of the commandments involves a social state different from that. But when Israel had entered upon its heritage, and had become possessed of the oxen and asses which were needed in agricultural labour and in settled life, this stage of their progress was reflected in the reasons and inducements which were added to the original commands. In the fourth and tenth commandments of Exodus we have consequently the essential commandments of the earlier day adapted to a new state of things, *i.e.* to a settled agricultural life. Then, even as between the Exodus and Deuteronomic texts, a progress is perceptible. The reasons for keeping the Sabbath which these two recensions give are different, as we have seen, and it is probable that the reason given in Deuteronomy was first. To the people in the wilderness came the bare Divine command that this one day was to be sacred to Yahweh. In both Exodus and Deuteronomy we have additions, going into details which show that when these versions were prepared Israel had ceased to be nomadic and had become agricultural. In Deuteronomy we find that the importance and usefulness of this command from a humane point of view had been recognised, and one at least of the grounds upon which it should be held a point of morality to keep it is set forth in the words "that thy manservant and thy maidservant may rest as well as thou." Finally, if the critical views be correct, in Exodus we have the motive for the observance of the Sabbath raised to the universal and eternal, by being brought into connection with the creative activity of God.

If the progression now traced out be real, then we have in it a classical instance of the manner in which Divine commands were given and dealt with in Israel. Given in the most general form at first, they inevitably open the way for progress, and as thought and experience grow in volume and rise in quality, so does the understanding of the law as given expand. Under the influence of this expansion addition after addition is made, till the final form is reached; and the whole is then set forth as having been spoken by Yahweh and given by Moses when the command was first promulgated. In such cases literary proprietorship was never in question. Each addition was sanctioned by revelation, and those by whom it came were never thought of. It would seem, indeed, that nothing but modern sceptical views as to the reality of revelation, the feeling that all this movement to a higher faith was merely natural, and that the hand of God was not in it, could have suggested to the ancient Hebrew writers the wish to hand on the names of those by whom such changes were made. Yahweh spoke at the beginning, Moses mediated between the people and Yahweh, and the law thus mediated was in all forms equally Mosaic, and in all forms equally Divine.

One other thing remains to be noticed, and that is the prevailingly negative form of the commandments. Of the ten only the fourth and fifth are in the affirmative. All the others are prohibitions, and we who have been taught by Christianity to put emphasis upon the positive aspects of duty as the really important aspects of it, may not improbably feel chilled and repelled by a moral code which so definitely and prevailingly forbids. But the cause of this is plain. A code like that of the Twelve Tables published in early Rome is only occasionally negative, because it rises to no great height in its demands, and is intent only upon ordering the life of the citizens in their outward conduct. But this code, which seeks to raise the whole of life into the sacredness of a continual service of God and man, must forbid, because the first condition of such a life is the renunciation and the restriction of self. Benevolent dreamers and theorists of all ages, and men of the world whose moral standard is merely the attainment of the average man, have denied the evil tendency in man's nature. They have asserted that man is born good; but the facts of experience are entirely against them. Whenever a serious effort has been made to raise man to any conspicuous height of moral goodness, it has been found necessary to forbid him to follow the bent of his nature. "Thou shalt not" has been the prevailing formula; and in this sense original sin has always been witnessed to in the world. Hence the Old Testament, in which the most strenuous conflict for goodness which the world in those ages knew was being carried on, could not fail, in every part of it, to proclaim that man is not born good. However late we may be compelled to put the writing of the story of the fall as it stands in Genesis, there can be no question that it represents the view of the Old Testament at all times. Man is fallen; he is not what he ought to be, and the evil taint is handed on from one generation to another. Every generation, therefore, is called, by prophet and priest and lawgiver alike, to the conflict against the natural man.

The truth is that all along the leaders of Israel had a quite overawing sense of the moral greatness of Yahweh and of the stringency of His demands upon them. "Be ye holy, for I am holy," was His demand; and so among this people, as among no other, the sense of sin was heightened, till it embittered life to all who seriously took to heart the religion they professed. This feeling sought relief in expiatory sacrifices, like the sin offering and the guilt offering; but in vain. It then led to Pharisaic hedging of the law, to seeking a positive precept for every moment of time, to binding upon men's consciences the most minute and burdensome prescriptions, as a means of making them what they must be if they were to meet the Divine requirements. But that too failed. It became a slavery so intolerable that, when St. Paul received the power of a new life, his predominant feeling was that for the first time he knew what liberty meant. He was set free from both the bondage of sin and the bondage of ritual.

To the religious man of the Old Testament life was a conflict against evil tendencies, a conflict in which defeat was only too frequent, but from which there was no discharge. It was fitting, therefore, that at the very beginning of Israel's history, as the people of God, this stern prohibition of the rougher manifestations of the natural man should stand.

But it is characteristic of the Old Testament that it states the fundamental fact, without any of the over-refinements and exaggerations by which later doctrinal developments have discredited it. There is no appearance here, or anywhere in the Old Testament, of the Lutheran exaggeration that man is by nature impotent to all good, as a stock or a stone is. Keeping close to the testimony of the universal conscience, the Decalogue, and the Old Testament generally, speaks to men as those who can be otherwise if they will. There is, further, a robust assertion of righteous intention and righteous act on the part of those whose minds are set to be faithful to God. This may have been partly due to a blunter feeling in regard to sin, and a less highly developed conscience, but it was mainly a healthy assertion of facts which ought not to be ignored. Yet, with all that, original sin was too plain a fact ever to be denied by the healthy-minded saints of the Old Testament. Fundamentally, they held that human nature needed to be restrained, its innate lawlessness needed to be curbed, before it could be made acceptable to God.

Among the heathen nations that was not so. Take the Greeks, for instance, as the highest among them. Their watchword in morals was not repression, but harmonious development. Every impulse of human nature was right, and had the protection of a deity peculiarly its own. Restraint, such as the Israelite felt to be his first need, would have been regarded as mutilation by the Greek, for he was dominated by no higher ideal than that of a fully developed man. There was no vision of unattainable holiness hovering always before his mind, as there was before the mind of the Israelite. God had not revealed Himself to him in power and unalloyed purity, with a background of infinite wisdom and omnipotence, so that unearthly love and goodness were seen to be guiding and ruling the world. As a consequence, the calling and destiny of man were conceived by the Greeks in a far less soaring fashion than by Israel. To put the difference in a few words, man, harmoniously developed in all his powers and passions and faculties, with nothing excessive about him, was made God by the Greeks; whereas in Israel God was brought down into human life to bear man's burden and to supply the strength needed that man might become like God in truth and mercy and purity. It is of course true that both conceived of God under human categories. They could not conceive God save by attributing to Him that which they looked upon as highest in man. It is also true that the higher natures in both nations, starting thus differently, did in much approach each other. Still, the immense difference remains, that the impulse in the one case was given from the earth by dreams of human perfection, in the other it came from above through men who had seen God. The Greeks had seen only the glory of man; Israel had seen the glory of God.

The result was that human nature as it is seemed to the one much more worthy of respect and much less seriously compromised than it did to the other. Comparing man as he is, only with man as he easily might be, the Greeks took a much less serious view of his state than the Hebrews, who compared him with God as He had revealed Himself. The former never attained any clear conception of sin, and regarded it as a passing weakness which could without much trouble be overcome. The latter saw that it was a radical and now innate want of harmony with God, which could only be cured by a new life being breathed into man from above. And when Europe became Christian, this difference made itself felt in very widespread religious and theological divergences. In the South and among the Latin races the less strenuous view of human disabilities—the view which naturally grew out of the heathen conception of man as, on the whole, born good, with no very arduous moral heights to scale—has prevailed, and in those regions the Pelagian form of doctrine has mastered the Christian Church. But the Teutonic races have, in this matter, shown a remarkable affinity with the Hebrew mind and teaching. The deeper and more tragic view of the state of man has commended itself to the Teutonic mind, and the depth of the moral taint in the natural man has been estimated according to the Biblical standard. It is not only theologians among the Northern races who have been thus affected. The higher imaginative literature of England gives the same impression; and in our own day Browning, our greatest poet, has emphasised his acceptance of the Augustinian view of human nature by making its teaching as to original sin a proof of the truth of Christianity.[33] At the end of his poem "Gold Hair: a Story of Pornic," in which he tells how a girl of angelic beauty, and of angelic purity of nature as was supposed, is found after her death to have sold her soul to the most gruesome avarice, he says:—

"The candid incline to surmise of late
That the Christian faith may be false, I find;
For our Essays and Reviews' debate
Begins to tell on the public mind,
And Colenso's words have weight:

I still, to suppose it true, for my part,
See reasons and reasons; this, to begin:
'Tis the faith that launched point-blank her dart
At the head of a lie—taught original sin,
The corruption of man's heart."

But the Pagan view always reasserts itself; and modern Hellenists especially, in their admiration of the grace which does undoubtedly go with such conceptions of goodness as the Greeks could attain, are apt to look askance at the harshness and strenuousness which they find in the Old Testament. For the most pathetic and pure of the Greek conceptions of the gods are those which, like Demeter, embody mother's love or some other natural glory of humanity. Being thus natural, they are set before us by the Greek imagination with an unconstrained and graceful beauty which makes goodness appeal to the æsthetic sense. To do this seems to many the supreme achievement. Without this they hold that Christianity would fail to meet the requirements of the modern heart and mind, for to interest "taste" on the side of goodness is, apparently, better than to let men feel the compulsion of duty. Reasoning on such premises, they claim that Greek religion gave to Christianity its completion and its crown. This is the claim advanced by Dyer in his *Gods of Greece* (p. 19). "The Greek poets and philosophers," he says, "are among our intellectual progenitors, and therefore the religion of to-day has requirements which include all that the noblest Greeks could dream of, requirements which the aspirations of Israel alone could not satisfy. Our complex life had need, not only of a supreme God of power, universal and irresistible, of a jealous God beside whom there was no other God, but also of a God of love and grace and purity. To these ideal qualities, present in the Diviner godhead of the Gospels, the evolution of Greek mythology brought much that satisfies our hearts." The best answer to that is to read Deuteronomy. The Hebrews had no need to borrow "a God of love and grace and purity" from Greek mythology. Centuries before they came in contact with Greeks, their inspired men had painted the love and grace and purity of God in the most attractive colours. Nor did they ever need to unlearn the belief that Yahweh was merely a supreme God of power. In the course of our exposition we shall have occasion to see that the worship of mere power was superseded by the religion of Yahweh from the first, and that the author of Deuteronomy gives his whole strength to demonstrate that the God of Israel is a "God of love and grace and purity." But perhaps "grace" means to Mr. Dyer "gracefulness." In that case we would deny that "the Diviner godhead of the Gospels," as revealed in Jesus Christ, had that æsthetic quality either. There is no word of an appeal to the sense of the artistically beautiful in anything recorded of Him; but neither in the Old Testament nor the New is there any want of moral beauty in the representation given of God. Moral beauty alone has a central place in religion; and when beauty that appeals to the senses intrudes into religion, it becomes a source of weakness rather than of strength. There may be a few people who can trust to their taste to keep them firm in the pursuit of goodness, but the bulk of men have always needed, and will always need, the severer compulsion of duty. They need an objective standard; they need a God, the embodiment and enforcer of all that duty demands of them; and when they bend themselves to the yoke of obligation thus imposed, they enter into a world of heavenly beauty which seizes and enraptures the soul. The mere æsthetic beauty of Greek mythology pales, for the more earnest races of mankind at least, before this Diviner loveliness, and it is the special gift of the Hebrew as well as of the Teutonic races to be sensitive to it, just as they fall behind others in æsthetic sensitiveness. Wordsworth felt this, and has expressed it inimitably in his "Ode to Duty" —

> "Stern Lawgiver! yet Thou dost wear
> The Godhead's most benignant grace
> Nor know we anything so fair
> As is the smile upon Thy face."

That expresses the Hebrew feeling also. Drawn upwards by the infinite and unchangeable love and goodness of Yahweh, the Hebrews felt the clog of their innate sinfulness as no other race has done. The stern "thou shalt nots" of the Decalogue consequently found an echo in their hearts. Won by the beauty of holiness, they gladly welcomed the discipline of the Divine law, and by doing so they established human goodness on a foundation immeasurably more stable than any the gracefulness of Greek imaginations could hope to lay.

CHAPTER VI
THE MEDIATORSHIP OF MOSES

Deut. v. 22-33

After the ten commandments, Deuteronomy, like Exodus, next indicates that for all of legislation, exhortation, and advice that follows, Moses was to be the mediator between God and the people. He is represented as Yahweh's prophet or speaker in all that succeeds; the Decalogue alone is set forth as the direct Divine command. Evidently a great distinction is here notified, and what it exactly was may be best explained by reference to the history of Roman law. In the earliest times that consisted of *Fas, Jus,* and *Jus moribus constitutum.* In Chapter IV. Professor Muirhead's description of fas has been given at length, so that we need not repeat it here. The point to remember is that it consisted of universal precepts such as the Decalogue contains, given direct by God. *Jus* again was, according to Breal, the Divine will declared by human agency, and it occupied much the position which law does in civilised states now. Finally, *jus moribus constitutum,* or *boni mores,* was customary law, which had a twofold function. "It was (1) a restraint upon the law, condemning, though it could not prevent, the ruthless and unnecessary exercise of legal right. (2) It was a supplement to law (*jus*), requiring things law did not, *e.g.* dutiful service, respect and obedience, chastity, fidelity to engagements, etc." Now it is a striking fact that, though there can be no question of imitation here, the legislation of Deuteronomy falls naturally into these very divisions; and that fact of itself gives strong support to the belief that here in Israel, as there in Rome, we have the recorded facts of the earliest efforts at the regulation of national life. The *fas,* then, corresponds to the Decalogue. The *jus* runs exactly parallel with the laws in the strict sense of the term, those which Moses received from Yahweh and afterwards promulgated. Lastly, the *boni mores* are represented in Deuteronomy by those beautiful precepts which limited the exercise of legal right, and, going far beyond law, demanded of Israel that they should make good their claim to be Yahweh's people by justice, charity, and purity.

To some it may seem that we do no service to Scripture by insisting upon such a parallel. They will feel as if thereby the unique character of the religion of Israel as a revealed religion were obscured, if not obliterated. But nothing can be imagined which could confirm us in belief of the substantial accuracy of what we find narrated of early times in Scripture, more than the discovery that, without any possibility of collusion, the earliest records of civilisation elsewhere give us precisely the same account of the forms in which law first makes its appearance. Surely we ought now to have learned this lesson at least, that it is no disparagement to a Divinely given system of law and religion, that its growth and development run in the same channels as the growth and development of similar systems which have none of the marks of a Divine origin. Revelation always seizes upon mind as it is, and makes that a sufficient and effective channel for itself. However it is to be explained, it is true that Divine action generally seeks to hide itself in the ordinary course of human things as quickly as possible. It is only at the moment of contact, or at the moment when it has burst forth in some flower of more than earthly grace and loveliness, or when it has overturned and overturned until that state of things which has a right to endure has been attained, that the Divine force reveals itself. For the most part it sinks into the general sum of forces that are making for the progress of humanity, and clothes itself gladly in the uniform of other beneficent but natural influences. Consequently it ought to be a welcome fact that so close a parallel exists between the origins of Roman law and the origins of Hebrew law. The one great gain already mentioned, that it explains the early appearance of the Decalogue, and shows that some such laws would naturally be among the primary laws of Israel, would be sufficient to justify that view; while in addition the distinctions from the early laws of Rome help us to classify in clear broad masses the somewhat disordered series of Deuteronomic laws.

On one point only does the parallel seem questionable. If we followed it alone as our guide, we should have to set down the mediatorship of Moses, as a mere part of the method, as belonging to the formal side only of the great revelation. In other words, we should have to ask whether the statement we have in Deut. v. 22-30 is only an emotional and pictorial way of setting forth the fact that, following and supplementing the elementary and Divinely given Hebrew *fas*, there was also a Divinely given but humanly mediated *jus*. But clearly it means much more than that. By the earlier prophets, and generally in all earlier delineations of him, Moses is regarded as a prophet who had more direct and continuous access to the Divine presence than any other prophet of Israel. Moreover he had always been represented from the earliest times as standing between Yahweh and His people, holding on to the one and refusing to let the other go. In the great scene, taken from the earliest constituents of the Pentateuch and narrated in Exod. xxxii., we see him anticipating by centuries the wonderful picture of the Servant of

God in Isa. liii., and by a still more amazing stretch of time, that Divinest wish of St. Paul, that he himself might be accursed even from Christ for his brethren's sake. He thus stood between Yahweh and His people both as the organ of Revelation and as the self-forgetting intercessor, who suffered for sins not his own, as well as for sins which his connection with his nation had brought upon him; who, instead of repining, was willing to be blotted out of God's book if that could benefit his people.

This representation of Moses is not accidental. It is in complete accord with a characteristic of Israelite literature from beginning to end. In the earliest historical records we find that the chief heroes of the nation are mediators, standing for God in the face of evil men, and pleading with God for men when they are broken and penitent, or even when they are only terrified and restrained by the terror of the Lord. At the beginning of the national history we see the noble figure of Abraham in an agony of supplication and entreaty before God on behalf of the cities of the plain. At the end of it, we see the Christ, the supreme "mediator between God and man," pouring out His soul unto death for men "while they were yet sinners," dying, the just for the unjust, taking upon Himself the responsibility for the sin of man, and refusing to let him wander away into permanent separation from God. And all between is in accord with this. For it is not Moses only who is regarded as having a mediatorial office. The very people itself is set, by the promise given to Abraham, in the same position. As early at least as the eighth century it was put before Israel, that their calling was not for their own sakes only, but that in them all nations of the earth might be blessed. And at their highest moments the prophets and teachers of Israel always recognised this as their nation's part. Even when they were being scattered among the heathen, it was that they might be the means of bringing the knowledge of Yahweh to the nations. From end to end of Scripture, therefore, this conception is wrought into the very fibre of its utterances. It is of the essence of the Biblical conception of God that He should work among men by mediators. In no other way could the primary Divine message be set forth than by the prophetic voice; in no other way than by the intercession and the suffering of those most in harmony with the Divine will could any effective hold upon God be given to His people. Only by those who thus proved that they had seen Yahweh could His character be expressed. Further, it was in this way that Moses and the prophets, the rulers and the saints of Israel, were types of Christ. They were not mere puppets set forth in certain crises of Israel's history to go through a certain career, live a certain life, and pass into and out of a number of scenes, in order that they might afford us, upon whom the end of the world has come, pictorial proofs that all things in this history were pressing towards and converging upon Christ. That would be a very artificial way of conceiving the matter. No, each of these types was a real man, with real tasks of his own to accomplish in the world. Not only were they all real men, they were the leading men of their various times. They bore the burden of their day more than others; they were the special organs of Divine power and grace; and their lives were spent in giving impulse and direction to the movements of their people's life towards the strange, unlooked-for consummation appointed for it. They were types of Christ, they gave promise of Him, not because of mere arbitrary appointment or selection, but because they did in their day, in a lower degree and at an earlier stage, the very same work that He did. Further, the whole nation was a type of Christ in so far as it was true to its calling at all. It was the prophet and the priest among nations. It spread abroad the knowledge of Him, and it died at last as a nation that life might be given to the world. Both Israel and all the men who truly represented it were partakers in the labours and in the sufferings of Christ beforehand, just as Christians are said to fill up the measure of His sufferings now. The mediatorial character of Moses, therefore, was essential. It is no merely formal thing, nor an afterthought. He would have been no fit founder of the mediatorial nation had he not been a mediator himself, for not otherwise could he have helped to realise the Abrahamic promise.

But there is another subsidiary reason why a mediator was necessary to Israel at this stage. Behind all that Moses taught his people lay necessarily the ancient popular religion of the Hebrews. Now, except in so far as it may have been changed in Egypt, that was in its main features the same as the religion of the other nomadic tribes of Semitic stock, for the Abrahamic faith was, clearly, known but to few. But the names given to their deities by these people—such as Baal, Adhonai, Milcom, etc.—"all expressed submission to the irresistible power revealing itself in nature," just as "Islam," which means "submission," indicates that Mohammedanism is a mere perpetuation of this view.[34] Consequently the Israelite people were unable to conceive God save as a devouring presence, before which no man could live. The Mosaic view was, in itself, immeasurably higher, and, besides that, it opened up the path to attainments then inconceivable. Moses therefore had to stand alone in his new relation to God, while the people cowered away in terror, dominated entirely by the lower conception. They could not stand where he stood. They were unable to believe that power was not Yahweh's only attribute; while Moses had had revealed to him, in germ at least, that God was "merciful and gracious, longsuffering and slow to anger," and that a life passed in His presence was the ideal life for man. Both the Yahwistic narrative in Exodus and the repetition of it in Deuteronomy give the same representation of the events at Sinai, and indicate quite clearly that, while the old relation to God was in itself good so far, it was to be superseded by that higher relation in which Moses stood. That is the meaning of the words in Deut. v. 28, 29: "And Yahweh said unto me, I have heard the voice of the words of this people which they have spoken unto thee; they have well said all that they have spoken. Oh that there were such a heart in them, that they would fear Me and keep all My commandments, always, that it might be well with them and with their children for ever!" The parallel passage in Exodus is xx. 20: "And Moses said unto the people, Fear not: for God is come to prove you, and that His fear may be before you, that ye sin not." In both, the standpoint of fear is approved as relatively good and wholesome. It was well that the people should have this awestruck fear of the Divine, for it would act as a deterrent from sin. But it was not sufficient. It was only the starting-point for the attainments which Yahweh by Moses, and in Moses, was about to call and incite them to. Moses therefore had to stand between Israel and Yahweh in this too, that he had entered into and lived in relations with his God which they were as yet unable either to conceive or to endure.

It is well to add, also, that in giving approval of this kind to fear as a religious motive these early teachers were entirely in accord with the final development of Israelite religion in the New Testament. The modern view that any appeal to fear in religion or morality is degrading would have been simply unintelligible to the Biblical writers. Even now, the whole fabric of society, the state with its officials and the law with its penalties, are a continual protest against it in the realm of practical morality. In truth the conflict raised about this matter in modern times is simply a conflict between superfine theories and facts. Now the Old Testament is throughout supremely true to the facts of human nature and human experience. It is practically a transcript of them as seen in the light of revelation. In a time, therefore, when in morals and religion physical fact is being allowed to override or pervert psychical fact, the Old Testament view is peculiarly wholesome. It helps to restore the balance and to keep man's thoughts sane.

Another point on which this narrative of Deuteronomy corrects and restores that which the tendency of modern thought has perverted is an even more important one. We have seen that the Old Testament view, as stated here, and as it is interwoven with the central fibres of the Old Testament conception, is that all men who are called to the task of permanently raising the level of human life and thought must give not only their light to, but their life for, those whom they seek to win for God. They must ask nothing from mankind but ever widening opportunities for service and self-sacrifice. But in our modern day this has been precisely reversed, and men like Goethe and Schopenhauer, and even Carlyle, have demanded that mankind should yield service to them, and then, by the furtherance and development they thereby attain, they promise to work out the deliverance of men from superstition and unreality and the bondage of ignorance. Goethe in this matter is typical. He preached and practised in the most uncompromising manner the doctrine of self-development. He thought that he could serve humanity in no way so well as by making every one he met, and all the experiences he encountered, minister to his own intellectual growth. Instead of saying with Moses, "Blot me out of Thy book," but spare these dim idolatrous masses, he would have said, "Let them all perish, and let me become the origin of a wiser, more intellectual, more self-restrained race than they." He consequently pursued his own ends relentlessly from his early years, and attained results so immense that almost every domain of thought, speculation, and science is now under some debt to him. But for all purposes of inspiring moral and spiritual enthusiasm he is practically useless. His selfishness, however high its kind, accomplished its work and left him cold, unapproachable, isolated. This want of love for men made him the accurate critic of human nature, but left him blind in great degree and hopeless altogether in regard to those possibilities of better things which are never wholly wanting to it. The result is that, notwithstanding his heroic powers, his influence is to-day rather a minus quantity in the spiritual and moral life. No one who has not warmth from other sources pouring in upon him can have much communion with Goethe without losing vitality, and in his presence the Divine passion of self-sacrificing love looks out of place, or even slightly absurd. His power is fascinating, but it freezes all the sources of the nobler spiritual emotions, and ultimately must tend to the impoverishing of human nature and the lowering of the level of human life. No; men are not to be reached so if it is wished to raise them to their highest powers, and all experience proves that the New Testament was right in summing up the teaching of the Old by the words, "He that saveth his life shall lose it, and he that loseth his life for My sake shall find it."

> "That is the doctrine, simple, ancient, true;
> Such is life's trial, as old earth smiles and knows.
> If you loved only what were worth your love,
> Love were clear gain, and wholly well for you;
> Make the low nature better by your throes!
> Give earth yourself, go up for gain above!"[35]

CHAPTER VII
LOVE TO GOD THE LAW OF LIFE

Deut. vi. 4, 5

In these verses we approach "the commandments, the statutes, and the judgments" which it was to be Moses' duty to communicate to the people, *i.e.* the second great division of the teaching and guidance received at Sinai. But though we approach them we do not come to them for a number of chapters yet. We reach them only in chapter xii., which begins with almost the same words as chapter vi. What lies between is a new exhortation, very similar in tone and subject to that into which chapters i-iii. have been transformed.

To some readers in our day this repetition, and the renewed postponement of the main subject of the book, have seemed to justify the introduction of a new author here. They are scornfully impatient of the repetition and delay, especially those of them who have themselves a rapid, dashing style; and they declare that the writer of the laws, etc., from chapter xii. onwards cannot have been the writer of these long double introductions. *They* would not have written so; consequently no one else, however different his circumstances, his objects, and his style may be, can have written so. It is true, they admit, that the style, the grammar, the vocabulary are all exactly those of the purely legal chapters, but that matters not. Their irritation with this delay is decisive; and so they introduce us, entirely on the strength of it, to another Deuteronomist, second or third or fourth—who knows? But all this is too purely subjective to meet with general acceptance, and we may without difficulty decide that the linguistic unity of the book, when chapters vi. to xii. are compared with what we find after xii., is sufficient to settle the question of authorship.

But we have now to consider the possible reasons for this second long introduction. The first introduction has been satisfactorily explained in a former chapter; this second one can, I think, quite as easily be accounted for. The object of the book is in itself a sufficient explanation. To modern critical students of the Old Testament the laws are the main interest of Deuteronomy. They are the material they need for their reconstruction of the history of Israel, and they feel as if all besides, though it may contain beautiful thoughts, were irrelevant. But that was not the writer's point of view at all. For him it was not the main thing to introduce new laws. He was conscious rather of a desire to bring old laws, well known to his fellow-countrymen, but neglected by them, into force again. Anything new in his version of them was consequently only such an adaptation of them to the new circumstances of his time as would tend to secure their observance. Even if Moses were the author of the book this would be true; but if a prophetic man in Manasseh's day was the author, we can see how naturally and exclusively that view would fill his mind. He had fallen upon evil times. The best that had been attained in regard to spiritual religion had been deliberately abandoned and trodden under foot. Those who sympathised with pure religion could only hope that a time would come when Hezekiah's work would be taken up again. If Deuteronomy was written in preparation for that time, the legal additions necessary to ward off the evils which had been so nearly fatal to Yahwism would seem to the author much less important than they appear to us to be. His object was to retrieve what had been lost, to rouse the dead minds of his countrymen, to illustrate that on which the higher life of the nation depended, and to throw light upon it from all the sources of what then was modern thought. His mind was full of the high teaching of the prophets. He was steeped in the history of his people, which was then receiving, or was soon to receive, its all but final touches. He was intensely anxious that in the later time for which he was writing all men should see how Providence had spoken for the Mosaic law and religion, and what the great principles were which had always underlain it, and which had now at last been made entirely explicit.

Under these circumstances, it was not merely natural that the author of Deuteronomy should dwell with insistence upon the hortatory part of his book; it was necessary. He could not feel Wellhausen's haste to approach his restatement of the law. To him the exhortation was, in fact, the important thing. Every day he lived he must have seen that it was not want of knowledge that misled his contemporaries. He must have groaned too often under the weight of the indifference even of the well disposed not to be aware that that was the great hindrance to the restoration of the better thoughts and ways of Hezekiah's day.

He had learned by bitter experience, what every man who is in earnest about inducing masses of men to take a step backward or forward to a higher life always learns, that nothing can be accomplished till a fire has been kindled in the hearts of men which will not let them rest. To this task the author of Deuteronomy devotes himself. And whatever impatient theorists of to-day may say, he succeeds amazingly. His exhortation touches men from one end of the world to the other, even to this day, by its affectionate impressiveness. His exhibition of the principles underlying the law is so true that, when our Lord was asked, "Which is the first commandment of all?" He answered from this chapter of Deuteronomy: "The first of all the commandments is this, The Lord our God is one Lord: and thou shalt love the Lord thy God with all thy heart, and with all thy soul, and with all thy strength. The second is this, Thou shalt love thy neighbour as thyself. There is none other commandment greater than these." Now these are precisely the truths Deuteronomy exhibits in these prefatory chapters, and it is by them that the after-treatment of the law is permeated. The author of Deuteronomy by announcing these truths brought the Old Testament faith as near to the level of the New Testament faith as was possible; and we may well believe that he saw his work in its true relative proportions. The hortatory chapters are really the most original part of the book, and exhibit what was most permanent in it. The mere fact that the author lingers over it, therefore, is entirely inadequate to justify us in admitting a later hand. Indeed, if criticism is to retain the respect of reasonable men, it will have to be more sparing than it has hitherto been with the "later hand"; to introduce it here under the circumstances is nothing short of a blunder.

In our verses, therefore, we have to deal with the main point of our book. Coming immediately after the Decalogue, these words render explicit the principle of the first table of that law. In them our author is making it clear that all he has to say of worship, and of the relation of Israel to Yahweh, is merely an application of this principle, or a statement of means by which a life at the level of love to God may be made possible or secured. This section, therefore, forms the bridge which connects the Decalogue with the legal enactments which follow; and it is on all accounts worthy of very special attention. Our Lord's quotation of it as the supreme statement of the Divine law, in its Godward aspect, would in itself be an overwhelmingly special reason for thorough study of it, and would justify us in expecting to find it one of the deepest things in Scripture.

The translation of the first clause presents difficulties. The Authorised Version gives us, "Hear, O Israel: The Lord our God is one Lord," but that can no longer be accepted, since it rests upon the Jewish substitution of Adhonai for Yahweh. Taking this view of the construction, it should be rendered, "Hear, O Israel: Yahweh our God is one Yahweh"; and this is the meaning which most recent authorities—e.g. Knobel, Keil, and Dillmann—put upon it. But equally good authorities—such as Ewald and Oehler—render, "Yahweh our God—Yahweh is one." This is unobjectionable grammatically. Still another translation, "Hear, O Israel: Yahweh is our God, Yahweh alone," has been received by the most recent and most scholarly German translation of the Scripture, that edited by Kautzsch. But the objection that in that case *l'bhaddo*, not *'echādh*, should have been used, seems conclusive against it. The two others come very much to the same thing in the end, and were it not for the time at which Deuteronomy was written, Ewald's translations would be the simpler and more acceptable. But the first—"Yahweh our God is one Yahweh"—exactly meets the circumstances of that time, and moreover emphasises that in Israel's God which the writer of Deuteronomy was most anxious to establish. As against the prevailing tendency of the time, he not only denies polytheism, or, as Dillmann puts it, asserts the concrete fact that the true God cannot be resolved in the polytheistic manner into various kinds and shades of deity, like the Baalim, but he also prohibits the amalgamation or partial identification of Him with other gods. Though very little is told us concerning Manasseh's idolatry, we know enough to feel assured that it was in this fashion he justified his introduction of Assyrian deities into the Temple worship. Moloch, for example, must in some way have been identified with Yahweh, since the sacrifices of children in Tophet are declared by Jeremiah to have been to Yahweh. Further, the worship at the High Places had led, doubtless, to belief in a multitude of local Yahwehs, who in some obscure way were yet regarded as one, just as the multitudinous shrines of the Virgin in Romanist lands lead to the adoration of our Lady of Lourdes, our Lady of Étaples, and so on, though the Church knows only one Virgin Mother. This incipient and unconscious polytheism it was our author's purpose to root out by his law of one altar; and it seems congruous, therefore, that he should sum up the first table of the Decalogue in such a way as to bring out its opposition to this great evil. Of course the oneness of deity as such is involved in what he says; but the aspect of this truth which is specially put forward here is that Yahweh, being God, is one Yahweh, with no partners, nor even with variations that practically destroy unity. No proposition could have been framed more precisely and exactly to contradict the general opinion of Manasseh and his followers regarding religion; and in it the watchword of monotheism was spoken. Since it was uttered, this has been the rallying point of monotheistic religion, both among Jews and Mohammedans. For "there is no God but God" is precisely the counterpart of "Yahweh is one Yahweh"; and from one end of the civilised world to the other this strenuous confession of faith has been heard, both as the tumultuous battle-shout of victorious armies, and as the stubborn and immovable assertion of the despised, and scattered, and persecuted people to whom it was first revealed. Even to-day, though in the hands of both Jews and Mohammedans it has been hardened into a dogma which has stripped the Mosaic conception of Yahweh of those elements which gave it possibilities of tenderness and expansion, it still has power over the minds of men. Even in such hands, it incites missionary effort, and it appeals to the heart at some stages of civilisation as no other creed does. It makes men, nay, even civilised men, of the wild fetich-worshipping African; but for want of what follows in our context it leaves them stranded—at a higher level, it is true, but stranded nevertheless—without possibilities of advance, and exposed to that terrible decay in their moral and spiritual conceptions which sooner or later asserts itself in every Mohammedan community.

Israel was saved from the same spiritual disease by the great words which succeed the assertion of Yahweh's oneness. The writer of Deuteronomy did not desire to set forth this declaration as an abstract statement of ultimate truth about God. He makes it the basis of a quite new, a quite original demand upon his countrymen. Because Yahweh thy God is one Yahweh, "thou shalt love Yahweh thy God with all thine heart, and with all thy soul, and with all thy might." To us, who have inherited all that was attained by Israel in their long and eventful history as a nation, and especially in its disastrous close, it may have become a commonplace that God demands the love of His people. But if so, we must make an effort to shake off the dull yoke of custom and familiarity. If we do, we shall see that it was an extraordinarily original thing which the Deuteronomist here declares. In the whole of the Old Testament there are, outside of Deuteronomy, thirteen passages in which the *love* of men to Yahweh is spoken of. They are Exod. xx. 6; Josh. xxii. 5, xxiii. 11; Judges v. 31; 1 Kings iii. 3; Neh. i. 5; Psalms xviii. 2, xxxi. 24, xci. 14, xcvii. 10, cxvi. 1, cxlv. 20; and Dan. ix. 4. Now of these the verses from Nehemiah and Daniel are manifestly later than Deuteronomy, and of the Psalms only the eighteenth can with any confidence be assigned to a time earlier than the seventh century B.C. All the others may with great probability be assigned at earliest to the times of Jeremiah and the post-exilic period. Three of the passages from the historic books again—Josh. xxii. 5, xxiii. 11; 1 Kings iii. 3—are attributed, on grounds largely apart from the use of this expression, to the Deuteronomic editor, *i.e.* the writer who went over the historical books about 600 B.C., and made slight additions here and there, easily recognisable by their differing in tone and feeling from the surrounding context. Indeed Josh. xxii. 5 is a palpable quotation from Deuteronomy itself.

Of the thirteen passages, therefore, only three—Exod. xx. 6, Judges v. 31, and Psalm xviii. 2—belong to the time previous to Deuteronomy, and in all three the mention of love to God is only allusive, and, as it were, by the way. Before Deuteronomy, consequently, there is little more than the mere occurrence of the word. There is nothing of the bold and decisive demand for love to the one God as the root and ground of all true relations with Him which Deuteronomy makes. At most, there is the hint of a possibility which might be realised in the future; of love to God as the permanent element in the life of man there is no indication; and it is this which the author of

Deuteronomy means, and nothing less than this. He makes this demand for love the main element of his teaching. He returns to it again and again, so that there are almost as many passages bearing on this in Deuteronomy as in the whole Old Testament besides; and the particularity and emphasis with which he dwells upon it are immeasurably greater. Only in the New Testament do we find anything quite parallel to what he gives us; and there we find his view taken up and expanded, till love to God flashes upon us from almost every page as the test of all sincerity and the guarantee of all success in the Christian life.

To proclaim this truth was indeed a great achievement; and when we remember the abject fear with which Israel had originally regarded Yahweh, it will appear still more remarkable that the book embodying this should have been adopted by the whole people with enthusiasm, and that with it should begin the Canon of Holy Scripture; for Deuteronomy, as all now recognise, was the first book which became canonical. I have said that the conception was an extraordinarily original one, and have pointed out that it had not been traceable to any extent previously in Israel's religious books or its religious men. It will appear still more original, I think, if we consider what a growth in moral and spiritual stature separates the Israel of Moses' day and that of Josiah's; what the attitude of other nations to their gods was in contrast to this; and, lastly, what it involves and implies, as regards the nature of both God and man.

As we have already seen, the earlier narratives represent the men to whom Moses spoke as acknowledging that they could not, as yet at any rate, bear to remain in the presence of Yahweh. Between their God and them, therefore, there could be no relation of love properly so called. There was reverence, awe, and chiefly fear, tempered by the belief that Yahweh as their God was on their side. He had proved it by delivering them from the oppressions of Egypt, and they acknowledged Him and were jealous for His honour and submissive to His commands. So far as the record goes, that would seem to have been their religious state. Progress from that state of mind to a higher, to a demand for direct personal relations between each individual Israelite and Yahweh, was not easy. It was hindered by the fact that Israel as a whole, and not the individual, was for a long time regarded as the subject of religion. That, of course, was no hindrance to the development of the thought that Yahweh loved Israel; but so long as that conception dominated religious thought in Israel, so long was it impossible to think of individual love and trust as the element in which each faithful man should live.

But the love of Yahweh was declared, century after century, by prophet and priest and psalmist, to be set upon His people, and so the way for this demand for love on man's part was opened. Man's relations with God began to grow more intimate. The distance lessened, as the use of the words "them that love Me" in the song of Deborah and the Davidic word in Psalm xviii., "I love thee, Yahweh my rock," clearly show. Hosea next took up the strain, and intensified and heightened it in a wonderful manner, but the nation failed to respond adequately. In the later prophets the love and grace and longsuffering of Yahweh and His ceaseless efforts on behalf of Israel are continually made the ground of exhortations, entreaties, and reproaches; but, as a whole, the people still did not respond. We may be sure, however, that an ever increasing minority were affected by the clearness and intensity of the prophetic testimony. To this minority, the Israel within Israel, the remnant that was to return from exile and become the seed of a people that should be all righteous, the love of Yahweh tended to become His main characteristic. That love sustained their hopes; and though the awe and reverence which were due to His holiness, and the fear called forth by His power, still predominated, there grew up in their hearts a multitude of thoughts and expectations tending more and more to the love of God.

As yet it was only a timid reaching out towards Him, a hope and longing which could hardly justify itself. Yet it was robust enough not to be killed by disappointment, by hope deferred, or even by crushing misfortune; and in the furnace of affliction it became stronger and more pure. And in the heart of the author of Deuteronomy it grew certain of itself, and soared up with an eagerness that would not be denied. Then, as always where God is the object of it, love that dares was justified; and out of its restless and timid longings it came to the "place of rest imperturbable, where love is not forsaken if itself forsaketh not."[36] From knowledge, confirmed by the answering love and inspiration of God, and impelled consciously by Him, he then in this book made and reiterated his great demand. All spiritual men found in it the word they had needed. They responded to it eagerly when the book was published; and their enthusiasm carried even the torpid and careless masses with them for a time. The nation, with the king at their head, accepted the legislation of which this love to God was the underlying principle, and so far as public and corporate action can go, Israel adopted the deepest principle of spiritual life as their own.

Of course with the mass this assent had little depth; but in the hearts of the true men in Israel the joy and assurance of their great discovery, that Yahweh their God was open to, nay, desired and commanded, their most fervent affection, soon produced its fruit. From the fragments of the earliest legislation which have come down to us, it is obvious that the Mosaic principles had led to a most unwonted consideration for the poor. In later days, though the ingrained tendency to oppression, which those who have power in the East seem quite unable to resist, did its evil work in both Israel and Judah, there were never wanting prophetic voices to denounce such villainy in the spirit of these laws. The public conscience was thereby kept alive, and the ideal of justice and mercy, especially to the helpless, became a distinguishing mark of Israelite religion. But it was in the minds of those who had learned the Deuteronomist's great lesson, and had taken example by him, that the love which came from God, and had just been answered back by man overflowed in a stream of blessing to man's "neighbours." Deuteronomy had uttered the first and great commandment; but it is in the Law of Holiness, that complex of ancient laws brought together by the author of P, and found now mainly in Lev. xvii.-xxvi., that we find the second word, "Thou shalt love thy neighbour as thyself."[37] If we ask, Who is my neighbour? we find that not even those beyond Israel are excluded, for in Lev. xix. 34 we read, "The stranger that sojourneth with you shall be unto you as the homeborn among you, and thou shalt love him as thyself." The idea still needed the expansion which it received from our Lord Himself in the parable of the Good Samaritan; but it is only one step from these passages to the New Testament.

From the standpoint of mere fear, then, to the standpoint of love which casteth out fear, even the masses of Israel were lifted, in thought at least, by the love and teaching of God. And the process by which Israel was led to this height has proved ever since to be the only possible way to such an attainment. It began in the free favour of God, it was continued by the answer of love on the part of man, and these antecedents had as their consequence the proclamation of that law of liberty—for self-renouncing love is liberty— "Thou shalt love thy neighbour as thyself." Without the first, the second was impossible; and the last without the other two would have been only a satire upon the incurable selfishness of man. It is worthy of remark, at least, that only on the critical theory of the Old Testament is each of these steps in the moral and religious education of Israel found in its right place, with its right antecedents; only when taken so do the teachers who were inspired to make each of these attainments find circumstances suited to their message, and a soil in which the germs they were commissioned to plant could live.

But great as is the contrast between the Israel of Moses' day and that of Josiah's, it is not so great as the contrast between the religion of Israel in the Deuteronomic period and the religion of the neighbouring nations. Among them, at our date 650 B.C., there was, so far as we know them, no suggestion of personal love to God as an effective part of religion. In the chapters on the Decalogue the main ideas of the Canaanites in regard to religion have been described, so that they need not be repeated here. I shall add only what E. Meyer says of their gods: "With advancing culture the cultus loses its old simplicity and homeliness. A fixed ritual was developed—founded upon old hereditary tradition. And here the gloomier conception became the ruling one, and its consequences were inexorably deduced. The great gods, even the protecting gods of the tribe or the town, are capricious and in general hostile to man—possibly to some degree because of the mythological conception of Baal as sun-god—and they demand sacrifices of blood that they may be appeased. In order that evil may be warded off from those with whom they are angry, another human being must be offered to them as a substitute in propitiatory sacrifice—nay, they demand the sacrifice of the firstborn, the best-loved son. If the community be threatened with the wrath of the deity, then the prince or the nobility as a whole must offer up their children on its behalf."[38] This also is the view of Robertson Smith,[39] who considers that while in their origin the Semitic religions involved kindly relations and continual intercourse between the gods and their worshippers, these gradually disappeared as political misfortune began to fall upon the smaller Semitic peoples. Their gods were angry and in the vain hope of appeasing them men had recourse to the direst sacrifices. Hints concerning these had survived from times of savagery; and to the diseased minds of these terror-stricken peoples the more ancient and more horrible a sacrifice was the more powerful did it seem. At this time, therefore, the course of the Canaanite religions was away from love to their gods. The decay of nationality brought despair, and the frantic efforts of despair, into the religion of the Canaanite peoples; but to Israel it brought this higher demand for more intimate union with their God. Whatever elements tending towards love the Canaanite religions originally may have had, they had either been mingled with the corrupting sensuality which seems inseparable from the worship of female deities, or had been limited to the mere superficial good understanding which their participation in the same common life established between the people and their gods. Their union was largely independent of moral considerations on either side. But in Israel there had grown up quite a different state of things. The union between Yahweh and His people had from the days of the Decalogue taken a moral turn; and gradually it had become clear that to have Abraham for their father and Yahweh for their God would profit them little, if they did not stand in right moral relations and in moral sympathy with Him. Now, in Deuteronomy, that fundamentally right conception of the relation between God and man received its crown in Yahweh's claim to the love of His people. No contrast could be greater than that which common misfortune and a common national ruin produced between the surrounding Semitic peoples and Israel.

But besides the small kingdoms which immediately surrounded Palestine, Israel had for neighbours the two great empires of Egypt and Assyria. She was exposed therefore to influence from them in even a greater degree. Long before the Exodus, the land which Israel came afterwards to occupy had been the meeting-place of Babylonian and Egyptian power and culture. In the fifteenth century B.C. it was under the suzerainty if not the direct sovereignty of Egypt; but its whole culture and literature, for it must have had books, as the name Kirjath-Sepher (Book-town) shows, was Babylonian. Throughout Israel's history, moreover, Assyrian and Egyptian manners and ways of thought were pressed upon the people; and we cannot doubt that in regard to religion also their influence was felt. But at this period, as in the Canaanite religions, so also in those of Assyria and Egypt, the tendency was altogether different from what Deuteronomy shows it to have been in Israel.

In regard to Egypt this is somewhat difficult to prove, for the Egyptian religion is so complicated, so varied, and so ancient, that men who have studied it despair of tracing any progress in it. A kind of monotheism, polytheism, fetichism, animism, and nature-worship such as we find in the Vedas, have in turn been regarded as its primitive state; but as a matter of fact all these systems of religious thought and feeling are represented in the earliest records, and they remained constant elements of it till the end. [40] Whatever had once formed part of it, Egyptian religion clung to with extraordinary tenacity. As time went on, however, the accent was shifted from one element to the other, and after the times of the XIXth dynasty, *i.e.* after the time of the Exodus, it began to decay. A systematised pantheism, of which sun-worship was the central element, was elaborated by the priests; the moral element which had been prominent in the days when the picture of the judgment of the soul after death was so popular in Thebes retired more into the background, and the purely magical element became the principal one. Instead of moral goodness and the fulfilment of duty being the main support of the soul in its dread and lonely journeys in the "world of the Western sky," knowledge of the proper formulas became the chief hope, and the machinations of evil demons the main danger. In the royal tombs at Thebes the walls of the long galleries are covered with representations of these demons, and the accompanying writing gives directions as to the proper formulas by knowledge of which deliverance can be secured. This, of course, confined the benefits of religion, so far as they related to the life to come, to the educated, and the wealthy. For these secret spells were hard to obtain, and had to be purchased at a high price. As Wiedemann says, "Still more important than in this world was the knowledge of the correct magical words and formulas in the other world. No door opened here if its name was not known, no dæmon let the dead pass in if he did not address him in the proper fashion, no god came to his help so long as his proper title was not given him, no food could be procured so long as the exactly prescribed words were not uttered."[41] The people were therefore thrown back upon the ancient popular faith, which needed gods only for practical life, and honoured them only because they were mighty.[42] Some of them were believed to be friendly; but others were malevolent deities who would destroy mankind if they did not mollify them by magic, or render them harmless by the greater power of the good gods. Consequently Set, the unconquerable evil demon, was worshipped with zeal in many places. With him there were numerous demons, "the enemies," "the evil ones," which lie in wait for individuals, and threaten their life and weal. The main thing, therefore, was to bring the correct sacrifices, to use such formulas and perform such acts as would render the gods gracious and turn away evil. Moreover the whole of nature was full of spirits, as it is to the African of to-day, and in the mystic texts of the Book of the Dead, there is constant mention made of the "mysterious beings whose names, whose ceremonials are not known," which thirst for blood, which bring death, which go about as devouring flame, as well as of others which do good. At all times this element existed in Egypt; but precisely at this time, in the reign of Psamtik, Brugsch[43] declares that new force was given to it, and on the monuments there appear, along with the "great gods," monstrous forms of demons and genii. In fact the higher religion had become pantheistic, and consequently less rigidly moral. Magic had been taken up into it for the life beyond the grave, and became the only resource of the people in this life. Fear, therefore, necessarily became the ruling religious motive, and instead of growing toward love of God, men in Egypt at this time were turning more decisively than ever away from it.

Of the Assyrian religion and its influence it is also difficult to speak in this connection, for notwithstanding the amount of translation that has been done, not much has come to light in regard to the personal religion of the Assyrians. On the whole it seems to be established that in its main features the religion of both Babylon and Assyria remained what the non-Semitic inhabitants of Akkad had made it. Originally it had consisted entirely of a spirit and demon worship not one whit more advanced than the religion of the South Sea islanders to-day. As such it was in the main a religion of fear. Though some spirits were good, the bulk were evil, and all were capricious. Men were consequently all their lifetime subject to bondage, and love as a religious emotion was impossible. When the Semites came at a later time into the country their star-worship was amalgamated with this mere Shamanism of the Akkadians. In the new faith thus evolved the great gods of the Semites were arranged in a hierarchy, and the spirits, both good and evil, were subordinated to them. But even the great gods remain within the sphere of nature, and have in full measure the defects and limitations of nature-gods everywhere.[44] They are not entirely beneficent powers, nor are they even moral beings. Some have special delight in blood and destruction, while the cruel Semitic child-sacrifice was practised in honour of others. Again, their displeasure has no necessary or even general connection with sin. Their wrath is generally the outcome of mere arbitrary whim. Indeed it may be doubted whether the conception of sin or of moral guilt ever had a secure footing in this religion. It certainly had none in the terror-struck hymn to the seven evil spirits who are described thus:—

> "Seven (are) they, seven (are) they.
> Male they (are) not, female they (are) not;
> Moreover the deep is their pathway.
> Wife they have not, child is not born to them.
> Law (and) order they know not,
> Prayer and supplication hear they not.
> Wicked (are) they, wicked (are) they."[45]

There is here an accent of genuine terror, which involved not love, but hatred. Even in what Sayce calls a "Penitential Psalm," and which he compares to the Biblical Psalms, there is nothing of the gratitude to God as a deliverer from sin which in Israel was the chief factor in producing the response to Yahweh's demand for the love of man. Morally, it contains nothing higher than is contained in the hymn of the spirits. The transgressions which are so pathetically lamented, and from the punishment of which deliverance is so earnestly sought, are purely ceremonial and involuntary. The author of the prayer conceives that he has to do with a god whose wrath is a capricious thing, coming upon men they know not why. So conceived God cannot be loved. It is entirely in accord with this that in the great flood epic no reason is given for the destruction of mankind save the caprice of Bel.[46] The few expressions quoted by Sayce from a hymn to the sun-god—such as this, "Merciful God, that liftest up the fallen, that supportest the weak.... Like a wife, thou submittest thyself, cheerful and kindly.... Men far and wide bow before thee and rejoice"—cannot avail to subvert a conclusion so firmly fixed. These are simply the ordinary expressions which the mere physical pleasure of the sunlight brings to the lips of sun-worshippers of all ages and of all climes. At best they could only be taken as germs out of which a loving relation between God and man might have been developed. But though they were ancient they never were developed. At the end as at the beginning the Assyrio-Babylonian religion moves on so low a level, even in its more innocent aspects, that a development like that in Deuteronomy is absolutely impossible. In its worse aspects Assyrian religion was unspeakable. The worship of Ishtar at Nineveh outdid everything known in the ancient world for lust and cruelty.

On this side too, therefore, we find no parallel to Israel's new outgrowth of higher religion. Comparison only makes it stand out more boldly in its splendid originality; and we are left with the fruitful question, "What was the root of the astonishing difference between Yahweh and every other god whom Israel had heard of?" Precisely at this time and under the same circumstances, the ethnic religions around Israel were developing away from any higher elements they had contained, and were thereby, as we know now, hastening to extinction. Under the inspired prophetic influence, Israel's religion turned the loss of the nation into gain; it rose by the darkness of national misfortune into a nobler phase than any it had previously known.

But perhaps the crowning merit of this demand for love of God is the emphasis it lays upon personality in both God and man, and the high level at which it conceives their mutual relations. From the first, of course, the personal element was always very strongly present in the Israelite conception of God. Indeed personality was the dominating idea among all the smaller nations which surrounded Israel. The national god was conceived of mainly as a greater and more powerful man, full of the energetic self-assertion without which it would be impossible for any man to reign over an Eastern community. The Moabite stone shows this, for in it Chemosh is as sharply defined a person as Mesha himself. The Canaanite gods, therefore, might be wanting in moral character; their existence was doubtless thought of in a limited and wholly carnal manner; but there never was, apparently, the least tendency to obscure the sharp lines of their individuality. In Israel, *a fortiori*, such a tendency did not exist; and that a writer of Matthew Arnold's ability should have persuaded himself, and tried to persuade others, that under the name of Yahweh Israel understood anything so vague as his "stream of tendency which makes for righteousness," is only another instance of the extraordinarily blinding effects of a preconceived idea. So far from Yahweh being conceived in that manner, it would be much easier to prove that, whatever aberrations in the direction of making God merely "a non-natural man" may be charged upon Christianity, they have been founded almost exclusively upon Old Testament examples and Old Testament texts. If there was defect in the Old Testament conception of God, it was, and could not but be, in the direction of drawing Him down too much into the limits of human personality.

But though the gods were always thought of by the Canaanites as personal, their character was not conceived as morally high. Moral character in Chemosh, Moloch, or Baal was not of much importance, and their relations with their peoples were never conditioned by moral conduct. How deeply ingrained this view was in Palestine is seen in the persistency with which even Yahweh's relation to His people was viewed in this light. Only the continual outcry of the prophets against it prevented this idea becoming permanently dominant even in Israel. Nay, it often deceived would-be prophets. Clinging to the idea of the national God, and forgetting altogether the ethical character of Yahweh, without, perhaps, conscious insincerity, they prophesied peace to the wicked, and so came to swell the ranks of the false prophets. But from very early times another thought was cherished by Israel's representative men in regard to their relations with God. Yahweh was righteous, and demanded righteousness in His people. Oblations were vain if offered as a substitute for this. All the prophets reach their greatest heights of sublimity in preaching this ethically noble doctrine; and the love to God which Deuteronomy demands is to be exhibited in reverent obedience to moral law.

Moreover, that God should seek or even need the love of man threw other light on the Old Testament religion. If, without revelation, Israel had widened its mental horizon so as to conceive Yahweh as Lord of the world, it may be questioned whether it could have kept clear of the gulf of pantheism. But by the manifestation of God in their special history, the Israelites had been taught to rise step by step to the higher levels, without losing their conception of Yahweh as the living, personal, active friend of their people. Moreover they had been early taught, as we have seen, that the deep design of all that was wrought for them was the good of all men. The love of God was seen pressing forward to its glorious and beneficent ends; and both by ascribing such far-reaching plans to Yahweh, and by affirming His interest in the fate of men, Israel's conception of the Divine personality was raised alike in significance and power; for anything more personal than love planning and working towards the happiness of its objects cannot be conceived. But the crown was set upon the Divine personality by the claim to the love of man. This signified that to the Divine mind the individual man was not hid from God by his nation, that he was not for Him a mere specimen of a genus. Rather each man has to God a special worth, a special character, which, impelled by His free personal love, He seeks to draw to Himself. At every step each man has near him "the great Companion," who desires to give Himself to him. Nay, more, it implies that God seeks and needs an answering love; so that Browning's daring declaration, put into the mouth of God when the song of the boy Theocrite is no more heard, "I miss My little human praise," is simple truth.[47]

But if the demand illustrates and illuminates the personality of God, it throws out in a still more decisive manner the personality of man. In a rough sense, of course, there never could have been any doubt of that. But children have to grow into full self-determining personality, and savages never attain it. Both are at the mercy of caprice, or of the needs of the moment, to which they answer so helplessly that in general no consistent course of conduct can be expected of them. That can be secured only by rigorous self-determination. But the power of self-determination does not come at once, nor is acquired without strenuous and continued effort; it is, in fact, a power which in any full measure is possessed only by the civilised man. Now the Israelites were not highly civilised when they left Egypt. They were still at the stage when the tribe overshadowed and absorbed the individual, as it does to-day among the South Sea islanders. The progress of the prophetic thought towards the demand for personal love has already been traced. Here we must trace the steps by which the personal element in each individual was strengthened in Israel, till it was fit to respond to the Divine demand.

The high calling of the people reacted on the individual Israelites. They saw that in many respects the nations around them were inferior to them. Much that was tolerated or even respected among them was an abomination to Israel; and every Israelite felt that the honour of his people must not be dragged in the dust by him, as it would be if he permitted himself to sink to the heathen level. Further, the laws regarding even ceremonial holiness which in germ certainly, and probably in considerable extension also, existed from the earliest time, made him feel that the sanctity of the nation depended upon the care and scrupulosity of the individual. And then there were the individual spiritual needs, which could not be suppressed and would not be denied. Though one sees so little explicit provision for restoration of individual character in early Yahwism, yet in the course of time—who can doubt it?—the personal religious needs of so many individual men would necessarily frame for themselves some outlet. Building upon the analogy of the relation established between Yahweh and Israel, they would hope for the satisfaction of their individual needs through the infinite mercy of God. The Psalms, such of them as can fairly be placed in the pre-Deuteronomic time, bear witness to this; and those written after that time show a hopefulness, and a faith in the reality of individual communion with God which show that such communion was not then a new discovery.

In all these ways the religious life of the individual was being cultivated and strengthened; but this demand made in Deuteronomy lifts that indirect refreshment of soul, for which the cultus and the covenants made no special provision, into a recognised position, nay, into the central position in Israelite religion. The word, "Thou shalt love Yahweh thy God," confirmed and justified all these persistent efforts after individual life in God, and brought them out into the large place which belongs to aspirations that have at last been authorised. By a touch, the inspired writer transformed the pious hopes of those who had been the chosen among the chosen people into certainties. Each man was henceforth to have his own direct relation to God as well as the nation; and the national hope, which had hitherto been first, was now to depend for its realisation upon the fulfilment of the special and private hope. Thus the old relation was entirely reversed by Deuteronomy. Instead of the individual holding "definite place in regard to Yahweh only through his citizenship," now the nation has its place and its future secured only by the personal love of each citizen to God. For that is obviously what the demand here made really means. Again and again the inspired writer returns to it; and his persistent endeavour is to connect all else that his book contains—warning, exhortation, legislation—with this as the foundation and starting-point. Here, as elsewhere, we can trace the roots of the new covenant which Jeremiah and Ezekiel saw afar off and rejoiced at, and which our blessed Lord has realised for us. The individual religious life is for the first time fully recognised for what ever since it has been seen to be, the first condition of any attempt to realise the kingdom of God in the life of a nation.

And not only thus does our text emphasise individuality. Love with all the heart, and all the mind, and all the soul is possible only to a fully developed personality; for, as Rothe says, "We love only in the measure in which personality is developed in us. Even God can love only in so far as He is personal."[48] Or, as Julius Muller says in his *Doctrine of Sin*, "The association of personal beings in love, while it involves the most perfect distinction of the I and Thou, proves itself to be the highest form of unity."[49] Unless other counteracting circumstances come in, therefore, the more highly developed individuality is, the more entirely human beings are determined from within, the more entirely will union among men depend upon free and deliberate choice, and the more perfect will it be. In being called to love God men are dealt with as those who have attained to complete self-determination, who have come to completed manhood in the moral life. For all that could mix love with alloy, mere sensuous sympathy, and the insistent appeal of that which is materially present, are wanting here. Here nothing is involved but the free outgoing of the heart to that which is best and highest; nothing but loyalty to that vision of Good which, amid all the ruin sin has wrought in human nature, dominates us so that "we needs must love the highest when we see it." The very demand is a promise and a prophecy of completed moral and religious liberty to the individual soul. It rests upon the assurance that men have at last been trained to walk alone, that the support of social life and external ordinances has become less necessary than it was, and that one day a new and living way of access to the Father will bring every soul into daily intercourse with the source of all spiritual life.

But this demand, in affirming personality of so high a kind, also re-created duty. Under the national dispensation the individual man was a *servant*. To a large extent he knew not what his Lord did, and he ruled his life by the commands he received without understanding, or perhaps caring to understand, their ultimate ground and aim. Much too of what he thus laid upon himself was mere ancient custom, which had been a protection to national and moral life in early days, but which had survived, or was on the point of surviving, its usefulness. Now, however, that man was called upon to love God with all his heart and mind and soul, the step was taken which was to end in his becoming the consciously free *son* of God. For to love in this fashion means, on the one hand, a willingness to enter into communion with God and to seek that communion; and on the other it implies a throwing open of the soul to receive the love which God so persistently has pressed upon men. In such a relation slavery, blind or constrained obedience, disappears, and the motives of right action become the purest and most powerful that man can know.

In the first place, selfishness dies out. Those to whom God has given Himself have no more to seek. They have reached the dwelling "of peace imperturbable," and know that they are secure. Nothing that they do can win more for them; and they do those things that please God with the free, uncalculating, ungrudging forgetfulness of self, which distinguishes those fortunate children who have grown up into a perfect filial love. Of course it was only the elect in Israel who in any great degree realised this ideal. But even those who neglected it had for a moment been illuminated by it; and the record of it remained to kindle the nobler hearts of every generation. Even the legalism of later days could not obscure it. In the case of many it bore up and transfigured the dry details of Judaism, so that even amid such surroundings the souls of men were kept alive. The later Psalms prove this beyond dispute, and the advanced view which brings the bulk of the Psalter down to the post-exilic period only emphasises the more this aspect of pre-Christian Judaism. In Christianity of course the ideal was made infinitely more accessible: and it received in the Pauline doctrine, the Evangelical doctrine, of Justification by Faith a form, which more than any other human teaching has made unselfish devotion to God a common aim. It would hardly be too much to say that those philosophical and religious systems which have preached the unworthiness of looking for a reward of well-doing, which have striven to set up the doing of good for its own sake as the only morality worthy of the name, have failed, just because they would not begin with the love of God. To Christianity, especially to Evangelical Christianity, they have assumed to speak from above downwards; but it alone has the secret they strove in vain to learn. Men justified by faith have peace with God, and do good with passionate fervour without hope or possibility of further reward, just because of their love and gratitude to God, who is the source of all good. This plan has succeeded, and no other has; for to teach men on any other terms to disregard reward is simply to ask them to breathe in a vacuum.

In the second place, those who rose to the height of this calling had duty not only deepened but extended. It was natural that they should not seek to throw off the obligations of worship and morality as they had been handed down by their ancestors. Only an authoritative voice which they were separated from by centuries could say, "It hath been said by them of old time, ... but *I* say unto you"; and men would be disposed rather to fulfil old obligations with new zeal, while they added to them the new duties which their widened horizon had brought into view. It is true that in course of time the Pharisaic spirit laid hold of the Jews, and that by it they were led back into a slavery which quite surpassed the half-conscious bondage of their earlier time. It is one of the mysteries of human nature that it is only the few who can live for any time at a high level, and hold the balance between extremes. The many cannot choose but follow those few; and the dumb, half-reluctant, half-fascinated way in which they are drawn after them is a most pathetic thing to see. But too often they avenge themselves for the pressure put upon them, by taking up the teaching they receive in a perverted or mutilated form, dropping unawares the very soul of it, and suiting it to the average man. When that is done the bread from heaven becomes a stone; the message of liberty is turned into a summons to the prison house; and the darkness becomes of that opaque sort which is found only where the light within men is darkness. That tragedy was enacted in Judaism as rarely elsewhere. The free service of sons was exchanged for the timorous, anxious scrupulosity of the formalist. How could men love a God whom they pictured as inexorable in claiming the mint and cummin of ceremonial worship, and as making life a burden for all who had a conscience? They could not, and they did not. Most substituted a merely formal compliance with the externalities of worship for the love to God and man which was the presupposition of the true Israelite's life, and the mass of the nation fell away from true faith. Strangely enough, therefore, the strength of men's love for God, and of their belief in His love, gave an impulse to the legalistic Pharisaism which our Lord denounced as the acme of loveless irreligion.

But it was not so perverted in all. There always was an Israel within Israel that refused to let go the truths they had learned, and kept up the succession of men inspired by the free spirit of God. Even among the Pharisees there were such—witness St. Paul—men who, though they were entangled in the formalism of their time, found it at last a pedagogue to bring them unto Christ. We must believe therefore that at the beginning the attainment marked by the demands of Deuteronomy and the Law of Holiness existed and was carried over into the daily life. As the national limits of religion were broken down, the word "neighbour" received an ever wider definition in Israel. At first only a man's fellow-tribesman or fellow-countryman was included; then the stranger; later, as in Jonah's picture of the conduct of the sailors, it was hinted that even among the heathen brethren might be found. Finally, in our Lord's parable of the Good Samaritan the last barrier was broken down. But it needed all St. Paul's lifework, and the first and most desperate inner conflict Christianity had to live through, to initiate men into anything like the full meaning of what Christ had taught. Then it was seen that as there was but one Father in heaven, so there was but one family on earth. Then too, though the merely ceremonial duties by which the Jew had been bound ceased to be binding on Christians, the sphere for the practice of moral duty was immensely widened. Indeed, had it not been for the free, joyous spirit with which they were inspired by Christ, they must have shrunk from the immensity of their obligation. For not only were men's neighbours infinitely more numerous now, but their relations with them became vastly more complicated. To meet all possible cases that might arise in the great and elaborate civilisations Christianity had to face and save, our Lord deepened the meaning of the commandments; and so far from Christians being free from the obligation to law, immeasurably more was demanded of them. To them first was the full sweep of moral obligation revealed, for they first had reached the full moral stature of men in Jesus Christ.

CHAPTER VIII
EDUCATION—MOSAIC VIEW

Deut. vi. 6-25

Those great verses, Deut. vi. 4, 5, form the central truth of the book. Everything else in it proceeds from and is informed by them, and they are dwelt upon and enforced with a clear perception of their radical importance. There is something of the joy of discovery in the way in which the unity of Yahweh and exclusive love to Him are insisted upon, not only in verses 6-25 of this chapter, but in xi. 13-20. The same strongly worded demand to lay to heart Yahweh's command to love Him and Him only, and to teach it strenuously to their children—to make it "a sign upon their hand," and "as a frontlet between their eyes"—is found in both passages. It is worthy of remark also that nearly the same words are found in Exod. xiii. 9, 16. Presumably on account of this, some have ascribed that section of Exodus to the author of Deuteronomy. But both Dillmann and Driver ascribe these passages to J and E, and with good reason. Indeed, apart from the purely literary grounds for thinking that these formulas were first used by the earlier writers and were copied by the author of Deuteronomy, another line of argument points in the same direction. In Exodus the thing to be remembered and taught to the children was the meaning and origin of the Passover and the consecration of the firstborn, *i.e.* the meaning and origin of some of their ritual institutions. Here in Deuteronomy, on the contrary, that which is to be written on the heart and taught to the children is moral and spiritual truth about God, and love to God. Now the probable explanation of this likeness and difference is, not that the author of Deuteronomy, after using this insistive phrase only of high spiritual truths in his own book, inserted it in Exodus with regard to mere institutions of the cultus; rather, the writers of Exodus had used it of that which was important in their day, and the Deuteronomist borrowed it from them to emphasise his own most cherished revelation. In the earlier stages of a religious movement, the establishment of institutions which shall embody and perpetuate religious truth, is one of the first necessities. It has become a commonplace of Christian defence, for example, that Baptism and the Lord's Supper were made the most successful vehicles for conveying fundamental Christian truth, and that the celebration of these two rites from the first days even until now is one of the most convincing proofs of the continuity of Christianity. Naturally, therefore, the establishment of the Passover was specially marked out as the *palladium* of Israelite religion in the earlier days. But in the time after Isaiah, when Deuteronomy was written, the institutions needed no longer such insistence. They had indeed become so important to the people that the mere observance of them threatened to become a substitute for religious and even moral feeling. The Deuteronomist's great message was, consequently, a reiteration of the prophetic truths as to the supremacy of the spiritual; and for the object of the warm exhortation of the earlier writings he substituted the proclamation of Yahweh's oneness, and of His demand for His people's love. This seems a reasonable and probable explanation of the facts as we find them. If true, it is a proof that the need of ritual institutions, and the danger of unduly exalting them, was not peculiar to post-exilic times. In principle the temptation was always present; and as living faith rose and fell it came into operation, or was held in abeyance, throughout the whole of Israel's history. Hence the mention of this kind of formalism or the denunciation of it must be very cautiously used as a criterion by which to date any Scriptural writings.

It is therefore with a full consciousness of its fundamental importance that the author of Deuteronomy follows the great passage chapter vi. 4, 5, with this solemn and inspiring exhortation. It is from no mere itch for religious improvement of the occasion that he presses home his message thus. Nor is it love for the mere repetition of an ancient formula of exhortation that dictates its use. He knew and understood the work of Moses, and felt that the moulding power in Israel's life as a nation, the unifying element in it, had been the religion of Yahweh. Whatever else may have been called in question, it has never been doubted that the salt which kept the political and social life of the people from rotting through many centuries was the always advancing knowledge of God. At each great crisis of Israel's history the religion of Yahweh had met the demands for direction, for inspiration, for uplifting which were made upon it. With Protean versatility it had adapted itself to every new condition. In all circumstances it had provided a lamp for the feet and a light for the path of the faithful; and in meeting the needs of generation after generation it had revealed elements of strength and consolation which, without the commentary of experience, could never have been brought out. Now the author of Deuteronomy felt that in these short sentences the high-water mark of Israelite religion so far had been reached, and that in renewing the work of Moses, and adapting it to his own time, the principles here enunciated must be the main burden of his message. Further progress depended, he obviously felt, upon the absorption and assimilation of these truths by his people, and he felt he must provide for the perpetuation of them in that better time he was preparing for. This he did by providing for the religious education of the young. Whatever else Israel had gained it had been careful to hand on from generation to generation. The land flowing with milk and honey was still in the possession of the descendants of the first conquerors. The literature, the science, the wisdom that the fathers had gathered, had been carefully passed down to the children; and a precious deposit of enriching experience in the form of history had reached to the elect even among the common people, as the example of Amos shows. But the most valuable heritage of Israel was that continually growing deposit of religious truth which had been the life-blood of its master spirits. From generation to generation the noblest men in the nation, those most sensitive to the touch of the Divine, had been casting soundings into the great deep of the hidden purposes of God. With sore travail of both mind and spirit, they had found solutions of the great problems which no living soul can escape. These were no doubt more or less partial, but they were sufficient for their day, and were always in the line of the final answer. As the sum of experience widened, the scope of the solutions widened also, and in the course of Providence these issued in a conception of God which elsewhere was never approached. This of all national treasures was the most priceless, and to preserve and hand on this was simply to keep the national soul alive. Compared with this, every other heritage from the past was as nothing; and so, with a simple directness which must amaze the legislators of modern states, the inspired lawgiver arranged for a religious education.

To him, as to all ancient lawgivers, a commonwealth without religion was simply inconceivable, and the hampering, confusing, and confused difficulties of to-day lay far beyond his horizon. Parents must take over this great heritage and lay it deeply to heart. They must then make it the subject of their common talk. They must write the profound words which summed it up upon the doorposts of their houses. They must let it fill their minds at their down-sitting and their uprising, and while they walked by the way. Further, as the crown of their work, they were to teach it diligently to their children, already accustomed by their parents' continual interest to regard this as the worthiest object of human thought. But though the parents were to be the chief instructors of children in religion, the State or the community was also to do its part. As the private citizen was to write, "Hear, O Israel: Yahweh our God is one Yahweh; and thou shalt love Yahweh thy God with all thine heart, and with all thy soul, and with all thy might," on the posts of his door, so the representatives of the community were to write them upon the town or village gates. In those early days schools were unknown, as State-regulated schools are still unknown in all purely Eastern countries. Consequently there was no sphere for the State in the direct religious teaching of the young. But so far as it could act, the State was to act. It was to commit itself to the religious principles that underlay the life of the people, and to proclaim them with the utmost publicity. It was to secure that none should be ignorant of them, so far as proclamation by writing in the most public place could secure knowledge, for on this the very existence of the State depended.

But the religious instruction was not to be limited to the reiteration of these great sentences; in that case they would have become a mere form of words. In the last verses of the chapter, vv. 20-25, we find a model of the kind of explanatory comment which was to be given in addition: "When thy son asketh thee in time to come, saying, What mean the testimonies, and the statutes, and the judgments, which Yahweh our God hath commanded you? then thou shalt say unto thy son, We were Pharaoh's bondmen in the land of Egypt; and Yahweh brought us out of Egypt with a mighty hand," and so on. That means that the *history* of Yahweh's dealings with His people was to be taught, to show the reasonableness of the Divine commands, to exhibit the love-compelling character of God. And this was entirely in accord with the Biblical conception of God. Neither here nor elsewhere in the Old Testament are there any abstract definitions of His character, His spirituality, His omnipresence, or His omnipotence. Nor is there anywhere any argument to prove His existence. All that is postulated, presupposed, as that which all men believe, except those who have wilfully perverted themselves. But the existence of God with all these great and necessary attributes is undoubtedly implied in what is narrated of Yahweh's dealings with His people. As we have seen, too, the very name of Yahweh implies that His nature should not be limited by any definition. He was what He would prove Himself to be, and throughout the Old Testament the *gesta Dei* through and for the Israelites, and the prophetic promises made in Yahweh's name, represented all that was known of God. This gave a peculiarly healthy and robust tone to Old Testament piety. The subjective, introspective element which in modern times is so apt to take the upper hand, was kept in due subordination by making history the main nourishment of religious thought. In constant contact with external fact, Israelite piety was simple, sincere, and practical; and men's thoughts being turned away from themselves to the Divine action in the world, they were less touched by the disease of self-consciousness than modern believers in God. In every sphere of human life, too, they looked for God, and traced the working of His hand. The later distinction between the sacred and secular parts of life, which has been often pushed to disastrous extremes, was to them unknown. For these among many other reasons, the Old Testament must always remain of vital importance to the Church of God. It can fall into neglect only when the religious life is becoming unhealthy and one-sided.

Further, its qualities especially fit it for use in the education of children. In many respects a child's mind resembles the mind of a primitive people. It has the same love of concrete examples, the same incapacity to appreciate abstract ideas, and it has the same susceptibility to such reasoning as this: God has been very loving and gracious to men, especially to our forefathers, and we are therefore bound to love Him and to obey Him with reverence and fear. To the children of a primitive people such teaching would therefore be doubly suitable; but the Deuteronomist's anxiety in regard to it has been justified by its results in times no longer primitive. Through ages of persecution and oppression, often amid a social environment of the worst sort, there has been little or no wavering in the fundamental points of Jewish faith. Scattered and peeled, slaughtered and decimated, as they have been through blood-stained centuries, this nation have held fast to their religion. Not even the fact that, through their refusal to accept their Messiah when He came, the most tender, the most expansive, the most highly spiritual elements of the Old Testament religion have escaped them, has been able to neutralise the benefit of the truth they have so tenaciously held. Of non-Christian nations they stand by far the highest; and among the orthodox Jews who still keep firm to the national traditions, and teach the ancient Scriptures diligently to their children, there is often seen a piety and a confidence in God, a submission and a hopefulness which put to shame many who profess to have hope in Christ. Even in our day, when agnosticism and denial of the supernatural is eating into Judaism more than into almost any other creed,[50] a book like Friedländer's *The Jewish Religion* gives us a very favourable idea of the spirit and teachings of orthodox Judaism. And its main stay is, and always has been, the religious training of the young. "In obedience to the precept 'Thou shalt speak of them,' *i.e.* of 'the words which I command thee this day,'" says Friedländer, "'when thou liest down and when thou risest up,' three sections of the law are read daily, in the morning and in the evening, viz. (1) Deut. vi. 4-9, beginning 'Hear'; (2) Deut. xi. 13-21, beginning 'And it shall be if ye diligently hearken'; (3) Numb. xv. 37-41, beginning 'And the Lord said.' The first section teaches the unity of God, and our duty to love this one God with all our heart, to make His word the subject of our constant meditation and to instil it into the heart of the young. The second section contains the lesson of reward and punishment, that our success depends on our obedience to the will of God. This important truth must constantly be kept before our eyes, and before the eyes of our children. The third section contains the commandments of Tsitsith, the object of which is to remind us of God's precepts." To-day, therefore, as so many centuries ago, these great words are uttered daily in the ears of all pious Jews, and they are as potent to keep them steady to their faith now as they were then. For in most cases where a drift towards the fashionable agnosticism of the day or to atheistic materialism is observable among Jews, it will be found to have been preceded either by neglect or formalism in regard to this fundamental matter. Briefly, without this teaching they cease to be Jews; with it they remain steadfast as a rock. Uprooted as they are from their country, their national coherence endures and seems likely to endure till their set time has come. So triumphantly has the enforcement of religious education vindicated itself in the case of God's ancient people.

In the remaining verses of the chapter, vv. 10-19, we have a warning against neglect and forgetfulness of their God, and an indication of the circumstances under which it would be most difficult to remain true to Him. These are uttered entirely from the Mosaic standpoint, and are among the passages which it is most difficult to reconcile with the later authorship; for there would appear to be no motive for the later writer to go back upon the exceptional circumstances of the early days in Canaan. His object must have been to warn and guide and instruct the people of *his* time in the face of their difficulties and temptations, to adapt Mosaic legislation and Mosaic teaching to the needs of his own day. Now on any supposition he must have written when all conquest on Israel's part had long ceased. It is most probable too that in his day the prosperity of his people was on the wane. They were not looking forward to a time of special temptation from riches; rather they were dreading expatriation and decay. Consequently this reference to the ease with which they became rich by occupying the cities and villages and farms of those they had conquered is quite out of place, unless we are to regard the author as a skilled and artistic writer who deliberately set himself to reproduce in all respects the mind and thoughts of a man of an earlier day, as Thackeray, for instance, does in his *Henry Esmond*. But that is not credible; and the explanation is that given in Chapter I., that the addresses here attributed to Moses are free reproductions of earlier traditions or narratives concerning what Moses actually said. If we know anything about Moses at all, it is in the highest degree probable that he left his people some parting charge. He longed to pass the Jordan with them. He could not fail to see that an immense revolution in their habits and manner of life was certain to occur when they entered the promised land. That must have appeared to him fraught with varied dangers, and words of warning and instructions would rush even unbidden to his lips.

There can be no doubt, at any rate, that this passage is true to human nature in regarding the sudden acquirement of great and goodly cities which they did not build, and houses full of good things which they filled not, and cisterns hewn out which they did not hew, vineyards and olive trees which they did not plant, as a great temptation to forgetfulness of God. At all times prosperity, especially if it come suddenly, and without being won by previous toil and self-denial, has tended to deteriorate character. When men have no changes or vicissitudes, then they fear not God. It is for help in trouble when the help of man is vain, or for a deliverance in danger, that average men most readily turn to God. But when they feel fairly safe, when they have raised themselves, as they think, "beyond all storms of chance," when they have built up between themselves and poverty or failure a wall of wealth and power, then the impulse that drives them upward ceases to act. It becomes strangely pleasant, and it seems safe, to get rid of the strain of living at the highest attainable level, and with a sigh of relief men stretch themselves out to rest and to enjoy. These are the average men; but there are some in every age, the elect, who have had the love of God shed abroad in their hearts, who have had such real and intimate communion with God that separation from Him would turn all other joys into mockery. They cannot yield to this temptation as most do, and in the midst of wealth and comfort keep alive their aspirations. In Israel these two classes existed; and to the former, *i.e.* to the great bulk of both rulers and people, the stimulus administered by the conquest to the material side of their nature must have been potent indeed.

It is here implied that the Israelite people when they entered Canaan had some moral education to lose. Whether that could be so is the question asked by many critics, and their answer is an emphatic No. They were, say they, a rude, desert people, without settled habits of life, without knowledge of agriculture, and possessed of a religion which in all outward respects was scarcely, if at all, higher than that of the surrounding nations. What happened to them in Canaan, therefore, was not a lapse, but a rise. They advanced from being a wandering pastoral people to become settled agriculturists. They gained knowledge of the arts of life by their contact with the Canaanites, and they lost little or nothing in religion; for they were themselves only image-worshippers and looked upon Yahweh as on a level with the Canaanite Baals. But if the Decalogue belongs, in any form, to that early time, and if the character of Moses be in any degree historical, then, of course, this mode of view is false. Then Israel worshipped a spiritual God, who was the guardian of morals; and there was in the mind of their leader and legislator a light which illuminated every sphere of life, both private and national. Consequently there could be a falling away from a higher level of religious life, as the Scriptures consistently say there was. Without perhaps having understood and made their own the fundamental truths of Yahwism, the people had had their whole social and political life remodelled in accordance with its principles. They had, moreover, had time to learn something of its inner meaning, and in forty years we may well believe that the more spiritually minded among them had become imbued with the higher religious spirit. Add to that the union, the movement, the excitement of a successful advance, crowned by conquest, and we have all the elements of a revived religious and national life among Eastern people.

Similar causes have produced precisely similar effects since. In important respects the origin of Mohammedanism repeats the same story. A semi-nomadic people, divided into clans and tribes, related by blood but never united, were unified by a great religious idea vastly in advance of any they had hitherto known. The religious reformer who proclaimed this truth, and those who belonged to the inner circle of his friends and counsellors, were turned from many evils, and exhibited a moral force and enthusiasm corresponding, in some degree at least, to the sublimity of the religious doctrine they had embraced. The masses, on their part, received and submitted to a revised and improved scheme of social life. Then they moved forward to conquest, and in their first days not only trampled down opposition, but deserved to do so, for in most respects they were superior to the ignorant and degraded Christians they overthrew. They came out of the desert, and were at first soldiers only. But in a generation or two they largely settled to purely agricultural life, as landowners for whom the native population laboured; and they gained in knowledge of the arts of life from the more civilised peoples they conquered. But in religious and moral character imitations of the conquered peoples involved, for the conquerors, a loss. And soon they did lose. The violence accompanying successful war produced arrogance and injustice; the immense wealth thrown into their hands so suddenly gave rise to luxury and greed. Within twenty-five years from the flight of Mohammed from Mecca, relaxation of manners manifested itself. Sensuality and drunkenness were rife; with Ali's death the Caliphate passed into the hands of Muawia, the leader of the still half-heathen part of the Koreish; and the secular indifferent portion of Mohammed's followers ruled in Islam.[51]

Allowing all that can be allowed for exceptional influences in Israel, we may well believe that the circumstances of the first invaders were such as would strain the influence of the higher religion upon the nation. And after the conquest and settlement the strain would necessarily be greater still. Whatever drawbacks warfare may have, it at least keeps men active and hardy, but the rest of a conqueror after warfare is a temptation to luxury and corruption which has been very rarely resisted. Even to-day, when men enter upon new and vacant lands, and that without war and under

Christian influences, the plenty which the first immigrants soon gather about them proves adverse to higher thought. In America in its earlier days, and in new American territories and Australia now, our civilisation at that stage always takes a materialistic turn. Every man may hope to become rich, the resources of the country are so great and those who are to share them are so few. In order to develop them, all concerned must give their time and thoughts to the work, and must become absorbed in it. The result is that, though the religious instinct asserts itself in sufficient strength to lead to the building of churches and schools, and men are too busy to be much influenced by theoretical unbelief, yet the pulse of religion beats feebly and low. The feeling spreads, under many disguises it is true, but still it spreads, that a man's life does "consist in the abundance of the things which he possesseth"; and the heroic element of Christianity, the impulse to self-sacrifice, falls into the background. The result is a social life respectable enough, save that the social blots due to self-indulgence are a good deal more conspicuous than they should be; a very high average of general comfort, with its necessary drawback of a self-satisfied and somewhat ignoble contentment; and a religious life that prides itself mainly in avoiding the falsehood of extremes. In such an atmosphere true and living religion has great difficulty in asserting itself. Each individual is drawn away from the region of higher thought more powerfully than in the older lands where ambitions are for most men less plausible; and so the struggle to keep the soul sensitive to spiritual influences is more hard. As for the national life, public affairs in those circumstances tend to be ruled simply by the standard of immediate expediency, and strenuousness of principle or practice tends to be regarded as an impossible ideal.

To all this Israel was exposed, and to more. There are doubts as to the extent of their conquests when they settled down; but there are none that when they did so they still had heathen Canaanites among them. Throughout almost the whole country the population was mixed, and constant intercourse with the conquered peoples was unavoidable. At first these were either Israel's teachers in many of the arts of settled life, or they must have carried on the work of agriculture for their Israelite lords. Moreover many of the sacred places of the land, the sanctuaries which from time immemorial had been resorted to for worship, were either taken over by the Israelites or were left in Canaanite hands. In either case they opened a way for malign influences upon the purer faith. Gradually, too, the tribal feeling asserted itself. The tribal heads regained the position they had held before the domination of Moses and his successor, just as the tribal heads of the Arabs asserted themselves after the death of Mohammed and his immediate successors, and plunged into fratricidal war with the companions of their prophet. The only difference was that, while the circumstances of the Arabs compelled them to retain a supreme head, the circumstances of the Israelites permitted them to fall back into the tribal isolation from which they had emerged. The national life was broken up, the religious life followed in the same path, until, as the Book of Judges graphically says in narrating how Micah set up an Ephod and Teraphim for himself and made his son a priest, "every man did that which was right in his own eyes." With a people so recently won for a higher faith, there could not but follow a recrudescence of heathen or semi-heathen beliefs and practices.

To sum up, given a great truth revealed to one man, which, though accepted by a nation, is only half understood by the bulk of them, and given also a great national deliverance and expansion brought about by the same leader, you have there the elements of a great enthusiasm with the seeds of its own decay within it. Such a nation, especially if plied with external temptation, will fall back, not into its first state certainly, but into a condition much below its highest level, so soon as the leader and those who had really comprehended the new truth are removed to a distance or are dead.

In the case of Mohammedanism this was instinctively felt. We find the Governor of Bassorah writing thus to Omar, the third Khalif: "Thou must strengthen my hands with a company of the Companions of the Prophet, for verily they are as salt in the midst of the people."[52] The same thing is expressly asserted of Israel also by the later editor in Josh. xxiv. 31: "And Israel served the Lord all the days of Joshua, and all the days of the elders that outlived Joshua, and had known all the work of the Lord, that He had wrought for Israel." It would almost seem as if Semitic peoples were specially liable to such oscillations, if Palgrave's account of the people of Nejed before the rise of the Wahabbis in the middle of last century can be trusted. "Almost every trace of Islam," he says,[53] "had long since vanished from Nejed, where the worship of the Djann, under the spreading foliage of large trees, or in the cavernous recesses of Djebel Toweyk, along with the invocation of the dead and sacrifices at their tombs, was blended with remnants of old Sabæan superstition. The Coran was unread, the five daily prayers forgotten, and no one cared where Mecca lay, east or west, north or south; tithes, ablutions, and pilgrimages were things unheard of."[54] If that was the state of things in a country exposed to no extraneous influences after a thousand years of Islam, we may well believe that the state of Israel in the time of the Judges was a fall from a better state religiously as well as politically. Looking to the future, Moses might well foresee the danger; and looking back the author of Deuteronomy would have reasons, many of them now unknown, for knowing that what was feared had occurred.

It is striking to see that both know but one security against such lapses in the life of a nation, and that is education. Nowadays we are inclined to ask if this was not a delusion on their part. The boundless faith in education as a moral, religious, and national restorative which filled men's minds in the early part of this century, has given place to disquieting questions as to whether it can do anything so high. Many begin to doubt whether it does more than restrain men from the worst crimes, by pointing out their consequences. And in the case of ordinary secular education that doubt is only too well founded. But it was not mere secular education the Old Testament relied on. Reading, writing, and arithmetic, valuable as these are as gateways to knowledge, were not in its view at all. What it was felt necessary to do was to keep alive an ideal view of life; and that was done by pouring into the young the history of their people, with the best that their highest minds had learned and thought of God. The demand is that parents shall first of all give themselves up to the love of God, without any reserve, and then that they shall teach this diligently to their children as the substance of the Divine demand upon *them*. Evidently by the words, "Thou shalt talk of them when thou sittest in thine house, and when thou walkest by the way, and when thou liest down and when thou risest up," it is meant that the truth about God and the thought of God should be a subject on which conversation naturally turned, and to which it gladly returned continually. Words about these things were to flow from a genuine delighted interest in them, which made speech a necessity and a joy. Further, parents were to meet the *naïve* and questioning curiosity of their children as to the meaning of religious and moral ordinances of their people, with grave and extended teaching as to the work of God among them in the past. They were to point out, vv. 21-25, all the grace of God, and to show them that the statutes, which to young and undisciplined minds might seem a heavy burden, were really God's crowning mercy: they marked out the lines upon which alone good could come to man: they were the directions of a loving guide anxious to keep their feet from paths of destruction, "for their good always." Such education as this might prove adequate to overcome even stronger temptations than those to which Israel was exposed. For see what it means. It means that all the garnered religious thought and emotion of past generations, which the experiences of life and the felt presence of God in them had borne in upon the deepest minds of Israel, was to be made the bounding horizon for the opening mind of every Israelite child. When the child looked beyond the desires of its physical nature, it was to see this great sight, this panorama of the grace of Yahweh. To compensate for the restrictions which the Decalogue puts upon the natural impulses, Yahweh was to be held up to every child as an object of love, no desire after which could be excessive. Love to Yahweh, drawn out by what He had shown

Himself to be, was to turn the energies of the young soul outward, away from self, and direct them to God, who works and is the sum of all good. Obviously those upon whom such education had its perfect work would never be fettered by the material aspects of things. Their horizon could never be so darkened that the twilight gods worshipped by the Canaanites should seem to them more than dim and vanishing shadows. Every evil, incident to their circumstances as conquerors, would fall innocuous at their feet.

The instrument put into the hands of Israel was, viewed ideally, quite adequate for the work it had to do. But the history of Israel shows that the effort to keep Yahweh continually present to the mind of the people failed; and the question arises, why did it fail? If, as we have every reason to believe, the main tendencies of human nature then were what they are now, the first cause of failure would be with the parents. Many, probably the most of them, would observe to do all that Moses commanded, but they would do it without themselves keeping alive their spiritual life. Wherever that was the case, though the prayers should be scrupulously rehearsed, though the religious talk should be increasing, though the instruction about the past should be exact and regular, the highest results of it all would cease to appear. The best that would be done would be to keep alive knowledge of what the fathers had told them. The worst would be to render the child's mind so familiar with all aspects of the truth, and with all the phases of religious emotion, that throughout life this would always seem a region already explored, and in which no water for the thirsty soul had been found.

But in the children, too, there would be fatal hindrances. One would almost expect, *a priori*, that when one generation had won in trial and hardship and conquest a fund of moral and spiritual wisdom, their children would be able to take it to themselves, and would start from the point their fathers had attained. But in experience that is not found to be so. The fathers may have gained a sane and strong manhood through the training and teaching of Divine Providence, but their children do not start from the level their fathers have gained. They begin with the same passions, and evil tendencies, and illusions, as their fathers began with, and against these they have to wage continual war. Above all, each soul for itself must take the great step by which it turns from evil to good. No rise in the general level of life will ever enable men to dispense with that. The will must determine itself morally by a free choice, and the Divine grace must play its part, before that union with God which is the heart of all religion can be brought about. No mechanical keeping up of good habits or fairer forms of social life can do much at this crucial point; and so each generation finds that there is no discharge in the war to which it is committed. As in all wars, many fall; sometimes the battle goes sorely against the kingdom of God, and the majority fall. The strength and beauty of a whole generation turns to the world and away from God, and the labours and prayers of faithful men and women who have taught them seem to be in vain.

The method of warding off evil by even high religious education is consequently very imperfect and uncertain in its action. Nevertheless this relative uncertainty is bound up with the very nature of moral influence and moral agency. Professor Huxley, in a famous passage of one of his addresses, says that if any being would offer to wind him up like a clock, so that he should always do what is right, and think what is true, he would close with the offer, and make no mourning about his moral freedom. Probably this was only a vehement way of expressing a desire for righteousness in deed, and truth in thought, somewhat pathetic in such a man. But if we are to take it literally, it is a singularly unwise declaration. The longing which gives pathos to the professor's words would on his hypothesis be a lunacy; for in the realm of morals mechanical compulsion has no meaning. Even God must give room to His creature, that he may exercise the spiritual freedom with which he is endowed. Even God, we may say without irreverence, must sometimes fail in that which He seeks to accomplish, in the field of moral life. Philosophically speaking, perhaps, this statement cannot be defended. But it is not the Absolute of Philosophy which can touch the hearts and draw the love of men. It is the living, personal God, of whom we gain our best working conception by boldly transferring to Him the highest categories predicable of our humanity. He is, doubtless, much more than we; but we can only ascribe to Him our own best and highest. When we have done that we have approached Him as near as we can ever do. The Scriptural writers, therefore, have no pedantic scruples in their speech about God. They constantly represent Him as pleading with men, desiring to influence them, and yet sometimes as being driven back defeated by the obstinate sin of man. The Bible is full of the failures of God in this sense; and God's greatest failure, that which forms the burden and inspires the pathos of the bulk of the Old Testament, is His failure with His chosen people. They *would* not be saved, they *would* not be faithful; and God had to accomplish His work of planting the true and spiritual religion in the world by means of a mere remnant of faithful men chosen from a faithless multitude.

But though this plan failed miserably in one way, in the way of gaining the bulk of the people, it succeeded in another. As has just been said, *the* purpose of God was in any case accomplished. But even apart from that, the religious education that was given was of immense importance. It raised the level of life for all; like the Nile mud in the inundation, it fertilised the whole field of this people's life. It kept an ideal, too, before men, without which they would have fallen even lower than they did. And it lay in the minds of even the worst, ready to be changed into something higher; for without previous intellectual acquaintance with the facts, the deeper knowledge was impossible. Moreover the ordinary civil morality of the people rested upon it. Without their religion and the facts on which it was based, the moral code had no hold upon them, and could have none. That had grown up in one complex tangle with religion; it had received its highest inspiration from the conception of God handed down from the fathers; and apart from that it would have fallen into an incoherent mass of customs unable to justify or account for their existence. In every community the same principle holds. Hence whatever the theory of the relation of the State to religion which may prevail, no State can, without much harm, ignore the religion of the people. It may sometimes even be wise and right for a government to introduce or to encourage a higher religion at the expense of a lower. But it can never be either wise or right to be inadvertent of religion altogether. In accordance with this precept, the rulers of Israel never were so. They not only encouraged parents to be strenuous, as this passage demands of them, but on more than one occasion they made definite provision for the religious instruction of the people. In a formal sense that grew into a habit which even yet has not lost its hold; and hence, as we have seen, the Jews have been kept true in an unexampled manner to their racial and religious characteristics.

CHAPTER IX
THE BAN

Deut. vii

As in the previous chapter we have had the Mosaic and Deuteronomic statement of the internal and spiritual means of defending the Israelite character and faith from the temptations which the conquest in Canaan would bring with it, in this we have strenuous provision made against the same evil by external means. The mind first was to be fortified against the temptation to fall away; then the external pressure from the example of the peoples they were to conquer was to be minimised by the practice of the ban. The first five verses, and the last two deal emphatically with that, as also does ver. 16, and what lies between is a statement of the grounds upon which a strict execution of this dreadful measure was demanded. These, as is usual in Deuteronomy, are dealt with somewhat discursively; but the command as to the ban, coming as it does at the beginning, middle, and end, gives this chapter unity, and suggests that it should be treated under this head as a whole. There are besides other passages which can most conveniently be discussed in connection with chapter vii. These are the historic statements as to the ban having been laid upon the cities of Sihon (Deut. ii. 34) and Og (Deut. iii. 6); the provision for the extirpation of idolatrous persons and communities (Deut. xiii. 15); and lastly, that portion of the law of war which treats of the variations in the execution of the ban which circumstances might demand (Deut. xx. 13-18). These passages, taken together, give an almost exhaustive statement in regard to the nature and limitations of the Cherem, or ban, in ancient Israel, a statement much more complete than is elsewhere to be found; and they consequently suggest, if they do not demand, a complete investigation of the whole matter.

It is quite clear that the Cherem, or ban, by which a person or thing, or even a whole people and their property, were devoted to a god, was not a specially Mosaic ordinance, for it is a custom known to many half-civilised and some highly civilised nations. In Livy's account of early Rome we read that Tarquinius, after defeating the Sabines, burned the spoils of the enemy in a huge heap, in accordance with a vow to Vulcan, made before advancing into the Sabine country. The same custom is alluded to in Vergil, *Æn.* viii. 562, and Cæsar, *B.G.* vi. 17, tells us a similar thing of the Gauls. The Mexican custom of sacrificing all prisoners of war to the god of war was of the same kind. But the most complete example of the ban in the Hebrew sense, occurring among a foreign people, is to be found in the Moabite stone which Mesha, king of Moab, erected in the ninth century B.C., *i.e.* in the days of Ahab. Of course Moab and Israel were related peoples, and it might in itself be possible that Moab during its subjection to Israel had adopted the ban from Israel. But that is highly improbable, considering how widespread this custom is, and how deeply its roots are fixed in human nature. Rather we should take the Moabite ban as an example of its usual form among the Semitic peoples. "And Chemosh said to me, Go, take Nebo against Israel. And I went by night and fought against it from the break of morn until noon, and took it and killed them all, seven thousand men and boys, and women and girls and maid-servants, for I had devoted it to 'Ashtor-Chemosh'; and I took thence the vessels" (so Renan) "of Yahweh, and I dragged them before Chemosh."[55] The ordinary Semitic word for the ban is *Cherem*. It denotes a thing separated from or prohibited to common use, and no doubt it indicated originally merely that which was given over to the gods, separated for their exclusive use for ever. In this way it was distinguished from that which was "sanctified" to Yahweh, for that could be redeemed; devoted things could not.

In the ancient laws repeated in Lev. xxvii. 28, 29, two classes of devoted things seem to be referred to. First of all, we have the things which an individual may devote to God, "whether of man or beast, or of the field of his possession." The provision made in regard to them is that they shall not be sold or redeemed, but shall become in the highest degree sacred to Yahweh. Men so devoted, therefore, became perpetual slaves at the holy places, and other kinds of property fell to the priests. In the next verse, 29, we read, "None devoted which shall be devoted of" (*i.e.* from among) "men shall be ransomed; he shall surely be put to death," but that must refer to some other class of men devoted to Yahweh. It is inconceivable that in Israel individuals could at their own will devote slaves or children to death. Moreover, if every man devoted must be killed, the provision of Numb. xviii. 14, according to which everything devoted in Israel is to be Aaron's, could not be carried out. Further, there is a difference in expression in the two verses: in 28 we have things "devoted to Yahweh," in 29 we have simply men "devoted."[56] There can be little doubt, therefore, that we have in ver. 29 the case of men condemned for some act for which the punishment prescribed by the law was the ban (as in Exod. xxii. 19, "He that sacrificeth unto any god save unto Yahweh only shall be put to the ban"), or which some legal tribunal considered worthy of that punishment. In such cases, the object of the ban being something offensive, something which called out the Divine wrath and abhorrence, this "devotion" to God meant utter destruction. Just as *anathēma*, a thing set up in a temple as a votive offering, became *anathěma*, an accursed thing, and as *sacer*, originally meaning sacred, came to mean devoted to destruction, so *Cherem*, among the Semites, came to have the meaning of a thing devoted to destruction by the wrath of the national gods. From ancient days it had been in use, and in Israel it continued to be practised, but with a new moral and religious purpose which antiquity could know nothing of. No more conspicuous instance of that transformation of ancient customs of a doubtful or even evil kind by the spirit of the religion of Yahweh, which is one of the most remarkable characteristics of the history of Israel, can be conceived than this use of the ban for higher ends.

As the fundamental idea of the *Cherem* was the devoting of objects to a god, it is manifest that the whole inner significance of the institution would vary with the conception of the Deity. Among the worshippers of cruel and sanguinary gods, such as the gods of the heathen Semites were, the ends which this practice was used to promote would naturally be cruel and sanguinary. Moreover, where it was thought that the gods could be bought over by acceptable sacrifices, where they were conceived of as non-moral beings, whose reasons for favour or anger were equally capricious and unfathomable, it was inevitable that the *Cherem* should be mainly used to bribe these gods to favour and help their peoples. Where victory seemed easy and within the power of the nation, the spoil and the inhabitants of a conquered city or country would be taken by the conquerors for their own use. Where, on the other hand, victory was difficult and doubtful, an effort would be made to win the favour of the god, and wring success from him by promising him all the spoil. The slaughter of the captives would be considered the highest gratification such sanguinary gods could receive, while their pride would be held to be gratified by the utter destruction of the seat of the worship of other gods. Obviously it was in this way that the Gauls and Germans worked this institution; and the probability is that the heathen Semites would view the whole matter from an even lower standpoint. But to true worshippers of Yahweh such thoughts must have grown abhorrent. From the moment when their God became the centre and the norm of moral life to Israel, acts which had no scope but the gratification of a thirst for blood, or of a petty jealous pride, could not be thought acceptable to Him. Every institution and custom, therefore, which had no moral element in it, had either to be swept away, or moralised in the spirit of the purer faith.

Now the ban was not abolished in Israel; but it was moralised, and turned into a potent and terrible weapon for the preservation and advancement of true religion.

By the Divine appointment the national life of Israel was bound up with the foundation and progress of true religion. It was in this people that the seeds of the highest religion were to be planted, and it was by means of it that all the nations of the earth were to be blessed. But as the chief means to this end was to be the higher ethical and religious character of the nation as such, the preservation of that from depravation and decay became the main anxiety of the prophets and priests and law-givers of Israel. Just as in modern days the preservation and defence of the State is reckoned in every country the supreme law which overrides every other consideration, so in Israel the preservation of the higher life was regarded. Rude and half-civilised as Israel was at the beginning of its career, the Divinely revealed religion had made men conscious of that which gave this people its unique value both to God and men. They recognised that its glory and strength lay in its thought of God, and in the character which this impressed upon the corporate life, as well as on the life of each individual. As we have seen, this bred in them a consciousness of a higher calling, of a higher obligation resting on them than upon others. They consequently felt the necessity of guarding their special character, and used the ban as their great weapon to ward off the contagion of evil, and to give this character room to develop itself. Its tremendous, even cruel, power was directed in Israel to this end; it was from this point of view alone that it had value in the eyes of the fully enlightened man of Israel. Stade in his history (vol. i., p. 490) holds that this distinction did not exist, that the Israelite view differed in little, if anything, from that of their heathen kinsmen, and that the ban resulted from a vow intended to gratify Yahweh and win His favour by giving Him the booty. But it is undeniable that in the earliest statement in regard to it (Exod. xx.) there is a distinct legislative provision that the ban should be proclaimed and executed irrespective of any vow; and in the later, but still early, notices of it in Joshua, Judges, and 1 Samuel the command to execute it comes in every case from Yahweh. In Deuteronomy, again, the ethical purpose of the ban is always insisted upon, most emphatically perhaps in chap. xx. 17 ff., where the *Cherem* is laid down as a regular practice in war against the heathen inhabitants of Canaan: "But thou shalt utterly destroy them, ... that they teach you not to do after all their abominations, which they have done unto their gods; so should ye sin against Yahweh your God." Whatever hints or appearances there may be in the Scripture narratives that the lower view still clung to some minds are not to be taken as indicating the normal and recognised view. They were, like much else of a similar kind, mere survivals, becoming more and more shadowy as the history advances, and at last entirely vanishing away. The new and higher thought which Moses planted was the rising and prevailing element in the Israelite consciousness. The lower thought was a decaying reminiscence of the state of things which the Mosaic revelation had wounded to the death, but which was slow in dying.

In Israel, therefore, the ban was, on the principles of the higher religion, legitimate only where the object was to preserve that religion when gravely endangered. If any object could justify a measure so cruel and sweeping as the ban, this could, and this is the only ground upon which the Scriptures defend it. That the danger was grave and imminent, when Israel entered Canaan, cannot be doubted. As we have seen, the Israelite tribes were far from being of one blood or of one faith. There was a huge mixed multitude along with them; and even among those who had unquestioned title to be reckoned among Israelites, many were gross, carnal, and slavish in their conceptions of things. They had not learned thoroughly nor assimilated the lessons they had been taught. Only the elect among them had done that; and the danger from contact with races, superior in culture, and religiously not so far below the position occupied by the multitude of Israel, was extreme. The nation was born in a day, but it had been educated only for a generation; it was raw and ignorant in all that concerned the Yahwistic faith. In fact it was precisely in the condition in which spiritual disease could be most easily contracted and would be most deadly. The new religion had not been securely organised; the customs and habits of the people still needed to be moulded by it, and could not, consequently, act as the stay and support of religion as they did at later times. Further, the people were at the critical moment when they were passing from one stage of social life to another. At such moments there is immense danger to the health and character of a nation, for there is no unity of ideal present to every mind. That which they are moving away from has not ceased to exert its influence, and that *to* which they are moving has not asserted itself with all its power. At such crises in the career of peoples emerging from barbarism, even physical disease is apt to be deadlier and more prevalent than it is among either civilised or entirely savage men. The old Semitic heathenism had not been entirely overcome, and the new and higher religion had not succeeded in establishing full dominion. Contact with the Canaanites in almost any shape would under such circumstances be like the introduction of a contagious disease, and at almost any price it had to be avoided. The customs of the world at that time, and of the Semitic nations in particular, offered this terribly effective weapon of the "ban," and for this higher purpose it was accepted; and it was enforced with a stringency which nothing would justify short of the fact that life or death to the great hope of mankind was involved in it.

But it may be and should be asked, Would any circumstances justify Christian men, or a Christian nation, in entering upon a war of extermination now? and if not, how can a war of extermination against the Canaanities have been sanctioned by God? In answer to the first question, it must be said that, while circumstances can be conceived under which the extermination of a race would certainly be carried out by nations called Christian, it is hardly possible to imagine Christian men taking part in such a massacre. Even the supposed command of God could not induce them to do so.[57] It would be so contrary to all that they have learned of God's will, both as regards themselves and others, that they would hesitate. Almost certainly they would decide that they were bound to be faithful to what God had revealed of Himself; they would feel that He could not wish to blunt their moral sense and undo what He had done for them, and they would put aside the command as a temptation. But the case with the Israelites was altogether different. The question is not, how could God destroy a whole people? Were it only that, there would be little difficulty. Everywhere in His action through nature God is ruthless enough against sin. Vice and sin are every day bringing men and women and innocent children to death, and to suffering worse than death. For that every believer in God holds the Divine law responsible. And when the Divine command was laid upon the Israelites to do, more speedily, and in a more awe-inspiring way, what Canaanite vices were already doing, there can be no difficulty except in so far as the effect upon the Israelites is concerned. It is by death, inflicted as the punishment of vice, and sparing neither woman nor child, that nations have, as a rule, been blotted out; and, except to the confused thinker, so far as the Divine action is concerned there is no difference between such cases and this of the Canaanites. The real question is, Can a living, personal God deliberately set to men a task which can only lower them in the scale of humanity—brutalise them, in fact? No, is of course the only possible answer; therefore a supposed Divine command coming to us to do such things would rightly be suspected. We could not, we feel sure, be called upon by God to slay the innocent with the guilty, to overwhelm in one common punishment individual beings who have each of them an inalienable claim to justice at our hands. But the Israelites had not and could not have the feeling we have on the subject. The feeling for the individual did not exist in early times. The clan, the tribe, the nation was everything, and the individual nothing. Consequently there was not existent in the world that keen feeling in regard to individual rights, which dominates us so completely that we can with difficulty conceive any other view. In this world the early Israelite scarcely perceived the individual man, and beyond this world he knew of no certain career for him. He consequently dealt with him only as part of his clan or tribe. His tribe suffered for him and he for his tribe, and in early penal law the two could hardly be separated. Indeed it may almost be said that, when the individual suffered for his own sin, the satisfaction felt by the wronged was rather due to the tribe having suffered so much loss in the individual's death than to the retribution which fell upon him. Moreover war was the constant employment of all, and death by violence the most common of all forms of death. Manners and feelings were both rude, and the pains as well as the pleasures of civilised and Christian men lay largely beyond their horizon. There was consequently no danger of doing violence to nobler feelings or of leaving a sting in the conscience by calling such men to such work. The stage of moral development they had reached did not forbid it, and the work therefore might be given them of God.

But the grounds for the action were immeasurably raised. Instead of being left on the heathen level, "the usage was utilised so as to harmonise with the principles of their religion, and to satisfy its needs. It became a mode of secluding and rendering harmless anything which peculiarly imperilled the religious life of either an individual or the community, such objects being withdrawn from society at large, and presented to the sanctuary, which had power, if needful, to authorise their destruction."[58] The Deuteronomic command is not given shamefacedly. The interests at stake are too great for that. Israel is utterly to smite the Canaanite nations, to put them to the ban, to make no covenant with them nor to intermarry with them. "Thus shall ye deal with them: ye shall break down their altars, and dash in pieces their obelisks, and hew down their Asherim, and burn their graven images with fire." There is a fierce, curt energy about the words which impresses the reader with the vigour needed to defend the true religion. The danger was seen to be great, and this tremendous weapon of the ban was to be wielded with unsparing rigour, if Israel was to be true to its highest call. "For," ver. 6 goes on to say, "thou art a holy people unto Yahweh thy God; Yahweh thy God hath chosen thee to be a peculiar people unto Himself, out of all peoples that are upon the face of the earth." They were the elect of God; they were a holy people, a people separated unto their God, and the Divine blessing was to come upon all nations through them if they remained true. Their separateness must therefore be maintained. As a people marked out by the love of God, they could not share in the common life of the world as it then was. They could not lift the Canaanites to their level by mingling with them. So they would only obscure, nay, in so far as this rigorous command was not carried out, they did all but fatally obscure, the higher elements of national and personal life which they had received. They were too recently converted to be the people of Yahweh, too weak in their own faith, to be able to do anything but stand in this austere and repellent attitude towards the world. Centuries passed before they could relax without danger. It may even be said that until the coming of our Lord they dared not take up any other than this separatist position, though as the ages passed and the prophetic influence grew, the yearning after a gathering in of the Gentiles, and the promise of it in the Messianic day, became more markedly prominent. Only when men could look forward to being made perfect in Jesus Christ did they receive the command to go unreservedly out into the world, for only then had they an anchor which no storm in the world could drag.

But we must be careful not to exaggerate the separation called for here. It does not authorise anything like the fierce, intolerant thirst for conquest and domination which was the very keynote of Islam.[59] In Deut. ii. 5, 6, 19, the lands of Edom, Moab, and Ammon are said to be Yahweh's gift to these peoples in the same way as Canaan was to Israel. Nor did the law ever authorise the bitter and contemptuous feeling with which Pharisaic Israelites often regarded all men beyond the pale of Judaism. There was no general prohibition against friendly intercourse with other peoples. It was against those only, whose presence in Canaan would have frustrated the establishment of the theocracy, and whose influence would have been destructive of it when established, that the "ban" was decreed. When war arose between Israel and cities farther off than those of Canaan, they were not to be put to the "ban." Though they were to be hardly treated according to our ideas, they were to suffer only the fate of cities stormed in those days, for the danger of corruption was proportionately diminished (Deut. xx. 17) by their distance. The right of other peoples to their lands was to be respected, and friendly intercourse might be entered on with them. But the right of Israel to the free and unhindered development to which it had been called by Yahweh was the supreme law. The suspicion of danger to that was to make things otherwise harmless, or even useful, to be abhorred. If men are to live nearer to God than others, they must sacrifice much to the higher call.

To press home this, to induce Israel to respond to this demand, to convince them anew of their obligation to go any length to keep their position as a people holy to Yahweh, our chapter urges a variety of reasons. The first (vv. 7-11) is that the history and grounds of their election exhibit the character of Yahweh in such a way as to heighten their sense of their privileges and the danger of losing them. He had chosen them, only because of His own love to them; and having chosen them and sworn to their fathers, He is true to His covenant. He brought them out of the house of bondage, and has led them until now. In Yahweh they had a spiritual ideal, whose characteristics were love and faithfulness. But though He loves He can be wrathful, and though He has made a covenant with Israel, it must be fulfilled in accordance with righteousness. In dealing with such a God they must beware of thinking that their election is irrespective of moral conditions, or that His love is mere good nature. He can and does smite the enemies of good, for anger is always possible where love is. It is only with good nature that anger is not compatible, just as warm and self-sacrificing affection also is. Those who turn away from Him, therefore, He requites immediately to their face, as surely as "He keepeth covenant and mercy with them that love Him and keep His commandments." All the blessed and intimate relations which He has opened up with them, and in which their safety and their glory lie, can be dissolved by sin. They are, therefore, to strike fiercely at temptation, to regard neither their own lives nor the lives of others when that has to be put out of the way, to smite and spare not, for the very love of God.

A second reason why they should obey the Divine commands, as in other matters, so in this terrible thing, is this. If they be willing and obedient, then God will bless them in temporal ways as well as with spiritual blessings. Even for their earthly prosperity a loyal attitude to Yahweh would prove decisive. "Thou shalt be blessed above all peoples; there shall not be a male or female barren among you, or among your cattle. And Yahweh will take away from thee all sickness, and He will put none of the evil diseases of Egypt which thou knowest upon thee; but will lay them upon all them that hate thee." The same promises are renewed in more detail and with greater emphasis in the speech contained in chapters xxviii. and xxix. There the significance of such a view, and the difficulties involved in it for us, will be fully discussed. Here it will be sufficient to note that the profit of obedience is brought in to induce Israel to enforce the "ban" most rigorously.

The last verses of our chapter, vv. 17-26, set before Israel a third incitement and encouragement. Yahweh, who had proved His might and His favour for them by His mighty deeds in Egypt, would be among them, to make them stronger than their mightiest foes (ver. 21): "Thou shalt not be affrighted at them, for Yahweh thy God is in the midst of thee, a great God and a terrible." The previous inducements to obey Yahweh their God and be true to Him were founded on His character and on His acts. He was merciful; but He could be terrible, and He would reward the faithful with prosperity. Now His people are encouraged to go forward because His presence will go with them. In the conflicts which obedience to Him would provoke, He would be with them to sustain them, whatever stress might come upon them. Step by step they would drive out those very peoples whom they had dreaded so when the spies brought back their report of the land. The terror of their God would fall upon all these nations. A great God and a terrible He would prove Himself to be, and with Him in their midst they might go forth boldly to execute the ban upon the Canaanites. The sins and vices of these peoples had brought this upon them; their horrible worship left an indelible stain wherever its shadow fell. Israel, led and directed by Yahweh Himself, was to fall upon them as the scourge of God.

Notwithstanding the Divine urgency, the command to destroy the Canaanites and their idols was not carried out. After a victory or two the enemy began to submit. Glad to be rid of the toils of war, Israel settled down among the people of the land. All central control would seem to have disappeared. The Canaanite worship and the Canaanite customs attracted and fascinated the people, and enemy after enemy broke in upon them and triumphed over them. The half-idolatrous masses were led away into depraved forms of worship, and for a time it looked as if the work of Moses would be utterly undone. Had the purer faith he taught them not been revived, Israel would probably not have survived the period of the Judges. As it was, they just survived; but by their lapse the leavening of the whole of the nation with the pure principles of Yahweh-worship had been stopped. Instead of being cured, the idolatrous inclinations they had brought with them from the pre-Mosaic time had been revived and strengthened. Multitudes, while calling Yahweh their God, had sunk almost to the Canaanite level in their worship, and during the whole period of their existence as a nation Israel as a whole never again rose clear of half-heathen conceptions of their God. The prophets taught and threatened them in vain, until at last ruin fell upon them and the Divine threats of punishment were fulfilled.

CHAPTER X
THE BAN IN MODERN LIFE

In our modern time this practice of the ban has, of course, become antiquated and impossible. The *Cherem*, or ban, of the modern synagogue is a different thing, based upon different motives, and is directed to the same ends as Christian excommunication. But though the thing has ceased, the principles underlying it, and the view of life which it implies, are of perpetual validity. These belong to the essential truths of religion, and especially need to be recalled in a time like ours, when men tend everywhere to a feeble, lax, and cosmopolitan view of Christianity. As we have seen, the fundamental principle of the *Cherem* was that, however precious, however sacred, however useful and helpful in ordinary circumstances a thing might be, whenever it became dangerous to the higher life it should at once be given up to Yahweh. The lives of human beings, even though they were men's dearest and nearest, should be sacrificed; the richest works of art, the weapons of war, and the wealth which would have adorned life and made it easy, were equally to be given up to Him, that He might seclude them and render them harmless to men's highest interests. Neighbourliness to the Canaanites was absolutely forbidden, and the Church of the Old Testament was commanded to take up a position of hostility, or at best of armed neutrality, to all the pleasures, interests, and concerns of the peoples who surrounded them. Now the prevailing modern view is that not only the ban itself, but these principles have become obsolete. Notwithstanding that the Church of the New Testament is the bearer of the higher interests of humanity, we are taught that when it is least definite in its direction ἅas to conduct, when it is most tolerant of the practices of the world, then it is most true to its original conception. We are told that an indulgent Church is what is wanted; rigour and religion are now supposed to be finally divorced in all enlightened minds. This view is not often categorically expressed, but it underlies all fashionable religion, and has its apostles in the golden youth who forward enlightenment by playing tennis on Sundays. Because of it too, Puritan has become a name of scorn, and careless self-gratification a mark of cultured Christianity. Not only asceticism, but ἄσκησις has been discredited, and the moral tone of society has perceptibly fallen in consequence. In wide circles both within and without the Church it seems to be held that pain is the only intolerable evil, and in legislation as well as in literature that idea has been registering itself.

For much of this progress, as some call it, no reasoned justification has been attempted, but it has been defended in part by the allegation that the circumstances which make the "ban" necessary to the very life of the ancient people of God have passed away, now that social and political life has been Christianised. Even those who are outside the Church in Christian lands are no longer living at a moral and spiritual level so much below that of the Church. They are not heathen idolaters, whose moral and religious ideas are contagiously corrupting, and nothing but Pharisaism of the worst type, it is said, can justify the Church in taking up a position to society in any degree like that which was imposed upon ancient Israel. Now it cannot be denied that there is truth here, and in so far as the Christian Church or individual Christians have taken up precisely the same position to those without as is implied in the Old Testament ban, they are not to be defended. Modern society, as at present constituted, is not corrupting like that of Canaan. No one in a modern Christian state has been brought up in an atmosphere of heathenism, and what an incredible difference that involves only those who know heathenism well can appreciate. If spiritual life is neither understood nor believed in by all, yet the rules of morals are the same in every mind, and these rules are the product of Christianity. As a consequence, the Church is not endangered in the same way and to the same degree by contact with the world as in the ancient days. Indeed to the Israelite of the post-Mosaic time our "world," which some sects at least would absolutely ignore and shut out, would seem a very definite and legitimate part of the Church. The Jewish Church was certainly to a very large extent made up of precisely such elements, while those who were to be put to the ban were far more remote than any citizens of a modern state, except a portion of the criminal class. Further, those not actively Christian are, on account of this community of moral sentiments, open to appeal from the Church as the heathen Canaanites were not. In English-speaking lands, while there are multitudes indifferent to Christianity, most acknowledge the obligation of the Christian motives. In nations at least nominally Christian, therefore, both because the danger of corruption is greatly less, and because the world is more accessible to the leaven of Christian life, no Church can, or dare, without incurring terrible loss and responsibility, withdraw from or show a merely hostile front to the world. The sects which do so live an invalid life. Their virtues take on the sickly look of all "fugitive and cloistered virtue." Their doctrines become full of the "idols of the cave," and they cease to have any perception of the real needs of men.

Nevertheless the austere spirit inculcated in this chapter must be kept alive, if the Church is to be the spiritual leader of humanity, for strenuousness is the great want of modern life. Dr. Pearson, whose book on *National Life and Character* has lately expounded the theory that the Church, "being too inexorable in its ideal to admit of compromises with human frailty, is precisely on this account unfitted for governing fallible men and women," i.e. governing them in the political sense, has elsewhere stated his view of the remedy for one of the great evils of modern life.[60] "The disproportionate growth of the distributing classes, as compared with the producing, is due, I believe, to two moral causes—the love of amusement and the passion for speculation. Men flock out of healthy country lives in farms or mines into our great cities, because they like to be near the theatre and the racecourse, or because they hope to grow rich suddenly by some form of gambling. The cure for a taint of this kind is not economical but religious, and can only be found, I am convinced, in a return to the masculine asceticism that has distinguished the best days of history, Puritan or Republican." This is emphatically true of Australia, where and of which the words were first spoken; and masculine asceticism of the Puritan type would cure many another evil there besides these. But the same thing is true everywhere; and if religion is to cure slackness in social or political life, how much more must it cultivate this austere spirit for itself! The function of the Church is not to govern the world; it seeks rather to inspire the world. It should lead the advance to a higher, more ennobling life, and should exhibit that in its own collective action and in the kind of character it produces. Its greatest gift to the world should be itself, and it is useful only when it is true to its own *ethos* and spirit. To keep that unimpaired must therefore be its first duty, and to fulfil that duty it must keep rigorously back from everything which, in relation to its own existing state, would be likely to lower the power of its peculiar life. The State must often compromise with human frailty. Often there will be before the legislator and the statesman only a choice between two evils, or at least two undesirable courses, unless a worse thing is to be tolerated. The Church, on the other hand, should keep close to the ideal as it sees it. Its reason for existence is that it may hold up the ideal to men, and exhibit it as far as that may be. Compromise in regard to that is impossible for the Church, for that would be nothing else than disloyalty to its own essential principle. The spirit, therefore, that inspired the "ban" must always be living and powerful in the Church. Whatever is dangerous to the special Christian life must cease to exist for Christians. It should be laid at the feet of their Divine Head, that He may seclude it from His people and render it innocuous. Many things that are harmless or even useful at a lower level of life must be refused a place by the Christian. Gratifications that cannot but seem good to others must be refused by him;

for he seeks to be in the forefront of the battle against evil, to be the pioneer to a more whole-hearted spiritual life.

But that does not imply that we should seek to renew the various imperfect and external devices by which past times sought to attain this exceedingly desirable end. Experience has taught the folly and futility of sumptuary laws, for example. Their only effect was to do violence to the inwardness which belongs of necessity to spiritual life. They externalised and depraved morality, and finally defeated themselves. Nor would the later Puritanism, with its rigidity as regards dress and deportment, and its narrow and limited view of life, help us much more. It began doubtless with the right principle; but it sought to bind all to its observances, whether they cared for the spirit of them or not; and it showed a measureless intemperance in regard to the things which it declared hostile to the life of faith. In that form it has been charged with "isolation from human history, human enjoyment, and all the manifold play and variety of human character." For a short time, however, Puritanism did strike the golden mean in this matter, and probably we could not in this present connection find a better example for modern days than in the Puritanism of Spenser, of Colonel Hutchinson (one of the regicides so called), and of Milton. Their united lives covered the heroic period of Puritanism, and taken in their order they represent very fairly its rise, its best estate, and its tendencies towards harsh extremes, when as yet it was but a tendency.

Spenser, born in the "spacious times of great Elizabeth," was politically and nationally a Puritan, and in aim and ideal, at least, was so in his stern view of life and religion.[61] His attachment to Lord Grey of Wilton, that personally kind yet absolutely ruthless executor of the English "ban" against the untamable Irish, and his defence of his policy, show the one; while his *Fairy Queen*, with its representation of religion as "the foundation of all nobleness in man" and its dwelling upon man's victory over himself, reveals the other. But he had in him also elements belonging to that strangely mingled world in which he lived, and which came from an entirely different source. He had the Elizabethan enthusiasm for beauty, the large delight in life as such even where its moral quality was questionable, and the artist's sensitiveness and adaptability in a very high degree. These diverse elements were never fully interfused in him. Amid all the gracious beauty of his work, there is the trace of discord and the mark of conflict; and at times perhaps his life fell into courses which spoke little of self-control. But his face was always in the main turned upwards. In the main, too, his life corresponded with his aspirations. He combined his poetic gift, his love of men and human life, with a faithfulness to his ideal of conduct which, if not always perfect, was sincere, and was, too, as we may hope, ultimately victorious. The Puritan in him had not entire victory over the worldling, but it had the mastery; and the very imperfection of the victory kept the character in sympathy with the whole of life.

In Colonel Hutchinson,[62] as depicted in that stately and tender panegyric which speaks to us across more than two centuries so pathetically of his wife's almost adoring love, we see the Puritan character in its fullest and most balanced form. We do not, of course, mean that his mind had the imaginative power of Spenser's, or his character the force of Milton's; but partly from circumstances, partly by singular grace of nature, his character possessed a stability and an equilibrium which had not come when Spenser lived, and which was beginning to go in the evil days upon which Milton fell. At the root of all his virtues his wife sets "that which was the head and spring of them all, his Christianity." "By Christianity," she says, "I intend that universal habit of grace which is wrought in a soul by the regenerating Spirit of God, whereby the whole creature is resigned up into the Divine will and love, and all its actions designed to the obedience and glory of its Maker." He had been trained in a Puritan home, and though when he went out into the world he had to face quite the average temptations of a rich and well-born youth, he fled all youthful lusts. But he did not retire from the world. "He could dance admirably well, but neither in youth nor riper years made any practice of it; he had skill in fencing such as became a gentleman; he had a great love to music, and often diverted himself with a viol, on which he played masterly; he had an exact ear, and judgment in other music; he shot excellently in bows and guns, and much used them for his exercise; he had great judgment in painting, graving, sculpture, and all liberal arts, and had many curiosities of value in all kinds. He took much pleasure in improvement of grounds, in planting groves and walks and fruit-trees, in opening springs and making fishponds. Of country recreations he loved none but hawking, and in that was very eager, and much delighted for the time he used it." Hutchinson was no ascetic, therefore, in the wrong sense, but lived in and enjoyed the world as a man should. But perhaps his greatest divergence from the lower Puritanism lay in this, that "everything that it was necessary for him to do he did with delight, free and unconstrained." Moreover, though he adopted strong Puritan opinions in theology, "he hated persecution for religion, and was always a champion for all religious people against all their great oppressors. Nevertheless self-restraint was the law of his life, and he many times forbore things lawful and delightful to him, rather than he would give any one occasion of scandal." In public affairs he took the courageous part of a man who sought nothing for himself, and was moved only by his hatred of wrong to leave the prosperity and peace of his home-life. He became a member of the Court which tried the King against his will, but signed the warrant for his death, simply because he conceived it to be his duty. When the Restoration came and he was challenged for his conduct, scorning the subterfuges of some who declared they signed under compulsion, he quietly accepted the responsibility for his acts. This led to his death in the flower of his age, through imprisonment in the Tower; but he never flinched, "having made up his accounts with life and death, and fixed his purpose to entertain both honourably." From the beginning of his life to the end there was a consistent sanity, which is rare at any time, and was especially rare in those days. His loyalty to God kept him austerely aloof from unworthiness, while it seemed to add zest to the sinless joys which came in his way. Above all, it never suffered him to forget that the true Christian temper and character was the pearl of price which all else he had might lawfully be sacrificed to purchase.

In the character of Milton we find the same essential elements, the same purity in youth, which, with his beauty, won for him the name of the Lady of his College; the same courage and public spirit in manhood; the same love of music and of culture. After his University career he retired to his father's house, and read all Greek and Latin literature, as well as Italian, and studied Hebrew and some other Oriental languages. All the culture of his time, therefore, was absorbed by him, and his mind and speech were shot through and through with the brilliant colours of the history and romance of many climes. Almost no kind of beauty failed to appeal to him, but the austerity of his views of life kept him from being enslaved by it. In his earlier works even, he caught in a surprising way all the glow, and splendour, and poetic fervour of the English Renaissance; but he joined with it the sternest and most uncompromising Puritan morality, not only in theory and desire like Spenser, but in the hard practice of actual life. When the idea of duty comes to dominate a man, the grace and impetuosity of youth, the overmastering love of beauty, and the appreciation of the mere joy of living are apt to die away, and the poetic fire burns low. But it was not so with Milton. To the end of his life he remained a true Elizabethan, but an Elizabethan who had always kept himself free from the chains of sensual vice, and had never stained his purity of soul. That fact makes him unique almost in English history, and has everywhere added a touch of the sublime to all that his works have of beauty. "His soul was like a star, and dwelt apart:" and we may entirely believe what he tells us of himself when he returned from his European travels: "In all the places in which vice meets with so little discouragement, and is protected with so little shame, I never once turned from the path of integrity and virtue, and perpetually reflected that, though my conduct might escape the notice of men, it could not elude the inspection of God." Like the true Puritan he was, Milton not only overcame evil in himself, but he thought his own life and health a cheap price to pay for the overthrow of evil wherever he saw it. When the civil war broke out, he returned at once from his travels, to help to right the wrongs of his country. In the service of the Government he sacrificed his poetic gift, his leisure for twenty years, and finally his sight, to the task of defending England from her enemies. But he did not stop there. His severity became excessive, at times almost vindictive. When he wrote prose he scarcely ever wrote without having an enemy to crush, and much that he uttered in this vein cannot possibly be approved. His pamphlets are unfair to a degree which shows that his mind had lost balance in the turmoil of the great struggle, so that he approached at moments the narrower Puritanism. But he still proved himself too great for that, and emerged anew as a great and lofty spirit, held down very little by earthly bonds, and strenuously set against evil as a true servant of God.

Now the temper of Puritanism such as this of these old English worthies is precisely what Christians need most to cultivate in these days. They must be animated by the spirit which refuses to touch, and refers to God, whatever proves hostile to life in God; but they must also combine with this aloofness a sympathetic hold on ordinary life. It is easy on the one hand to solve all problems by cutting oneself off from any relation with the world, lest the inner life should suffer. It is also easy to let the inner life take care of itself, and to float blithely on with all the currents of life which are not deadly sins. But it is not easy to keep the mind and life open to all the great life-streams which tend to deepen and enrich human nature, and yet to stand firm in self-control, determined that nothing which drags down the soul shall be permitted to fascinate or overpower. To this task Christian men and the Christian Church seem at present to be specially called. It is admitted on all hands that the ordinary Puritanism became too intolerant of all except spiritual interests; so that it could not, without infinite loss, have been accepted as the guide for all life. But hence what was good in it has been rejected along with the bad; and it needs to be restored, if a weak, self-indulgent temper, which resents hardship or even discipline, is not to gain the upper hand. In social life especially this is needful, otherwise so much debate would never have been expended on the question of amusements. On the face of it, a Christianity which can go with the world in all those of its amusements which are not actually forbidden by the moral law must be a low type of Christianity. It can be conscious of no special character which it has to preserve, of no special voice which it has to utter in the antiphony of created things. Whatever others allow themselves, therefore, the vigilant Christian must see to it that he does nothing which will destroy his special contribution to the world he lives in. It is precisely by that that he is the salt of the earth; and if the salt have lost its savour wherewith will you season it? No price is too great for the preservation of this savour, and in reference to the care of it each man must ultimately be a law unto himself. No one else can really tell where his weakness lies. No one else can know what the effect of this or that recreation upon that weakness is.

When men lose spiritual touch with their own character they are apt to throw themselves back for guidance in such matters upon the general opinion of the Christian community, or the tradition of the elders. In doing so they are in danger of losing sincerity in a mass of formalism. But if a vivid apprehension of the need of individuality in the regulation of life is maintained, the formulated Christian objection to certain customs or certain amusements may be a most useful substitute for painful experience of our own. Some such amusements may have been banned in the past without sufficient reason; or they may have been excluded only because of the special openness to temptation of a certain community; or they may have so changed their character that they do not now deserve the ban which was laid upon them once justly enough. Any plea, therefore, for the revisal or abolition of standing conventions on such grounds must be listened to and judged. But, on the whole, these standing prohibitions of the Church represent accumulated experience, and all young people especially will do wisely not to break away from them. What the mass of Christians in the past have found hurtful to the Christian character will in most cases be hurtful still. For if it can be said of the secular world in all matters of experience that "this wise world is mainly right," it may surely be said also of the Christian community. In our time there is a quite justifiable distrust of conventionality in morals and in religion; but it should not be forgotten that conventions are not open to the same objection. They represent, on the whole, merely the registered results of actual experience, and they may be estimated and followed in an entirely free spirit. It is not wise, therefore, to revolt against them indiscriminately, merely because they may be used cruelly against others, or may be taken as a substitute for a moral nature by oneself. Thackeray in his constant railing at the judgment of the world seems to make this mistake. He is never weary in pointing out how unjust the broad general judgments of the world are to specially selected individuals. Harry Warrington in *The Virginians*, for instance, though innocent, lives in a manner and with associates which the world has generally found to indicate intolerable moral laxity; and because the world was wrong in thinking that to be true in his case which would have been true in ninety-five out of a hundred similar cases, the moralist rails at the evil-hearted judgments of the world. But "this wise world is mainly right," and its rough and indiscriminating judgments fit the average case. They are part of the great sanitary provision which society makes for its own preservation. And the case is precisely similar with the conventions of the religious life. They too are in the main sanitary precautions, which a conscience thoroughly alive and a strong intelligence may make superfluous, but which for the unformed, the half-ignorant, the less original natures, in a word, for average men and women, are absolutely necessary. Spontaneity and freedom are admirable qualities in morals and religion. They are even the conditions of the highest kinds of moral and religious life, and the necessary presuppositions of health and progress. But something is due to stability as well; and a world of original and spontaneous moralists, trusting only to their own "genial sense" of truth, would be a maddening chaos. In other words, conventions if used unconventionally, if not exalted into absolute moral laws disobedience to which excludes from reputable society, if taken simply as indications of the paths in which least danger to the higher life has been found to lie, are guides for which men may well be thankful.

In the world of thought too, as well as in the world of action, a wise austerity of self-control is absolutely necessary. The prevailing theory is that every one, young men more especially, should read on all sides on all questions, and that they should know and sympathise with all modes of thought. This is advocated in the supposed interests of freedom from external domination and from internal prejudice. But in a great number of cases the result does not follow. Such catholicity of taste does produce a curious *dilettante* interest in lines of thought, but as a rule it weakens interest in truth as such. It delivers from the domination of a Church or other historic authority; but only, in most cases, to hand over the supposed freeman to the narrower domination of the thinker or school by which he happens to be most impressed. For it is vain and impotent to suppose that in regard to morals and religion every mind is able to find its way by free thought, when in regard to bodily health, or even in questions of finance, the free thought of the amateur is acknowledged to end usually in confusion. Those only can usefully expose their minds to all the various currents of modern thought who have a clear footing of their own. Whatever that may be, it gives them a point on which to stand, and a vantage-ground from which they can gather up what widens or corrects their view. But to leave the land altogether, and commit oneself to the currents, is to render any after-landing all but impossible. With regard to the books read, the lines of thought followed, and the associations formed, the Christian must exercise self-denial and self-examination. Whatever is manifestly detrimental to his best life, whatever he feels to be likely to taint the purity of his mind or lower his spiritual vitality, should be put under the "ban," should be resolutely avoided in all ordinary cases. Of course modes of thought that deserve to be weighed may be found mingled with such elements; also views of life which have a truth and importance of their own, though their setting is corrupt. But it is not every one's business to extricate and discuss these. Those who are called to it will have to do it; and in doing it as a duty they may expect to be kept from the lurking contagion. Every one else who investigates them runs a risk which he was not called upon to run. The average Christian should, therefore, note all that tends to stunt or deprave him spiritually, and should avoid it. It is not manliness but folly which makes men read filthy literature because of its style, or sceptical literature because of its ability, when they are not called upon to do so, and when they have not fortified themselves by the purity of the Scriptures and the power of prayer. To make such literature or such modes of thought our staple mental food, or to make the writers or admirers of such books our intimate friends, is to sap our own best convictions and to disregard our high calling.

Lastly, however common it may be for men to sit down in selfish isolation and devote themselves to their own interests, even though these be spiritual, in the face of remediable evils, that is not the Christian manner of acting. Of the great Puritans we mentioned, Spenser endured hardness in that terrible Irish war which the men of Elizabeth's day regarded as the war of good against evil; Hutchinson fought for and died in the cause of political and religious freedom; and Milton devoted his life and health to the same cause. All of them, the two latter especially, might have kept out of it all, in the peace and comfort of private life; but they judged that the destruction of evil was their first duty. At the trumpet call they willingly took their side, and prepared to give their lives, if necessary, for the righteous cause. Now it is not enough for us to avoid evil any more than it was for them. Though personal influence and example are undoubtedly among the most potent weapons in the warfare for the Kingdom of God, there must be, besides these, the power and the will to put public evils under the ban. Whatever institution or custom or law is ungodly, whatever in our social life is manifestly unjust, should stir the Christian Church to revolt against it, and should fill the heart of the individual Christian with an undying energy of hatred. It is not meant that the Christian Churches as such should transform themselves into political societies or social clubs. To do that would simply be to abdicate their only real functions. But they should be the sources of such teaching as will turn men's thoughts towards social justice and political righteousness, and should prepare them for the sacrifice which any great improvement in the social state must demand of some. Further, every individual Christian should feel that his responsibility for the condition of his brethren, those of his own nation, is very great and direct; that to discharge municipal and political duty with conscientious care is a primary obligation. Only so can the power be gained to "ban" the bad laws, the unjust practices, the evil social customs, which disfigure our civilisation, which degrade and defraud the poor.

A militant Puritanism here is not only a necessity for further social progress, but it is also a necessity for the full exhibition of the power and the essential sympathies of Christianity. For want of it the working classes in their movement upward have not only been alienated from the Churches, but they have learned to demand of their leaders that they shall "countenance the poor man in his cause." They are tempted to require their leaders to share not only their common principles, but their prejudices; and they often look with suspicion upon those who insist upon applying the plumb-line of justice to the demands of the poor as well as to the claims of the rich. The whole popular movement suffers, for it is degraded from its true position. From being a demand for justice, it becomes a scramble for power—power too which, when gained, is sometimes used as selfishly and tyrannically by its new possessors as it sometimes was by those who previously exercised it. Into all branches of public life there is needed an infusion of a new and higher spirit. We want men who hate evil and will destroy it where they can, who seek nothing for themselves, who feel strongly that the kind of life the poor in civilised countries live is intolerably hard, and are prepared to suffer, if by any means they may improve it. But we want at the same time a type of reformer who, by his hold upon a power lying beyond this world, is kept steady to justice even where the poor are concerned, who, though he passionately longs for a better life for them, does not make more food, more leisure, more amusement, his highest aim. Men are needed who think more nobly of their brethren than that: men, on the one hand, who know that the Christian character and the Christian virtues may exist under the hardest conditions, and that the Christian Church exists mainly to brighten and rob of its degradation the otherwise cheerless life of the multitude; but, on the other, who recognise that our present social state is fatal in many ways to moral and spiritual progress for the mass of men, and must be in some way recast.

All this means the entrance into public life of Christian men of the highest type. Such men the Christian community must supply to the State in great numbers, if the higher characteristics of our people are not to be lost. Through a long and eventful history, by the manifold training afforded by religion and experience, the English nation has become strong, patient, hopeful, and self-reliant, with an instinct for justice and a hatred of violence which cannot easily be paralleled. It has, too, retained a faith in and respect for religion which many other nations seem to have lost. That character is its highest achievement, and its decay would be deplorable. Christianity is specially called to help to preserve it, by bringing to its aid the power of its own special character, with its great spiritual resources. The sources of its life are hid, and must be kept pure; the power of its life must be made manifest in actual union with the higher elements in the national character for mutual defence. Above all, Christianity must not, timidly or sluggishly, draw upon itself the curse of Meroz by not coming to the help of the Lord against the mighty. Nor can it permit the immediate interests of the respectable to blind or hold it back. That which is best in its own nature demands all this; and in seeking to answer that demand the Churches will attain to a quite new life and power. The Lord their God will be in the midst of them, and they will feel it; for they will then have made themselves channels for the Divine purity and power.

CHAPTER XI
THE BREAD OF THE SOUL

Deut. viii

In the chapters which follow, viz. viii., ix., and x. 1-11, we have an appeal to history as a motive for fulfilling the fundamental duty of loving God and keeping His commandments. In its main points it is substantially the same appeal which is made in chapters i.-iii., is, in fact, a continuation of it. Its main characteristics, therefore, have already been dealt with; but there are details here which deserve more minute study. Coming after Yahweh's great demand for the love of His people, the references to the Divine action in the past assume a deeper and more affectionate character than when they were mere general exhortations to obedience and submission. They become inducements to the highest efforts of love; and the first appeal is naturally made to the gracious and fatherly dealing of Yahweh with His people in their journey through the wilderness. Of all the traditions or reminiscences of Israel, this of the wilderness was the most constantly present to the popular mind, and it is always referred to as the most certain, the most impressive, and the most touching of all Israel's historic experiences. Yet Stade and others push the whole episode aside, saying, if any Israelites came out of Egypt, we do not know who they were. Such a mode of dealing with clear, coherent, and in themselves not improbable historical memories, is too arbitrary to have much effect, and the wilderness journey remains, and is likely to remain, one of the indubitable facts which modern critical research has established rather than shaken.

To this, then, our author turns, and he deals with it in a somewhat unusual way. As we have seen, the prevalent notion that piety and righteousness are rewarded with material prosperity is firmly rooted in his mind. But he did not feel himself limited to that as the solitary right way of regarding the providence of God. Men's minds are never quite so simple and direct in their action as many students and critics are tempted to suppose. Every great conception which holds the minds of men produces its effects, even from the first moment it is grasped, by *all* that is in it. Implications and developments which are made explicit, or are called out into visibility, only by the friction of new environments, have been there from the beginning; and minds have been secretly moulded by them though they were not conscious of them. Hard and fast lines, then, are not to be drawn between the stages of a great development, so that one should say that before such and such a moment, when a new aspect of the old truth has emerged into consciousness, that aspect was not effective in any wise. The outburst of waters from a reservoir is indubitable evidence of steady persistent pressure from within in that direction before the overflow. Similarly, in the region of thought and feeling the emergence of a new aspect of truth is of itself a proof that the holders of the root conception were already swayed in that direction.

The history of Christianity affords proof of this. It is a commonplace to-day that the world is only beginning to do justice to some aspects of the teaching of our Lord. But the teaching, always present, always exerted its influence, and was felt before it could be explained. In the Old Testament development the same thing was most emphatically true. Individual responsibility to God was not, so far as we can now see, distinctly present in Israelite religious thought till the time of Jeremiah, but it would be absurd to say that any mind that accepted the religion of Yahweh had ever been without that feeling. So with the doctrine of God's providence over men: we are not to say that before the Book of Job the explanation of suffering as testing discipline had been entirely hid from Israel, by the view that material prosperity and adversity were regulated in the main according to moral and religious life. Consequently, notwithstanding previous strong assertions of the latter view which we find in Deuteronomy, we need not be in the least surprised to find that here the hardships of the wilderness journey are regarded, not as a punishment for Israel's sins, but simply as a trial or test to see what their heart was towards Him. This is essentially the point of view of the Book of Job, the only difference being that here it is applied to the nation, there to the individual. But our chapter rises even above that, for the first verses of it plainly teach that the experiences of the wilderness were made to be what they were, in order that the people might learn to know the spiritual forces of the world to be the essential forces, and that they might be induced to throw themselves back upon them as that which is alone enduring. In the words of ver. 3, they were taught by this training that man does not live by bread alone, but by everything that proceeds from the mouth of God.

These two then, that hardship was testing discipline for Israel, and that it was also intended to be the means of revealing spirit as the supreme force even in the material world, are the main lessons of the eighth chapter. Of these the last is by far the most important. Casting back his eye upon the past, the author of Deuteronomy teaches that the trials and the victories, the wonders and the terrors of their wilderness time were meant to humble them, to empty them of their own conceits, and to make them know beyond all doubting that God alone was their portion, and that apart from Him they had no certainty of continuance in the future and no sustainment in the present. "All the commandment which I command thee this day shall ye observe to do, *that ye may live,*" is the fundamental note, and the physical needs and trials of the time are cited as an object-lesson to that effect. "He humbled thee, and suffered thee to hunger, and fed thee with manna which thou knewest not; that He might make thee to know that man doth not live by bread alone, but by everything that proceedeth out of the mouth of Yahweh doth man live." Of course the first reference of the "everything that proceedeth" is to the creative word of Yahweh. The meaning is that the sending of the manna was proof that the ordinary means of living, *i.e.* bread, could be dispensed with when Yahweh chose to make use of His creative power. Many commentators think that this exhausts the meaning of the passage, and they regard our Lord's use of these words in the Temptation as limited in the same fashion. But both here and in the New Testament more must be intended. Here we have the statement in the first verse that Israel is to keep the commandments, which certainly are a part of "all that proceeds" from the mouth of God, that they may *live*. This implies that the mere possession of material sustenance is not enough for even earthly life. Impalpable spiritual elements must be mingled with "bread" if life is not to decay. This, our chapter goes on to say, would be plain to them if they would carefully consider God's dealing with them in the wilderness, for the sending of the manna was meant to emphasise and bring home to them that very truth. It was meant, in short, to convey a double lesson—the direct one above referred to, and the more remote but deeper one which had been asserted in the first verse.

In the Temptation narrative the same deeper meaning is surely implied. The temptation suggested to Jesus was that He should use the miraculous powers given to Him for special purposes to make stones into bread for Himself. Now that would have been precisely an instance of the literal primary meaning of our passage; it would have been a case of supplying the absence of bread by the use of the creative word of God. To meet that temptation and to put it aside our Lord uses these words: "It is written, Man shall not live by bread alone, but by every word that proceedeth out of the mouth of God." Thereupon He was no more importuned to supply the place of bread by a creative word. The implication is that the life of the Son of God found sustenance in spiritual strength derived from His Father. In other words, the passage is really parallel to John iv. 31 ff: "In the mean while the disciples prayed Him, saying, Rabbi, eat. But He said unto them, I have meat to eat that ye know not. The disciples therefore said one to another, Hath any man brought Him to eat? Jesus saith unto them, My meat is to do the will of Him that sent Me, and to accomplish His work." Understanding it thus, the Temptation passage is entirely in accord with that from which it is quoted, if the first and third verses be taken together. Both teach that abundance of material resources, all that visibly sustains the material life, is not sufficient for the life of such a creature as man. Not only his inner life, but his outer life, is dependent for its permanence upon the inflow of spiritual sustenance from the spiritual God. For animals, bread might be enough; but man holds of both the spiritual and the material as animals do not. It is not mere mythical dreaming when man is said to be made in the image of God; it expresses the essential fact of his being. Consequently, without inbreathings from the spiritual, even his physical life pines and dies. But how wonderful is this insight in a writer so ancient, belonging to so obscure a people as the Jews! How can we account for it? There was nothing in their character or destiny as a people to explain it, apart from the supernatural link that binds them and their thoughts at all times to the coming Christ, and draws them, notwithstanding all aberrations, even when they know it not, towards Him.

How great an attainment it is we may see, if we reflect for a moment upon the state of Christian Europe at the present day. Nowhere among the masses of the most cultured nations is this deeply simple truth accepted by the vast majority of men. Nowhere do we find that history has succeeded in bringing it home to the conscience as a commonplace. The rich or well-to-do cling to riches, the means of material enjoyment, as if their life did consist in the abundance of things they possess. They strive and struggle for them with an industry, a forethought, a perseverance, which would be justified only if man could live by bread alone. That is largely the condition of those who have bread in abundance or hope to gain it abundantly. With those who do not have it the case is perhaps even worse. Worn and fretted by the hopeless struggle against poverty, driven wild by the exigencies of a daily life so near starvation point that a strike, a fall in prices, a month's sickness, bring them face to face with misery, the toiling masses in Europe have turned with a kind of wolfish impatience upon those who talk of God to them, and demand "bread." As a German Socialist mother said publicly some years ago, "He has never given me a mouthful of bread, or means to gain it: what have I to do with your God?" Their only hope for the future is that they may eat and be full; and of this they have made a political and religious ideal which is attracting the European working classes with most portentous power.

In all countries men are passionately asserting that man *can* live by bread alone, and that he will. For this dreadful creed increasing numbers are prepared to sacrifice all that humanity thought it had gained, and shut their ears to any who warn them that, if they had all they seek, earth might be still more of a Pandemonium than they think it at present. But they have much excuse. They have never had wealth so as to know how very little it can do for the deepest needs of men; and their faith in it, their belief that if they were assured of a comfortable maintenance all would be right with the world, is pathetic in its simplicity. Yet the secret that is hid to-day from the mass of men was known among the small Israelite people two thousand five hundred years ago. Since then it has formed the very keynote of the teaching of our Lord; but save by the generations of Christians who have found in it the key to much of the riddle of the world it has been learned by nobody.

Yet history has never wearied in proclaiming the same truth. Israel as we have seen, had verified it in the history of the pre-Canaanite races whose disappearance is recorded in the first section of our book, and in the doom which was impending over the Canaanites. But to our wider experience, enriched by the changes of more than two thousand years, and by the still more striking vicissitudes of ancient days revealed by archæology, the fact that intelligence of the highest kind, practical skill, and the courage of conquerors cannot secure "life," is only more impressively brought home. If we go back to the pre-Semitic empire of Mesopotamia, to what is called the Akkadian time, we find that, before the days of Abraham, a great civilisation had arisen, flourished for more than one thousand years, and then decayed so utterly that the very language in which its records were written had to be dealt with by the Semites, who inherited the former culture, as we deal with Latin. Yet these early people had made a most astonishing advance into the ocean of unknown truth. They had invented writing; they had elaborate systems of law and social life; they had in other directions made remarkable discoveries in science, especially in mathematical and astronomical science, and had built great cities in which the refinement and art of modern times was in many directions anticipated. In all ways they stood far higher above neighbouring peoples than any civilised nation of Europe stands now in comparison with its neighbours. But if they were at all inclined to put their trust in the immortality of science, if they ever valued themselves, as we do, on the strength of the advances they had made, time has had them in derision. Very much of what they knew had to be rediscovered painfully in later times. Their very name perished out of the earth; and it has been discovered now to make them an object of abiding interest only to the few who make ethnology their study. Neither material wealth and comfort nor assiduous culture of the mind could save them. For their religion and morals were, amid all this material success, of the lowest type. They heard little of what issues from the mouth of God in the specially Divine sphere of morality, and did not give heed to that little, and they perished. For man does not live by bread alone, but by that also, and neglect of it is fatal.

It may be said that they flourished for more than a thousand years, and neglect of the Divine word, if it be a poison, must (as Fénélon said of coffee) be a very slow one, so far as nations are concerned. But it has always been a snare to men to mistake the Divine patience for Divine indifference and inaction. The movement, though to us creatures of a day it seems slow, is as continuous, as crushing, and as relentless as the movement of a glacier. "The mills of God grind slowly, but they grind exceeding small," and all along the ages they have thrown out the crushed and scattered fragments of the powers that were deaf to the Divine voice. So persistently has this appeared that it would by this time have passed beyond the region of faith into that of sight, were it not always possible to ignore the moral cause and substitute for it something mechanical and secondary. The great world-empires of Egypt and Assyria passed away, primarily owing to neglect of the higher life. Secondarily, no doubt, the ebbs and flows of their power, and their final extinction, were influenced by the course of the Indian trade; and many wise men think they do well to stop there. But in truth we do not solve the difficulty by resting in this secondary cause; we only shift it a step backwards. For the question immediately arises, Why did the trade change its course from Assyria to Egypt, and back again from Egypt to Assyria? Why did a rivulet of it flow through the land of Israel in Solomon's day and afterwards cease? The answer must be that it was when the character of these various nations rose in vigour by foresight and moral self-restraint that they drew to themselves this source of power. They "lived," in fact, by giving heed to some word of God. Nor does the history of Greek supremacy in Europe and Asia, or the rise and fall of the Roman Empire, contradict that view. The modern historian, whatever his faith or unfaith may be, is driven to find the motive power which wrought in these stupendous movements in the moral and spiritual sphere. This transforms history from being merely secular into a Bible, as Mommsen finely says,[63] "And if she cannot any more than the Bible hinder the fool from misunderstanding and the devil from quoting her, she too will be able to bear with and to requite them both." She utters her voice in the streets, and in the end makes her meaning clear. For she gives us ever new examples.

Probably her grandest object-lesson at present is the wasting and paralysis that is slowly withering up all Mohammedan states. Where they have been left to themselves, as in Morocco and Persia, depopulation and the break-up of society has come upon them, and where Muslim populations are really prospering it is under the influence of Christian Powers. And the reason is plain. Islam is a revolt from, and a rejection of, the higher principles of life contained in Christianity, and a return to Judaism. But the Judaism to which it returned had already lost its finest bloom. All that was left to it of tenderness or power of expansion Islam rejected, and of the driest husks of Old Testament religion it made its sole food. Naturally and necessarily, therefore, it has been found inadequate. It cannot permanently live under present conditions, and it is capable of no renewal. Here and there, especially in India, attempts to break out of the prison house which this system builds around its votaries are being made, but in the opinion of experts like Mr. Sell[64] they cannot succeed. "Such a movement," he tells us, "may elevate individuals and purify the family life of many, but it will, like all reform movements of the past, have very little real effect on Islam as a polity and as a religion." If he be right, we learn from a Mohammedan whom he quotes, the Naual Mulisin-ul-Mulk, what alone can be looked for. "To me it seems," he says, "that as a nation and a religion we are dying out; our day is past, and we have little hope of the future." More conspicuously and deliberately perhaps than any one did Mohammed choose to go back from the best light that shone in the world of his day. Some at least of his contemporaries knew what a spiritual religion meant. He was guilty, therefore, of the "great refusal"; and his work, great as it was, seems to some even of his own disciples to be hastening to its end. Material success, bread in all senses, the kingdoms founded by him and his successors had in abundance, and still might have. But man cannot live by that alone, and the absence of the higher element has taken even that away.

In Christendom, too, the same lesson is being taught. Of all European countries France perhaps is that where the corroding power of materialistic thought has been most severely felt. Yet few countries are so rich in material wealth, and if bread was all that "life" demanded, no country should be so full of it. But it is in no sense so. Even its intellectual life is drooping, and its population, if not decreasing, is standing still. This, all serious writers deplore; and the dawn of what may perhaps be a new era is seen in the earnestness with which the sources of this evil are sought out and discussed. Men like the Vicomte de Vogüé[65] depict the new generation as weary of negations, sick of the material positivism of their immediate predecessors, disgusted with "realism," which, as another recent writer defines it, "in thought is mere provincialism, in affection absolute egoism, in politics the deification of brute force; in the higher grades of society tyranny; in the lower, unbridled licence." And the only cure is faith and moral idealism. "Society can apply to itself to-day," says De Vogüé, "the beautiful image of Plotinus; it resembles those travellers lost in the night, seated in silence on the shore of the sea, waiting for the sun to rise above the billows." In Germany similar conditions have produced similar though much mitigated results. Yet even there, Lange, the historian of materialism, tells us that there runs through all our modern culture a tendency to materialism, which carries away every one who has not found somewhere a sure anchor. "The ideal has no currency; all that cannot prove its claim on the basis of natural science and history is condemned to destruction, though a thousand joys and refreshments of the masses depend upon it." He concludes by saying that "ideas and sacrifices may still save our civilisation, and change the path of destructive revolution into a path of beneficent reforms." Through all history, then, and loudest in our own day, the cry of our passage goes up; and where the path marked out by the faith of Israel, and carried to its goal by Jesus Christ, has been forsaken, the peoples are resting in hungry expectation. Words from the mouth of God can alone save them; and if the Churches cannot make them hear, and no new voice brings it home to them, there would seem to be nothing before them but a slower or quicker descent into death.

But it may be that the nations are deaf to the Churches' voice because these have not learned thoroughly that life for them too is conditioned in the same fashion. They can live truly, fully, triumphantly only when they take up and absorb "everything that issues from the mouth of God." All Christians must admit this; but most proceed at once to annul what they have stated by the limitations of meaning they impose upon it. An older generation vehemently affirmed this faith, meaning by it every word and letter which Scripture contained. We do not find fault with what they assert, for the first necessity of spiritual life is the study and love of the Holy Scriptures. No one who knows what the higher life in Christ is, needs to be told that the very bread of life is in the Bible. Neglect it, or, what is perhaps worse, study it only from the scientific and intellectual point of view, and life will slowly ebb away from you, and your religion will bring you none of the joy of living. Bring your thoughts, your hopes, your fears, and your aspirations into daily contact with it, and you will feel a vigour in your spiritual nature which will make you "lords over circumstance." Every part of it contributes to this effect when it is properly understood, for experience proves the vanity of the attempt to distinguish between the Bible and the word of God. As it stands, wrought into one whole by labours the strenuousness, the multiplicity, the skill, and the religious spirit of which we are only now coming to understand, it is the word of God; it has issued from His mouth, and from it, searched out and understood, the most satisfying "bread" of the soul must come. Only by use of it can the Christian soul live.

But though the Bible is the word of God *par excellence,* it is not the only word that issues from the mouth of God to man. Because the Church has often too much refused to listen to any other word of God, those who are without are "sitting looking out over the sea towards the west for the rising of the sun which is behind them." For if it is death to the spirit to turn away from Scripture, it means sickness and disease to refuse to learn the other lessons which are set for us by the God of truth. All true science must contain a revelation of Him, for it is an exposition of the manner of His working. History too is a Bible, which has been confirming with trumpet tongue the truths of Scripture as we have seen. Nay, it is a commentary upon the special revelation given to us through Israel, set for our study by the Author of that revelation. Further, we may say that the progress of our Christian centuries has shown us heights and depths of wisdom in the revelation mankind has received in Christ which, without its light, we should not have known.

The spirit of Christ in regard to slavery, for instance, was made manifest fully only in our day. The true relations of men to each other, as conceived by our blessed Lord, are evidently about to be forced home upon the world by the turmoils, the strikes, and the outrages, by the wild demands, and the wilder hopes which are the characteristic of our epoch. In the future, too, there must lie experiences which will make manifest to men the brand which the spirit of Christ puts upon war, with its savagery and its folly. These are only noteworthy instances of the explanation of revelation by the developments of the Divine purpose in the world. But in countless ways the same process is going on, and the Church which refuses to regard it is preparing a decay of its own life. For man lives by *every* word that proceedeth out of the mouth of God, and every such word missed means a loss of vitality. The Christian Church, therefore, if it is to be true to its calling, should be seriously watchful lest any Divinely sent experience should be lost to it. It cannot be indifferent, much less hostile, to discoveries in physical science; it cannot ignore any fact or lesson which history reveals; it cannot sit apart from social experiments, as if holding no form of creed in such things, without seriously impairing its chances of life. For all these things are pregnant with most precious indications of the mind of God, and to turn from them is to sit in darkness and the shadow of death. In the most subtle and multifarious way, the inner spiritual life of man is being modified by the discoveries of scientists, historians, philologists, archæologists, and critics, and by the new attention which is being given to the foundations of society and social life. All the truth that is in these discoveries issues from the mouth of God. They too are a Bible, as Mommsen says, and if the Christian Church cannot "hinder the fool from misunderstanding and the devil from quoting them," it can itself listen with open ear to these teachings, and work them into coherent unity with the great spiritual Revelation. This is the perennial task which awaits the Church at every stage of its career, for on no other terms can it live a healthy life.

Here we find the answer to timid Christians who address petulant complaints to those who are called to attempt this work. If, say they, these new thoughts are not essential to faith, if in the forms to which we have been accustomed the essence of true religion has been preserved, why do you disturb the minds of believers by outside questions? The reply is that we dare not refuse the teaching which God is sending us in these ways. To refuse light is to blaspheme light. Though we might save our generation some trouble by turning our back upon this light, though we might even save some from manifest shipwreck of faith, we should pay for that by sacrificing all the future, and by rendering faith impossible perhaps for greater multitudes of our successors.

Yet this does not imply that the Church is to be driven about by every wind of doctrine. Some men of science demand, apparently, that every new discovery, in its first crude form, should be at once adopted by the Church, and that all the inferences unfavourable to received views of religion, which occur to men accustomed to think only truths that can be demonstrated by experiment, should be registered in its teachings. But such a demand is mere folly. The Church has in its possession a body of truth which, if not verifiable by experiment, has been verified by experience as no other body of truth has been. Even its enemies being judges, no other system of a moral or spiritual kind has risen above the horizon which can for a moment be compared with Christianity as the guide of men for life and death.[66] Through all changes of secular thought, and amid all the lessons which the world has taught the Church, the fundamental doctrines have remained in essence the same, and by them the whole life of man, social, political, and scientific, has ultimately been guided. Immense practical interests have therefore been committed to the Church's keeping, the interests primarily of the poor and the obscure. She ought never to be tempted, consequently, to think that she is moving and acting in a vacuum, or manage her affairs after the manner of a debating society. It is no doubt a fault to move too slowly; but in circumstances like that of the Church, it can never be so destructive to the best interests of mankind as to move with wanton instability. Her true attitude must be to prohibit no lines of inquiry, to open her mind seriously to all the demonstrated truths of science with gladness, to be tolerant of all loyal effort to reform Christian thought in accordance with the new light, when that has become at all possible. For her true food is everything that issues from the mouth of God; and only when she receives with gratitude her daily bread in this way also, can her life be as vigorous and as elevated as it ought to be.

CHAPTER XII
ISRAEL'S ELECTION, AND MOTIVES FOR FAITHFULNESS

Deut. ix-xi

The remaining chapters of this special introduction to the statement of the actual laws beginning with chapter xii., contain also an earnest insistence upon other motives why Israel should remain true to the covenant of Yahweh. They are urged to this, not only because life both spiritual and physical depended upon it, as was shown in the trials of the wilderness, but they are also to lay it to heart that in the conquests which assuredly await them, it will be Yahweh alone to whom they will owe them. The spies had declared, and the people had accepted their report, that these peoples were far mightier than they, and that no one could stand before the children of Anak. But the victory over them would show that Yahweh had been among them like a consuming fire, before which the Canaanite power would wither as brushwood in the flame.

Under these circumstances the thought would obviously lie near that, as they had been defeated and driven back in their first attempt upon Canaan because of their unrighteousness and unbelief, so they would conquer now because of their righteousness and obedience. But this thought is sternly repressed. The fundamental doctrine which is here insisted on is that Israel's consciousness of being the people of God must at the same time be a consciousness of complete dependence upon Him. If His gifts were ultimately to be the reward of human righteousness, then obviously that feeling of complete dependence could not be established. They are to move so completely in the shadow of God that they are to see in their successes only the carrying out of the Divine purposes. Instead of feeling fiercely contemptuous of the Canaanites they destroy, because they stand on a moral and spiritual height which gives them a right to triumph, the Israelites are to feel that, while it is for wickedness that the Canaanite people are to be punished, they themselves had not been free from wickedness of an aggravated kind. Their different treatment, therefore, rests upon the fact that they are to be Yahweh's chosen instruments. In the patriarchs he chose them to become the means, the vehicle, by which salvation and blessing were to be brought to all nations. While, therefore, the evil that comes upon the peoples they are to conquer is deserved, the good they themselves are to receive is equally undeserved. That which alone accounts for the difference is the faithfulness of God to the promises He made for the sake of His purposes. He needs an instrument through which to bless mankind. He has chosen Israel for this purpose, partly doubtless because of some qualities, not necessarily spiritual or moral, which they have come to have, and partly because of their historical position in the world. These taken together make them at this precise moment in the history of the world's development the fittest instruments to carry out the Divine purpose of love to mankind. And they are elected, made to enter into more constant and intimate communion with God than other nations, on that account. In the words of Rothe, "God chooses or elects at each historical moment from the totality of the sinful race of mankind that nation by whose enrolment among the positive forces which are to develop the kingdom of God the greatest possible advance towards the complete realisation of it may be attained, under the historical circumstances of that moment." Whether that completely covers the individual election of St. Paul, as Rothe thinks, or not, it certainly precisely expresses the national election of the Old Testament, and exhausts the meaning of our passage. Israelite particularism had universality of the highest kind as its background, and here the latter comes most insistently to its rights.

It was not only the election of Israel to be a peculiar people which depended upon the wise and loving purpose of God; the providences which befell them also had that as their source. To fit them for their mission, and to give them a place wherein they could develop the germs of higher faith and nobler morality which they had received, Yahweh gave them victory over those greater nations, and planted them in their place. This, and this only, was the reason of their success; and with scathing irony the author of Deuteronomy stamps under his feet (ix. 7 ff.) any claim to superior righteousness on their part. He points back to their continuous rebellions during the forty years in the wilderness. From the beginning to the end of their journey towards the promised land, they are told, they have been rebellious and stiff-necked and unprofitable. They have broken their covenant with their God. They have caused Moses to break the tables of stone containing the fundamental conditions of the covenant, because their conduct had made it plain that they had not seriously bound themselves to it. But the mercy of God had been with them. Notwithstanding their sin, Yahweh had been turned to mercy by the prayer of Moses (vv. 25 ff.), and had repented of His design to destroy them. A new covenant was entered into with them (chap. x.) by means of the second tables, which contained the same commands as were engraven on the first. The renewal, moreover, was ratified by the separation of the tribe of Levi (x. 8 ff.) to be the specially priestly tribe, "to bear the Ark of the Covenant of the Lord, to stand before the Lord to minister unto Him and to bless in His name." From beginning to end it was always Yahweh, and again Yahweh, who had chosen and loved and cared for them. It was He who had forgiven and strengthened them; but always for reasons which reached far beyond, or even excluded, any merit on their part.

The grounds of Moses' successful intercession for them (ix. 25 ff.) are notable in this connection. They have no reference at all to the needs, or hopes, or expectations of the people. These are all brushed aside, as being of no moment after such unfaithfulness as theirs had been. The great object before his mind is represented to be Yahweh's glory. If this stiff-necked people perish, then the greatness of God will be obscured and His purposes will be misunderstood. Men will certainly think, either that Yahweh, Israel's God, attempted to do what He was not able to do, or that He was wroth with His people, and drew them out into the wilderness to slay them there. It is God's purpose with them, God's purpose for the world through them, which alone gives them importance. Were it not for that, they would be as little worth saving as they have deserved to be saved. For his people, and, we may be sure, for himself, Moses recognises no true worth save in so far as he or they were useful in carrying out Divine purposes of good to the world. Nor is the absence of any plea on Israel's behalf, that it is miserable or unhappy, due merely to a desire to keep the rebellious people in the background for the moment, and to appeal only to the Divine self-love for a pardon which would, on the merits of the case, be refused. It is the God of the whole earth, before whom "the inhabitants of the earth are as grasshoppers," who is appealed to; a God removed far above the petty motives of self-interested men, and set upon the one great purpose of establishing a kingdom of God upon the earth into which all nations might come. If His glory is appealed to, that is only because it is the glory of the highest good both for the individual and for the world. If fear lest doubt should be cast upon His power is put forward as a reason for His having mercy, that is because to doubt His power is to doubt the supremacy of goodness. If the Divine promise to the patriarchs is set forth here, it is because that promise was the assurance of the Divine interest in and Divine love of the world.

Under such circumstances it would need a very narrow-hearted literalism, such as only very "liberal" theologians and critics could favour, to reduce this appeal to a mere attempt to flatter Yahweh into good-humour. It really embodies all that can be said in justification of our looking for answers to prayer at all; and rightly understood it limits the field of the answer as strictly as the expressed or implied limitations of the New Testament, viz. that effectual prayer can only be for things according to the will of God. Moreover it expresses an entirely natural attitude towards God. Before Him, the sum of all perfections, the loving and omniscient and omnipresent God, what is man that he should assert himself in any wise? When the height and the depth, the sublimity and the comprehensiveness of the Divine purpose is considered, how can a man do aught save fall upon his face in utter self-forgetfulness, immeasurably better even than self-contempt? The best and holiest of mankind have always felt this most; and the habit of measuring their attainments by the faithfulness and knowledge, the virtue and power which is in God, has impressed some of the greatest minds and purest souls with such humility, that to men without insight it has seemed mere affectation. But the pity, the condescension, the love of Christ has so brought God down into our human life, that we are apt at times to lose our awe of God as seen in Him. Were we children of the spirit we should not fall into that sin. We cannot, consequently, be too frequently or too sharply recalled to the more austere and remote standpoint of the Old Testament. For many even of the most pious it would be well if they could receive and keep a more just impression of their own worthlessness and nullity before God.

In the section from the twelfth verse of chapter x. to the end of chapter xi. the hortatory introduction is summed up in a final review of all the motives to and the results of obedience and love to God. The fundamental exhortation as to love to God is once more repeated; only here fear is joined with love and precedes it; but the necessity of love to God is expanded and dwelt upon, as at the beginning, with a zeal that never wearies. The Deuteronomist illustrates and enforces it with old reasons and new, always speaking with the same pleading and heartfelt earnestness. He does not fear the tedium of repetition, nor the accusation of moving in a narrow round of ideas. Evidently in the evil time when he wrote this love towards God had come to be his own support and his consolation; and it had been revealed to him as the source of a power, a sweetness, and a righteousness which could alone bring the nation into communion with God. In affecting words resembling very closely the noble exhortation in Micah vi., "He hath showed thee, O man, what is good; and what doth Yahweh require of thee, but to do justly, and to love mercy, and to walk humbly with thy God?" he teaches much the same doctrine as his contemporary: "And now, Israel, what doth Yahweh thy God require of thee, but to fear Yahweh thy God, to walk in all His ways, and to love Him, and to serve Yahweh thy God with all thy heart and with all thy soul, to keep the commandments of Yahweh and His statutes which I command thee this day for thy good?"[67]

In spirit these passages seem identical; but it is held by many writers on the Old Testament that they are not so, that they represent, in fact, opposite poles of the faith and life of Israel. Micah is supposed by Duhm, for instance, to mean by his threefold demand that justice between man and man, love and kindliness and mercy towards others, and humble intercourse with God are, in *distinction from sacrifice*, true religion and undefiled. Robertson Smith also considers that these verses in Micah contain a repudiation of sacrifice. In Deuteronomy, on the contrary, fear and love of God and walking in His ways are placed first, but they are joined with a demand for the heartfelt service of God and the keeping of His statutes as about to be set forth. Now these certainly include ritual and sacrifice. The one passage, written by a prophet, excludes sacrifice as binding and acceptable service of God; the other, written perhaps by a priest, certainly by a man upon whom no prophetic lessons of the past had been lost, includes it. To use the words of Robertson Smith in discussing the requisites of forgiveness in the Old Testament, "According to the prophets Yahweh asks only a penitent heart and desires no sacrifice; according to the ritual law, He desires a penitent heart approaching Him in certain sacrificial sacraments."[68] The author of Deuteronomy teaches the second view; the author of Micah chap. vi., who is probably his contemporary, teaches the former. How is such divergence accounted for? The answer generally made is that Deuteronomy was the product of a close alliance between priests and prophets. A common hatred of Manasseh's idolatry and a common oppression had brought them together as never perhaps before. With one heart and mind they wrought in secret for the better day which they saw approaching, and Deuteronomy was a reissue of the ancient Mosaic law adapted to the prophetic teaching. It represented a compromise between, or an amalgamation of, two entirely distinct positions.

But even on this view it would follow that from the time of Josiah, when Deuteronomy was accepted as the completest expression of the will of God, the doctrine that ritual and sacrifice as well as penitence were essential things in true religion was known, and not only known but accepted as the orthodox opinion. Putting aside, then, the question whether sacrifice was acknowledged by the prophets before this or not, they must have accepted it from this point onward, unless they denied to Deuteronomy the authority which it claimed and which the nation conceded to it. Jeremiah clearly must have assented to it, for his style and his thought have been so closely moulded on this book that some have thought he may have been its author. In any case he did not repudiate its authority; and all the prophets who followed him must have known of this view, and also that it had been sanctioned by that book which was made the first Jewish Bible.

We have here, at all events, the keynote of the supremacy of moral duty over Divine commands concerning ritual which distinguishes the prophetic teaching in Micah and elsewhere, joined with the enforcement of ritual observances. But there are few purely prophetic passages which raise the higher demand so high as it is raised here.

To love and fear God are anew declared to be man's supreme duties, and the author presses these home by arguments of various kinds. Again he returns to the election of Israel by Yahweh, without merit of theirs; and to bring home to them how much this means, the Deuteronomist exhibits the greatness of their God, His might, His justice, and His mercy, which, great as it is to His chosen people, is not confined to them, but extends to the stranger also. This most gracious One they are to serve by deeds, to Him they are to cleave, and they are to swear by Him only, that is, they are solemnly to acknowledge Him to be their God in return for His undeserved favour. For their very existence as a nation is a wonder of His power, since they were only a handful when they went down to Egypt, and now were "as the stars of heaven for multitude."

Then once more, in chapter xi., he repeats his one haunting thought that love is to be the source of all worthy fulfilment of the law; and he endeavours to shed abroad this love to God in their hearts by reminding them once more of all the marvels of their deliverance from Egypt, and of their wilderness journey. Their God had delivered them first, then chastised them for their sins, and had trained them for the new life that awaited them in the land promised to their fathers.

Even in the security of the land they were to find themselves not less dependent upon God than before. Rather their dependence would be more striking and more impressive than in Egypt. As we have seen repeatedly, this inspired writer belonged in many respects to the childhood of the world, and the people he addressed were primitive in their ideas. Yet his thoughts of God in their highest flight were so essentially true and deep, that even to-day we can go back upon them for edification and inspiration. But here we have an appeal based upon a distinction which to-day should have almost entirely lost its meaning. The Deuteronomist yields quite simply and unreservedly to the feeling that the regular, unvarying processes of nature are less Divine, or at least are less immediately significant of the Divine presence, than those which cannot be foreseen, which vary, and which defy human analysis. For he here contrasts Egypt and Canaan, in both of which he represents Israel as having been engaged in agricultural pursuits, and speaks as if in the former all depended upon human industry and ingenuity, and might be counted upon irrespective of moral conduct, while in the latter all would depend upon Divine favour and a right attitude towards God. It is quite true that in preceding chapters he has been teaching that, even for worldly material success, the higher life is necessary, that man nowhere lives by bread alone; and that we may assuredly assume is his deepest, his ultimate thought. But he has a practical end in view at this moment. He wishes to persuade his people, and he appeals to what both he and they felt, though in the last resort it might hardly perhaps be justified. In Egypt, he says, your agricultural success was certain if only you were industrious. The great river, of which the land itself is the gift, came down in flood year after year, and you had only to store and to guide its waters to ensure you a certain return for your labour. You had not to look to uncertain rains, but could by diligence always secure a sufficiency of the life-giving element. In Canaan it will not be so. It "drinketh water only of the rain of heaven." God's eye has to be upon it continually to keep it fertile, and the sense of dependence upon Him will force itself upon you more constantly and powerfully in consequence. They could hope to prosper only if they never forgot, never put away His exhortations out of their sight. Otherwise, he says, the life-giving showers will not fall in their due season. Your land will not yield its fruits, and "ye shall perish quickly off the good land which Yahweh giveth you."

Now what are we to say of this appeal? There can be no doubt that the Divine omnipotence was really, in the Deuteronomist's view as well as in ours, as irresistible in Egypt as in Canaan. Fundamentally, no doubt, life or death, prosperity or adversity, were as much in the hand of God in the one case as in the other; and the Deuteronomist, at least, had no doubt that rebellion against God could and would destroy Egypt's prosperity as much as Canaan's. But he felt that somehow there was a tenderer and more intimate communion of love between Yahweh and His people under the one set of circumstances than under the other. We are not entitled to impute to him a questionable distinction which modern minds are apt to make, viz. that where long experience has taught men to regard the course of providence as fixed, there the sphere of prayer for material benefit ends, and that only in the region where the Divine action in nature seems to us more spontaneous, and less capable of being foreseen, can prayer be heartily, because hopefully, made. But the feeling that suggests that was certainly in his mind. He felt the difference between the fixed conditions of life in Egypt and the more variable conditions in Canaan, to be much the same as the difference between the circumstances of a son receiving a fixed yearly allowance from his father, in an independent and perhaps distant home, and those of a son in his father's house, who receives his portion day by day as the result and evidence of an ever-present affection. Both are equally dependent upon the father's love, and both should theoretically be equally filled with loving gratitude. But as a fact, the latter would be more likely to be so, and would be held more guilty if he were not so. Upon that actual fact the Deuteronomist takes his stand. As they were now to enter into Yahweh's land, His chosen dwelling-place, he sees in the different material conditions of the new country that which should make the union between Yahweh and His people more intimate and more secure, and He presses home upon them the greater shame of ingratitude, if under such circumstances they should forget God and His laws.

Finally (xi. 22-25) he promises them the victorious extension of their dominion if they will love Yahweh and keep His laws. From Lebanon to the southern wilderness, from the Euphrates to the western sea, they should rule, if they would cleave unto their God. At no time was this promise fulfilled save in the days of David and Solomon. For only then had Lebanon and the wilderness, the Euphrates and the sea, been the boundaries of Israel. This must, then, be regarded as the time of Israel's greatest faithfulness. But it is striking that it is in Josiah's day, after the adoption of Deuteronomy as the national law, that we meet with a conscious effort to realise this condition of things once more. There would seem to be little doubt that the good king took an equally literal view of what the book commanded and of what it promised. He inaugurated a period of complete external compliance with the law, and like the young and inexperienced man he was, he regarded that as the fulfilment of its requirements, and looked for a similar instantaneous fulfilment of the promises. Bit by bit he had absorbed the ancient territory of the Northern Kingdom; and in the decay of the Assyrian power he saw the opportunity for the enlargement of his dominion to the limit here defined. He consequently went out against Pharaoh Necho in the full confidence that he would be victorious. But if the Divine promise and its conditions were taken up too superficially by him, Divine providence soon and terribly corrected the error. The defeat and death of Josiah revealed that the reformation had not been real and deep enough, and that the nation was not faithful enough to make such triumph possible. Indeed, so far as we can see, the time for any true fulfilment of Israel's calling in that fashion had then passed by. The harvest was past, and Israel was not saved, and could not now be saved, for it was in its deepest heart unfaithful.

It may be questioned by some, of course, whether an Israel faithful even in the highest degree could at any time have kept possession of so wide a dominion in the face of the great empires of Assyria and Egypt. These were rich, and had a far larger command both of territory and men: how then could the Israelites ever have maintained themselves in face of them? But the question is how to measure the power of the higher ideas they held. It is not force but truth that rules the world; and absolutely no limit can be set to the possibilities which open out to a free, morally robust, and faithful people, who have become possessed of higher spiritual ideas than the peoples that surround them. Even in this sceptical modern day the transformation as regards physical strength which takes place when certain classes of Hindus become either Mohammedans or Christians is so startling and so rapid that it appears almost a miracle. As regards courage, too, it is even more rapid and equally remarkable. The great majority of the struggles of nations are fought out on the level of mere physical force and for material ends, and the strongest and richest wins: but whenever a people possessed of higher ideas and absolutely faithful to them does appear, the opposing power, however great it may be in wealth and numbers, is whirled away in fragments as by a tornado, or it dissolves like ice before the sun. What Israel might have been, therefore, had it been penetrated by the principles of the higher religion, and been passionately true to it, can in no way be judged by that which it actually was. Among the untried possibilities which it was too unfaithful to realise, the possession of such an empire as Deuteronomy promises would seem to be one of the least.

Our chapter sums up what precedes with the declaration on the part of Yahweh, "See, I am setting before you this day a blessing and a curse," according as they might obey or disobey the Divine command. It is stated, in short, that the whole future of the people is to be determined by their attitude to Yahweh and the commands He has given them. In these two words "blessing" and "curse," as Dillmann observes, He sets before them the greatness of the decision they are called upon to make. Just as at the end of chapter iii. the vision of Yahweh's stretched-out hand, which has strewn the world with the wrecks and fragments of destroyed nations, is relied on to prepare the people for contemplating their own calling, so here the gain or loss which would follow their decision is solemnly set before them. By Dillmann and others it is supposed that vv. 29 and 31, which instruct the people to "lay the blessing upon Mount Gerizim and the curse upon Mount Ebal," have been transferred by the later editor from chapter xxvii., where they would come in very fittingly after ver. 3. But whether that be so or not, they are evidently so far in place here that they add to the solemnity with which the fate of the nation in the future is insisted upon. Their "choice is brief and yet endless"; it can be made in a moment, but in its consequence it will endure.

But here a difficulty arises. Dr. Driver in his *Introduction* says of this hortatory section of our book that its teaching is that "duties are not to be performed from secondary motives, such as fear or dread of consequences; they are to be the spontaneous outcome of a heart from which every taint of worldliness has been removed, and which is penetrated by an all-absorbing sense of personal devotion to God." Yet in these later chapters we have had little else but appeals to the gratitude and hopes and fears of Israel. Chapters viii. to xi. are wholly taken up with incitements to love and obey God, because He has been immeasurably good to them, never letting their ingratitude overcome His lovingkindness; because they are wholly dependent upon Him for prosperity and the fertility of their land; and because evil will come upon them if they do not. That would seem to be the opposite of what Driver has declared to be the informing spirit and the fundamental teaching of Deuteronomy.

Yet his view is the true one. Even if the Deuteronomist had added these lower motives to attract and gain over those who were not so open to the higher, that would not deprive him of the glory of having set forth disinterested love as the really impelling power in true religion. We are not required to lower our esteem of that achievement, even if, like the reasonable and wise teacher he is, he boldly uses every motive that actually influences men, whether it should do so or not, to win them to the higher life. But it is not necessary to suppose that he does so. His demand is that men shall love Yahweh their God with all their heart and strength, and to win them to that he sets forth what their God has revealed Himself to be. Men cannot love one whom they do not know; they cannot love one who has not proved himself lovable to them. As his whole effort is to get men to love God, and show their love by obedience to His expressed will, the Deuteronomist brings to mind all His loving thoughts and acts towards them, and so continually keeps his appeal at the highest level. He does not ask men to serve God because it will be profitable to them, but because they love God; and he endeavours to make them love God by reciting all His love and friendliness and patience to His people, and by pointing out the evil which His love is seeking to ward off. The plea is not the ignoble one that they must serve Yahweh for what they can gain by it, but that they should love Yahweh for His love and graciousness, and that out of this love continual obedience should flow as a necessary result. That is his central position; and if he points out the necessary results of a refusal to turn to God in this way, he does not thereby set forth slavish fear or calculating prudence as in themselves religious motives. They are only natural and reasonable means of turning men to view the other side. He uses them to bring the people to a pause, during which he may win them by the love of God. That is always the true appeal; and Christianity when it is at its finest can do nothing but follow in this path. Having before his mind the results of evil conduct, he does urge men to escape from the wrath that may rest upon them. But the only means so to escape is to yield to the love of God. No self-restraint dictated by fear of consequences, no turning from evil because of the lions that are seen in the path, satisfies the demand of either Old Testament or New Testament religion. Both raise the truly religious life above that into the region of self-devoting love; and they both deny spiritual validity to all acts, however good they may be in themselves, which do not follow love as its free and uncalculating expression. Yet they both deal with men as rational beings who can estimate the results of their acts, and warn them of the death which must be the end of every other way of supposed salvation. In this manner they keep the path between extremes, ignoring neither the inner heart of religion nor winding themselves too high for sinful men.

How hard it is to keep to this reasonable but spiritual view is seen by popular aberrations both within and without the Church. At times in the history of the Church Christian teachers have allowed their minds to be so dominated by the terror of judgment that judgment has seemed to the world to be the sole burden of their message. As a reaction from that again, other teachers have arisen who put forward the love of God in such a one-sided way as to empty it of all its severe but glorious sublimity; as if, like Mohammed, they believed God was minded mainly "to make religion easy" unto men. Outside the Church the same discord prevails. Some secular writers praise those religions which declare that a man's fate is decided at the judgment by the balance of merit over demerit in his acts; while others mock at any judgment, and commit themselves with a light heart to the half-amused tolerance of the Divine good-nature. But the teaching which combines both elements can alone sustain and bear up a worthy spiritual life. To rely upon terror only, is to ignore the very essence of true religion and the better elements in the nature of man; for that *will* not be dominated by fear alone. To think of the Divine love as a lazy, self-indulgent laxity, is to degrade the Divine nature, and to forget that the possibility of wrath is bound up in all love that is worthy of the name.

One other point is worthy of remark. In these chapters, which deal with the history of God's chosen people in their relations with Him, there come out the very elements which distinguish the personal religion of St. Paul. The beginning and end of it all is the free grace of God. God elected His people that they might be His instrument for blessing the world, not because of any goodness in them, for they were perverse and rebellious, but because He had so determined and had promised to the fathers. He had delivered them from the bondage of Egypt by His mighty power, and dwelt among them thenceforth as among no other people. He gave them a land to dwell in, and there as in His own house He watched and tended them, and strove to lead them upwards to the height of their calling as the people of God by demanding of them faith and love. It is a very enlightening remark of Robertson Smith's that the deliverance out of Egypt was to Israel in the Old Testament what conversion is to the individual Christian according to the New Testament. Taking that as our starting-point, we see that the thought of Deuteronomy is precisely the thought of Romans. It is said, and truly enough, that the Pauline theology was a direct transcript of Paul's own experience; but we see from this that he did not need to form the moulds for his own fundamental thoughts. Long before him the author of Deuteronomy had formed these, and they must have been familiar to every instructed Jew. But the recognition of this is not a loss but a gain. If St. Paul had founded a theory of the universal action of God upon the soul only on the grounds of his own very peculiar experience, it might be argued that the basis of his teaching had been too personal to permit us to feel sure that his view was really as exhaustive as he thought. We see, however, that what he experienced the Deuteronomist had long before traced in the history of his people; and most probably he would not have traced it with so firm a hand had he not himself had experience of a similar kind in his personal relations with God. This method of conceiving the relation of God to the higher life of man, therefore, is stated by the Scriptures as normal. The free grace of God is the source and the sustainer of all spiritual life, whether in individuals or communities. Ultimately, behind all the successful or unsuccessful efforts of the human heart and will, we are taught to see the great Giver, waiting to be gracious, willing that all men should be saved, but acting with the strangest reserves and limitations, choosing Israel among the nations, and even within Israel choosing *the* Israel in whom alone the promises can be realised. Made to serve by human sin, He waits upon the caprices of the wills He has created. He does not force them; but with compassionate patience He builds up His Holy Temple of such living stones as offer themselves, and "without haste as without rest" prepares for the consummation of His work in the redemption of a people that shall be all prophets, a kingdom of priests, a holy nation unto whom all nations shall join themselves when they see that God is in them of a truth. That is the Old Testament conception of the source, and guarantee, and goal of all spiritual life in the world, and St. Paul's view is merely a more mature and definite form of the same thing. And wherever spiritual life has manifested itself with unusual power, the same consciousness of utter unworthiness on the part of man, and entire dependence upon the grace and favour of God, has also manifested itself. The intellectual difficulties connected with this view, great as they are, have never suppressed it; the pride of man and his faith in himself have not been able permanently to obscure it. The greater men are, the more entirely do they dread any approach to that self-exaltation which puts away as unnecessary the Divine hand stretched out to them. As Dean Church points out,[69] "not Hebrew prophets only, but the heathen poets of Greece looked with peculiar and profound alarm upon the haughty self-sufficiency of men." Nothing can, they think, ward off evil from the man who makes the mistake of supposing, even when carrying out the Divine will, that he needs only his own strength of brain and will and arm to succeed, that he is accountable to no one for the character which he permits success to build up within him.

Even the agnostic of to-day, as represented by Professor Huxley, cannot do without some modicum of "grace" in his conception of man's relation to the powers of nature, though to admit this is to run a rift of inconsistency through his whole system of thought. "Suppose," he says in his *Lay Sermons*, "it were perfectly certain that the life and future of every one of us would, one day or other, depend on his winning or losing a game at chess.... The chessboard is the world, the pieces are the phenomena of the universe, the rules of the game are what we call the laws of nature. The player on the other side is hidden from us. We know that his play is always fair, just, patient. But we know to our cost that he never overlooks a mistake, or makes the smallest allowance for ignorance. To the man who plays well the highest stakes are paid with that overflowing generosity with which the strong shows delight in strength, and one who plays ill is checkmated without haste, but without remorse. My metaphor will remind you of the famous picture in which the Evil One is depicted playing a game of chess with man for his soul. Substitute for the mocking fiend in that picture a calm, strong angel, playing, as we say, for love, and who would rather lose than win, and I should accept it as the image of human life." Even in a world without God, therefore, the facts of life suggest "justice," "patience," "generosity," and a pity which "would rather lose than win." With all the inexorable rigour and hardness of man's lot there is mingled something that suggests "grace" in the power that rules the world; and from the Deuteronomist to St. Paul, from Augustine to Calvin and Professor Huxley, the resolutely thorough thinkers have found, in the last analysis, these two elements, the rigour of law and the election of grace, working together in the moulding of mankind.

The statement of these facts in Deuteronomy is as thorough as any that succeeded it. The rigour of law could not be more precisely and pathetically declared than in this insistence on the blessing or the curse which must inevitably follow right choice or wrong. But the tenderness of grace could not be more attractively displayed than in this picture of Yahweh's dealings with Israel. Love never faileth here, no more than elsewhere. It persists, notwithstanding stiff-necked rebellion, and in spite of coarse materialism of nature. Even a childish fickleness, more utterly trying than any other weakness or defect, cannot wear it out. But inexorable blessing or curse is blended with it, and helps to work out the final result for Israel and mankind. That is the manner of the government of God, according to the Scriptures. History in its long course as known to us now confirms the view; and the author of Deuteronomy, in thus blending love and law together in the end of this great exhortation, has rested the obligation to obedience on a foundation which cannot be moved.

CHAPTER XIII
LAW AND RELIGION

Deut. xii-xxvi

With this section (chapters xii.-xxvi.) we have at length reached the legislation to which all that has gone before is, in form at least, a prelude. But in its general outline this code, if it can be so called, has a very unexpected character. When we speak of a code of laws in modern days, what we mean is a series of statutes, carefully arranged under suitable heads, dealing with the rights and duties of the people, and providing remedies for all possible wrongs. Then behind these laws there is the executive power of the Government, pledged to enforce them, and ready to punish any breaches of them which may be committed. In most cases, too, definite penalties are appointed for any disregard or transgression of them. Each word has been carefully selected, and it is understood that the very letter of the laws is to be binding. Every one tried by them knows that the exact terms of the laws are to be pressed against him, and that the thing aimed at is a rigorous, literal enforcement of every detail. Tried by such a conception, this Deuteronomic legislation looks very extraordinary and unintelligible.

In the first place, there is very little of orderly sequence in it. Some large sections of it have a consecutive character; but there is no perceptible order in the succession of these sections, and there has been very little attempt to group the individual precepts under related heads. Moreover in many sections there is no mention of a penalty for disobedience, nor is there any machinery for enforcing the prescriptions of the code. There is, too, much in it that seems rather to be good advice, or direction for leading a righteous life, a life becoming an Israelite and a servant of Yahweh, than law. For instance, such a prescription as this, "If there be with thee a poor man, one of thy brethren, within any of thy gates, in thy land which Yahweh thy God giveth thee, thou shalt not harden thine heart nor shut thine hand from thy poor brother," can in no sense be treated as a law, in the hard technical sense of that word. It stands exactly on a level with the exhortations of the New Testament, *e.g.* "Be not wise in your own conceits," "Render to no man evil for evil," and rather sets up an ideal of conduct which is to be striven after than establishes a law which must be complied with. There is no punishment prescribed for disobedience. All that follows if a man do harden his heart against his poor brother is the sting of conscience, which brings home to him that he is not living according to the will of God. In almost every respect, therefore, this Deuteronomic code differs from a modern code, and in dealing with it we must largely dismiss the ideas which naturally occur to us when we speak of a code of laws. Our conception of that is, clearly, not valid for these ancient codes; and we need not be surprised if we find that they will not bear being pressed home in all their details, as modern codes must be, and are meant to be. Great practical difficulties have arisen in India, Sir Henry Maine assures us, from applying the ideas of Western lawyers to the ancient and sacred codes of the East. He says that the effect of a procedure under which all the disputes of a community must be referred to regular law-courts is to stereotype ascertained usages, and to treat the oracular precepts of a sacred book as texts and precedents that must be enforced. The consequence is that vague and elastic social ordinances, which have hitherto varied according to the needs of the people, become fixed and immutable, and an Asiatic society finds itself arrested and, so to speak, imprisoned unexpectedly within its own formulas. Inconsistencies and contradictions, which were never perceived when these laws were worked by Easterns, who had a kind of instinctive perception of their true nature, became glaring and troublesome under Western rule, and much unintentional wrong has resulted. May it not be that the same thing has happened in the domain of literature in connection with these ancient Hebrew laws? Discrepancies, small and great, have been the commonplace of Pentateuch criticism for many years past, and on them very far-reaching theories have been built. It may easily be that some of these are the result rather of our failure to take into account the elastic nature of Asiatic law, and that a less strained application of modern notions would have led to a more reasonable interpretation.

But granting that ordinary ancient law is not to be taken in our rigorous modern sense, yet the fact that what we are dealing with here is Divine law may seem to some to imply that in all its details it was meant to be fulfilled to the letter. If not, then in what sense is it inspired, and how can we be justified in regarding it as Divinely given? The reply to that is, of course, simply this, that inspiration makes free use of all forms of expression which are common and permissible at the time and place at which it utters itself. From all we know of the Divine methods of acting in the world, we have no right to suppose that in giving inspired laws God would create entirely new and different forms for Himself. On the contrary, legislation in ancient Israel, though Divine in its source, would naturally take the ordinary forms of ancient law. Moreover in this case it could hardly have been otherwise. As has already been pointed out, a large part of the Mosaic legislation must have been adopted from the customs of the various tribes who were welded into one by Moses. It cannot be conceived that the laws against stealing, for example, the penalties for murder, or the prescriptions for sacrifice, can have been first introduced by the great Lawgiver. He made much ancient customary law to be part and parcel of the Yahwistic legislation by simply taking it over. If so, then all that he added would naturally, as to form, be moulded on what he found pre-existing. Consequently we may apply to this law, whether Divinely revealed or adopted, the same tests and methods of interpretation as we should apply to any other body of ancient Eastern law.

Now of ancient Eastern codes the laws of Manu are the nearest approach to the Mosaic codes, and their character is thus stated by themselves (chap. i., ver. 107): "In this work the sacred law has been fully stated, as well as the good and bad qualities of human actions and the immemorial rule of conduct to be followed by all." That means that in the code are to be found ritual laws, general moral precepts, and a large infusion of immemorial customs. And its history, as elicited by criticism, has very interesting hints to give us as to the probable course of legal development in primitive nations. It is sometimes said that the results of the criticism of the Old Testament, if true, present us with a literature which has gone through vicissitudes and editorial processes for which literary history elsewhere affords absolutely no parallel. However that may be as regards the historical and prophetical books, it is not true with regard to the legal portions of the Pentateuch. The very same processes are followed in Professor Buhler's Introduction to his translation of the *Laws of Manu*, forming Vol. XXV. of *The Sacred Books of the East*, as are followed in the critical commentaries on the Old Testament law codes. Pages lxvii. *seq.* of Buhler's Introduction read exactly like an extract from Kuenen or Dillmann; and the analysis of the text, with its resultant list of interpolations, runs as much into detail as any similar analysis in the Old Testament can do. Moreover the conjectures as to the growth of Manu's code are, in many places, parallel to the critical theories of the growth of the Mosaic codes. The foundation of Manu is, in the last resort, threefold — the teaching of the Vedas, the decisions of those acquainted with the law, and the customs of virtuous Aryas. At a later time the teachers of the Vedic schools gathered up the more important of these precepts, decisions, and customs into manuals for the use of their pupils, written at first in aphoristic prose, and later in verse. These, however, were not systematic codes at all. As the name given them implies, they were strings of maxims or aphorisms.

Later, these were set forth as binding upon all, and were revised into the form of which the *Laws of Manu* is the finest specimen.

In Israel the process would appear to have been similar, though much simpler. It was similar; for though there are radical differences between the Aryan and the Semitic mind which must not be overlooked, the former being more systematic and fond of logical arrangement than the latter, a great many of the things which are common to Moses and Manu are quite independent of race, and are due to the fact that both legislations were to regulate the lives of men at the same stage of social advancement. But Manu was much later than Moses. Indeed, as we now have them, the laws of Manu are as late as the post-Ezraite Judaic code, and in temper and tone these two codes very nearly resemble each other. Consequently the earlier codes of the Pentateuch are simpler than Manu. When Israel left Egypt, custom must have been almost alone the guide of life. Moses' task was to promulgate and force home his fundamental truths; in this view he must adopt and remodel the customary law so as to make it innocuous to the higher principles he introduced, or even to make it a vehicle for the popularising of them. So far as he made codes, he would make them with that end. Consequently he would take up mainly such prominent points as were most capable of being, or which most urgently needed to be, moralised, leaving all the rest to custom where it was harmless. This is the reason, too, most probably, why the earlier codes are so short and so unsystematic. They are selections which needed special attention, not complete codes covering the whole of life. In fact the form and contents of all the Old Testament codes can be accounted for only on this supposition. As the codes lengthen, they do so simply by taking up, in a modified or unmodified form, so much more of the custom; and under the pressure of Yahwistic ideas these selected codes became more and more weighted with spiritual significance and power.

That would seem to have been the process by which the inspired legislators of Israel did their work; and if it be so, some of the variations which are now taken to be certain indications of different ages and circumstances may simply represent local varieties of the same custom. Custom tends always to vary with the locality within certain narrow limits. It would be quite in accord with the general character of ancient customary law to believe that, provided the law was on the whole observed, there would be no inclination to insist upon excluding small local variations; and equally so that in a collection like the Pentateuch the custom of one locality should appear in one place, that of another in another. In that case, to insist that a certain sacrifice, for example, shall always consist of the same number of animals, and that any variation means a new and later legislation on the subject, is only to make a mistake. The discrepancy is made important only by applying modern English views of law to ancient law. Professor A. B. Davidson has shown in the Introduction to his *Ezekiel* (p. liii.) that this latter was probably Ezekiel's view. "On any hypothesis of priority," he says, "the differences in details between him (*i.e.* Ezekiel) and the law (*i.e.* P) may be easiest explained by supposing that, while the sacrifices in general and the ideas which they expressed were fixed and current, the particulars, such as the kind of victims and the number of them, the precise quantity of meal, oil, and the like, were held non-essential and alterable when a change would better express the idea." The same principle would apply to the differences between Ezekiel and Deuteronomy, *e.g.* the omission of the feast of weeks and of the law of the offering of the firstlings of the flock. If so, then obviously Ezekiel must have thought that the previous ritual law was not meant to be as binding as we make it.

But, as has already been remarked, this law was elastic in more important matters; often, even when it seems to legislate, it is only setting up ideals of conduct. Before we leave this subject an example should be given, and the law of war may serve, especially if we compare it with the corresponding section of Manu. The provisions in Deuteronomy chap. xx. according to which on the eve of a battle the officers should proclaim to the army that any man who had built a new house and had not dedicated it, or who had planted a vineyard and had not yet used the fruit of it, or who had betrothed a wife and not yet taken her, or who was afraid, should retire from the danger, as also the provisions that forbid the destruction of fruit-trees belonging to a besieged city, cannot have been meant as absolute laws. Yet that is no ground for supposing that they could have been introduced only after Israel, having ceased to be a sovereign state, waged no war, and that consequently they are interpolations in the original Deuteronomy. For the similar provisions of the laws of Manu were given while kings reigned, and were addressed to men constantly engaged in war. Yet this is what we find: "When he (the king) fights with his foes in battle, let him not strike with weapons concealed (in wood), nor with (such as are) barbed, poisoned, or the points of which are blowing with fire. Let him not strike one who (in flight) has climbed on an eminence, nor a eunuch, nor one who joins the palms of his hands (in supplication), nor one (who flees) with flying hair, nor one who sits down, nor one who says 'I am thine,' nor one who sleeps, nor one who has lost his coat of mail, nor one who is naked, nor one who is disarmed, nor one who looks on without taking part in the fight, nor one who is fighting with another foe, nor one whose weapons are broken, nor one afflicted (with sorrow), nor one who has been grievously wounded, nor one who is in fear, nor one who has turned to flight; but in all these cases let him remember the duty (of honourable warriors)." With an exact and unremitting obligation to observe these precepts war would be impossible, and we may be sure that in neither case were they meant in that sense. They simply set forth the conduct which a chivalrous soldier would desire to follow, and would on fitting occasions actually follow; but by no means what he must do, or else break with his religion. Only by hypotheses like these can the form and the character of such laws be properly explained, and if we keep them constantly in mind, some at least of the difficulties which result from a comparison of the law and the histories may be mitigated.

Such being the character of the Deuteronomic code, the question has been raised whether its introduction and acceptance by Josiah was not a falling away from the spirituality of ancient religion. Many modern writers, supported by St. Paul's *dicta* concerning the law, say that it was. Indeed the very mention of law seems to depress writers on religion in these days, and Deuteronomy appears to be to them a name of fear. But whatever tendencies of modern thinking may have brought this about, it is nevertheless true that experience embodied in custom and law is the kindly nurse, not the deadly enemy, of moral and spiritual life. Without law a nation would be absolutely helpless; and it is inconceivable that at any stage of Israel's history they were without this guide and support. As we have seen, they never were. First they had customary law; then along with that short special codes, *e.g.* the Book of the Covenant and the Deuteronomic code; and even when the whole Pentateuchal law as we have it had been elaborated, a good deal must still have been left to custom. Consequently there was nothing so startling and revolutionary in the introduction of Deuteronomy as many have combined to represent. Indeed it is difficult to see how it altered anything in this respect. Of all forms of law, customary law is perhaps that which demands and receives most unswerving obedience. Under it, therefore, the pressure of law was heavier than it could be in any other form. It does not appear how the fact that those observing it did not think of that which they obeyed as law, but simply custom, altered the essential nature of their relation to it. They were guided by ordinances which did not express their own inward conviction, and were not a product of their own thought. They obeyed ordinances from without, and these ought therefore to have had the same effect upon the moral and spiritual life as written laws. For they cannot be said to have regulated only civil life. Religious life (even if the Book of the Covenant be Mosaic or sub-Mosaic, as I believe; much more if it be post-Davidic, as many say) must have been largely regulated by the customs of Israel. If law then be in its own nature, as the antinomians tell us, destructive of spontaneity and progress, if it necessarily externalises religion, then there would have been as little room for the religion of the prophets before Deuteronomy as after it.

But, as a matter of fact, no falling off in spirituality took place after Deuteronomy. Wellhausen says that with law freedom came to an end, and this was the death of prophecy. But he can support his thesis only by denying the name of prophet to all the prophets after Jeremiah. It is difficult to see the basis of such a distinction. It is judged by this, if by nothing else—that it compels Wellhausen to deny that the author of Second Isaiah is a prophet. That he wrote anonymously is held to prove that he felt this himself. Now a view so extraordinarily superficial has no root, and every reader of that most touching and sublime of all the Old Testament books will simply stand amazed at the depth of the critical prejudice which could dictate such a judgment. If the post-Deuteronomic prophets are not prophets, then there are no prophets at all, and the whole discussion becomes a useless logomachy. But even if Ezekiel and Second Isaiah and the rest are not prophets, they are at least full of spiritual life and power, so that the decay of spiritual religion which the adoption of Deuteronomy is supposed to have brought about must be considered purely imaginary on that ground also. And this contention is strengthened by the theories of the critical school themselves. If the bulk of the Psalms, as all critics incline to believe, or all of them, as some say, are post-exilic, then the first centuries of the post-exilic period must have been the most spiritually minded epoch in Israelite history. The depth of religious feeling exhibited in the Psalms, and the comprehension of the inwardness of man's true relation to God by which they are penetrated, are the exact contrary of the externality and superficiality which the introduction of written law is said to have produced. So long as the Psalms were being written religious life must have been vigorous and healthy, and to date the beginnings of Pharisaic externalism from Josiah's day must consequently be an error.

After what has been said it is scarcely necessary to discuss Duhm's views of the opposition between prophecy and Deuteronomy. It will be sufficient to ask how the latter can have turned against prophecy, when it is in its essence an embodiment of prophetic principles in law, and was introduced and supported by prophets. But, it may be said, after all prophecy did decay, and ultimately die, and that too during the period after Deuteronomy. Is there not in that admitted fact a presumption that this law did work against prophecy? If so, then it is more than met by the fact that the decay of spiritual religion became noticeable only some centuries after this, and that the immediate effect of Deuteronomy was rather to deepen and intensify religion, and to keep it alive amid all the vicissitudes of the Captivity and Return. Moreover the break-up of the national life was sufficient to account for the slow decay and final cessation of prophecy. From the first, prophecy had been concerned with the building up of a nation which should be faithful to Yahweh. Its main function had been to interpret and to foretell the great movements and crises of national life—to read God's purpose in the great world-movements and to proclaim it. With Israel's death as a nation the field of prophecy became gradually circumscribed, and ultimately its voice ceased. Consequently, though in the main the final cessation of prophecy was connected with the rise of externalism in religion and with the great decay of spiritual life in the two or three centuries before Christ, the destruction of the nation would account for the feebleness of prophecy during a period when the inner spiritual life was flourishing as it flourished after Deuteronomy. Moreover, as religion became more inward and personal, prophecy, in the Old Testament sense, had less place. Though in New Testament times spiritual life and spiritual originality and power were more present than at any time in the world's history, prophecy did not revive. In the whole New Testament there is not one purely prophetic book save the Revelation, and that is apocalyptic more than simply prophetic; and though there was an order of prophets in the early Church, if they had any special function other than that of preachers their office soon died out. If then the denationalising of religion and its growth in individualism and inwardness in New Testament times prevented the revival of prophecy, we may surely gather that the same things, and not the introduction of written law, brought it to an end in the Old Testament.

Nor does St. Paul's judgment as to the meaning and use of law, in Galatians, when rightly understood, contradict this. No doubt he seems to say that the Mosaic law by its very nature as law is incompatible with grace, that it necessarily stands out of relation to faith, and that its principle is a purely external one, so much wages for so much work. Further, he clearly regards it as having been interpolated into the history of Israel between the promises given to Abraham and the fulfilment of them in the redemption by Christ, and as having served only to increase sin and to drive men thus to Christ. But when he says this he is replying mainly to the Pharisaic view of the law which was represented by the Judaizers, and finds himself all the more at home in refuting it that it was his own view before he became a Christian. According to that view, the whole law, both the moral and ceremonial provisions of it, was necessary to obtain moral righteousness, and the mere doing of the legally prescribed things gave a claim to the promised reward. So interpreted, law had all the evil qualities he states, and stood in absolute hostility to grace and faith, the great Christian principles. The only difficulty is that St. Paul does not say, as we should expect him to do, that originally the law was not meant to be so regarded. He seems to admit by his silence that the Pharisaic view of the law was the right one. But if he does, he cannot have meant to include Deuteronomy. For there law is made to have its root and ground in grace. It is given to Israel as a token of the free love of God, and it is a law of life which, if kept, would make them a peculiar people unto God. Further, love to God is to be the motive from which all obedience springs, so that this law is bound up with both grace and faith. But the probability is that St. Paul admits the Pharisaic view only because it is that view with which alone he has to contend in the case in hand. For in Romans vii. he gives us quite another conception of the Mosaic law.[70] There he is thinking of it mainly from an ethical point of view, and he regards it as full of the Spirit of God, as a norm of moral life which not only continues to be valid in Christianity, but which finds in the Christian life the very fulfilment which it was intended to have. It presses home too the moral ideal upon the man with extraordinary power, and marks and emphasises the terrible divergence between his aspirations and his actual performance. This is a much higher office than that which he assigns to law in Galatians; and hence one gathers that he is not speaking in Galatians exhaustively and conclusively, but is condemning rather a way of regarding the Mosaic law with which he had once sympathised than that law in its own essential character. In its moral aspects, as represented by the Decalogue, the law is of eternal obligation. From it comes the light which brings to the Christian that moral unrest and dissatisfaction which is one of God's Divinest gifts to His people. In this aspect, the law is holy and just and good: instead of favouring the critical view St. Paul leaves it without any fragment of real support.

Our conclusion is, therefore, that the antinomianism, which makes the acknowledgment of Deuteronomy by Josiah and his people the turning-point for the worse in the religious history of Israel, is unfounded. The nation had always been under law, and previous to Deuteronomy under even written law. This code was not in any previously unheard-of way made the law of the kingdom. Its very contents are conclusive against that view, for it contains much that could not be enforced by the State. Instead of trying to do by external means that which the persuasions of the prophets had failed to do, Josiah and his people did just what they would have had to do, when they became convinced that the prophetic principles ought to be carried out. They made an agreement to follow these Divine commands, these God-given principles, in actual life. But there is no hint that they regarded Deuteronomy as the sum of the Divine ordinances for the life of men. Indeed there are many references to other Divine laws; and the priestly oracle remained, after Deuteronomy as before it, a source of Divine guidance. Deuteronomy therefore did not destroy prophecy; the post-exilic Psalms are proof that it did not destroy spiritual life: and the Pauline view of the law, in at least one series of passages, coincides entirely with the view that law stated as it is stated in Deuteronomy may be one of the mightiest influences to mould, and enrich, and deepen, moral and spiritual life.

CHAPTER XIV
LAWS OF SACRIFICE

Deut. xii

It is a characteristic of all the earlier codes of law—the Book of the Covenant, the Deuteronomic Code, and the Law of Holiness—that at the head of the series of laws which they contain there should be a law of sacrifice. Probably, too, each of the three had, as first section of all, the Decalogue. The Book of the Covenant and Deuteronomy undeniably have it so, and the earlier element which forms the basis of Lev. xvii.-xxvi. not improbably had originally the same form. If so, we may assume that the order of the precepts has in a measure been determined by the order of the commandments. On this account the laws for the cultus would naturally come first. For just as the first commandment is, "Thou shalt have no other god before Me," and the second forbids all idolatrous images, so the laws begin with provisions meant in the main to ward off idolatry. Israel's great calling was to receive and to spread the truth concerning God. That was the centre of the sacred deposit of Divine and revealed truth committed to that nation; and it is most instructive to see how, not only in historical statements, but even in the form in which early Israelite legislation is handed down to us, the Decalogue dominates all the details of it. It formulated in as concrete a shape as was possible the Divine demand that Israelites should love God and their neighbour, and *therefore* the legislative provisions and statutes begin with ordinances dealing with sacrifice.

To us in modern times it may seem almost bathos to connect such an antecedent with such a consequent; but it seems so, only because we have difficulty in apprehending the meaning and importance of sacrifice in primitive religion. For sacrifice had in Israel a meaning and importance of its own, and a present value at every period, which in no way depended upon its typical or prophetic value as pointing forward to the sacrifice of Christ. It supplied the religious needs of men even apart from the clearness of their knowledge about its ultimate purpose. Sacrifice, especially in its simplest meaning, was in heathenism absolutely essential as a means of approach to God. To come before a great *man* without a gift was in ancient days an outrage. It was therefore inevitable that men should approach their gods in the same manner. Sacrificial gifts expressed the dependent's joy in a gracious lord, and also the homage and reverence due from a subject to a king. Further, as all good things were regarded as the gifts of the gods to their worshippers, the sacrifices conveyed thanks for good gifts received, and joined the gods and their worshippers by a common participation in the Divine gift which connected them as eaters at the same table. But sacrifices had a higher reach of expression even than that. As they were brought to the gods they were the symbols of the self-devotion of the offerer to the service of his god; and where there was need of propitiation because of offence consciously given, or offence felt by the deity for unknown reasons, these gifts took on in some measure a reconciling or propitiatory quality.

Now the Old Testament sacrifices had in them, unquestionably, all these elements: but as Yahweh was high above all heathen deities in moral character, they also took on a depth and intensity of meaning which they could never have on the soil of heathen religious conceptions. Along this line of sacrificial ritual, therefore, all the spiritual emotions of Israel flowed; and to hold that sacrifice had no real place in the religion of Yahweh would be almost equivalent to saying that neither love, nor penitence, nor prayer, had any real place in it either. All these found utterance in sacrifice and along with it; and it has yet to be shown that they had any regular and acceptable utterance otherwise. To regulate sacrifice and keep it pure must, therefore, have been one chief means of guarding against the degradation of Yahweh to the level of the gods of the heathen.

But there is another and very important reason for it. Both in the days when Moses parted from his people, and also in the time of Manasseh, the people stood confronted by very special danger just at this point.

At the earlier period they were about to enter upon intimate contact with the Canaanites, their superiors in culture and in all the arts of civilised life, but corrupted to the core. Further, the Canaanite corruption was focussed in their religious rites and worship, and evil could not fail to follow if the people suffered themselves to be drawn into any participation in it. For if Professor Robertson Smith be right, the central point of ancient sacrifice was the communion between the god and his worshippers in the sacrificial feast. They became of one kin with each other and with the god, and this close relationship made the communication of spiritual and moral infection almost a certainty.

In Manasseh's day again it was natural that legislation on the same subject, and warnings of even a more solemn kind, should be repeated. A prophetic lawgiver writing at that date had before him, not only the possibility of evil, but actual experience of it. The laws and warnings of the earlier code had been defied and neglected. The faith of the chosen people had been miserably perverted by contact with the Canaanites; the whole history of prophecy had been a struggle against corrupt and insincere worship; and now the monstrous sacrifices to Moloch and the invasion of Assyrian idolatry had degraded Yahweh and destroyed His people, so that scarce any hope of recovery remained. In bracing himself for one more struggle with this desperate corruption, the Deuteronomist naturally repeated in deeper tones the Mosaic warnings. The command utterly to uproot and trample under foot the symbols and instruments of Canaanite worship, he brings, from the less prominent place it occupies in the Book of the Covenant, to the first place in his own code. To break with that and all other forms of idolatry, utterly and decisively, had come to be the first condition of any upward movement. The degrading and defiling bondage to idolatry into which his people had fallen must end. With trumpet tongue he calls upon them to break down the Canaanite altars, dash in pieces their obelisks, and burn their Asherim with fire.

To some moderns it may seem that such excessive energy might, with better effect, have been expended upon the denunciation of moral evils, such as cruelty and lust and oppression, rather than of idolatry. We have grown so accustomed to the distinctions drawn by the Church of Rome, and in later times by the neo-classicists, between worshipping God through an image or a picture, or in any natural object or natural force, and the actual worship of the image or picture or natural object itself, that we have sophisticated our minds. But the author of Deuteronomy knew by bitter experience that such subtle, and, in great part, sophistical distinctions had no application to his people and his time. Their worst immoralities were, he knew well, rooted in their idol-worship. For idolatry in any form binds all that is highest in man to the sphere of nature, *i.e.* of moral indifference. Just as a conception of God which rigorously separated Him from nature, which made His will the supreme impelling force in the world, and which conceived His essential attributes to be entirely ethical, was the fountain of the higher life in Israel, so a lapse into idolatry of any kind was the negation of it all. No doubt some moral life would have remained in Israel, even if the lapse had become universal. But, even at its best, this natural morality of self-preservation has no future and no goal. It does not lead the van of human progress; it merely comes after, to ratify the results of it. Only when social morality is taken up into a wider sphere than its own,—only when it is conceived as the path by which man can co-operate with a sublime purpose lying beyond himself,—can it maintain itself as the inspiration of human life, impelling to progress and guiding it.[71] Now, so far as history teaches, this energy of moral life has been attained only where the conception of God which makes moral perfection to be His essential nature has been accepted and cherished. But no natural religion can rise to that; hence idolatry must always be destructive of ethical religion. It must destroy faith in the moral character of God.

Further, it must destroy the moral character of man. In the last resort all idolaters are equally acceptable to their god, if only they bring the prescribed gifts and accurately perform the prescribed ceremonies. The lewd and the chaste, the cruel and the merciful, the revengeful and the forgiving, are all equally accepted when they sacrifice. Non-moral or positively immoral gods can care nothing about such differences. Of this fact and its results no man acquainted with the history of Israel could doubt. The main zeal of the prophets was at all times directed against those who were steeped in moral evil, but were zealous in all that concerned sacrifice, and against the amazing folly of a people who thought to bind the living God to their cause and their interests by mere bribes, in the shape of thousands of bullocks and ten thousand rivers of oil. This conception was bound up essentially with idolatry. But the evil of it was intensified in the Semitic idolatries with which Israel specially defiled itself. Their cruelty and obscenity were unspeakable. Now by Israel's idolatry Yahweh was made to appear tolerant of Moloch and Baal, as if they were equals. Every quality which the Mosaic revelation had set forth as essential to the character of Yahweh—His purity, His mercy, His truth—was outraged by the society which His worshippers in Manasseh's days had thrust upon Him. No reform, then, had the least chance of stability till the axe was laid at the root of this wide-spreading upas tree.

Deuteronomy, therefore, grapples first and grapples thoroughly with the evil, and strikes it a blow from which it was never to recover. The inspired writer repeats with new energy the old decrees of utter destruction against the Canaanite sanctuaries; for though these were for the most part no longer in Canaanite hands, the High Places still existed; and the principle of that old prohibition was more clamant for recognition and realisation than it had ever been in the history of Israel before.

Then he goes on to proclaim the new law, that no sacrifice should any longer be offered save at the one central sanctuary chosen by Yahweh. There is no such provision in the Book of the Covenant, and there is no hint in the legislation of Deuteronomy that its author knew of the Tabernacle and its sole right as a place of sacrifice. From beginning to end of the code he never mentions the Tabernacle nor the sacrifices there; and in the very terms in which he permits the slaughter of animals for food in vv. 15, 16, and 20-25, though he obviously repeals a custom which has been embodied in the

Priestly Code as a law (Lev. xvii. 3 ff.), he makes no reference to that passage. Consequently this at least may be said, that he may quite conceivably have been ignorant of Lev. xvii. 3 ff. In ignorance of it, he might write as he has done; and if not ignorant, it would be much more natural to refer to it. When we add to this negative testimony the positive testimony of verses 8 and 13, which we have already discussed in Chapter I., there would seem to be little room for doubt that the priestly law on this subject was not before the writer of Deuteronomy. Consequently we are justified in regarding this as the first written law actually promulgated on this subject. Hezekiah had attempted the same reform; but he had, so far as we know, neither published nor referred to any law commanding it, and his work was entirely undone. The Deuteronomist, more convinced than he that this step was absolutely necessary to complete the Mosaic legislation on idolatry, and filled with the same inspiration of the Almighty, completed it; and though a reaction followed Josiah's enforcement of this law also, its existence saved the life of the nation. Its principles kept the nation holy, *i.e.* separate to their God, during the Exile, and at the return they were dominant in the formation of the "congregation."

Certainly there is no lack of earnestness in the way in which these principles are urged. With that love of repetition which is a distinguishing mark of this writer, he expresses the commandment first positively, then negatively. Then he brings in the consequential alteration in the law regarding the slaughtering of animals for food. Again he returns to the command, explaining, enlarging, insisting, and concludes with a reiteration of the permission to slaughter. Efforts, of course, have been made to show that this repetition is due to the amalgamation here of no fewer than seven separate documents! But little heed need be given to such fantastic attempts. It is, once for all, a habit of this writer's mind to shrink from no monotony of this kind. There is not one important idea in his book which he does not repeat again and again; and where repetition is so constant a feature, and where the language and thought is so consistent as it is here, it is worse than useless to assert separate documents. The writer's earnestness is sufficient explanation. He saw plainly that, so long as the provincial High Places existed and were popular, it would be impossible to secure purity of worship. The heathen conceptions of the Canaanites clung about their ancient sanctuaries, and, like the mists from a fever swamp, infected everything that came near. Inspection sufficiently minute and constant to be of use was impracticable; there remained nothing but to decree their abandonment. When the whole worship of the people was centred at Jerusalem, corruption of the idolatrous kind would, it was hoped, be impossible. There, a pious king could watch over it; there, the Temple priesthood had attained to worthier ideas in regard to sacrifice and the fulfilment of the law than the priests elsewhere. Josiah accordingly rigorously enforced this new law.

Such a change, aimed solely at religious ends, did not stop there. In many ways it affected the social life of the people; in vv. 15, 16, and 20, 24, the author meets one hardship connected with the new law, by allowing men to slay for food at a distance from the altar. According to ancient custom, no flesh could be eaten by any Israelite, save when the fat and the blood had been presented at the altar. During the wilderness journey there would be little difficulty regarding this. In the desert very little meat is eaten; and so long as life was nomadic there would be no hardship in demanding that those who wished to make sacrificial feasts should wander towards the central place of worship rather than from it. It has been disputed whether there was in those days a tabernacle such as the Priestly Code describes; but there certainly was, according to the earliest documents, a tent in which Yahweh revealed Himself and gave responses. As we have seen, there must have been sacrifice in connection with it; and though worship at other places where Yahweh had made His name to be remembered was permitted, this sanctuary in the camp must have had a certain pre-eminence. A tendency, but according to the words of Deuteronomy nothing stronger than a tendency, must have shown itself to make this the main place of worship.

When the people crossed the Jordan into the land promised to the fathers, and had abandoned the nomadic life, great difficulty must have arisen. For those at a distance from the place where the Tabernacle was set up, the eating of meat and the enjoyment of sacrificial feasts would, by this ancient customary law, have been rendered impossible, if the attendance at one sanctuary had been obligatory. Only if men could come to local sanctuaries, each in his own neighbourhood, could the religious character of the festivals at which meat was eaten be preserved. The nature of men's occupations, now that they had become settled agriculturists, and the dangers from the Canaanites so long as they were not entirely subdued and absorbed, alike forbade such long and frequent journeys to a central sanctuary. The conquest must consequently at once have checked any tendency to centralisation that may have existed; and there is reason to believe that the acceptance of the Canaanite High Places as sanctuaries of Yahweh was in great part caused by the demands of this ancient law concerning the "zebhach." In any case it must have helped to overcome any scruples that may have existed. But when the Tabernacle and Ark were brought to Zion, and still more when the Temple was built, the centripetal tendency, never altogether dead, must have revived. For there was peace throughout the land and beyond it. No danger from the Canaanites existed; and the political centralisation which Solomon aimed at, and actually carried out, as well as the superior magnificence of the Solomonic Temple and its priests, must have attracted to Jerusalem the thoughts and the reverence of the whole people. What

Deuteronomy now makes law may have then first arisen as a demand of the Jerusalem priests. At all events, the very existence of the Temple must have been a menace to the High Places; and we may be sure that among the motives which led the ten tribes to reject the Davidic house, jealousy for the local sanctuaries must have been prominent.

But the separation of the ten tribes would only strengthen the claim of the Temple on Zion to be for Judah the one true place of worship. The territory ruled from Jerusalem was now so small that resort to the central sanctuary was comparatively easy. The glorious memories of the Davidic and Solomonic time would centre round Jerusalem. Any local sanctuaries would be entirely dwarfed and overshadowed by the splendour and the, at least comparative, purity of the worship there. Priests of local altars too must inevitably have sunk in the popular estimation, and even in their own, to a secondary and subordinate position, as compared with the carefully organised and strictly graded Jerusalem priests. Even without a positive command, therefore, the people of Judah must have been gradually growing into the habit of seeking Yahweh at Jerusalem on all more solemn religious occasions; and though the High Places might exist, their repute in the Southern Kingdom must have been decreasing. Of course if a command was given in the Mosaic time which had been neglected, the tendencies here traced must have been stronger and more definite than we have depicted them. When the prophetic teachings of Isaiah which proclaimed Jerusalem to be "Ariel," the "sacrificial hearth," or "the hearth of God," were so wondrously confirmed by the destruction of Sennacherib's host before the city, the unique position of Zion must have been secured; and after that only those who were set upon idolatry can have had much interest in the High Places. Hezekiah's effort to abolish these latter is quite intelligible in these circumstances; and we may feel assured that, as Wellhausen says,[72] "The Jewish royal temple had early overshadowed the other sanctuaries, and in the course of the seventh century they were extinct or verging on extinction."

Along with this there must have grown up a measure of laxity in regard to the provision that all slaughtering for food should take place at the sanctuary. Many would doubtless go to Zion, many would continue to resort to the High Places, and a number, from a mere halting between two opinions, would probably take their "zebhachim" to neither. Consequently the law before us would by no means be so revolutionary as Duhm, for instance, pictures it. He says: "I do not know if in the whole history of the world a law can be pointed to which was so fitted to change a whole people in its innermost nature and in its outward appearance, at one stroke, as this was. The Catholic Church even has never by all her laws succeeded in anything in the least like it." But we have seen evidence of a very strong and continuous pressure to this point, at least in Judah. History during centuries had justified and intensified it; so that in all probability the true worshippers of Yahweh found in the new law not so much a revolution as a ratification of their already ancient practice. To idolaters, of course, its adoption must have meant a cessation of their idolatry; but the change in the people and in their life would, though extensive, be only such as any ordinary reform would produce. Duhm overlooks altogether the very small territory which the law affected. A long day's walk would bring men from Jericho, from Hebron, from the borders of the Philistine country, and from Shechem and Samaria to Jerusalem. If Deuteronomy made a revolution, it must have been confined within the modest limits of substituting a whole for a half-day's journey to the Sanctuary.

Moreover it is a mistake to say that sacrifice at one central sanctuary "took religion away from the people," as Duhm says. If spiritual religion be meant, it ultimately brought religion more vitally home to them. For when the priestly system was fully carried out, the demands of household religion were met, as the post-exilic Psalms show, by the adoption of the practice of household prayer without reference to sacrifice, and finally by the institution of the synagogue. A more spiritual method of approach to God was substituted for a less spiritual in the remote places and in the homes of the people. And the public worship even gained. It became deeper, and more penetrated with a sense of the necessity of deliverance from sin. It is true, of course, that in the end Pharisaic legalism perverted the new forms of worship, as heathen externalism had perverted the old. But in neither case was the perversion a necessity. In both it was simply a manifestation of the materialistic tendency which dogs the footsteps of even the most spiritual religion, when it has to realise itself in the life of man. It is enough for the justification of the whole movement led by Josiah to say that it held the Judæan exiles together; that it kept alive in their hearts, as nothing else did, their faith in God and in their future; and that on their return it gave them the form which their institutions could most profitably take. Further, under the forms of religious and social life which this movement generated, the true, heartfelt piety which the prophets so mourned the want of became more common than ever it had been before.

The establishment of the central altar as the only one was the main object of this law; but there is much to be learned from the very terms in which this is expressed. They breathe the same love for man and sympathy with the poor which forms one of the most attractive characteristics of our book. The gracious bonds of family affection, the kindly feeling that should unite masters and servants, the helpfulness which ought to distinguish the conduct of the rich to the poor, and above all the cheerful enjoyment of the results of honest labour, are to be preserved and sanctified even in the ritual of sacrifice. "Thou shalt rejoice before Yahweh in all that thou puttest thine hand unto," is here the motto, if we may so speak, of religious service. That, indeed, is to be made the opportunity for the discharge of all humane and brotherly duties; and the religious life is at its highest when the worshipper rejoices himself, and shares and sheds abroad his joy upon others. The love of God is here most intimately blended with love of the brethren. Masters and servants, slaves and free, the high and the low, are to be reminded of their equal standing in the sight of God, by their common participation in the sacrificial meals; and the poorest are to be permitted an equal enjoyment of the luxuries of the rich in these solemn approaches to Yahweh. The Deuteronomist here reaches the highest stage of religious life, in that he shows himself in nowise afraid of human joy. As we have seen, he knows the value of austerity in religion. He is well enough aware that war against evil is not made with rose-water. But then he is equally far from the extreme of suspecting all affection not directly turned to God, of regarding natural gladness as a ruinous snare to the soul. This finely balanced, this just attitude to all aspects of life, is a most notable thing at this epoch in the history of the world, and considering the circumstances of the time it is little short of a marvel. It is true, of course, that the religion of Israel was always finely human. It could run into excesses, and was marked by many imperfections; but asceticism, the doctrine which holds pain and self-denial to be in themselves good, when it did intrude into Israel, always came from without. Nevertheless the heartiness and thoroughness with which all gracious human feelings and all kindly human relations are here taken up into religion is remarkable, even in the Old Testament. More, perhaps, than anything else in this book, it shows the sweetening and wholesome effect of demanding supreme love to God as man's first duty. "If any man come to Me and hate not his father and mother," says Christ, "he cannot be My disciple,"[73] and many purblind critics have found this to be a hard saying. But all who know men know, that when God in Christ is made so much the supreme object of love that even the most sacred human obligations seem to be disregarded in comparison, the human affection so thrust into the background is only made richer far than it otherwise could be.

CHAPTER XV
THE RELATION OF OLD TESTAMENT SACRIFICE TO CHRISTIANITY

But it may be asked, What is the relation of this Divinely sanctioned ritual law of sacrifice to our religion in its present phase? To that question various answers are being returned, and indeed it may be said that on this point almost all the main differences of Christians turn. The Church of Rome maintains in essence the sacerdotal view of the later Old Testament times, though in a spiritualised Christian shape, and to this the High Anglican view is a more or less pronounced return. The Protestant Churches, on the other hand, regard priests and sacrifices as anachronisms since the death of Christ. In that, for the most part, they regard the significance of sacrifice as being summed up and completed; and the present dispensation is for them the realisation in embryo of that which Old Testament saints looked forward to—a people of God, every true member of which is both priest and prophet, *i.e.* has free and unrestricted access to God, and is authorised and required to speak in His name. The interest of Protestant Christians, therefore, in priesthood and sacrifice in the Old Testament sense, though very great and enduring, has no connection with the continuation of sacrifice. They look upon the Old Testament ritual as wholly obsolete now. It was simply a stage in the religious development of the chosen people, and as such it has no claim to be continued among Christians.

By a curious allegorical process, however, some devout Protestants keep alive their interest in Old Testament ritual by finding in it an elaborate symbolism covering the whole field of evangelical theology. But this revivification of the old law is too arbitrary and subjective, as well as too improbable, to have an abiding place in Christianity. It is, moreover, useless for the guidance of life; for all that is thus ingeniously put into the Levitical ordinances is found more clearly and directly expressed elsewhere. The amount of religious symbolism in the earlier stages of Israelite religion is small, and very simple and direct. Even in the most elaborate parts of the Levitical legislation, *e.g.* in the directions regarding the Tabernacle, the purposely allegorical element is kept within comparatively narrow limits; and we may boldly say that the mind which delights in finding spiritual mysteries in every detail of the sacrificial ritual is Rabbinical rather than Christian. On the other hand we need not enter upon a discussion of the view held by "Modern" or Broad Church theologians and by Unitarians, that sacrifice was merely a heathen form taken over into Mosaism, that it had no special significance there, and that the ideas connected with it have absolutely no place in enlightened Christian theology. The Christianity which attaches no sacrificial signification to the death of Christ has, so far as I know, never shown itself to be a type of religion able to create a future, and it is only with types of Christianity that do and can live we have to do. Our question here therefore is limited to this, Which of the two types of view, the Roman Catholic or the Protestant, is truest to the Old Testament teaching?

Externally, perhaps, the evidence seems to favour the Roman Catholic position; for the prophets either directly say, or imply, that sacrifice shall be restored with new purity and power in the Messianic time. This is so patent a fact that it led Edward Irving to say that it was the Old Testament economy that should abide, and that of the New Testament which should pass away. But the inner progress and development of Old Testament religion is quite as decisively on the other side. As we have seen, Old Testament piety had at the beginning almost no recognised expression save in connection with sacrifice, and the Exile first trained the people to faithfulness to God without it, sowing the seed of a religious life largely separate from the sacrificial ritual. Then the ordinance demanding sacrifice at one central altar, which, though introduced by Deuteronomy, was made the exclusive law only by the post-exilic community, furthered the growth of these germs, so that they produced the synagogue system. This completed the severance of the ordinary daily religion of the bulk of the people from sacrificial ritual, so far as that was attained within the limits of Judaism, and prepared the way for Pauline Christianity, in which all allegiance to ritual Judaism is cast off. Now, as between the external and internal evidence, there can be little doubt that the latter has by far the greater weight, especially as the external evidence can, perfectly well, be read in a different sense. The Old Testament promises that sacrifice should be restored may be held to have been fulfilled by the sacrificial death of Christ, which completed and filled up all that had gone before. In that case the evidence that sacrifice and ritual are now obsolete for Christians is left standing alone, and the Protestant view is justified.

And the case for this view is strengthened immeasurably by observing that the modern sacerdotalism has taken up as essential what was the main vice of sacrificial worship in the old economy. That was, as we have seen, the tendency to rest on the mere performance of the external rite, without reference to the disposition of the heart or even to conduct. Rivers of oil and hecatombs of victims were thought sufficient to meet all possible demands on God's part, and against this the polemic of the prophets is unceasing. Now in almost all modern sacerdotalism the doctrine of the efficacy of sacraments duly administered, apart from right dispositions in either him who administers them or in him who receives them, has been affirmed. It is not now, as it was in the "old time," an evil tendency which had to be assiduously fought against, but which could not be overcome. It is openly incorporated in the orthodox teaching, and is distinctly provided for in the ideal of Christian worship. That marks a considerable falling away from the prophetic ideal: it can hardly be regarded as the appointed end of that great religious movement which the prophets dominated and directed for so long. The teaching of Deuteronomy certainly is, that wherever mere external acts are supposed to have power to secure entrance into the spiritual world of life and peace, there the character of God is misconceived and religion degraded. What it demands is the inward and spiritual allegiance of faithful men to God. What it depicts as the essence of religious life is a set of the whole nature Godward, as deep and irresistible as the set of the tides—

> "Such a tide as moving seems asleep,
> Too full for sound and foam."

Under no sacerdotal system can that view be unreservedly accepted, and therein lies the condemnation of every such system. So far as it is allowed to prevail, the force of the prophetic polemic has to be ignored or evaded, and in greater or less degree the same spiritual decay which the prophets mourned over in Israel must appear.

But it is not only where trust in the mere *opus operatum* is theoretically justified that it makes its baleful presence felt. It may surreptitiously creep in where the door is theoretically shut against it. The tendency is very deep-seated in human nature; and many evangelical preachers, who repudiate all sacramentarianism, and throw the full emphasis of Christian religious life upon grace and faith, yet bring back again in subtler shape that very thing which they have rejected. For example, instead of the reception of the sacrament at the hands of ordained ministers, a man's acceptance with God is sometimes made to depend upon a declaration of belief that Christ has died for him, or that he has been redeemed and saved by Christ. Wherever such statements are forced upon men, there is a tendency to assume that a decisive step in the spiritual life is taken by the mere utterance of them. The motives which actuate the utterer are taken for granted; the existence of such a set of the spiritual nature to God as Deuteronomy demands is supposed to be proved by the mere spoken words; and men who cannot or will not say such things glibly are unchurched without mercy. What is that but the *opus operatum* in its most offensive shape? But in whatever shape it appears, the Deuteronomic demand for love to God, with the heart and soul and strength, as essential to all true spiritual service and sacrifice, condemns it. Love to God and men are the main things in true religion. All else is subordinate and secondary. Sacrifice and ritual without these are dead forms. That is the Deuteronomic teaching, and by it, once for all, the true relation of the cultus to the life is fixed.

Nevertheless the priestly and sacrificial system of the Old Testament has even for Christians a present importance, for it is an adumbration of that which was to be done in the death of Christ. It has an unspeakable value, when rightly used, as an object-lesson in the elements which are essential to a right approach to a Holy God on the part of sinful men. Even in heathenism there were such foreshadowings; and nothing is more fitted to exalt our views of the Divine wisdom than to trace, as we can now do, the ways in which man's seekings after God, even beyond the bounds of the chosen people, took forms that were afterwards absorbed and justified in the redeeming work of our Blessed Lord. For example, Professor Robertson Smith says of certain ancient heathen piacular sacrifices, "The dreadful sacrifice is performed, not with savage joy, but with awful sorrow, and in the mystic sacrifices the deity himself suffers with and for the sins of his people and lives again in their new life." Now if we admit that he is not unduly importing into these sacrifices ideas which are really foreign to them, surely awe is the only adequate emotion wherewith a believer in Christ can meet such a strange prophecy, in the lowest religion, of that which is deepest in the highest.[74] The sacrificial system in general was founded, in part at least, on belief in the possibility and desirability of communion with God. In the sacrificial feasts this was supposed to be attained, and the essential religious needs of mankind found expression in much of the ritual. If the death of the god, and his returning to life again in his people found a prominent place in piacular sacrifices in various lands, that suggests that in some dim way even heathen men had learned that sin cannot be removed and forgiven without cost to God as well as to man, and that communion in suffering as well as in joy is a necessary element of life with God. The human heart, Divinely biassed, asserted itself in effort after such association with Deity, and in the feeling that sin was that element in life which it would make the highest demand upon the Divine love to set effectively aside.

But if such preparation for the fulness of the time was going on in heathenism, if the mind and heart of man, driven forward by Divinely ordered experience and its own needs, could produce such forecasts in the ritual of heathen religion, we surely must admit that the religious ritual in Israel had an even more intimate connection with that which was to come. For we claim that in guiding the destinies of Israel God was, in an exceptional manner, revealing Himself, that among them He established the true religion, unfolded it in their history, and prepared as nowhere else for the advent of Him who should make real and objective the union of God and man. Here consequently, if anywhere, we should expect to find the permanent factors in religion recognised even in the forms of worship, and the less permanent allowed to fall away. We should also expect the ritual of the cultus to grow in depth of meaning with time, and that it would more and more recognise the moral and spiritual elements in life. Finally, we should expect that it would be the parent of conceptions rising above and beyond itself, and more fully consonant with the revelation given by Christ than anything in heathenism.

Now all these expectations would seem to have been fulfilled; and it is reasonable to assume that those sacrificial ideas which corresponded to the deepened consciousness of sin, and synchronised apparently with the decay of Israel's political independence, are rightly applied to the elucidation of the meaning of Christ's death. Of course mistakes may be and have been made in the application of this principle; the most common being that of forcing every detail of the imperfect and temporary provision into the interpretation of the perfect and eternal. Sometimes, too, the significance of the life and coming of Christ are obscured by a too exclusive attention to His sacrificial death. But the principle in itself must be sound, if Christianity is in any sense to be regarded as the completion and full development of the Old Testament religion. Besides the immediate significance of sacrifice which the worshippers perceived and by which they were edified, there was another significance which belonged to it as a step in the long progress which had been marked out for this people in the Divine purpose. Regarded from that standpoint, the sacrifices, and the ritual connected with them, had a meaning for the future also, were in fact typical of the final sacrifice which would need to be offered only once for all. How much of this was understood by the men of ancient Israel we have no means of knowing. Some, doubtless, had a faint perception of it; but at its clearest it was probably more a dissatisfaction with what they had, leading them to look for some better sacrifice, than any more definite understanding. But what they only dimly guessed was, as we can now see, the inner meaning of all; and it is perfectly legitimate to use both the provisional and the perfected revelations to explain each other. On these grounds the New Testament freely makes use of the ancient ritual to bring out the full significance of the sacrifice of Christ.

No doubt a different view has to be reckoned with. Many say that the whole of this typical reference is a begging of the question. In the infancy of mankind sacrifice was a natural way of expressing adoration and of seeking the favour of the gods. In the heathen world it reached its highest manifestation in those piacular sacrifices of which Robertson Smith speaks, but which nevertheless were merely an outgrowth of Totemism. In Israel sacrifice was taken up by the religion of Yahweh and embodied in it. The spiritual forces which were at work in that nation used it as a means whereby to express themselves; and when Christ came to complete the revelation, His purely ethical and spiritual work was unavoidably expressed in sacrificial terms. But that is no guarantee that the essential thing in the work of Christ was sacrifice. On the contrary, the sacrificial language used about it is of no real importance. It is simply the natural and unavoidable form of expression, in that place and at that time, for any spiritual deliverance. In short, had there been really nothing sacrificial in the death of Christ, the religious meaning and significance of it would have been expressed in sacrificial language, for no other was available. Consequently the presence of such language in the New Testament does not prove that the sacrificial meaning belongs to its main and permanent significance. The sacrificial idea, on this view of things, belongs, both in Israel and in heathenism, to the elements which Christianity superseded and did away with; and it is consequently an anachronism to bring it in to explain and elucidate anything done or taught under this new dispensation.

But such a view is singularly narrow, and unjust to the past. It surely is more honouring to both God and man to suppose that the capital religious ideas of the race, those ideas which have been everywhere present and have been seen to deepen and refine with every advance man has made, have permanent value. Moreover, on any view, it is probable that in them the essential religious needs of human nature have found expression. If so, we should expect that they would in the end be met, and that the perfect religion, when it did come, would not ignore but satisfy the demand which the nature of man and the providence of God had originated and combined to strengthen. Further, it is the very essence of the Scriptural view of Christ that He perfected and carried to their highest power all the essential features in the religious constitution of Israel. He *was* indeed the true Israel, and all Israel's tasks fell to Him. As Prophet, Priest, and Messianic King alike, He excelled all His predecessors, who were what they were only because they had, in their degree, done part of the work which He was to come to finish. Apart from the religion of the Old Testament, therefore, Christ is unintelligible, and that, in turn, without Him, has neither a progress nor a goal. Belief in a Divine direction of the world would in itself be sufficient to forbid the separation of one from the other. If so, it will follow that the sacrificial idea is essential to the interpretation of our Lord's work. That idea grew in complexity with the growth of the higher religion. It was at its deepest when religious thought and feeling had done its most perfect work; and on every principle of evolution we should expect that, instead of disappearing at the next stage, it would, though transformed, be more influential than ever. It is so if Christ's death is regarded from the point of view of sacrifice; whereas, if that is laid aside like a worn-out garment, it can never have been anything anywhere but an excrescence and a superstition. That has not been so; the essential ideas connected with sacrifice, and forgiveness by means of it, were lessons Divinely taught in the childhood of the world, to prepare men to understand the Divinest mystery of history when it should be manifested to the world.

CHAPTER XVI
LAWS AGAINST IDOLATROUS
ACTS AND CUSTOMS

Deut. xiii, xiv

Having thus set forth the law which was to crown and complete the long resistance of faithful Israel to idolatry, our author goes on to prohibit and to decree punishment for any action likely to lead to the worship of false gods. He absolutely forbids any inquiry into the religions of the Canaanites. "Take heed to thyself that thou inquire not after their gods, saying, How do these nations serve their gods? even so will I do likewise." All that was acceptable to Yahweh was included in the law of Israel, and beyond that they were on no account to go in their worship. "What thing soever I command you, that shall ye observe to do: thou shalt not add thereto nor diminish from it." But it should be observed that the inquiry here forbidden has nothing in common with the scientific inquiries of Comparative Religion in our time. Curiosity of that kind, supported by the motive of discovering how religion had grown, was unknown at that early age of the world, probably everywhere, certainly in Israel. The only curiosity powerful enough to result in action then was that which tried to learn how the ritual might be made more potent in its influence over Yahweh by gathering attractive features from every known religion. That was one of the distinguishing characteristics of Manasseh's reign. The Canaanite religions, the religions of Egypt and Assyria, were all laid under contribution; and wherever there was a feature which promised additional power with God or the gods, that was eagerly adopted. Israel had lost faith in Yahweh, owing to the successes of Assyria. In unbelieving terror men were wildly grasping at any means of safety. They worshipped Yahweh, lest He should do them harm, but they joined with Him the gods of their foes, to secure if possible their favour also. Inquiry into other religions, with the intent of adopting something from them which would make either Yahweh or the strange gods, or both, propitious to them, was rife. Like the heathen population who had been transported by Assyria into the territory of the ten tribes, men "feared Yahweh, and served their graven images." All that is here sternly condemned, and Judah is taught to look only to the Divine commands for effective means of approach to their God. The prohibition, therefore, does not import mere fanatical opposition to knowledge. It is a necessary practical measure of defence against idolatry; and only those can disapprove of it who are incapable of estimating the value which the true religion in its Old Testament shape had and has for the world. To preserve that was the high and unique calling of Israel. Any narrowness, real or supposed, which this great task imposed upon that people, is amply compensated for by their guardianship of the spiritual life of mankind.

But if inquiry into lower religions was forbidden, there could be nothing but the sternest condemnation for those who had inquired, and then endeavoured to seduce the chosen people. Deuteronomy, therefore, takes three typical cases—first, seduction by one who was respected because of high religious office, then seduction by one who had influence because of close bonds of natural affection, and lastly that of a community which would be likely to have influence by force of numbers—and gives inexorably stern directions how such evil is to be met. There can be little doubt that the cases are not imaginary. In the evil days which the Deuteronomist had fallen upon they were probably of frequent occurrence, and they are, consequently, provided against as real and present evils. Naturally the writer takes the most difficult case first. If an Israelite prophet, with all his religious prestige as a confidant of Yahweh, and still more with the prestige of successful prediction in his favour, shall attempt to lead men to join other gods to Yahweh in their worship—for that and not rejection of Yahweh for the exclusive service of strange gods is almost certainly meant—then they were not to listen to him. They were to fall back upon the original principle of the Mosaic teaching as it was restated in Deuteronomy, that Yahweh alone was to be their God. Some lynx-eyed critics have discovered here the cloven hoof of legalism. They think they see here the free spirit of prophecy, to which untrammelled initiative was the very breath of life, subjected to the bondage of written law, and so doomed to death. But probably such a mood is unnecessarily elegiac. It is not to written law that prophecy is subjected here. It is the actual life-principle of Yahwism in its simplest form which prophecy is required to respect; that is, ultimately, it is called upon simply to respect itself. Its own existence depended upon faithfulness to Yahweh. If it had a mission at all, it was to proclaim Him and to declare His character. If it had a distinction which severed it from mere heathen soothsaying, it was that it had been raised by the inspiration of Yahweh into the region of "the true, the good, the eternal," and its whole power lay in its keeping open the communication with that region. It is therefore only the law of its own inner being to which prophecy is here bound; and the people are instructed that, whatever reputation or even supernatural power it might have attained to, it was to be obeyed only when true to itself and to the faith. Nothing was to make men stagger from that foundation. Not even the working of miracles was to mislead the people, for only on the plane of Yahweh's revelation had even miracle any worth. This is the sound and wholesome doctrine of true prophecy, and other utterances on the subject in our book must be taken in conjunction with it. Religious faithfulness, not foretelling, is the essence of it, and by that the prophet is to be inexorably judged. If any prophet, therefore, leads men to strange gods, his character and his powers only make him more dangerous and his punishment more inexorable. "That prophet, or that dreamer of dreams, shall be put to death." He comes under the ban. "So shalt thou put away the evil from the midst of thee."

Similarly, when family ties and family affection are perverted to be instruments of seduction, they are to be disregarded, just as religious reputation and miraculous power were to be set aside. If a brother, or a son, or a daughter, or a wife, or a friend, shall secretly entice a man to "serve other gods," then he shall not only not yield, but he must slay the tempter. It is characteristic of the Deuteronomist that, by the qualifications of the various relationships he mentions, he should show his sympathy and his insight into the depths of both family affection and friendship. "Thy brother, the son of thy mother," "the wife of thy bosom," "the friend which is as thine own soul," even these, near as they are to thee, must be sacrificed if they are false to Israel and to Israel's God. Nay more, "Thou shalt surely kill him; thine hand shall be upon him to put him to death, and afterwards the hand of all the people, and thou shalt stone him with stones that he die." Upon him, too, the ban shall be laid.

Nor, finally, shall their multitude shield those who suffered themselves to be perverted. If a city should have been led away by sons of Belial, i.e. by worthless men, to worship strange gods, then the whole city was to be put to the ban. It was to be immediately stormed, every living creature put to death, and all the spoil of it burnt "unto Yahweh their God"; and the ruins were to be a "mound for ever"—that is, a place accursed. Only on these terms could Yahweh be turned away from the fierceness of His anger at such treason and unfaithfulness among His people. The Canaanites had been condemned to death that their idolatries and vices might not corrupt the spiritual faith of Israel. There was no other way, if the treasure which had been committed to this nation was to be preserved. As Robertson Smith has said, "Experience shows that primitive religious beliefs are practically indestructible except by the destruction of the race in which they are engrained." But if so, it was perhaps even more necessary that idolaters within Israel should be also extirpated. We may think the punishment harsh; and our modern doctrines concerning toleration can by no ingenuity be brought into harmony with it. But the times were fierce, and men were not easily restrained. In more civilised communities excessive severity in punishment defeats itself, for it enlists sympathy on the side of the criminal. But among a people like the Hebrews, probably severity succeeded where mercy would have been flouted. In India our administrators have had to confess that the horrible recklessness and severity of punishment in the Mahratta states of the old type suppressed crime as the infinitely more just and better organised but milder British police organisations could not then do. "Probably the success of barbarous methods of repressing crime is best explained by their origin in and close connection with a primitive state of society. Because punishments were inhuman, they struck terror where no other motive would deter from crime."[75] In other and Scriptural words, the hardness of men's hearts made such harshness unavoidable.

Taking the whole of this thirteenth chapter into consideration, therefore, we see how high and severe were the demands which Old Testament religion, as taught in Deuteronomy, made upon its votaries. It presupposes on the part of the people an insight into the fundamentally spiritual nature of their faith entirely unobscured by ritual and sacrifice. They were expected to pass beyond the teachings of accredited spiritual guides, beyond even the evidence of supernatural power, and to test all by the moral and spiritual truth, once delivered to them by prophet and by miracle, and now a secure possession. Spiritual truth received and lived by is thus set above everything else as the test and the judge of all. Other things were merely ladders by which men had been brought to the truth in religion. Once there, nothing should move them; and any further guidance which purported to come from even the heavenly places was to be tried and accepted, only if it corroborated the fundamental truths already received and attested by experience in actual life. Loyalty to ascertained truth, that is, is greater than loyalty to teachers, or to that which seems to be supernatural; and the chief power for which a prophet is to be reverenced is not that by which he gives a true forecast of the future, but that which impels him to speak the truth about God.

Even at this day, and for believers in Christ, after all the teaching and experience of eighteen Christian centuries, this is a high, almost an unattainable, standard to set up. Even to-day it is thought an advanced position that miracles as a security for truth are subordinate and inferior to the light of the truth itself as exhibited in the lives of faithful men. Yet that is precisely what the Deuteronomist teaches. He has no doubt about miracles. He regards them as being Divinely sent, even when they might be made use of to mislead; but he calls upon his people to disregard them if they seem to point towards unfaithfulness to God. Their supreme trust is to be that Yahweh cannot deny Himself. If he seem to do so by giving the sanction of miracle to teaching which denies Him, that is only to prove men, to know whether they love Yahweh their God with all their heart and with all their soul. The inner certainty of those who have had communion with Yahweh is to override everything else. "Whosoever loves God with a pure heart," says Calvin, "is armed with the invincible power of the Divine Spirit, that he should not be ensnared by falsehoods."[76] This has always been the confidence of religious reformers who have had real power. Luther, for example, took his stand upon the New Testament and his own personal experience; and by what he *knew* of God he judged all that the most venerable tradition, and the authority of the Church, and the examples of saintly men claimed to set forth as binding upon him. "Here stand I: I can do no other: God help me." He felt that he had hold of the heart of the revelation of God as it was made in Christ, and he rejected, without scruple, whatever in itself or in its results contradicted or obscured that. Inspired and upheld by this consciousness, he faced a hostile world and a raging Church with equanimity. It is always so that abuses have been removed and innovations that are hurtful warded off in the Church of God.

But there is a difficulty here. As against the historical examples which show how much good may be wrought by this unshaken mind when accompanied by adequate insight, many, perhaps even more, instances can be adduced where unbending assertion of individual conviction has led to fanaticism and irreligion; or, as has even more frequently been the case, has blinded men's eyes, and made them resist with immovable obstinacy teachings on which the future of religion depended. On the altar of uncompromising fidelity to the letter of the faith delivered to them, men in all ages have offered up love and gentleness and fairness, and that open mind to which alone God can speak. How then can they be sure, when they disregard their teachers and defy even signs from heaven, that they are really only holding up the banner of faith in an evil day, and are not hardening themselves against God? The answer is that, since the matter concerns the spiritual life, there are no clear, mechanical dividing lines which can be pointed out and respected. Nothing but spiritual insight can teach a man what the absolutely essential and the less essential elements of religion are. Nothing else can give him that power of distinguishing great things from small which here is of such cardinal importance. Probably the nearest approach to effective guidance may be found in this principle, that when all points in a man's faith are to him equally important, when he frets as much in regard to divergence from his own religious practices as in regard to denial of the faith altogether, he must certainly be wrong. Such a temper must necessarily resist all change; and since progress is as much a law in the religious life as in any other, it must be found at times fighting against God. Otherwise, stagnation would be the test of truth, and the principles of the Christian faith would be branded as so shallow and so easily exhausted, that their whole significance could be seized and set forth at once by the generation which heard the apostles. That was far from being the case. The post-apostolic Church, for instance, did not understand St. Paul. It turned rather to the simpler ideas of the mass of Christians, and elaborated its doctrines almost entirely on that basis. During the centuries since then many lessons of unspeakable value have been learned by the Christian world. The Church has been enriched by the thoughts and teachings of multitudes of men of genius. The providential chances and changes of all these centuries have immensely widened and deepened Christian experience. Stagnation consequently cannot be made the test of Christian truth. We must be open to new light on the meaning of Divine revelation, or we fail altogether, as the Israelites would have done had they refused to accept the teaching of any prophet after the first. This much may, however, be said on the affirmative side, that when a man has thoughtfully and prayerfully decided that the central element of his faith is attacked, he cannot but resist, and if he is faithful he will resist in the spirit of the passage we are discussing. His assertion of his individual conviction, even if it be mistaken, will do little harm. Time will be in favour of the truth. But mistake will be rare, indeed, when men are taught to assert in this manner only the things by which the soul lives, when only the actual channels of communion with God are thus defended to the uttermost. These any thoughtful patient man who looks for and yields to the guidance of the Holy Spirit of Christ will almost infallibly recognise, and by these he will take his stand, for he can do no other.

But precautions against idolatry are not exhausted by the war declared upon men who might attempt to lead the Israelite into evil. Besides insidious human enemies, there were also insidious customs originating in heathenism, and still redolent of idolatry even when they were severed from any overt connection with it. Ancient rituals, ancient superstitions, hateful remnants of bloodthirsty pagan rites, were being revived in the Deuteronomist's day on every hand, because faith in the higher religion that had superseded them had been shaken. Like streams from hidden reservoirs suddenly reopened, idolatrous and magical practices were overflowing the land, and were finding in popular customs, harmless in better days, channels for their return into the life of those who had formerly risen above them.

Some of these were more hurtful than others, and two are singled out at the beginning of chapter xiv. as those which a people holy unto Yahweh must specially avoid: "Ye shall not cut yourselves, nor make any baldness between your eyes for the dead." The grounds for avoiding these practices are first given, and we may probably assume that they are the grounds also for the other enactments which follow. They are these: "Ye are the children of Yahweh your God," and "Thou art a holy people unto Yahweh thy God, and Yahweh hath chosen thee to be a peculiar people unto Himself, out of all peoples that are upon the face of the earth." The last of these reasons is common to the Exodus code with Deuteronomy, and comes even more prominently into view in the Levitical law. Just as Yahweh alone was to be their God, they alone were to be Yahweh's people, and they were to be holy to Him, *i.e.* were to separate themselves to Him; for in its earliest meaning to be holy is simply to be separate to Yahweh. This whole dispensation of law, that is, was meant to separate the people of Israel from the idolatrous world, and in this separation we have the key to much that would otherwise be hard to comprehend. Looked at from the point of view of revelation, petty details about tonsure, about clean and unclean animals, and so on, seem incredibly unworthy; and many have said to themselves, How can the God of the whole earth have really been the author of laws dealing with such trivialities? But when we regard these as provisions intended to secure the separation of the chosen people, they assume quite another aspect. Then we see that they had to be framed in contrast to the idolatries of the surrounding nations, and are not meant to have further spiritual or moral significance.

But the first reason given is a higher and more important one, which occurs here for the first time in Deuteronomy: "Ye are the children of Yahweh your God." In heathen lands such a title of honour was common, because physically most worshippers of false gods were regarded as their children. But in Israel, where such physical sonship would have been rejected with horror as impairing the Divine holiness, the spiritual sonship was asserted of the individual much more slowly. In Yahweh's command to Moses to threaten Pharaoh with the death of his firstborn son, and in Hosea xi. 1, Israel collectively is called Yahweh's firstborn and His son. In Hosea i. 10 it is prophesied that in the Messianic time, "in the place where it was said unto them, Ye are not My people, it shall be said unto them, Ye are the sons of the living God." But here for the first time this high title is bestowed upon the actual individual Israelites. It was perhaps implied in the Deuteronomist's view of God's fatherly treatment of the nation in the desert, and still more in his demand for the love of the individual heart. Yet only here is it brought plainly forth as a ground for the regulation of life according to Yahweh's commands. Each son of Israel is also a son of God; and by none of his acts or habits should he bring disgrace upon his spiritual Father. Likeness to God is expected and demanded of him. It is his function in the world to represent Him, to give expression to the Divine character in all his ways. This is the Israelite's high calling, and the religious application of *noblesse oblige* to such matters as follow, gives a dignity and importance to all of them such as in their own nature they could hardly claim.

"Ye shall not cut yourselves, nor make any baldness between your eyes for the dead." Israel was not to express grief for the dead in these ways, first because that was the custom of other nations, and secondly still more because the origin and meaning of such rites was idolatrous, and as such altogether unworthy of Yahweh's sons. "Both," says Robertson Smith, "occur not only in mourning, but in the worship of the gods, and belong to the sphere of heathen superstition."[77] Elsewhere he explains the cutting of themselves to be the making of a blood covenant with the dead, just as the priests of Baal in their worship tried to get their god to come to their help by making a covenant of blood with him at his altar.[78] This naturally tended to bring in the superstitions of necromancy, and opened the way also for the worship of the dead. Many traces of its previous existence among the Israelite tribes are to be found in the Scriptures; and the probability is that as ancestor-worship ruled the life and shaped the thoughts of Greeks and Romans till Christianity appeared, so Yahwism alone had broken its power over Israel. But such superstitions die hard, and in the general recrudescence of almost forgotten forms of heathenism at this time, this cult may very well have been reasserting itself. As for the shaving of the front part of the head, that had a precisely similar import. "It had exactly the same sense as the offering of the mourner's blood."[79] "When the hair of the living is deposited with the dead, and the hair of the dead remains with the living, a permanent bond of connection unites the two."

The prohibition as food of the animals and birds called "unclean" was another measure obviously of the same nature as the prohibition of heathen mourning practices; but in its details it is more difficult to explain. Probably, however, it was a more potent instrument of separation than any other. In India to-day the gulf between the flesh-eater and the orthodox vegetarian Hindu is utterly impassable; and in the east of Europe and in Palestine, where the Jewish restrictions as to food are still regarded, the orthodox Jew is separated from all Gentiles as by a wall. In travelling he never appears at meals with his fellow-travellers. All the food he requires he carries with him in a basket; and at every place where he stops it is the duty of the Jewish community to supply him with proper food, that he may not be tempted to defile himself with anything unclean. But it is very difficult for us now to bring the individual prohibitions under one head, and it seems impossible to explain them from any one point of view.

Some of the animals and birds prohibited were probably, then, animals eaten in connection with idolatrous feasts by the neighbouring heathen. Isa. lxv. 4 shows that swine's flesh was eaten at sacrificial meals by idolaters, and from the expression "broth of abominable things is in their vessels" it is clear that the flesh of other animals was so used. All these would necessarily be prohibited to Israel; but beyond a few, such as the swine, which was sacrificed to Tammuz or Adonis, and the mouse and the wild ass, we have no means of knowing what they were. That this is a *vera causa* of such prohibitions is shown by the facts mentioned by Professor Robertson Smith, that "Simeon Stylites forbade his Saracen converts to eat the flesh of the camel, which was the chief element in the sacrificial meals of the Arabs, and our own prejudice against the use of horse-flesh is a relic of an old ecclesiastical prohibition framed at the time when the eating of such food was an act of worship to Odin." The very ancient and stringent prohibition of blood as an article of diet is probably to be accounted for in this way also. Blood was eaten at heathen sacrificial feasts; without other reason that would be sufficient. These are the general lines which must have determined the list of clean animals in the view of the lawgiver, since he brings them in under the head of idolatry and under the two general grounds we have discussed (p. 289, *supra*).

Jewish writers, however, especially since Maimonides, have regarded these prohibitions as aiming primarily at sanitary ends, and as a proof of their efficacy have adduced the unusually high average health of the Jews, and their almost complete exemption from certain classes of disease. No such point of view is suggested in the Scriptures themselves, for it would surely be rather farfetched to class possible disease as an infringement of the holiness demanded of Israel, or as a thing unworthy of Yahweh's sons. Nevertheless a general view of the list of clean animals here given would support the idea that sanitary considerations also had *something* to do with the classification. The practical effect of the rule laid down is to exclude all the *carnivora* among quadrupeds, and so far as we can interpret the nomenclature, the *raptores* among birds.[80] "Amongst fish, those which were allowed contain unquestionably the most wholesome varieties." Further, the nations of antiquity which developed such categories of clean and unclean animals seem in the main to have taken the same line. The ground of this probably is the natural disgust with which unclean feeders are always regarded. Animals and birds especially which feed, or may be supposed to feed, on carrion, are everywhere disliked, and as a rule they are unsuitable for food. Grass-eating animals, on the other hand, are always regarded as clean. Scaleless fish, too, are generally more or less slimy to the touch, and with them reptiles are altogether forbidden. All this seems to show that a natural sentiment of disgust, for whatever reason felt, was active in the selection of the animals marked unclean by men of every race. The pre-Mosaic customary law on this subject would, of course, have this characteristic in common with similar laws of primitive nations. When the worship of Yahweh was introduced, most of this would be taken over, only such modifications being introduced as the higher religion demanded. In some main elements, therefore, the Mosaic law on this subject would be a repetition of what is to be found elsewhere. Hence a general tendency to health may be expected; for besides the guidance which healthy disgust would give, a long experience must also have been registered in such laws. The influence of them in promoting health has recently been acknowledged by the *Lancet*; and though that reason for observing them is not mentioned in Scripture, we may view it as a proof that the Jewish legislators were under an influence which brought them, perhaps even when they knew it not, into relation with what was wholesome in the practices and customs of their place and time.

Beyond these three reasons for the laws regarding food, all is the wildest speculation. If other reasons underlie these laws, we cannot now ascertain what they were. For a time it was the custom to ascribe the Jewish laws to Persian influence, though from the nature of the case such laws must have been part of the heritage of Israel from pre-Mosaic time. Even to-day Jewish writers ascribe them to the evil effect which bad food has upon the soul, either by infecting it with the characteristics of the unclean beasts, or by rendering it impenetrable to good influences.[81] But, as usual, it is the allegorical interpreters who carry off the palm. Animals that chew the cud were to be eaten, because they symbolised those who "read, mark, learn, and inwardly digest" the Divine law: those which divide the hoof are examples of those who distinguish between good and bad actions; and in the ostrich one interpreter finds an analogue to the bad commentators who pervert the words of Holy Scripture.

Hitherto in chapter xiv. we have been dealing with material to which a parallel can be found only in the small code of laws contained in Lev. xvii.-xxvi., commonly called the Law of Holiness, and in the Priestly Code.[82] But the two remaining directions regarding food, which are contained in the twenty-first verse are parallel to prohibitions in the Law of the Covenant. The first, "Ye shall not eat of anything that dieth of itself ... for thou art an holy people unto Yahweh thy God," is parallel to Exod. xxii. 31. "And ye shall be holy men unto Me: therefore ye shall not eat any flesh that is torn of beasts in the field," and to Lev. xvii. 15, "Every soul that eateth that which dieth of itself, or that which is torn of beasts, whether he be homeborn or a stranger, he shall wash his clothes, and bathe himself in water, and be unclean until the evening." The ground for prohibiting such food, was, of course, that the blood was in it. But there is a divergence between the parallel laws, which is seen clearly when we take into account the destination of the flesh of the animal so dying. In Exodus it is said, "To the dogs shall ye cast it." In Deuteronomy the command is, "To the stranger within thy gates ye shall give it, and he shall eat of it, or ye may sell it unto a foreigner." In Leviticus it is taken for granted that an Israelite and also a stranger may eat either of the *nebhelah*, that which dieth of itself, or the *terephah*, that which is torn; and if either do so it is prescribed only that he should wash, and should be unclean until the evening.

Here, therefore, we have one of the cases in which the traditional hypothesis—that the Law of the Covenant was given at Sinai when Israel arrived there, the laws of the Priestly Code probably not many weeks after, and the code of Deuteronomy only thirty-eight or thirty-nine years later, but before the laws had come fully into effect by the occupation of Canaan— raises a difficulty. Why should the Sinaitic law say that *terephah* is not to be eaten by any one, but cast to the dogs, and the Levitical law in so short a time after make the eating of that and *nebhelah* mere cause of subordinate uncleanness to both Israelite and stranger, while Deuteronomy permits the Israelite either to give the *nebhelah* to the stranger that he may eat it, or to make it an article of traffic with the foreigner? Keil's explanation is certainly feasible, that in Exodus we have the law, in Leviticus the provision for accidental, or perhaps wilful, disobedience of it under the pressure of hunger, while in Deuteronomy we have a permission to sell, lest on the plea of waste the law might be ignored. But the position of the "*gēr*," or stranger, is not accounted for. In Leviticus he is bound to the worship of Yahweh, and can no more eat *nebhelah* or *terephah* than the native Israelite can, while in Deuteronomy he is on a lower stage than the Israelite as regards ceremonial cleanness, and much on the same level as the *nokhri*, the foreigner, who in Deuteronomy is dealt with as an inferior, not bound to the same scrupulosity as the Israelite (Deut. xv. 3, 23, 29). There does not appear to be any explanation of such a change in less than forty years; more especially as the moment at which the change would on that hypothesis be made was precisely the moment when the stranger was about for the first time to become an important element in Israelite life. If, on the other hand, the order of the codes be Exodus, Deuteronomy, Leviticus, then the Exodus law, which does not consider the stranger, would suit the earliest stage of Israel's history, when the stranger would generally be a spy. Later, he crept into Israelite life, and gradually received more and more consideration; especially in the days of Solomon, when the Chronicler estimates the number of the strangers at over a hundred and fifty thousand. But he was not recognised at that stage as fully bound to all an Israelite's duties, or as possessed of all an Israelite's privileges, and that is precisely the position he occupies in Deuteronomy. In the Priestly Code, however, at a time when the stranger had practically become a proselyte, the ideal Kingdom of God includes the "stranger," and gives him a position which differs little from that of the homeborn. That would make these different laws answer to different periods of Israel's history, and would coincide with what has been otherwise found to be the order of Israel's legal development.

The second prohibition, which runs parallel to what we find in Exodus, is the somewhat enigmatical one that a kid should not be sodden in its mother's milk. What it was in this act which made it seem necessary to issue such a command cannot now be ascertained with any certainty. Most probably it was connected in some way with heathen ceremonies, perhaps at a harvest feast; for, as we have seen, it is a ruling motive throughout all this section that the Israelites should reject everything which among their neighbours was connected with idolatry.

CHAPTER XVII
THE SPEAKERS FOR GOD—I. THE KING

Deut. xvii. 14-20

In approaching the main section of the legislation it will be necessary, in accordance with the expository character of the series to which this volume belongs, to abandon the consecutive character of the comment. It would lead us too far into archæology to discuss the meaning and origin of all the legal provisions which follow. Moreover nothing short of an extensive commentary would do them justice, and for our purpose we must endeavour to group the prescriptions of the code, and discuss them so. As it stands there is no arrangement traceable. So utterly without order is it, that it can hardly be thought that it is in the exact shape in which it left its author's hands. Transpositions and misplacements must, one thinks, have taken place to some extent. We are thus left free to make our own arrangements, and it would appear most fitting to discuss the code under the five heads of National Life, Economic Life, and three fundamental qualities of a healthy national life—Purity, Justice, and the Treatment of the Poor. Every phase of the laws which remain for discussion can easily be brought under these heads, and this chapter will discuss the first of them, the organisation of the national life.

It is a striking instance of the accuracy of the national memory that there is a clear and conscious testimony to the fact that for long there was no king in Israel. Had the later historians been at the mercy of a tradition so deeply influenced by later times as it pleases some critics to suppose, it would seem inexplicable that Moses should not have been represented as a king, and especially that the conquest should not have been represented as a king's work. Evidently there was a perfectly clear national consciousness of the earlier circumstances of the nation, and it presents us with an outline of the original constitution which is very simple and credible. According to this the tribes whom Moses led were ruled in the main by their own sheikhs or elders. Under these again were the clans or fathers' houses similarly governed; and lastly, there were the families in the wider sense, made up of the individual households and governed by their heads. So far as can be gathered, Moses did not interfere with this fundamental organisation at all. He added to it only his own supremacy, as the mediator and means of communication between Yahweh and His people. As such, his decision was final in all matters too difficult for the sheikhs and judges. But the fundamental point never lost sight of was that Yahweh alone was their ruler, their legislator, their leader in war, and the doer of justice among His people. From the very first moment of Israel's national existence therefore, from the moment that it passed the Red Sea, Yahweh was acknowledged as King, and Moses was simply His representative. That is the cardinal fact in this nation's life, and amid all the difficulties and changes of its later history that was always held to. Even when kings were appointed, they were regarded only as the viceroys of Yahweh. In this way the whole of the national affairs received a religious colour; and those who look at them from a religious standpoint have a justification which would have been less manifest under other circumstances.

It is, therefore, no delusion of later times which finds in Israelite institutions a deep religious meaning. Nor is the persistence with which the Scriptural historians regard only the religious aspects of national life to be laid as a fault to their charge. It is nothing to the purpose to say that the bulk of the people had no thoughts of that kind, that the whole fabric of the national institutions appeared to them in a different light. We have no right to lower the meaning of things to the gross materialism of the populace. One would almost think, to hear some Old Testament critics speak, that in this most ideal realm of religion we can be safe from illusion only when ideal points of view are abandoned, that only in the commonest light of common day have we any security that we are not deceiving ourselves. But most of these same men would resent it bitterly if that standard were applied to the history of the lands they themselves love. What Englishman would think that Great Britain's career and destiny were rightly estimated if imperial sentiment and humanitarian aims were thrust aside in favour of purely material considerations? Why then should it be supposed that the views and opinions of the multitude are the only safe criterion to be applied to the institutions of God's ancient people?

In truth, there is no reason why we should think so. The Divine kingship made it impossible that the higher minds should be content with the low aims of the opportunists of their day, whether these were of the multitude or not. Even the entrance into Canaan, which to the mass of the people was, in the first place, a mere acquisition of territory and wealth, was idealised for the leaders of the people by the thought that it was the land promised by Yahweh to their fathers, the land in which they should live in communion with Him. Generally, it may be said that the desire for communion with God was the impelling and formative power in Israel. The thoughts of even the dullest and most earthly were touched by that ideal at times; and no leader, whether royal, or priestly, or prophetic, ever really succeeded among this people who did not keep that persistently in view as the true goal of his efforts. Moreover this gave its depth of meaning to the whole movement of history in Israel. Every triumph and defeat, every lapse and every reform had, owing to this direction of the people's efforts, a significance far beyond itself. These were not merely incidents in the history of an obscure people; they were the pulsations and movements of the world's advance to the full revelation of God. All that would have been wholly national or tribal in the institutions and arrangements of an ordinary people was in Israel lifted up into the religious sphere; and the orders of men who spoke for the invisible King—the earthly king, the priest, and the prophet—became naturally the organs of the national life.

The king's position was entirely dependent upon Yahweh. He was to be chosen by Yahweh, he was to act for Yahweh, and no king could rightly fill his place in Israel who was not loyal to that conception. It is in this sense that David was the man after God's own heart. He, in contrast to Saul and to many of the later kings, accepted with entire loyalty, notwithstanding his great natural powers, the position of viceroy for Yahweh. It is, therefore, an essential truth which underlies the Scriptural judgment that the kings who made themselves, or attempted to make themselves, independent of Yahweh, were false to Israel and to their true calling. And this is why Samuel, when the people demanded a king, regarded the movement with stern disapproval, and why he received an oracle denouncing the movement as a falling away from Yahweh. For, in the first place, the motive for the people's request, their desire to be like other nations, was in itself a rejection of their God. It repudiated, in part at least, the position of Israel as His peculiar people, and implied that an earthly king would do more for them than Yahweh had done; whereas if they had been faithful and united enough in spirit they would have found victory easy. In the second, the request in itself was a confession of unfitness for their high national calling; it was a confession of failure under the conditions which had been Divinely appointed for them. Not only in the eyes of the Biblical historian therefore, but as a plain matter of fact, the demand was an expression of dissatisfaction on the people's part with their invisible King. They needed something less spiritual than Yahweh's invisible presence and the prophetic word to guide them. But since they had declared themselves thus unfaithful, Yahweh had to deal with them at that level, and granted their request as a concession to their unbelief and hardness of heart.

That is the representation of the Books of Samuel; and the absence of any similar law from the codes before Deuteronomy confirms the view that the earthly kingship was not an essential part of the polity of Israel, but a mere episode. Nowhere in legislation save here in Deuteronomy is the king ever mentioned, and nowhere, not even here, is any provision made for his maintenance. No civil taxes are appointed by any law, while the most ample provision is made for the presentation direct to Yahweh, as Lord paramount, of tithes and firstfruits.

The history and the law alike agree therefore in regarding the kingship as somewhat of an excrescence upon the national polity; and this law, where alone the king's existence is recognised, confines itself strictly to securing the theocratic character of the constitution. He must be chosen by Yahweh; he must be a born worshipper of Yahweh, not a foreigner; and he must rule in accordance with the law given by Yahweh. Further, the ideal Israelite king must be on his guard against the grossly voluptuous luxury which Oriental sovereigns have never been able to resist, either in ancient or modern times; and also against the lust for war and conquest which was the ruling passion of Assyrian and Egyptian kings. Evidently too the ideal king of Israel was, like Bedouin sheikhs now, expected to be rich, able to maintain his state out of his own revenues. The tribute paid by subject peoples, together with the booty taken in war and the profits of trade, were his only legitimate sources of income beyond his own wealth. Every other exaction was more or less of an oppression. He had no right to make any claims upon the land, for that was held direct of Yahweh. Nor were there any regular taxes, so far as the Old Testament informs us. The only approach to that would appear to be that the presents with which his subjects voluntarily approached the king were sometimes and by some rulers made permanent demands; at least that would seem to be the meaning of the somewhat obscure statement in 1 Sam. xvii. 25 that King Saul would reward the slayer of Goliath by making "his father's house free in Israel." Some kind of regular exaction from which the victorious champion's family should be free must here be referred to; but it would not be safe, in the absence of all other evidence, to suppose that regular taxes in the modern sense are referred to. More probably something of the nature of the "benevolences" which Edward IV. introduced into England as a source of revenue is meant. If a popular and powerful king of Israel was in want of money, he could always secure it by ordering those able to afford handsome presents to appear yearly before him with such gifts as a loyal subject should offer. For the convenience of all parties an indication of how much would be expected might be made, and then he would have what to all intents and purposes would be a tax. Along with this he might also enforce the *corvée*; but such things were always regarded as excesses of despotic power. That Samuel in his *mishpat hammelekh* (1 Sam. viii. 15) warns the people that the king would demand of them a tithe of their cereal crops and of the fruit of their vineyards and of their sheep, does not contradict this reading of the passage in 1 Sam. xvii. For though chapter viii. belongs to the later portion of 1 Samuel and may therefore represent what the kings had actually claimed, yet it in no way endorses such demands. On the contrary, it indicates that such exactions would bring the people into slavery to the king by the phrase "And ye shall be to him for slaves." All that is mentioned there, consequently, is part of the evil the kingship would bring with it, and cannot in any way be regarded as a legal provision for the maintenance of royalty.

It is not probable, therefore, that in these prescriptions the author of Deuteronomy is repeating a more ancient law. No such law has come down to us. Dillmann supposes the provision that the king should always be an Israelite to be ancient; and indeed at first sight it is difficult to see why such a provision should be introduced for the first time in the last days of the Southern Kingdom, where the kingship had so long been confined, not only to Israelites, but to the Davidic line. But Jer. xxxii. 21—"Their potentate shall be of themselves, and their governor shall proceed from the midst of them"—shows that, whatever the cause might be, there was in the first years of the sixth century a longing for a native king similar to that here expressed. In any case, as the obvious intention here is to make entire submission to Yahweh the condition of any legitimate kingship, it was only consistent to require expressly that the king should be one of Yahweh's people. That motive would be quite sufficient to account for raising what had been the invariable practice into a formulated law; and no other of the prescriptions need have been ancient. On the other hand, the curious phrase "Only he shall not multiply horses to himself, nor cause the people to return to Egypt to the end that he should multiply horses; forasmuch as Yahweh hath said unto you, Ye shall henceforth return no more that way," can hardly belong to the Mosaic time. There was no doubt then much danger that the people should wish to return to Egypt; but that a king should cause them to return for horses, is too much of a subordinate detail to have been portion of a Mosaic prophecy. If, as is most probable, the phrase condemns the sending of Israelites into Egypt to buy horses and chariots, it can have been written only after Solomon's days. Before that time Israel, as an almost exclusively mountain people, regarded horses and chariots with dislike, and usually destroyed them when they fell into their hands. With the extension of their power over the plains and the growth of a lust for conquest, they sought after chariots eagerly. To procure them they entered into alliances with Egypt which the prophets denounced, and which brought to the nation nothing but evil. It was natural, therefore, that the Deuteronomist should specially mention this detail, and should support it by reference to a Divine promise, which does not appear in our Bible, but which probably was found in either the Yahwistic or the Elohistic narrative.

But whether the whole is Deuteronomic or not, there can be no question that the command that the king shall have "a copy of this law" prepared for him and shall read constantly therein is so; and perhaps of all the prescriptions this is the most important. In purely Eastern states there is no legislature at all, and the greater part of the criminal jurisdiction especially is carried on without any reference to fixed law save in cases affecting religion. This was the case in the Mahratta states in India so long as they were independent. The ruler and the officers he appointed administered justice, solely according to custom and their own notions of rectitude, "without advertence to any law except the popular notions of customary law."[83] Now in Israel the state of things was entirely similar, save in so far as the fundamental principles of Yahwistic religion had been formulated. In all other respects customary law ruled everything. But it was the religious influence that gave its highest and best developments to the life of Israel. It was this, too, which brought to such early maturity in Israel the principles of justice, mercy, and freedom. Elsewhere these were of exceedingly slow growth. In Israel, the influence of the lofty religious ideas implanted in the nation by Moses did for them what the influence of the higher political and social ideas of the governing Englishmen are said to do, under favourable circumstances, for the Indian peoples. Without disturbing the general harmony which must subsist between all parts of the organism of the State if the nation's life is to be healthy, and without putting it out of relation with its surroundings, that influence has been, and is still, moving the more backward Indian societies along the natural paths of human progress at a greatly accelerated speed.[84] In a similar way the Israelite people was moved by the Mosaic influence, in its aspirations at least, with an elsewhere unexampled speed and certainty, towards an ideal of national life which no nation since has even endeavoured to realise. But whenever the kings threw off the yoke of Yahweh and plunged into idolatry, then the evils of despotic Oriental rule made their appearance unchecked. These evils have been enumerated in the following words by one well acquainted with Oriental states: "Cruelty, superstition, callous indifference to the security of the weaker and poorer classes, avarice, corruption, disorder in all public affairs, and open brigandage." With the exception perhaps of the last, these are precisely the sins which the prophets are continually denouncing. Long before Hezekiah they were rampant, especially in the Northern Kingdom, and in the evil days between Hezekiah and Josiah, when we suppose Deuteronomy to have been written, they were indulged in without shame or compunction.

The result was that an inarticulate cry, like that we hear to-day from Persia in the articulate form of newspaper articles, must have filled the hearts of all righteous men and the multitude of the oppressed. What it would be we may learn from the following extract from a letter written from Persia to the *Kamin*, *i.e.* "Law," a Persian newspaper published in London, and translated by Arminius Vambéry in the *Deutsche Rundschau* for October 1893: "Oh, brothers, behold how deeply we have sunk into the sea of ignominy and shame. Tyranny, famine, disease, poverty, calamity, decay of character, and all the misery in the world has overflowed our country. The cause of all this misfortune lies in this, that we have no laws; only in this, that our conscienceless and foolish great ones have wilfully and purposely rejected, trodden under foot, and destroyed the laws of the sacred code.... We are men, and would have laws! It is not new laws we ask for, but we desire that our secular and spiritual heads should assemble and press for the enforcement of the holy laws of the sacred code. Therefore we ask of you this one thing, that you should proclaim: 'We are men, and would have laws.'" The East is so perennially the same, that the two thousand five hundred years which separate that pathetic cry from the prayers of the true Israel in Manasseh's and Amon's days make no radical difference. The situation was the same, and the need was the same. Hence came this prophetic and priestly redaction of the Law of the Covenant. "They were men, and would have laws." They sought to be freed from the greed, the cruelty, and the lawlessness of their rulers; and having produced their revised code, they wished to secure that it should not disappear from memory, as the more ancient law had been suffered to do. It must be kept continually before the king's mind. "It shall be with him, and he shall read therein all the days of his life; that he may learn to fear Yahweh his God, to keep all the words of this law and these statutes to do them." In this way it was thought that future "great ones" would be prevented from "rejecting, treading under foot, and destroying the laws of the sacred code."

But the king of Israel was not only to be a law-abiding and a law-enforcing king. He was to learn from this new law even a deeper lesson. He was to read daily in the law, "that his heart might not be lifted up above his brethren." Oriental despots either openly claim that they are of higher and purer blood than their subjects, or they deal with these latter as if they had nothing in common with them. In the laws of Manu it is said, "Even an infant king must not be despised, (from an idea) that he is a (mere) mortal; for he is a great deity in human form." It was not to be so in Israel. His subjects were the Israelite king's "brethren." They all stood in the same relation to their God. All equally had shared Yahweh's favour in being delivered from the bondage of Egypt. Each had the same rights, the same privileges, the same claims to justice and consideration as the king himself had. That, this law was to teach the king; and when he had learned the lesson, it is taken for granted that the root from which the other evils spring would be destroyed.

Such, then, the ruler of Israel was to be. He was to feel, first of all his responsibility to God. Then he was to deny himself to the lust of conquest, to the voluptuous pleasures of the flesh, to the most devouring lust of all, the love of money. Last of all, and above all, he was to acknowledge his equality with the poorest of the people in the sight of God. Could there be even yet a nobler ideal set before the kings of the world than this? The reign of only one king of Israel, Josiah, promised its realisation. That seemed, indeed, to be "the fair beginning of a time." But it was not so; it proved to be only an afterglow, a mere prelude to the night. None of his successors made even an attempt to imitate him, and the destruction of the Jewish State put an end to all hope of the appearance of the Yahwistic king in Israel. Elsewhere, before the coming of Christ, he did not appear. Since Christ's coming, here and there, at rare intervals, such rulers have been found. But in the East perhaps the only rulers who can be said to have made any attempt in this direction are the best of the great uncrowned kings of India, the British viceroys.

Such, for example, was Lord Lawrence's aim, and his reward. From the beginning to the end of his Indian career he lived a pure and simple life, laboured with untiring energy for the good of the people, and kept in his mind, as his aspirations for his Punjaub peasantry show, the Old Testament ideal of both ruler and ruled. He was, too, entirely free from the lust of conquest, as some Indian viceroys have not perhaps been; and he did all his work under a solemn sense of responsibility to God. To a large extent, the Biblical ideal made him what he was as a ruler, and the life and power of that ideal now, in such men, sufficiently show the truth of the prophetic and priestly insight which is embodied here. Many who have disregarded these rules have done great things for the world; but we are only the more sure, after two thousand five hundred years, that on these lines alone can the ruler attain his highest and purest eminence. All the aspirations of men to-day are towards a state of things in which rulers, whether they be any longer kings or no, shall stand on a level of brotherhood with their subjects, and shall set the good of the ruled before them as their sole aim. All men are dreaming now of a future in which personal ambition shall have little scope, in which none will be for himself or for a party, but "all will be for the State." If ever that good dream be realised, rulers of the Deuteronomic type will be universal; and the depth of wisdom embodied in the laws of this small and obscure Oriental people, so many ages ago, will be manifested in a general political and social happiness such as has never yet been seen, on any large scale at least, in the history of men.

CHAPTER XVIII
SPEAKERS FOR GOD.—II. THE PRIEST

Deut. xviii. 1-8

The priesthood naturally follows the kingship in the regulations regarding the position of the governing classes. But it was an older and much more radical constituent in the polity of Israel than we have seen the kingship to be. Originally, the priests were the normal and regular exponents of Yahweh's will. They received and gave forth to the people oracles from Him, and they were the fountain of moral and spiritual guidance. The Torah of the priests, which on the older view was the Pentateuch as we have it, or its substance at least, which Moses had put into their hands, is much more probably now regarded as the guidance given by means of the sacred lot and the Urim and Thummim. Because of their special nearness to and intimacy with God, the priests were in contact with the Divine will and could receive special Divine guidance; and in days when the voice of prophecy was dumb, or in matters which it left untouched, the priestly Torah, or direction, was the one authorised Divine voice. But this was not the only function of the priests. Sacrificial worship was a more fundamental function. Wellhausen and his school indeed seem inclined to deny that as priests of Yahweh they had any Divinely ordered connection with sacrifice. But the truer view is that their power to give Torah to Israel depended entirely upon their being the custodians of the places where Yahweh had caused His name to be remembered. The theory was that, as they approached Him with sacrifices in His sanctuaries, they consequently could speak for Him; so that the guarding of His shrines, and the offering of the people's sacrifices there were their first duties. In fact they were the mediators between Yahweh and Israel. Yahweh was King, but He was invisible, and the priests were His visible earthly representatives. The dues, which in a merely secular state would have gone to the king, as rent for the lands held of him, were employed for their appointed uses by the priests, as the servants and representatives of the heavenly King who had bestowed the land upon Israel and allotted to each family its portion. Occupying a middle position, then, between the two parties to the Covenant by which

Israel had become Yahweh's chosen people, they spoke for the people when they appeared before Yahweh, and for Him when they came forth to the people. They were, as we have said, the oldest and most important of the ruling classes, and must have been from early times a special order set apart for the service of Israel's God.

The main passages in Deuteronomy which bear upon the position and character of the priesthood and of the tribe of Levi are the following. In chaps. xviii. 1-8, x. 6-9, and xxvii. 9-14 the strictly priestly functions of the tribe of Levi are dealt with; in xvii. 9 ff. xix. 17, the judicial functions; in xxi. 1-5 their function in connection with sanitary matters is referred to. Besides these there are the various injunctions to invite the Levites to the sacrificial feasts, because they have no inheritance, and a number of references to the priesthood as a well-known body, the constitution and duties of which did not need special treatment. These last are of themselves sufficient to prove beyond question that in dealing with the priests and Levites the author of this book writes from out of the midst of a long established system. He does not legislate for the introduction of priests, neither does he refer to a priestly system recently elaborated by himself, and only now coming into operation. He does not tell us how priests are to be appointed, nor from whom, nor with what ceremonies of consecration they are to be inducted into their office. In fact the writer speaks of what concerns the priests and Levites in a manner which makes it certain that in his day there were, and had long been, Levites who were priests, and Levites of whom it may at least be said that they were probably nothing more than subordinates in regard to religious duty. In a word, while presupposing an established system of priestly and Levitical service, he nowhere attempts to give any clear or complete view of that system. His whole mind is turned towards the people. It is about their duties and their rights he is anxious, about their duties perhaps more than their rights; and he touches upon matters connected with others than the people only in a cursory way. In this matter, especially, he clearly needs to be supplemented by information drawn from other sources, and his every word about it shows that he is not introducing or referring to anything new. Any modifications he makes are plainly stated and are limited to a few special points.

The chief passage for our purpose is, however, xviii. 1-8, where we have the agents of the cultus defined, and directions for the dues to be given them. In ver. 1 these agents are clearly said to be the whole tribe of Levi; for the phrase "The priests, the Levites, the whole tribe of Levi," cannot mean the priests and the Levites who together make up the whole tribe of Levi. Notwithstanding the arguments of Keil and Curtiss and other ingenious scholars, the unprejudiced mind must, I think, accept Dillmann's rendering,

"The Levitical priests, the whole tribe of Levi," the latter clause standing in apposition to the former. In that case Deuteronomy must be held to regard every Levite as in some sense priestly. This view is confirmed by x. 8 f., where distinctly priestly duties are assigned to the "tribe of Levi." Some indeed assert that this verse was written by a later editor, but valid reasons for the assertion are somewhat difficult to find.[85] Neither Kuenen nor Oettli nor Dillmann find any. We may, then, accept it as Deuteronomic since critics of such various leanings do so. To quote Dillmann, "Beyond question, therefore, the tribe as a whole appears here as called to sacred, especially priestly service; only it does not follow from that that every individual member of the tribe could exercise these functions at his pleasure, without there being any organisation and gradation among these servants of God." No, that does not follow; and this very passage (Deut. xviii. 1-8) shows that it does not, for it makes a very clear distinction. In vv. 3 ff. the dues of the priest are dealt with, while in vv. 6 ff. those of the Levite in one special case are provided for. As if to emphasise the distinction between them, the priest in ver. 3 is not called "Levitical," as he is in other passages.

Further, the verses concerning the Levite also emphasise the distinction; for few will be able to adopt the view that here in vv. 6 ff. every Levite who chooses is authorised to become a priest, by the mere process of presenting himself at the central sanctuary. The author of Deuteronomy must have known, better probably than any one now considering this matter, that the priests in the central sanctuary would never consent to divide their privileges and their income with every member of their tribe who might choose to come up to Jerusalem. Indeed, if they had received each and every one, the crowd would have been an embarrassment instead of a help. As a matter of fact, when the Deuteronomic reform came to be put in practice, this free admission of every Levite to the service of the Jerusalem Temple was not adopted, and it is *prima facie* improbable that the author of it can have meant his provision in that sense. The meaning seems to be that, as only those Levites who were employed in the central sanctuary could be *de facto* priests, those living in the country were not priests in the same sense; and the regulation made is that if any Levite came up to Jerusalem and was received into the ranks of the Temple Levites, *i.e.* the sacrificial priests, he should receive the same dues as the others performing the same work did. But though no conditions of admission to the Temple service are mentioned, obviously there must have been some conditions, some division of labour, some organisation involving gradations in rank, and perhaps also some limitation as to time in the case of such voluntary service as is here dealt with. For, as Dillmann points out, it is not said that the service of every Temple Levite is the same; numbers of them may have had no higher work than the Levites under the laws of the Priest Codex.

Moreover the other functions assigned to the priests confirm the argument, and prove that in the time of Deuteronomy distinctions of rank among the Levites must have been firmly established. They had a place in the public justiciary, even in the supreme court, "in the place which Yahweh their God" had chosen (Deut. xvii. 9, xix. 17). Not only so, the law concerning a man found slain in chap. xxi., vv. 1-5, implies that there were in the cities throughout the land priests, the sons of Levi, whom "Yahweh thy God hath chosen to minister unto Him and to bless in the name of Yahweh, and according to their word shall every controversy and every stroke be." Now it cannot possibly have been the intention of the author of Deuteronomy that every member of the tribe of Levi should have equal power to decide such matters. If in his view every Levite was a priest, then we should have this impossible state of affairs, that the highest courts for judicial process should be in the hands of a class which was more largely indebted to the generosity of the rich for its maintenance than any other in the country. It seems plain therefore that every Levite could not exercise *full* priestly functions because of his birth. Clearly, if any Levite might become a priest it was only in the same sense in which every Napoleonic soldier was said to carry a marshal's baton in his knapsack.[86]

Finally, in this passage (ver. 5), by the words "him and his sons for ever," which refer back to "the priest," a hereditary character of the priesthood is asserted. This phrase is remarkably parallel to that so frequently used by P, "Aaron and his sons"; and though we are not told in what family or families the priesthood was hereditary, it must have been so in some. But in x. 6, 7, the family of Aaron is mentioned by the Deuteronomist as having hereditary right to the priesthood at the central shrine. There can therefore be no doubt that in the time of the author of Deuteronomy priesthood was hereditary, perhaps in several families, but certainly in the family of Aaron.

The remaining point in these verses of chap. xviii. is the dues. As the whole tribe had no land, so the whole tribe had a share in the dues paid by the people to their Divine King. In vv. 3 ff. we have a statement of what these were. The whole tribe of Levi are to eat "the offerings of Yahweh made by fire, and His inheritance. And they shall have no inheritance among their brethren: Yahweh is their inheritance, as He hath spoken unto them." The only place in Scripture in which such a promise is given is Numb. xviii. 20, 24, so that these passages, if not referred to by the author of Deuteronomy, must be founded upon a tradition already old in his time. As the servants of Yahweh, the Levites were to be wholly Yahweh's care; as His representatives, they were to use for the supply of their needs all such portions of the offerings made to Him by fire as were not to be consumed on the altar. Their remaining provision was to be "His," *i.e.* Yahweh's, "inheritance," or rather "portion," or that which belongs to Him. Now Yahweh's "portion" consisted of all the other sacred dues (besides the sacrifices) which should be paid to Yahweh, such as the tithes, the firstlings, and the firstfruits. On these the whole tribe of Levi was to live, and so be free to give their time to the special business of the sanctuary, and to related duties, in so far as they were called upon.

But there were to be distinctions. In vv. 3-5 we have a special statement of what was to be paid by the people to the priests, *i.e.* the sacrificing priests. Of every animal offered in sacrifice, except those offered as whole burnt-offerings, they were to receive "the shoulder, the two cheeks, and the maw," all choice pieces. Further, they were to receive the "firstfruits of corn, wine, oil, and the first of the fleece of the sheep." For the priests of one sanctuary these would be quite provision enough, though the word translated "firstfruits," *rēshith*, is very indefinite, and probably meant much or little, according as the donor was liberal or churlish. But how does this agree with that which is bestowed upon the priests according to the Priest Codex? In the passage corresponding to this (Lev. vii. 31-34) the wave breast and the heave thigh are the portions which are to be bestowed upon "Aaron the priest and his sons, as a due for ever from the children of Israel"; and where the firstfruits are dealt with (Numb. xviii. 12 ff.) "the first of the fleece of the sheep" is not mentioned. That is an addition made by the author of Deuteronomy; but what of "the shoulder, the two cheeks, and the maw"? Are they a substitute for the "wave breast and the heave thigh," or are they an addition? If we hold that the laws in the Pentateuch were all given by Moses in the wilderness, and in the order in which they stand, it will be most natural to think that what we have here is meant to be an addition to what Numbers prescribes. But if it is established that Deuteronomy is a distinct work, written at a different period from the other books of the Pentateuch, then, though there is not sufficient evidence to justify a dogmatic decision on either side, the weight of probability is in favour of the supposition that the Deuteronomic provision is a substitute, or at least an alternative, for what we have in Numbers. The fact that the prescription in Numbers is not repeated makes for that view, as well as the fact that Deuteronomy does not as a rule tend to increase the burdens on the people. Keil's view, that Deuteronomy and Numbers are dealing with quite different sacrifices, will hardly stand examination. He thinks that the feasts at which the firstlings, turned into money, and the third-year tithes were eaten, are referred to here, while in Numbers it is the ordinary peace-offerings which are dealt with. But the postponed firstlings were eaten at the sanctuary, and would consequently come under the head of ordinary sacrifices; and the third-year tithes were eaten in the local centres, so that the bringing of the priestly portions would be as difficult in this case as in the case of the slaughterings for ordinary meals, which Keil, partly for that reason, thinks cannot be referred to here. On the whole, the best opinion seems to be that Deuteronomy has here different prescriptions from those in Numbers, and that probably there is a considerable interval of time between the two.

In vv. 6-8 the Levite as distinguished from the priest is dealt with, though by no means fully. Only in one respect are special regulations given. When such an one came to do duty at the central sanctuary, he was to receive his share of the sacrifices with the rest.

In Chapter I. the main outlines of the Deuteronomic system of priestly arrangements have been placed alongside those of the Book of the Covenant and JE, and those of P, with a view to decide whether they could all have been the work of one lawgiver's life. Here they must be compared in order that we may ascertain whether a view of the development of the priestly tribe which will do justice to these various documents and their provisions can be suggested.

Some schools of critics offer the hypothesis that there was no special priesthood till late in the time of the kings. From the beginning, they say, the head of each household was the family priest, and secular men, such as the kings, and men of other tribes than the Levites, could be and were priests, and offered sacrifice even at Jerusalem. With Deuteronomy the tribe of Levi was established as the priestly tribe, and only after the Exile was priesthood restricted to the sons of Aaron. But this scheme does justice to one set of passages only at the expense of another. It accounts for all that is anomalous in the history, and pushes aside the main and consistent affirmation of all our authorities, that from the earliest days the tribe of Levi had a special connection with sacred things and a special position in Israel. To what straits its advocates are reduced may be seen in the fact that Wellhausen has to declare that there were two tribes of Levi, one purely secular that was all but destroyed in an attack upon Shechem, and which afterwards disappeared, and a later ecclesiastical and somewhat factitious tribe, or caste, which "towards the end of the monarchy arose out of the separate priestly families of Judah."[87] A more improbable suggestion than that can hardly be conceived.

But historical analogy, the favourite weapon of these very critics, also condemns it. Let us look at the growth of the priesthood in other ancient nations. In small and isolated communities the head of the household was generally the family priest, and in all probability this was the case in the various separate tribes of which Israel was composed; at least it was so in the households of the patriarchs. But, in communities formed by amalgamation of different tribes—and according to modern ideas Israel was so formed—there was almost always superinduced upon that more primitive state of things another and different arrangement. In antiquity no bond could hold together tribes or families conscious of different descent, save the bond of religion. Consequently, whenever such an amalgamation took place, the very first thing which had to be done was to establish religious rites common to the whole new community, which of course were not the care of the heads of households as such. Each separate section of the composite body kept up, no doubt, the family rites; but there had to be a common worship, and of course a special priesthood, for the new community. This is sufficiently attested for the Greeks and Romans by De Coulanges, who in his *La Cité Antique* gathers together such a mass of authorities in regard to this matter that few will be inclined to dispute his conclusion. On page 146 he says: "Several tribes might unite, on condition that the worship of each was respected. When such an alliance was entered into, the city or state came into existence. It is of little importance to inquire into the causes which induced several tribes to unite; what is certain is that the bond of the new association was again a religion. The tribes which grouped themselves to form a state never failed to light a sacred fire, and to set up a common religion." But the family and tribal rites continued to exist as *sacra privata*, just as the central government dominated but did not destroy the family and tribal governments.[88]

It may be objected that these customs are proved only for the Aryan races, and that, though proved for them, they form no valid analogy for Semitic peoples. But besides the fact that part of the statements we have quoted are obviously true of Israel, we have a guarantee that the principle enunciated is also valid for it. The whole process traced in the religious progress of the Aryan nations is based upon the worship of ancestors. Now one of the critical discoveries is that ancestor-worship was a part of the religion of the tribes which afterwards united to form the Israelite nation. Some, like Stade, tell us that that was the early religion of Israel itself. In that form the theory is, I think, to be rejected; but there would seem to be little doubt that, before the birth of the nation, ancestor-worship was much practised by the Hebrew tribes. If so, we may quite safely take over the analogy we have established, and believe that when Moses united the tribes into a nation, the religion of Yahweh was the absolutely necessary connecting link which bound them together. For though the tribes were related, and are represented as the descendants of Abraham, they must have varied considerably from each other in religious beliefs and usages. By Moses these variations were extinguished, as far as that was possible, by the establishment of an exclusive Yahweh-worship as the national cult; and to carry on this, not the heads of households, but a priesthood that represented the nation, must have been selected. But if so, who would most naturally be selected for this duty? A sentence from De Coulanges will show that in this case the tribe of Levi would almost necessarily be chosen. Speaking of cases in which a composite state relieved itself of the trouble of inventing a new worship by adopting the special god of one of the component tribes, he says: "But when a family consented to share its god in this fashion it reserved for itself at least the priesthood." Now if that was the case in Israel, the priesthood of the tribe of Levi would at once become a necessity. Whether Yahweh had been ever known to the other tribes or not, there can be little doubt that the knowledge of Him which made them a nation and started them on their unique career of spiritual discovery came from the Mosaic tribe, and family.

The God whom the family worshipped became the God of the confederacy, and they would be the natural guardians of His sanctuary. This would not in the least involve special sanctity and meekness on the part of the tribe, as some insist. They would remain a tribe, like the others; but their leading men would discharge the functions of priests for the confederated nation. It is difficult, indeed, to see why any one else should have been thought of: most likely the arrangement was made as a thing of course.

But if there was such a common worship, there must have been a sanctuary for it, and at it the Levitic priests must have discharged their functions. Now though the Tabernacle, as P knows it, is not spoken of either in JE or in Deuteronomy, a "tent of meeting" at which Jehovah revealed Himself to Moses and to which the people went to seek Yahweh (Exod. xxxiii. 7 ff.) is known to all our authorities. Further, Wellhausen himself says, "If Moses did anything at all he certainly founded the sanctuary at Qadesh and the Torah there, which the priests of the ark carried on after him," so that even he recognises the necessity we have pointed out. From the days of Moses onwards, therefore, there must have been special priests of Yahweh, a special Yahwistic sanctuary, ritual with a special sacrifice presented to Yahweh, and lastly a central oracle, which is precisely what the passages explained away by Wellhausen assert. But of course at that early time, even if the ultimate purpose was to have an exclusively Levitical priesthood, concessions to the old state of things would have to be made. The Passover was left in the hands of the household priest, and in other ways probably he would be considered. The old order would insist on surviving, and the rigour of the later arrangements cannot then have been attained. In other respects we know that it was so; and we may well believe that the priesthood of the individual householder and of the rulers was tolerated, and as far as possible regulated, so as to offer no public scandal to the religion of Yahweh. So, among the Homeric Greeks special hereditary priesthoods coexisted with a political priesthood of the head of the State, and with the household priesthood.[89]

The laxity on these points ascribed to Moses is, however, less than has been supposed. At Mount Sinai he certainly did appoint the "young men of the children of Israel"[90] to slaughter the beasts for sacrifice; but he reserved for himself, a Levite, the sprinkling of the blood on the altar. [91] He also made Joshua his servant, an Ephraimite, the keeper of the sanctuary; but even under the Levitical law, a priest's slave was reckoned to be of his household and could eat of the holy things. These were not very great laxities, and there is nothing in them to make us suppose that a regular priesthood did not exist from Sinai. Moreover, that a special place should be assigned to Aaron and his sons was natural. He was the brother of Moses, and would be the natural representative of the tribe, since Moses was removed from it as being leader of all. Everything therefore concurs to confirm the Biblical view that the Levitic priesthood had its origin at Sinai, and that at the chief sanctuary and oracle the chief place in the priesthood fell to Aaron and his sons. Worship at other sanctuaries was permitted, and there the heads of households may have performed priestly functions, or in later times in Canaan some other Levitic families; but that there was a central sanctuary in the hands of Levitic priests, among whom the family of Aaron had a chief place, is what the circumstances, the historical data we have, and all historical analogy alike demand.

For the discharge of their sacred functions certain dues were doubtless assigned to the priests, and the Levites sharing in the subordinate duties of the sanctuary would share also in the emoluments. In other respects Levi in the wilderness would differ in nothing from other tribes. But in preparation for the arrival in Canaan, it was decreed that Levi should "have no part or inheritance in Israel." Yahweh was to be their inheritance.

The point to notice here is that this tribe was to retain the nomadic life when the other tribes became agricultural. The reason for it is plain. That ancient manner of life was looked upon as superior in a religious aspect to the agricultural life. In the first place, the ancestral life of Israel had been of that kind. Abraham, Isaac, and Jacob had been heads of nomadic families or tribes; and the pure and peaceful religious life, the intimate communion with God which they enjoyed, always dominated the imagination of the pious Israelite. Moreover the fundamental revelation had come to Moses when he was a shepherd in the waste. Further, the life of the shepherd is necessarily less continuously busy than that of the agriculturist; it has, therefore, more scope in it for contemplation; and in many countries and at various times shepherds have been a specially thoughtful, as well as a specially pious class. But, perhaps the chief reason was that the shepherd life was not only simple and frugal in itself, but it was also by its very conditions free from some of the greatest dangers to which the religious life of the Israelite in Canaan was exposed. When the bulk of the people adopted the settled life, they were not only thrown among the Canaanites, but they went to school them in all that concerned elaborate agriculture. This necessarily made the intercourse and connection between the two peoples extremely intimate, and was fruitful in evil results. From this the semi-nomadic portions of the people were to a great extent free, and they would seem to have been regarded as the guardians of a higher life and a purer tradition than others. They represented to the popular mind the Israel of ancient days, which had known nothing of the vices of cities, and in which the pure uncorrupted religion of Yahweh had held exclusive sway.

A remarkable narrative of the Old Testament establishes this. When Jehu was engaged in his sanguinary suppression of the house of Ahab, and the Baal-worship which they had introduced, we read in 2 Kings x. 15 ff. that he lighted on Jonadab the son of Rechab coming to meet him. This Jonadab was the chief of the Rechabites, a nomadic clan, who were bound by oath to drink no wine, nor to build houses, nor sow seed, nor plant vineyards, and to dwell in tents all their days (Jer. xxxv. 6, 7). This was clearly intended as a protest against the prevailing corruption of manners, and was founded on a special zeal for the uncorrupted religion of Yahweh. Recognising Jonadab's position as a champion of true religion, Jehu anxiously seeks his approval and co-operation. He says, "Is thine heart right, as my heart is with thy heart?" And Jonadab answered, "It is." "If it be," said Jehu, "give me thine hand." And he gave him his hand, and he took him up to him into the chariot. And he said, "Come with me, and see my zeal for Yahweh." At a much later time, Jeremiah, at the Divine command, used the faithfulness of these nomads to the ordinances of their chiefs to put to shame the unfaithfulness of Israel to Yahweh's ordinances; and promises (Jer. xxxv. 19) that because of it "Jonadab the son of Rechab shall never want a man to stand before Yahweh," *i.e.* as His servant. The Nazarites, again, were in some measure an indication of the same thing. Their rigorous abstinence from the fruit of the vine (the special sign and gift of a settled life in a country like Palestine) was their great distinguishing mark, as persons peculiarly set apart to the service of God. Something analogous is seen in that other desert faith, Mohammedanism. When the great reformer, Abd-el-Wahab, attempted to bring back Islam to its primitive power, he fell back largely upon the simplicity of the desert life, though he did not insist upon the abandonment of agriculture and fixed habitations.

It is, therefore, not surprising that the priestly tribe was kept to the nomadic life by the ordinance that they should not have a portion in the distribution of the Canaanite territory. But according to the narrative of the attack upon Shechem by Levi and Simeon, and the verses in the blessing of Jacob (Gen. xlix.) dealing with these tribes, the course of history reinforced this command. Whether the treachery at Shechem occurred, as the Genesis narrative places it, before the Exodus, when Israel was only a family, or was an incident in the history of the two tribes after Canaan had been invaded, as many critics think,[92] the significance of it is that because of an historical exhibition of fierce and intolerant zeal on the part of Levi and Simeon, which the other tribes would not defend, their settlement in that part of the land was rendered difficult, if not impossible. Hence Simeon had to seek other settlements, while Levi fell back to the position assigned to it by its priestly character. It is not a valid exception to this view—which reconciles the two statements that Levi had no inheritance with the other tribes because of its specially near relation to Yahweh, and also because of its cruel treachery at Shechem—that a priestly tribe is likely to have been not more, but rather less, fierce than the others. That would entirely depend upon the cause or occasion which called out the fierceness. In all that concerned religion Levi would naturally be more inclined to extreme measures than the other tribes, and in this case the higher morality, secured by the separateness of Israel, might easily appear to be at stake.[93] It is, therefore, quite credible that the excessive vengeance taken should have been planned mainly by Levi, and that the resulting hatred should have broken up Simeon, and driven back Levi with emphasis to its higher call.

In any case there never was again any doubt that the Levites were to be excluded from the number of land-owning tribes. Even in the legislation regarding the forty-eight priestly cities this principle asserts itself. The keeping of sheep and cattle on the pastures, which were the only lands attached to these cities, was to be the Levites' only secular occupation, and they were neither to own nor work agricultural land. But to compensate for any hardship this arrangement might bring with it, the Levites, as the special servants of Yahweh, were to have Him for their inheritance, *i.e.* as we have seen, the dues coming to Yahweh were to become the property of the Levites in great part. I say in great part, because the gift to the Levites exclusively of a tithe of the income of the people is thought by many to be only a late provision.

After Canaan had been conquered, the state of things in connection with the priesthood would be something like this. The tent with the ark would be the principal sanctuary, served by a hereditary Levitic priesthood, at the head of which would be a descendant of Aaron. The tribe of Levi, being nomadic, would probably encamp in the neighbourhood of the central sanctuary in part, and recruits for the priestly work would be taken occasionally from them, while other sections would gravitate to the neighbourhood of other sanctuaries. As we see from the story of Micah in Judges, it was considered desirable to have a Levite for priest everywhere, and consequently there would arise at all the High Places Levitic priesthoods, most probably in part hereditary. But notwithstanding their dues, the bulk of the tribe, being nomads, would be looked upon by the agricultural population as poor, just as the Bedouin, in Palestine now are, comparatively speaking, very poor. This state of things would correspond entirely with what Deuteronomy tells us; and after that legislation the position of the Levites as a priestly body would be more assured than ever. In the post-exilic period all that had been regulated by practice in earlier days found written expression. Differentiation of function was minutely carried out. The priesthood was confined rigorously to the Aaronic house, and the other Levites were given to them as attendants. In this way the whole Levitic system was introduced, and with the exclusive altar came the exclusive priesthood. So far as I can see, it is only by some such hypothesis that justice can be done to *all* the statements of Scripture; and considering the elastic nature of Old Testament law, there is nothing improbable in it. In any case there is an amount of evidence of various kinds for the Mosaic origin of the Levitic, and even the Aaronic priesthood, which no proof of irregularities can overturn.

In the Divinely sanctioned arrangements of the Old Testament Church, therefore, the existence of a body of ecclesiastical persons, having little share in the ordinary pursuits of their neighbours, and dependent upon their clerical duties for a large part of their maintenance, was deemed necessary to secure the continuity of worship and religious belief. As has been already pointed out, the priesthood was necessarily more conservative than progressive. As an institution, it was suited rather to gather up and perpetuate the results of religious movements otherwise originated, than to originate them itself. But in that sphere it was an absolutely necessary element in the life of Israel. Difficult as it was to permeate the people with the truths of revealed religion, it would have been impossible without the services of the priestly tribe. Wherever they went they were a visible embodiment of the demand for faithfulness to Yahweh, and, with all their aberrations, they probably lived at a higher spiritual level than the average layman. As has been well said, though Malachi had much reason to complain of the priests in his own day, his estimate of what Levi had been in the past is no exaggeration (ii. 6): "The law of truth was in his mouth, and unrighteousness was not found in his lips: he walked with Me in peace and uprightness, and did turn many away from iniquity." But such a body as the Levites could not have been kept thus spiritually alive, unless the members of it had lived somewhat aloof from the strifes and envies of the market-place, and this they could not have done had they not lived by their sacred function. The prophets, under the power and impulse of new truth adapted to their own time, did not need this protection; consequently some of them were called from ordinary secular work—from the plough, like Elisha, or from the midst of the rich and highborn inhabitants of Jerusalem, like Isaiah. If one may so say, they were men of religious genius; while the bulk of the priests and Levites must always have been commonplace men in comparison. Yet even of the prophets a number were trained in the nomadic life; others were priests who were shut off also from agriculture. Clearly, therefore, some measure of separation from the full pulsing life of the world was, even in the most favourable circumstances, helpful in developing religious character. For the ordinary average ecclesiastic it was indispensable; and that he should exist, and should live at as high a level as possible, was as much a condition of Israel's discharge of her great mission, as that the voice of the prophet should be heard at all the great turning-points of her career.

The modern tendency in Old Testament study is to depreciate the priest and to exalt the prophet, just as in ecclesiastical life we tend to make much of those who are or give themselves out to be religious reformers and thinkers, and to make little of the ordinary parish or congregational ministry. But the good done by the latter is, and must be, for each individual generation more than that done by the former. No one can estimate too highly the conserving and elevating effect of a faithful high-minded spiritual minister. Often without genius either intellectual or religious, without much speculative power, with so firm a hold of the old truth, which has been their own guiding star, that they cannot readily see the good in anything new, such men, when faithful to the light they have, are the stable, restful, immediately effective element in all Church life. And such a body can be best spiritualised by being separated somewhat from the stress and strain of competition in the race of life. Being what they are, the necessity of taking their full part in the business of the world would inevitably secularise them, to the great and lasting damage of all spiritual interests. For though to modern students of Old Testament religion, who are interested most in its growth and progress towards its consummation in Christianity, the prophet is by far the most interesting figure, to the ancient people itself it must have seemed that the priests and Levites, if they in any degree deserved Malachi's eulogy, were the entirely indispensable element in their religious life. They gave the daily bread of religion to the people. They embodied the principles which came to them from prophetic inspiration in ceremonies and institutions; they treasured up whatever had been gained, and kept the people nurtured in it and admonished by it. In short, they prepared the soil and cultivated the roots from which alone the consummate flower of prophecy could spring; and when the voice of prophecy was dying away they brought the piety of the average Israelite to the highest point it ever reached.

In modern times the necessity for such a body of special churchmen is challenged from two opposite sides. There is, on the one hand, the body of over-spiritualised believers who abhor organisation, and the machinery of organisation, as if it were an intolerable evil. Conscious very often of quick spiritual impulse and vivid life in themselves, they fret against the slow movements of large bodies of men; they separate themselves from all the organised Churches and reject a regular ministry. All the Lord's people are now, under the Christian dispensation, priests and prophets, they say, and a separate paid ministry in sacred things they refuse to hear of. For spiritual nourishment they rely solely upon the prophetic gifts of their members, and are satisfied that thus they are preparing the way for the universal prevalence of a higher form of Church life. But, so far as can be judged, their experiment has not prospered, nor is it likely to do so. For these separatist Christians have found that spiritual life, like other kinds of life, cannot express itself without an organism. That implies organisation; and though they do with less of it than other Christians, still they are often driven into arrangements which really bring back the regular ministry with its separate position; and in other respects they are saved from the inconveniences they have fled from, only by their want of success. If their system ever became general, it would necessarily drift into organisation, for only at that price can any coherent, continuous, and lasting effect be produced. Unfettered by the dull, the critical, and the judicious, the impulsive and enthusiastic would always be outrunning the possibilities of the present time. In the interests of the best, they would be continually ignoring or destroying the good. To prevent that, a special body of religious men set apart for sacred services, and freed from the rough struggle for existence so far as a maintenance from funds devoted to religious purposes can free them, is one of the best provisions known. Where in the mass they are really religious men, they secure that the pressure upward, which the Church exerts upon the lives of its own members and upon the community in general, shall be effective to the highest degree then possible, and shall be exerted in the directions in which such pressure will most fully answer to the needs and aspirations of the time. Where, on the contrary, the mass of them are secularised, they no doubt are a power for evil; but the contrast between their profession and their practice in that case is so shocking, that unless they be supported by the "dead hand" of endowments with no living spiritual demand behind them, they soon sink by their own weight, to give place to a better type. And even when they are thus supported, though unfaithful, their calling in name at least remains spiritual, and sooner than the other elements in the nation they are apt to be stirred by breathings of a new life.

The other objectors to the regular ministry are those, in the press and elsewhere, who demand of all ministers that they should be prophets, or inspired religious geniuses, and, because they are not, deny their right to exist. According to this view every sermon that is not a new revelation is a failure, every minister of the sanctuary who is not a discoverer in religion is a pretender, every one who only exemplifies and lives by the power of the Gospel, as it was last formulated so as to lay hold upon the popular mind, is an obscurantist. But no reasonable man really believes this. Such reproaches are merely the penalty which must be paid for claiming so high a calling as that of an ambassador for Christ. No man can quite adequately fill such a position; and the bulk of ministers of Christ know better than others how much below their ideal their real service is. But this also is true, that, take them all in all, no class of men are doing anything like so much as Christian ministers throughout the world are doing to keep up the standard of morals and to keep alive faith in that which is spiritual. We have no right to complain that in their sphere they are conservative of that which has been handed on to them. They have tried and proved that teaching; they know that wherever it secures a foothold it lifts men up to God, and they are naturally doubtful whether new and untried teaching will do as much. They have pressing upon them, too, as others have not, the interest of individual men and women whom they see and know, men and women who for the most part, and so far as they can see, are accessible to spiritual impulse only on lines with which they are familiar; and they dread the diversion of their thoughts from their real spiritual interests, to matters which, for them at least, must remain largely intellectual and speculative. No doubt it would be well if all pastors could, as the most highly endowed do, look beyond that narrower field; could take account of the movements which are drifting men into new positions, from which the old landmarks cannot be seen and consequently exert no influence; and could endeavour to rethink their Christianity from new points of view, which may be about to become the orthodoxy of the next generation. But no ministry will ever be a ministry of prophets. It may even be doubted whether such a ministry could be borne if it ever should arise. Under it one might fear that spiritual repose and spiritual growth would alike be impossible for the average man, in his breathless race after teachers each of whom was always catching sight of new lights. The mass of men need, first of all, teachers who have firmly seized the common truth by which the Church of their day lives, who live conspicuously nearer the Christian ideal, as generally conceived, than others do, who devote themselves in sincerity and self-sacrifice to the work of making the things that are most surely believed among Christians a common and abiding possession. Such men need never be ashamed of themselves or of their calling. Theirs is the foundation work, so far as any attempt to realise the Kingdom of God on earth is concerned; for without the general acceptance of the truth attained which they bring about, no further attainment would be possible. The very environment out of which alone the prophet could be developed would be wanting, and stagnation and death would certainly and necessarily follow.

One other thing remains to be said. Though we have taken these significant words of ver. 2—"And they shall have no inheritance among their brethren: Yahweh is their inheritance, as He hath spoken unto them"—in their first and most obvious reference, it is not to be supposed that that meaning has exhausted all that the words conveyed to ancient Israel. The perpetuation of the nomadic form of life among the Levites, and the bestowal of tithes and sacrificial meats upon them, was undoubtedly the first purpose of this command. But it had, even for ancient Israel, a more spiritual meaning. Just as in the promise of Canaan as a dwelling-place the spiritual Israelite never regarded *merely* the gift of wealth and the prospect of comfort,—Canaan was always for them Yahweh's land, the land where they would specially live near Him and find the joy of His presence,—so in this case the spiritual gift, of which the material was only an expression, is the main thing. To have Yahweh for their heritage can never have meant *only* so much money and provisions, so much leisure and opportunity for contemplation, to any true son of Levi. Otherwise it is inexplicable how the words used to indicate this very earthly thing should have become so acceptable a formula for the deepest spiritual experience of Christian men. It meant also a spiritual bond between Yahweh and His servants—a special nearness on their part, and a special condescension on His. To the other tribes Yahweh had given His land, to them He had given Himself as a heritage; and though doubtless any unspiritual son of Levi must have thought the tangible advantages of a fertile farm more attractive than visionary nearness to God, the spiritual among the Levites must have felt that they had received the really good part, which no hostile invasion, no oppression of the rich, could ever take away. Their ordinary life-work brought them more into contact with sacred things than others. The goodness, the mercy, the love of God were, or at least ought to have been, clearer to them than to their brethren; and the joy of doing good to men for God's sake, the rapture of contemplation which possessed them when they were privileged to see the face of God, must have made all the coarser benefits of the earthly heritage seem worse than nothing and vanity. Of course there was the danger that familiarity with religious things should dull instead of quickening the insight; and many passages in the Old Testament show that this danger was not always escaped. But often, and for long periods, it must have been warded off; and then the superiority of God's gift of Himself must have been manifest, not only to the chosen tribe, but to all Israel. For the nature of man is too intrinsically noble ever to be quite satisfied with the world, and the riches and comforts of the world, for its inheritance. At no time has man ever failed to do homage to spiritual gifts. Even to-day, in spheres outside of religion, there are multitudes of men and women who would put aside without a sigh any wealth the world could give, if it were offered as a substitute for their delight in poetry, or for their power to rethink and re-enjoy the ideas of those whose "thoughts have wandered through eternity." And the power to follow and to yield oneself up to the thoughts of the Eternal God Himself is a reward far above these. To the faithful servant of God at all times and in all lands that joy has been open, for God Himself has been their heritage; and though in ancient Israel the beauty of "Yahweh their God" was not quite unveiled, yet we know from the Psalms that many penetrated even then to the inner glory where God meets His chosen, and there, though having nothing, yet found that in Him they had all.

CHAPTER XIX
SPEAKERS FOR GOD—III. THE PROPHET

Deut. xviii. 9-22

The third of the Divine voices to this nation was the prophet. Just as in the other Semitic nations round about Israel there were kings and priests and soothsayers, there were to be in Israel kings and priests and prophets; and the first two orders having been discussed, there remains for consideration the prophet, in so far at least as he was to be the substitute for the soothsayer. That this parallel was in the mind of the writer, and that he probably intended only to deal with certain aspects of the prophetic office, is witnessed by the fact that he introduces what he has to say regarding the prophet by a stern and detailed denunciation of any dealings with soothsayers and wizards. In the earlier codes the same denunciation is found, but the catalogue of names for those who practised such arts is nowhere so extensive as it is here. In the Book of the Covenant the *mekhashsheph*, or magician, alone is mentioned (Exod. xxii. 17); while the peculiar code which is contained in the last chapters of Leviticus,[94] mentions only five varieties of sorcerers. The Deuteronomic list of eight is thus the most complete; and Dillmann may be right in regarding it as also the latest. But the special indignation of the writer of Deuteronomy against these forms of superstition would be quite sufficient to account for his elaborate detail. If he lived in the days of Manasseh, he would have before his eyes the passing of children through the fire to Moloch. That was connected with soothsaying and was the crowning horror of Israel's idolatry. The author of Deuteronomy might, therefore, well be more passionate and detailed in his denunciations than others, whether earlier or later.

Nor let any one imagine that in this he was wrong and unenlightened. Whether we believe in the occasional appearance of abnormal powers of the soothsaying kind or not, it is evident that in every nation's life there has been a time in which faith in the existence of such powers was universal, and in which the moral and spiritual life of men has been threatened in the gravest way by the proceedings of those who claimed to possess them. At this hour the witch-doctor, with his cruelties and frauds, is the incubus that rests upon all the semi-civilised or wholly uncivilised peoples of Africa. Even British justice has to lay hands upon him in New Guinea, as the following extract from a Melbourne newspaper will show: "Divination by means of evil spirits is practised to such an extent and with such evil effects by the natives of New Guinea that the Native Regulation Board of British New Guinea has found it necessary to make an ordinance forbidding it. The regulation opens with the statement, 'White men know that sorcery is only deceit, but the lies of the sorcerer frighten many people; the deceit of the sorcerer should be stopped.' It then proceeds to point out that it is forbidden for any person to practise or to pretend to practise sorcery, or for any person to threaten any other person with sorcery, whether practised by himself or any one else. Any one found guilty of sorcery may be sentenced by a European magistrate to three months' imprisonment, or by a native magistrate to three days' imprisonment, and he will be compelled to work in prison without payment." Through the sorcerer attempts at advance to a higher life are in our own day being rendered futile; at his instigation the darkest crimes are committed; and because of him and the beliefs he inculcates men are kept all their lives subject to bondage. So also of old. The ancient soothsayer might be an impostor in everything, but he was none the less dangerous for that. To what depths of wickedness his practices can bring men is seen in the horrors of the secret cult of the negroes of Hayti. Even when soothsaying and magic were connected with higher religions than the fetichism of the Haytian negro, they were still detrimental in no ordinary degree. No worthy conception of God could grow up where these were dominant, and toleration of them was utterly impossible for the religion of Yahweh.

The justice of the punishment of death decreed against wizards and witches in Scripture was, therefore, quite independent of the reality of the powers such persons claimed. They professed and were believed to have them, and thus they acquired an influence which was fatal to any real belief in a moral and spiritual government of the world. They must therefore be an "abomination" to Yahweh; and as, in any case, by the very fact that they were soothsayers and diviners they practised low forms of idolatry, those who sought them must share the condemnation of the idolater in Israel. In the earlier days of the sacred history there was no enemy so subtle, so insidious, so difficult to meet as magic and soothsaying. Only by actual prohibition, on pain of death, could the case be adequately met; and under these circumstances there is no need for us to apologise for the Old Testament law, "Thou shalt not suffer a witch to live" (Exod. xxii. 17). What is aimed at here is the profession on the part of any woman that she had and used these supernatural powers. This was a crime against Israel's higher life. The punishment of it had no resemblance to the judicial cruelties perpetrated in comparatively modern times, when the charge of being a witch became a weapon against people, who for the most part were guilty only of being helpless and lonely.

But it is characteristic of the large outlook of Deuteronomy that not only is the evil protested against; the universal human need which underlay it is acknowledged and supplied. Behind all the terrible aberrations of heathen soothsaying and divination the author saw hunger for a revelation of the will and purpose of God. That was worthy of sympathy, however inadequate and evil the substitutes elaborated for the really Divine means of enlightenment were. So he promises that the real need will be supplied by God's holy prophets. Nothing that savoured of ignorance or misapprehension of God's spirituality, or of unfaithfulness to Yahweh, could be tolerated; for Israel's God would supply all their need by a prophet from the midst of them, of their brethren, like unto Moses, in whose mouth Yahweh would put His words, and who should speak unto them all that He should command him. This is the broadest and most general legitimation of the prophet, as a special organ of revelation in Israel, that the Scripture contains. By it he is made one of the regularly constituted channels of Divine influence for his people. For it is evidently not one single individual, such as the Messiah, who is here foretold. That has been the interpretation received from the earlier Jews, and cherished in the Church up till quite modern times. But as Keil rightly says, the fact that this promise is set against any supposed need to have recourse to diviners and wizards, is in itself sufficient proof that the prophetic order is meant. It was not only in the far-off Messianic time that Israel was to find in this Divinely sent prophet that knowledge of God's will and purposes which it needed. Israel of all times, tempted by the customs of its heathen neighbours to go to the diviners, was to have in Yahweh's prophet a continual deliverance from the temptation. That implies that this *Nabhi*, or prophet like unto Moses, was to be continually recurring, at every turn and crisis of this nation's career.

Further, the direction in the end of the passage for testing the prophets, whether they were really sent of God or not, confirms this view. It would be singularly out of place in a promise which referred to the Messiah in an exclusive and primary fashion. He would never need testing of this sort, for He was to be the realisation and embodiment of Israel's highest aspirations. But if the passage means to give the prophets a place among the national organs of intercourse with Yahweh alongside of the priests, the necessity of distinguishing these true and Divinely given prophets from pretenders was urgent. The context, both before and after the promise, seems, therefore, to be decisively in favour of the general reference; and the phrases "like unto me," "like unto thee," *i.e.* Moses, when carefully examined, instead of weakening that inference, strengthen it. They are not used here as the similar phrase is used in Deut. xxxiv. 10: "And there hath not arisen a prophet since in Israel like unto Moses, whom Yahweh knew face to face." There the closeness of Moses' approach to Yahweh is the point in hand, and it is clearly stated that in that regard Moses was more favoured than any who had succeeded him. But here the comparison is between Moses and the prophets, in so far as mediation between Yahweh and His people was concerned. At Israel's own wish Moses had been appointed to hear the Divine voice. Israel had said "Let me not hear again the voice of Yahweh my God, neither let me see this great fire any more, that I die not." The prophet here promised was to be like Moses in that respect, but there is nothing to assert that he would be equal to Moses in power and dignity. On all grounds, therefore, the reference to the line of prophets is to be maintained.

Still, the interpretation thus reached does not exclude—it distinctly includes—the Messianic reference. If the passage promises that at all moments of difficulty and crisis in Israel's history, the will of God would be made known by a Divinely sent prophet, that would be specially true of the last and greatest crisis, the birth of the new time which the Messiah was to inaugurate. Whatever fulfilment the promise might receive previously to that, it could not be perfectly fulfilled without the advent of Him whose office it was to close up the history of the present world, and bring all things by a safe transition into the new Messianic world. That was the greatest crisis; and necessarily the prophet who spoke for Yahweh in it must be the crown of the long line of prophets. There is still a higher sense in which this promise has reference to the Messiah. He was to sum up and realise in Himself all the possibilities of Israel. Now they were the prophetic nation, the people who were to reveal God to mankind; and when they proved prevailingly false to their higher calling, the hopes of all who remained faithful turned to that "true" Israel which alone would inherit the promises. At one period, just before and in the Exile, the prophetic order would appear to have been looked upon as the Israel within Israel, to whom it would fall to accomplish the great things to which the seed of Abraham had been called. But the author of Second Isaiah, despairing even of them, saw that the destiny of Israel would be accomplished by one great Servant of Yahweh, who should outshine all other prophets, as He would surpass all other Israelite priests and Davidic kings. As the crown and embodiment of all that the prophets had aspired to be, the Messiah alone completely fulfilled this promise, and consequently the Messianic reference is organically one with the primary reference. They are so intimately interwoven that nothing but violence can separate them; and thus we gain a deeper insight into the wide reach of the Divine purposes, and the organic unity of the Divine action in the world. These form a far better guarantee for the recognition of Messianic prophecy here than the supposed direct and exclusive reference did. By not grasping too desperately at the view which more strikingly involves the supernatural, we have received back with "full measure pressed down and running over" the assurance that God was really speaking here, and that this, like all the promises of the Old Testament when rightly understood, is yea and amen in Christ.

But for our present purpose the primary reference of this passage to the prophetic line is even more important than the secondary but most vital reference to the Messiah. For it sets forth prophecy as the most potent instrument for the growth and furtherance of the religion of Israel. The prophet is here declared to be the successor of Moses, to be the inspired declarer of the Divine will to His people in cases which did not come within the sphere or the competency of the priest. The latter was, as we have seen, bound to work within the limits and on the basis of the revelation given by Moses. He was to carry out into execution what had been commanded, to keep alive in the hearts of the people the knowledge of their God as Moses had given it, to give "Torah" from the sanctuary in accordance with its principles. But here a nobler office is assigned to the prophet. He is to enlarge and develop the work of Moses. The Mosaic revelation is here viewed as fundamental and normative, but, in contrast to the views of later Judaism, as by no means complete. For the completion of it the prophet is here declared to be the Divinely chosen instrument, and he is consequently assigned a higher position in the purpose of God than either king or priest. He is raised far above the diviners by having his calling lifted into the moral sphere; and he excels both the other organs of national life in that, while they are largely bound by the past, he is called of God to initiate new and higher stages in the life of the chosen people. The ascending steps of the revelation begun by Moses were to be in his hands, and through him God was to reveal Himself in ever fuller measure.

Viewed thus, the prophetic order in Israel has a quite unique character. It is a provision for religious progress such as had no parallel elsewhere in the world; and this public acknowledgment of its Divine right is almost more remarkable. Wherever elsewhere in the world religion has been supposed to be Divinely given through one man, though modifications have indeed been made in later times, yet they have never been anticipated and provided for beforehand. Save in the case of Mohammedanism, which borrowed its idea of the office of the prophet from Judaism, there has never been a deliberate admission that God had yet higher things to reveal concerning Himself, still less has provision been made for the coming of that which was new to fulfil the old. And in modern times the revealer of new aspects of truth finds nowhere a welcome. Instead of being received as a messenger of God, even in the Christian Church he has always to face neglect, often persecution, and only if he be unusually fortunate does he live to see his message received. But in Israel, even in such ancient days as those we are dealing with, the progressive nature of God's Revelation of Himself was acknowledged, the reception of new truth was legitimised and looked for, and the highest place in the earthly kingdom of God was reserved for those whom God had enlightened by it. It is true of course that the nation as a whole never acted in accordance with this teaching. They did not obey the command given here, "Unto him shall ye hearken," and reiterated still more solemnly in the words, "And it shall come to pass, that whosoever will not hearken unto My words, which he shall speak in My name, I will require of him." The prophets for the most part spoke to their contemporaries in vain. Where they were not neglected they were persecuted, and many sealed their testimony with their blood. But the thought that Yahweh was educating His people step by step, and that at all times in their history He would have further revelations of Himself to make, is familiar to this writer. Therefore he welcomes the thought of advance in this region of things, and here solemnly enrols those who are to be the instruments of it among the ruling powers of the nation.

Now in religious thought this is quite unparalleled. Tenacious conservatism, based on the conviction that full truth has already been attained, has always been the mark of religious thinking. That a religious teacher should be able to see that the light of revelation, like the natural light, must come gradually, broadening by degrees into perfect day, and that he himself was standing only in the morning twilight, is a thing so remarkable that one is at a loss to account for it, save on the ground of the special nature of prophetic enlightenment. It was part of the office of the prophets to foresee and foretell the future. Smend is certainly in the right, as against those who have been teaching that the prophet was merely a preacher of genius, when he says that "in Amos and his successors prophecy is the starting-point of their whole discourse and action," and that "all new knowledge which they preach comes to them from the action of Yahweh which they foretell.... Consequently the greatness of a prophet is to be gathered from the measure in which he foresees the future."[95] This statement gives us the truth that lies between the two other extremes; for according to it the prophet proclaims and preaches religious truth, but he does so on the basis of what he perceives that God is about to do in the future. In other words, he proclaims new truth on the ground of the revelation God is about to make of Himself, which he is inspired to foresee and to interpret. His business is neither all foreseeing nor all teaching; it is teaching grounded upon foresight. Consequently it was impossible for the prophet to believe that change in religion was in itself evil. He *knew* to the contrary. Only change which should remove men from the Divinely given basis of the faith was evil; and such change, whatever credentials might accompany it, even though they might be miraculous, every faithful Israelite had been already warned most sternly to reject (Deut. xiii. 5). But when the impulse to advance came from Yahweh's manifestation of Himself, change was not only good, it was the indispensable test of faithfulness. They were not the true followers of Isaiah who, on the ground of his prophecy that Zion, as Yahweh's dwelling-place, should be delivered from destruction, rejected the prophecy of Jeremiah that Zion would fall before the Chaldeans. The really faithful men were those who had taken to heart the lessons Yahweh had set for His people in the century that lay between these two prophets; who saw that the time when the deliverance of Zion was necessary to the safety of the true religion was past, and that now the capture of Zion was necessary to its true development. And that is not a solitary case; it is an example of what was normal in the religious history of this people.

This did not escape the quick eye of John Stuart Mill. He says the religion of Israel "gave existence to an inestimably precious unorganised institution—the order (if it may be so termed) of prophets.... Religion, consequently, was not there, what it has been in so many other places, a consecration of all that was once established, and a barrier against further improvement." There always was the movement of pulsing life within it, and under the Divine guidance that movement was always upward. At some times it was comparatively shallow and slow, at others it was a deep and rushing tide. But it was always moving in directions which led straight to the great consummation of itself in the coming of Christ, who gathered up into His own life all the varied streams of revelation, and crowned and fulfilled them all. At no point in the progress from Moses to the Messiah do we touch rounded and completed truth; nor, according to the teaching of Scripture in this passage, were we meant to do so. The faithful among Israel had as their watchword the *disio* and *pace* of Dante. They saw before them a world of Divine "peace," which they knew lay still in the future, and the "desire" and yearning of their souls were always directed towards it. With inextinguishable hope they marched onward with uplifted faces, to which light reflected from that future gave at times a radiant gladness; and always they kept an open ear for those who saw what God was about to do at each turning of the way.

But granting that religion was thus progressive before men were spoken unto "by the Son," can we say or believe that, now that He has spoken, progress in this way is still possible? At first sight it would seem necessary to answer that question in the negative. The progressive revelation of God has come to its perfection in Jesus Christ; what then remains to us but to cling to that? Are we not bound to make resistance to progress, to any new view in religion, our first duty? Many act and speak as if that were the only possible course consistent with faithfulness. But we must distinguish. The revelation of God has, according to our Christian faith, reached not only its highest actual point, but also its highest possible point in Christ. God can do nothing more for His vineyard than He has done. As a manifestation of God, revelation is completed and closed in Christ. For it is impossible to manifest God to men more fully than in a man who reveals God in every thought and word and act.

But it is quite otherwise with the interpretation of the manifestation. In the earlier days this was provided for by a special inspiration of God, which made the holy men of old infallible in their interpretation of the revelation received up to their day, and that continued till the establishment of the Church. Since then the Holy Spirit is to be the guide of faithful men into all truth. Now in the way of interpreting Christ and His message progress is as much open to us as it was to Israel. A complete revelation of God must necessarily, at any given time up till the consummation of all things, contain in it a residuum of significance which, at that point of their experience, mankind has not felt the need of, nor has had the capacity to understand. As the world grows older, however, new outlooks, new environments, new circumstances continually appear, and they all insist upon being dealt with by the Church. In order to deal with them adequately and worthily, a faithful Church must turn to Christ to see what God would have it do; and if Christ be what we take Him to be, there will issue from Him a light, unseen or unnoticed before, to meet the hitherto unfelt need. Moreover, while our Lord Jesus Christ reveals God completely as the God of Redemption, and throws light upon all God's relations to man, a light which needs and admits of no supplementary addition, there are other aspects of the Divine character which He does not so entirely reveal. For example, God's relations to the world of nature, which are now being unveiled in a most striking manner, are dealt with comparatively rarely in the Gospels. Are we to shut our eyes to these as of no importance, and to allow them no influence upon our thoughts? Surely that cannot be demanded of us; for, to speak plainly, it is impossible. No one can remain unmoved when God and man are revealing themselves in the wondrous panorama of the world's life.

Even those who most profess to do so in no case take their stand simply and solely upon the truths believed and held by the first Christians. All of them have adopted later developments as part of their indefeasible treasure.

Some go back to the theology of the great Evangelical Revival only; some to the Reformation; some to the pre-Reformation Scholastics; others to the first five centuries. But whatever the point may be at which they take up Christian theology, they take up, along with the original creed of the first believers, some truths or doctrines which emerged and were accepted at a later date. Themselves being judges, therefore, additions to the primitive deposit of faith have to be admitted; and it is a purely arbitrary proceeding on their part to say that now we have attained to all truth, and stolid conservatism is henceforth the only faithful attitude. No, we have still a living God and a living Church, and a multifarious and wonderful world to deal with. Interaction of these cannot be avoided, nor can it occur without new truth being evolved. To have ears and not to hear, to have eyes and not to see, must be as offensive to God now as it was in Old Testament times. Though we have now no inspired prophets to foresee and interpret, we have in all our Churches men whose ears are better attuned to the celestial harmony than others, whose eyes have a keener and surer insight into what God the Lord would speak; and we ought to hear them, to see at least whether they can make their position good. To reject their teaching, only because some element or aspect of it is new, is to deny the guiding providence of God, to turn our back upon the rich stores of instruction which the facts of history, both secular and religious, are fitted to impart. That can never be a Christian duty. Even if it were possible it would be futile. The light will be received by the younger, the fresher and less stereotyped natures in all the Churches; and those who refuse it, in holding obstinately and with exclusive devotion to what they have, will find it shrink and shrivel in their hand. Only in the rush and conflict, only amid the impulses and the powers which are moving in the world, can a healthy religion breathe. Doubtless new teaching will come to *us* in ways congruous to the completed Revelation of our Redeeming God; but it will come; and it should be welcomed as gladly as the teaching of the prophets was welcomed by faithful men in Israel. If it be not, then the Divine threat will apply in this case as fully as in the other: "Whosoever will not hearken unto My words which he shall speak in My name, I will require it of him."

Many say now, and at all times many have said, to those who had caught glimpses of some new lesson God was desiring to teach: "You admit that souls have been renewed and character built up and spiritual life preserved without this new teaching. Why then can you not let us alone? In your pursuit of the best you may destroy the good; and no harm can happen if you keep the improved faith to yourself." But they have forgotten Yahweh's solemn "Whosoever will not hearken, I will require it of him." If we refuse to hear when the Lord hath spoken, evil must come of it. Indeed, though the evils of heresy may be more dramatically and strikingly manifest, those of stagnation and a refusal to learn may be much more destructive of the common faith. For refusal to acknowledge truth has far wider issues than the loss of any particular truth. It indicates and reinforces an attitude of soul which, if persisted in, will allow the Church that adopts it to drift slowly away from living contact with the minds of men. So drifting, it shrinks into a *coterie*, and its every activity becomes infected with the curse of futility.

On both sides, therefore, there is danger for us, as there was for the Old Testament Church; and we turn with quickened interest to the test, the criterion, by which Deuteronomy would have the prophets tried. It puts the very question which the line of thought we have been pursuing could not fail to suggest: "How shall we know the word which Yahweh hath not spoken?" If a prophet spoke in the name of other gods he was to die; that had already been determined in the thirteenth chapter, and it is repeated here. But the prophet who should speak a word presumptuously in the name of Yahweh, which He had not commanded, was to be in the same condemnation. It was, therefore, of the last importance that there should be means of detecting when this last evil occurred. The test is this: "When a prophet speaketh in the name of Yahweh, if the thing follow not, nor come to pass, that is the thing which Yahweh hath not spoken." The strange notions of Duhm and others in regard to this have been already dealt with (*vide* pp. 248 f.). There, too, it has been shown that the prophecy here spoken of must have been prophecy in its narrower sense, prophecy dealing with promises of *immediate* judgment and deliverance. Furthermore, this is set forth here as a test applicable to prophets in all ages of the history of Israel. It lies, too, in the nature of the case that it must always have been the popular test. The announcement of things to come before they came was made, at least partially, with the view of impressing the populace, and of gaining their confidence and attention. They must consequently have been continually on the alert to apply this test, and all that is here done is to acknowledge it in the fullest manner as a right and Divinely approved criterion.

But the way in which it ought to be applied is best exemplified by Jeremiah's own method of applying it, which, as Dr. Edersheim[96] has pointed out, is to be found in the twenty-eighth chapter of that prophet's book. There we read of Jeremiah's conflict with "Hananiah the son of Azzur the prophet," in the beginning of the reign of Zedekiah. Just previously Nebuchadnezzar had carried away Jeconiah the king of Judah, with all the treasures of the house of Yahweh and the strength of the people. Jeremiah had prophesied that they would not return; nay, he had foretold a further calamity, viz. that Nebuchadnezzar would come again and would take away the people and the vessels of the house which still remained.

In opposition to that, Hananiah declared, as a word of Yahweh, "Within two full years will I bring again into this place all the vessels of Yahweh's house that Nebuchadnezzar king of Babylon took away from this place, and carried them to Babylon; and I will bring again to this place Jeconiah the son of Jehoiakim king of Judah, with all the captives of Judah that went to Babylon, saith Yahweh." Jeremiah's conduct under these circumstances is noteworthy. He did not immediately denounce his rival as prophesying falsely. He seems to have thought that possibly he might have a true word from Yahweh, since, as we see in the Book of Jonah, the most positive prophecies were conditional, and Jeremiah would seem to have thought it possible that personal repentance was about to bring upon the captive king and people a blessing, instead of the evil he had foreseen. He consequently expressed a fervent wish that Hananiah's prophecy might come true, but reminded his rival that the causes of the evil prophecies of himself and previous prophets were far wider than the ground which the personal repentance of the captives could cover. Because of that he evidently felt the gravest doubt about Hananiah; but he disposes of the matter by saying, "The prophet which prophesieth of peace, when the word of the prophet shall come to pass, then shall the prophet be known, that Yahweh hath truly sent him." Only afterwards, when he had himself received a special revelation concerning Hananiah, did he denounce him as an impostor and a false prophet.

The whole narrative is of extreme importance, for it shows us how the prophets themselves regarded their own supernatural powers, and how they used the tests supplied in Deuteronomy. In the first place, they asked how the new word of Yahweh stood in regard to the older words which He had certainly spoken. If there was any possible way in which the new and the old could be reconciled, they gave the new the benefit of the doubt, and left the decision to the event. Obviously had there been no way of reconciling Hananiah's prophecy with the mass of contrary prophecy which had gone before, Jeremiah would have denounced him under the law of Deut. xiii. 5 as leading away from Yahweh. As it was, he fell back upon the test in this twenty-eighth chapter, and would have maintained an attitude of watchful neutrality until the event had justified or condemned his rival, had not Yahweh Himself settled the question.

For our own day and in our different circumstances the tests are radically the same, though, as prophecy is extinct in the Church, they must to some extent act differently. The New Testament parallel to the criterion in Deut. xiii. 5 is to be found in 1 John iv. 1, 2, and 3: "Prove the spirits, whether they are of God: because many false prophets are gone out into the world. Hereby know ye the Spirit of God: every spirit which confesseth that Jesus Christ is come in the flesh is of God: and every spirit which confesseth not Jesus is not of God: and this is the spirit of the antichrist, whereof ye have heard that it cometh." Under the Christian dispensation to deny "that Jesus Christ is come in the flesh" is the same as it was to say under the earlier dispensation "Let us go after other gods," so completely do God and Christ coincide in our most holy faith. In each case the ultimate test of prophecy is to be the fundamental principle of the faith. Whatever credentials teachers who deny that may bring, they are to be unhesitatingly rejected. They belong to the world, that scheme and fabric of things which rejects allegiance to the Spirit of God. Least of all is popularity with the world as distinguished from the Church, or with the worldly portion of the Church, to stand in the way of its rejection. That is only the natural consequence of its being "of the world." Within the Church no quarter is to be shown to such teaching, for it really carries with it the absolute negation of the faith.

But what of erroneous teaching which acknowledges that "Jesus Christ is come in the flesh"? To it the Old Testament parallel is the utterance of the prophet who "speaketh in the name of Yahweh, and the thing followeth not nor comes to pass." According to Old Testament precept and example, that was to be left to the judgment of time. In our day a corresponding course must be found. The case supposed is that of teaching believed to be erroneous, but neither fundamentally subversive of Christianity nor destructive of the special principles of a Church. If so, earnest opposition by those who hold the opposite view, and adequate discussion, are the true way of meeting the case. For the rest, the final decision should be left to experience. In time, even subsidiary error of this kind, if important, will manifest itself by weakening spiritual life in those who hold it; they will gradually dwindle in numbers and their influence in the Church will die away. They begin by promising renewed strength and insight in spiritual things, renewed energy in the spiritual life. If that "follow not nor come to pass," when due time has been given for any such development, then that is the thing which the Lord hath not spoken, and it should be dealt with as the fundamental heresy is to be dealt with. But probably by that time it will have judged itself, and will need no judgment of men at all.

These then were the connecting links between Yahweh and His people, and the organs by which the life of the Israelite nation was guided: the Kingship, the Priesthood, and the Prophetic Order. The first gave visibility to the Divine rule, and stability to national and social life; the second secured the stability of religion, and built up the moral life of the nation on the basis of Mosaic law; the third secured progress and averted stagnation, both in religion and in social and individual morals. In fact, order and progress, the two things Positivist thinkers have set forth as those which can alone secure health to a community, are provided for here with a directness and success which it would be difficult to parallel elsewhere. When we remember how small, how obscure, and how uncivilised the people was to whom this scheme of things was given, and how little their surroundings or circumstances were calculated to suggest such far-reaching provisions, we see that the source of it all was the Revelation of the Divine character given by Moses. Yahweh as revealed through him did not permit His worshippers to believe that they could, at one moment, receive all that was to be known about Him. They were taught to found their conduct and their polity upon what they did know, and to be eagerly on the watch for that which might be revealed at new crises of their history. Now that teaching finds its most complete expression in the laws concerning the three institutions we have been reviewing. Behind all healthy national life and all stable institutions there was, so had this people learned, the power and the righteousness of Almighty God. In His eagerness to draw near to men, He had changed the priest, the king, the prophet from being, as they were among the heathen, merely political and religious officials appointed for purely earthly ends, into channels of communication with Him. Through them there were poured into the life of this nation wholesome and varied streams of Divine grace and enlightenment, and a just balance between conservatism and reform in religion was admirably secured. Consequently, amid all drawbacks, the Israelites became an instrument of the finest power for good in the hands of their Almighty King; and even when their outward glory faded, they were inwardly renewed and pressed onward age after age. "Without hasting and without resting," the purpose of God was realised in their history, guided by these three organs of their national life. Each contributed its share in preparing for the fulness of the time when He came who was the Salvation of God, and each supplied elements of the most essential kind to the mingled expectation which was so marvellously satisfied by the life and work of Christ. They wrought together in the fullest harmony, moreover, though they were not always conscious of doing so. For they all moved at the bidding of the still small voice wherewith God speaks most effectively to the souls of men. Because of this their purposes took a wider sweep than they knew, their hopes received wings which carried them far away beyond the horizon of Old Testament time; and, starting from the remotest points, all the streams of the national life converged, till, at the close of the Old Testament time, they were running in such directions that they could not fail in little space to meet. It was therefore no surprise to the faithful in Israel when, at the beginning of the New Testament, they were found to have met in Jesus the Christ. Once that point was reached, the whole former history, which was now lying completed before the eyes of all, could be fully appreciated. Everything in the past seemed to speak of Him. If, in that first burst of joyous surprise, Messianic references of the most definite kind were found where we now can see only faint hints and adumbrations, we need not wonder. So much more had been spoken of Him than they had thought, it would have been strange had they not swung a little to the opposite extreme. But that need not hinder us from acknowledging that the history of Israel, viewed from their standpoint, was and is the most conspicuous, the most convincing, the most inspiring proof of the Divine action in the world. The finger of God was so manifestly *here*, harmonising, directing, impelling, that the evidence for Divine guidance in much more obscure regions becomes irresistible. With this history before us we can believe that it was not only in those far-off days, and in that little corner of Asia that God was active for the production of good. Now and here, as well as then and there, there are Divine and guiding forces at work in the world; and the only safe politics, the only truly prosperous peoples, are those in which rulers and priests and prophets are secured, to whom the secret of God is open.

CHAPTER XX
THE ECONOMIC ASPECTS OF ISRAELITE LIFE

It has often and justly been said that the life of Israel is so entirely founded on the grace and favour of God that no distinction is made between the secular and the religious laws. Whatever their origin may have been, whether they had been part of the tribal constitution before Moses' day or not, they were all regarded as Divinely given. They had been accepted as fit building stones for the great edifice of that national life in which God was to reveal Himself to all mankind, and behind them all was the same Divine authority. That being so, it is not wonderful, in times like these, when the air is full of plans and theories for the reconstruction of society in the interest of the toiling masses of men, that believers in the Scriptures should turn with hope to the legislation of the Old Testament. In the present state of things the material conditions of life are far more deadening and demoralising for the multitude in civilised countries than they are in many uncivilised lands. That this should be so is intolerable to all who think and feel; and men turn with hope to a scene where God is teaching and training men, not merely in regard to their individual life, as in the New Testament, but also in regard to national life. It is seen, too, that the tone and feeling of these laws are sympathetic for the poor as no other code has ever been; and many maintain that, if we would only return to the provisions of these laws, the social crisis which is as yet only in its beginning, and which threatens to darken and overshadow all lands, would be at once and wholly averted. Men consequently are diligently inquiring what the land tenure of ancient Israel was, what its trade laws were, how the poor were dealt with, and how and to what extent pauperism was averted or provided for. Many say, If God has spoken in and by this people, so that their first steps in religion and morals have been the starting-point for the highest life of humanity, may we not expect that their first steps in political and social life will have the same abiding value, if rightly understood? Now the main thing in regard to which the economical arrangements of a nation are important is land. In modern times there may be some exceptionally situated communities, such as the British people, among whom commerce and manufactures are more important than agriculture; but in ancient times no such case could arise.

In every community the land and the land tenure were the fundamentally important things.

Now the fundamental thing concerning it was that Yahweh, being the King of Israel, who had formed and was guiding this people as His instrument for saving the world, and who had bestowed their country upon them, was regarded as the sole owner of the soil. It is not necessary to quote texts to prove this, since it is the fundamental assumption throughout the Old Testament Scriptures that the Israelite title to their land was the gift of Yahweh. He had promised it to the fathers. He had driven out the Canaanite nations before Israel. He had by His mighty hand and His stretched-out arm established His chosen people in the place which He had chosen, and He had granted them the use and enjoyment of it so long as they proved faithful to Him. Consequently, in a quite real and palpable sense, there was no owner of land in Israel save Yahweh. And this thought was not without practical consequences of great moment. It was not a mere religious sentiment, it was a hard and palpable fact, that Yahweh ruled. Absolute proprietorship could never be built up on that basis, and never as a matter of fact, was acknowledged in Israel. All were tenants, who held their places only so long as they obeyed the statutes of Yahweh. The sale in perpetuity of that which had been portioned out to tribes and families was consequently entirely prohibited. As against other nations, indeed, Israel was to possess this land, so that no heathen could be permitted to buy and possess even a scrap of it; but as against Yahweh and the purposes for which He had chosen Israel, all were equally strangers and sojourners, practically tenants at will, who could neither give nor take their holdings as if they were absolutely theirs. Yet, relatively, the land was given to the community as a whole, and according to Joshua xiii. 7 sqq. (a passage generally assigned to the Deuteronomic editor) it was parcelled out by lot to the various tribes just before Joshua's death, according to their respective numbers.[97] Then within the tribal domain the families in the wider sense had their portion, and within these family domains again the individual households. In this way the Israelite tenure of land occupies a middle point between the theories of Socialism, and the high doctrine of private property in land which declares that the individual owner can do what he will with his own. The nation as a whole claimed rights over all the land, but it did not attempt to manage the public estate for the common good. It delegated its powers to the tribes. But not even they undertook the burdens of proprietorship. Under them the families undertook a general superintendence; but the true proprietary rights, the cultivation of the soil, and the drawing of profit from it, subject only to deductions made by the larger bodies, the families, the tribes, and the nation, were exercised only by individuals. The nation took care that none of its territory should be sold to foreigners, lest the national inheritance should be diminished, and the tribes did the same for the tribal heritage, as we see from the narrative concerning the daughters of Zelophehad. It was only within limits therefore, that the individual proprietor was free; and though the rights of property were respected, the corresponding duties of property were set forth with irresistible clearness. The community, in fact, never abandoned its claims upon the common heritage, any more than Israel's Divine King did, and consequently the field within which proprietary rights were exercised was more restricted here than in any modern state.

Further, besides the prohibition of absolute sale which flowed from the recognition of Yahweh's ownership, and the limitations which tribal and family claims involved, there were distinct provisions in which the national ownership under Yahweh was plainly asserted. For example, it is enacted in Deut. xxiii. 24 — "When thou comest into thy neighbour's vineyard, then thou mayest eat grapes thy fill at thine own pleasure; but thou shalt not put any in thy vessel. When thou comest into thy neighbour's standing corn, then thou mayest pluck the ears with thine hand; but thou shalt not move a sickle unto thy neighbour's standing corn." Allied to these were the provisions (Lev. xix. 9 ff., xxiii. 10) concerning gleaning, and not reaping the corners of the field. It will be observed that, though these latter may be discounted as intended for the relief of the poor alone, the former provision was for all, and that consequently it may be regarded as an undoubted assertion of the common ownership, or common *usufruct*, which, though latent, was always held to be a fact. In other ways also the same hint is given. The provisions for letting the land lie fallow in the seventh year and in the jubilee year, and for securing the use of what grew in the field for all who chose to take it, were interferences with the free-will of the individual owners or occupiers, which find their justification only in the fact that the general ownership was never suffered entirely to fall into the background.

To sum up then this system aimed at securing the advantages both of the socialist view and of the individualistic view, while avoiding the evils of both. Private enterprise was encouraged, by the individual being guaranteed possession of his land against any other individual; while public spirit and a regard for general interests were promoted by the restrictions which limited the private ownership. Further, and more important still, the whole relation of the nation and of the individual to the land was raised out of the merely sordid region of material gain into the spiritual and moral region, by the principle that Yahweh their God alone had full proprietary rights over the soil. All were "sojourners" with Him. He had promised this land to their fathers as the place wherein He should specially reveal Himself to them. Here, communion with Him was to be established, and to each household there had been assigned by Yahweh a special portion of it, which it would be equally a sin and an unspeakable loss to part with. Compulsion alone could justify such a surrender; and the completed legislation, whatever its date, and even if it remained always an unrealised ideal, shows how determined the effort was to secure the perpetuity of the tenure in the original hands. The ideal of Israelite life was consequently that the land should remain in the hands of the hereditary owners, and that the main support of all the people should be agricultural labour.[98]

The hypothesis that this was the case is strengthened to a certainty by the manner in which commerce, one of the other main sources of wealth, is dealt with in the Israelite law. There is but little sympathy expressed with it, and some of the regulations issued are such as to render trade on any very large scale within Palestine itself impossible. From the use of the word "Canaanite" in the Old Testament (cf. Job xli. 6; Prov. xxxi. 24; Zeph. i. 11; Ezek. xvii. 4, and Isa. xxiii. 8) it is clear that, even in the later periods of Israelite history, the merchants were so prevailingly Canaanites that the two words are synonymous. Nay, more; there can be no doubt that the commercial career was looked down upon. Even as early as the prophet Hosea the Canaanite name is connected with false weights and vulgar commercial cheating (Hos. xii. 7), and it is looked upon as a last degradation that Ephraim should take delight in similar pursuits. In all that we read of merchants in the Old Testament we seem to hear the expression of a feeling that commerce, with its necessary wanderings, its temptations to dishonesty, its constant contact with heathen peoples, was an occupation that was unworthy of a son of Israel. Even Solomon's success as a royal merchant would not seem to have overcome this feeling, nor did the later commercial successes of kings like Jehoshaphat. In fact the ordinary Israelite had the home-staying farmer's contempt and suspicion of these far-wandering commercial people, so much more nimble-witted than himself, who were therefore to be regarded with half-admiring wariness.

But the very sinews of extensive commerce were cut by the law against the taking of interest from a brother Israelite.[99] Without credit, or the lending of money, or what is called sleeping partnership (and all these are bound up with receiving interest), it is impossible to have extensive trade. Without them every merchant would have to limit his operations to cash transactions and to his own immediate capital, and the great combinations which especially bring wealth would be impossible. Now we do not need at present to discuss the wisdom of prohibiting the taking of interest, nor the still more debated question whether that ancient prohibition would be wise or advantageous now. It is enough for our purpose that usury in its literal sense was actually forbidden among Israelites, and that they were thus shut out from the developed commercial life of the surrounding nations. As a result trade remained in a merely embryonic condition.

But in still other ways the Sinaitic legislation interfered with its development. The inculcation of ceremonial purity, especially in food, and the effort to make Israel a peculiar people unto Yahweh, which distinguishes even the earlier forms of the law, made intercourse with foreigners and living abroad, always difficult, and under some circumstances impossible. Consequently all the legislation that can possibly be considered commercial was of a very rudimentary character. From every point of view it is clear that ancient Israel was not a commercial people, and that the Divine law was intended to restrain them from commercial pursuits. They could not have been the holy and peculiar people they were meant to be, had they become a nation of traffickers.

With regard to manufacturing industries the case was not essentially different. Such pursuits were, it is true, more honoured than commerce was, for skill in all arts, whether agricultural or industrial, was regarded as a special gift of the Almighty. But so far as the records go, there is no evidence that a manufacturing industry existed, beyond what the very limited needs of the nation itself demanded. From the fact that, according to Prov. xxxi. 24, which was probably written late in the history of Israel, the manufacturing of linen garments for sale and of girdles for the Canaanites was the business of the thrifty and virtuous housewife, we may gather that systematic wholesale manufacture of such things was unknown. Probably the case was not otherwise in regard to all branches of industry. There are no traces of trade castes, nor of manufacturing towns; so that the manufacturing industries, so far as they existed, had no other place than that of handmaids to agriculture, by which the nation really lived.

According to the Old Testament, then, the ideal state of things for a people like Israel was that every household should be settled upon the land, that permanent eviction from or even alienation of the holdings should be impossible, and that the whole population should have a common interest in agriculture, that most honourable and fundamental of all human pursuits. There were, of course, some men in Israel more prominent than others, and some richer, but there was to be no impassable barrier between classes such as we find in Eastern countries where caste prevails, or in Western countries where the aristocratic principle has drawn a deep dividing line between those of "good" blood and all others. So far as is known, there were no class barriers to intermarriage. From the highest to the lowest, all were servants of Yahweh, and were consequently equal. The conditions of the land tenure were such that it was impossible, if they were respected, that large estates should accumulate in the hands of individuals, and a landless proletariate could not arise. The very rich and the very poor were alike legislated out of existence, and a sufficient provision for all was that which was aimed at. By the cycle of Sabbatic periods (the weekly Sabbath, the Sabbatic year, and the year of jubilee) ample rest for the land and its inhabitants was secured; and in the limits set upon the period for which a Hebrew slave might be retained, in the release, whatever that was, which the seventh year brought to the debtor, and in the restoration of land to the impoverished owner in the year of jubilee, such a series of breakwaters were erected against the inrushing flood of pauperism, that, had they been maintained, the world would have seen for the first time a fairly civilised community in which even moderate ill-desert in a man could not bring irretrievable ruin upon his posterity. The prodigal was hindered from selling his heritage; he could only sell the use of it for a number of years. He could not ruin himself by borrowing at extravagant rates of interest, for no one was tempted to lend him, and usury was forbidden. He might indeed run into debt and be sold into slavery along with his family, but that could only be for a few years, and then they all resumed their former position. In this very land where the fact, Divinely impressed upon human life, that the sins of the fathers were visited on the children was most unflinchingly taught, the most elaborate precautions were taken to mitigate the severity of this necessary law. From the first the ideal was that there should be no son or daughter of Israel oppressed or impoverished permanently; and whatever the stages of advance in Israelite law may have been, and whatever the date of particular ordinances may be, there is an admirable consistency of aim throughout. Even should it be proved that the Sabbatic ordinances remained mere generous aspirations, which never entered into the practical life of the people at all, that fact would only emphasise the earnestness and persistency with which the inspired legislators pursued their generous aim. No change in circumstances turned them aside. The glitter of the wealth acquired by Solomon and other kings by commerce never seduced them. No ideal but that early one of every man sitting under his own vine and his own fig-tree, with none to make him afraid, which is witnessed to before the Exile (Micah iv. 4), in the Exile (1 Kings iv. 25), and after the Exile (Zech. iii. 10), was ever cherished by them; and the whole economic legislation is entirely consistent with what we know of the earliest time. And the deepest roots of it all were religious. The Biblical writers have no doubt at all that the ideal economic state can be reached only by a people attuned by religion to self-sacrifice, to pity, and to justice. In this they differ radically from the socialists or semi-socialists of to-day. These imagine that man needs only a favourable environment to become good; whereas the Scriptural writers know that to use well the best environment is a task which, more than anything, puts strain upon the moral and spiritual nature. For to deal in a supremely wise fashion with great opportunities is the part only of a nature perfectly moralised. Consequently all the social laws of Israel are made to have their root in the relation of the people to their God.

There was only one power that could secure that this admirable machinery would move, and keep it moving. That was the love and fear of God. The conduct prescribed was the conduct befitting the *true* Israelite, the man who was faithful in all his ways. The laws marked out the paths wherein he should walk if he willed to do God's will. They were, therefore, ideal in all their highest prescriptions, and could never become real except where the true religion had had its perfect work. In that respect the Sermon on the Mount resembles the Israelite law. It presupposes a completely Christian society, just as the old law presupposes a completely Yahwistic society, *i.e.* a society made up of men who made devotion to their God the chief motive of their lives. In such a community there would have been no difficulty in entirely realising the state of things aimed at here, just as in a community penetrated by the love of Christ the Sermon on the Mount would be not only practicable but natural. But without that supreme motive much that the enactments of both the Old Testament and the New demand must remain mere aspiration. Just in proportion as Israel was true to Yahweh was the law realised, and the demands of the law always acted as a spur to the better part of the people to enter into fuller sympathy and communion with Him in order that they might respond to them. The law and the religion of the people acted and reacted upon one another, but the greater of these two elements was religion.

It was not wonderful, therefore, that to a large extent this legislation failed, as men measure failure. The religious state of the nation never was what it should have been; and the law, though it was held to be Divine, was never wholly observed. In the Northern Kingdom, by the time of the Syrian wars, the old constitution of Israel had broken up. The hardy yeomanry had been ruined and dispersed. Their lands had been seized or bought by the rich, and every law that had been made to ensure restoration was habitually disregarded. As Robertson Smith states it,[100]: "The unhappy Syrian wars sapped the strength of the country, and gradually destroyed the old peasant proprietors who were the best hope of the nation. The gap between the many poor and the few rich became wider and wider. The landless classes were ground down by usury and oppression, for in that state of society the landless man had no career in trade, and was at the mercy of the landholding capitalist." And in Judah the state of things, though not so bad, was similar. In the days of Zedekiah we know that Hebrew slaves were held for life, instead of being released in the seventh year.[101] The properties of those compelled to sell were never returned to the owners, and all the laws that were meant to secure the welfare and prosperity of the masses of Israel were contemptuously disregarded. In short, the worst features of a purely competitive civilisation, with materialism eating into its soul, became glaringly manifest. All the canonical prophets without exception denounce the vices and tyrannies of the rich.[102] As far as can be learned, moreover, the year of release and the Sabbatic year were not regularly or generally observed, while the jubilee year would seem never to have been kept after the Exile. The laws regarding taking interest were also evaded.[103]

Nevertheless it would be a great error to suppose that these Divinely given social laws should be branded as a failure. They were not lived up to, and it is not improbable that the corruption of the people's life was in a degree intensified by the reaction from so high an ideal. But the axiom which is current now in all the newspapers, that laws too far above the general level of the national conscience cannot be enforced, and becoming a dead letter tend to produce lawlessness, does not apply to such codes as those of Israel. These, as has more once been pointed out, were not of the same character as our legal codes are. Among us, laws are meant to be observed with minute and careful diligence, and any breach of them is punished by the courts, which, on the whole, can be easily set in motion. Ancient religious codes are never of that kind. They do contain laws of that character, but the bulk of the provisions are not laws which the executive is to enforce, but ideals of conduct which the true worshipper of God ought to strive to attain to. It is, therefore, of their very essence that they should be far above the average national conscience. Nations whose ideals soar no higher than the possible attainment of the average man as he is, have virtually no ideals at all, and are cut off from all enduring upward impulses. Those, on the contrary, who have a vision of the perfect life, are certain to be both humbler, and at the same time more sure to persist in the painful path of moral discipline. As "a man's reach should exceed his grasp," so also should a nation's; and though it is almost always forgotten, it is precisely Israel's glory that she set up for herself and exhibited to the world an ideal of brotherhood, of love to God and man, to which she could not attain. Great as the practical failure in Israel was, therefore, no fault can be found in the legislation. It moulded the characters of men who were sensitive to the influences coming from God, so that they became fit instruments of inspiration; and it made their lives examples of the highest virtue that the ancient world knew. Further, it gave shape to the hopes and aspirations of the people, especially where it was not realised. The year of jubilee, for example, is the groundwork of that great and affecting promise contained in Isa. lxi: "The Spirit of the Lord Yahweh is upon me, because Yahweh hath anointed me to preach good tidings unto the meek; He hath sent me to bind up the broken-hearted, to proclaim liberty (*deror*) to the captives, and the opening of the prison to them that are bound; to proclaim the acceptable year of Yahweh and the day of vengeance of our God; to comfort all that mourn." That which was unattainable here, amid the greeds and lusts of an unspiritual generation, gave colour to the Messianic future; and men were taught to look and wait for a kingdom of God in which a peace and truth that could not as yet be reached would be the certain possession of all.

When we turn to modern times and modern circumstances, it is not easy to see how this ancient law can be applicable to them. In the first place, much of it was made binding upon Israel only because of its peculiar character as the people to whom the true religion was revealed. As custodians of that, they were justified in keeping up walls of partition between themselves and the world, which if universally accepted would only be hurtful to the highest interests of mankind. On the contrary, the development of the true religion having been completed by the coming of Christ, it is the duty of those nations which enjoy the light to spread abroad the "good news" of God which they have received, and to exhibit its power among all the nations of the earth. The highest and most Divine call which can now come to any people must, therefore, be radically different in some chief aspects from that of Israel. In the second place, the civilisation and culture of the great nations of to-day are far more complicated than any ancient civilisation ever was, and the general level is fixed by an action and reaction extending over the whole civilised world. No successes can be achieved, no blunders can be committed, in any part of the world which do not affect almost immediately the farthest ends of the earth. Moreover the intimate and universal correlation of interest makes interference with any part of the complicated whole an exceedingly perilous matter. Any proposal that this law, as being Divinely given, ought in its economic aspect to be made universally binding, should therefore be met by a demand for a careful inquiry into possible differences between ancient life and modern, which might make guidance Divinely given to the one inapplicable to the other. It is not necessarily true that because Israel by Divine command established every household upon the soil, forbade interest, and did nothing to encourage trade and manufactures, we should do these things. Take, for instance, the case of interest. In our day, and in civilisations of a high type, lending money to a person not in distress at all, but who sees an opportunity of making-enough by the use of borrowed money to pay the interest and make a profit, is often a most praiseworthy and charitable act.

But if the Israelite legislation in regard to interest cannot justly be taken as a law for all time, still less can any great modern state neglect or discourage commerce and manufactures. The merely embryonic character of commercial legislation, and the contempt for the merchant which did in ancient days exist, would be exceedingly out of place now. There is no career more honourable than that of the merchant of our day when he carries on his business in a high-minded fashion, nor is there any member of the community whose calling is more beneficent than his. So long as he looks for gain to himself in ways which, taken on the great scale, bring benefit both to producer and consumer, his activity is purely beneficial. There is absolutely no reason why commercial life should not be as honest, as sound, as much in accord with the mind of God, in itself, as any other manner of life. For in many ways it has been a civilising agent of the highest power. Of course, if the charges brought against merchants by Ruskin, for example, who seizes upon and believes every story which involves charges of fraud against modern commerce, were true; if it were impossible, as he says it is, for an honest man to prosper in trade, then we might have some ground for condemning this branch of human activity. But happily only a confirmed and incorrigible pessimist can believe that. In our time some of the noblest men of whom we have any knowledge have been merchants, and among no class has so much princely generosity been exhibited. If mercantile help had been withdrawn from the poor, if the time, the money, the organising skill which merchants have freely expended upon charities were suddenly to fail them, the case against our modern civilisation would be indefinitely stronger than it is. Moreover the immense expansion of credit which is at once the glory and the danger of modern commerce, is itself a proof that such wholesale condemnation as we have spoken of is unwarrantable. The bulk of commerce must, after all, be fairly sound, otherwise it could not continue and spread as it does. And, as against the evils which affect it in common with all human activities, we must put the fact that it brings the produce of all lands to the door even of the poor, and by the constant contact between nations which it causes it is influencing the thought as well as the lives of men. Human brotherhood is being furthered by it, slowly, it is true, but surely, and the barriers which separate the nations are being sapped by its influence. These are indispensable services for the future progress of mankind, and make commerce now as much the necessary handmaid of the highest life as it would have been a hindrance to it in the case of the chosen people, before they had assimilated the truths of which they were to be the bearers to the world. That commerce, and trade in general, need to be purified goes without saying. That it may, of late years, have deteriorated, as the general decay of faith and the pursuit of luxury have weakened the sanctions of morality, is not improbable. But in itself it is not only a legitimate human activity; it is also an admirable instrument for bringing home to the consciences of men the truth that they are all their brothers' keepers. It presses home as nothing else could do the great truth proclaimed by St. Paul in regard to the Church, as true also of the world, that if one member suffers all the body suffers with it. Every day through this channel men are receiving lessons, which they cannot choose but hear, to the effect that no permanent benefit can come from the loss and suffering of men in any part of the world; that peace and righteousness and good faith are things which have supreme value even in the mercantile sense; and that, conversely, the merchant's pursuit of wealth, if carried on in accord with the fundamental truths of morality, inevitably becomes a potent factor in that advance to a worldwide knowledge of the Lord, which gleamed before the eyes of prophets and seers as the

> "Far-off Divine event,
> To which the whole creation moves."

But if we cannot make the Old Testament our law in regard to commerce, we must ask whether the legislation in regard to land has for us any binding force? Viewing it with this question in our minds, I think we must be struck by one fact, this namely, that the universal possession of land which was provided for in Israel and so anxiously maintained is the only provision known against the growth of a wage-earning class largely, if not entirely, at the mercy of the employer. In Greece and Rome the population at first were all settled on their own lands, and it was only when by money-lending the small properties were bought up and turned into huge farms, worked by farm-bailiffs and slaves, that misery began to invade all parts of the social fabric. In mediæval and feudal England, on the other hand, and indeed wherever the feudal system existed, the cultivators, even when they were serfs, had an inalienable right to the land. They could not be evicted if they rendered certain not very burdensome services to the lord. "As long as these dues were satisfied, it is plain the tenant was secure from dispossession," says Professor Thorold Rogers (*Six Centuries*, etc., p. 44). But in time that system was broken down; and ever since, until within the last half-century, the course of things with the labouring classes in England has been one long descent. So long as the people were attached to the soil, and so long as all alike practised agriculture, as in Palestine under the Mosaic law, Englishmen lived in rough plenty, and were for the most part content. The fifteenth century was the golden age of mediæval agriculture; but a change for the worse came in with the seventeenth, and it continued.[104]

Two measures—the introduction of competitive rents with its corollary, eviction, and the enclosure of the common lands—worked gradually on until they have entirely divorced the workman from the soil, and Professor Cairnes[105] has told us clearly what that means. "In a contest between vast bodies of people so circumstanced and the owners of the soil the negotiation could have but one issue, that of transferring to the owners of the soil the whole produce, *minus* what was sufficient to maintain in the lowest state of existence the race of cultivators. This is what has happened wherever the owners of the soil, discarding all considerations but those dictated by self-interest, have really availed themselves of the full strength of their position. It is what has happened under rapacious governments in Asia; it is what has happened under rapacious landlords in Ireland; it is what now happens under the bourgeois proprietors of Flanders; it is, in short, the inevitable result which cannot but happen in the great majority of all societies now existing on earth where land is given up to be dealt with on commercial principles unqualified by public opinion, custom, or law." The result is that the labourers have only their daily wages to depend upon. "They have no means of productive home industry; they have not even a home from which they cannot be ejected at any moment on failure to pay the weekly rent; they have no land, garden, or domestic animals, the produce of which might support them till fresh work could be obtained."[106] We need not wonder that this question of the occupancy of land as the only visible remedy for the hideous social state of the most highly civilised nations of the world is gradually becoming *the* question of our time. A great reaction against the purely commercial theory of land tenure has taken place. The land legislation in Ireland has been based on the doctrines that the nation cannot permit absolute property in land, and that there is no hope for any permanent improvement in the condition of the poor until labourers have land of their own. Now these are precisely the principles of the Scriptural land legislation. Under it landlords with absolute rights over land were impossible, and the rise of a proletariate at the mercy of the capitalist was also impossible. It is not so strange, therefore, as it might at first sight appear that the demands of advanced land reformers, as they are voiced in Mr. Wallace's book (p. 192), are, *mutatis mutandis*, identical with the provisions of the Israelite law. He demands (1) that landlordism shall be superseded by occupying ownership; (2) that the tenure of the holders of land must be made secure and permanent; (3) that arrangements must be made by which every British subject may secure a portion of land for personal occupation at its fair agricultural value; and (4) that in order that these conditions be rendered permanent sub-letting must be absolutely prohibited, and mortgages strictly limited. This essential oneness of view in the modern land reformer and in the ancient law is all the more remarkable that, so far as can be gathered from his book, Mr. Wallace has never regarded the Old Testament from this point of view. He never quotes it, and is apparently quite unconscious that the plan which experience of present evils, and acute and disinterested reflection on them, has suggested to him, was set forth thousands of years ago as the only righteous one.

But this is not by any means the end of the matter. Even if the social reformers of our day could restore society to the conditions set forth so emphatically and so long ago in Israel, history proves that nothing more than a temporary improvement might be accomplished. In Israel, as we have seen, with the decay of religion came the decay of this righteous social state. Human selfishness then shook off the curb of religion, and gave itself without restraint to the oppression of the poor. Have we any reason to believe that now human selfishness would do less? There appears little ground to think so; and though we may believe that without the acceptance of Deuteronomic principles in modern life we cannot restrain the growth of poverty, even with Deuteronomic principles embodied in our laws nothing will be done if the people turn their backs upon religion, make selfish enjoyment their highest good, and the comforts and pleasures of a merely material life their only heart-warming aspiration. In that fact we have an indication of the true functions of the Church and of religious teachers in the social and political life of our time and of times to come. As individuals, religious men should certainly be found always among the advocates of all laws and plans which tend to justice and mercy, and to the raising of the toilers everywhere to a higher standard of living. Further, at no time should the Church be found committed to a purely conservative policy, of retaining things as they are. The undeniable facts as to the condition of the poor are so utterly unjustifiable, that to leave things as they are is to fall into the treason of despair in regard to the future of our race, and into scarcely veiled disbelief of the essential truth of Christianity. No Church whose heart has not been corrupted by worldliness can think for a moment that the present state of things in all highly civilised communities is even tolerable. It cannot last, and it ought not to last; the Church that timidly supports it, lest worst things should come, is named and known thereby for recreant to Christ and to the highest hopes of His Gospel. But, on the other hand, it is only in very exceptional circumstances, and for short intervals, that the Churches and their ministers can ever be called upon to make the external, material condition of the people their first and chief care. They have a place of their own to fill, a function of their own to discharge; and upon their efficiency and diligence in these the stability and permanence of all that politicians and publicists can accomplish ultimately depends. They must keep alive and nourish the religious life, as that life has been shaped and constituted by our Lord Jesus Christ. Their province is to witness, in season and out of season, for a life of purity and love, for the Divine and ideal sides of things, for the necessity, for man's highest well-being, of a life hid with Christ in God. If they do not keep up this testimony, no others will; and if it be dropped out of sight, then the social agony and struggle, the patriotic and humanitarian strivings of all the reformers, will lack their final sanction. Men will inevitably come to think that man's life does consist in the abundance of the things that he possesses, the leisure, the amusement, the culture which by combining material resources he may attain to. But it is to deny and denounce that view that the Church exists in the world. It was to lift men out of it, to set them above it for ever, that Christ died. It is finally only by abandoning it that the highest social condition can be reached and made permanent for the multitudes of men. In no way therefore can the Church so dangerously betray the cause of the poor and the oppressed as by plunging into the heat of the social and political struggle. She has to witness to higher things than that involves, and her silence in the ideal region which would certainly follow her devotion to material interests, however unselfish, would be but ill compensated for by any imaginable success she might attain.

CHAPTER XXI
JUSTICE IN ISRAEL

Among the nations of the modern world one of the most vital distinctions is the degree in which just judgment is estimated and provided for. Indeed, according to modern ideas, life is tolerable only where all men are equal before the law; where all are judged by statutes which are known, or at least may be known, by all; where corruption or animus in a judge is as rare as it is held to be dishonourable. But we cannot forget that in the majority of even the more advanced countries of the world these three conditions are not yet found, and that where they do exist they are only recent acquirements. In the latest born, and in many respects the most advanced of the great commonwealths, in the United States of America, the corruption of a number of the inferior courts is undeniable, and is tolerated with a most disappointing patience by the people. In England Judge Jeffries is no very remote memory, and Lord Bacon's acceptance of presents from litigants in his court has only been made more certain by recent investigations. An absolutely honest intention to give even-handed justice to all is, therefore, even in England, only a recent attainment, and in no country is the honest intention always successful in realising itself. But if this be so among the civilised nations of the West, we may say that in Oriental countries there has been little of systematic and continuous effort to give even-handed justice at all. Yet nowhere has the sinfulness and the destructiveness of corruption in judgment been more impassionedly and more frequently set forth by the highest authorities in religion and morals, than in the East. Tupper, our most recent authority, in writing of *Our Indian Protectorate*, p. 289, describes the Indian attitude to law thus: "There was not that reverence for law which in Europe is in all probability very largely due to the influence of the Roman law, and to the teaching of the Roman Catholic and other Christian Churches. So far as there was a germ out of which the respect for law ought to have grown, it was to be found in dislike to actions plainly opposed to custom and tradition. There was a deeply rooted and widespread conviction that there could be no rule to which exceptions could not be made, if agreeable to the discretion of the chief or any of his delegates. The chief was set above the law; it did not limit his authority by any constitution. There was no legislation for the improvement of law. The administration of justice was extremely imperfect." The same writer describes the result of such a state of mind in his picture of Mahratta rule (p. 247). "There was," he says, "no prescribed form of trial. Men were seized on slight suspicions. Presumptions of guilt were freely made. Torture was employed to compel confession. Prisoners for theft were often whipped at intervals to make them discover where the stolen property was hidden. *Ordinarily no law was referred to except in cases affecting religion.*" That there were both Hindu codes and Mohammedan codes in existence which claimed and were believed to have Divine authority made no difference in India. Nor does it make any in Persia to-day.[107]

Now, in coming to the consideration of the views of justice embodied in Old Testament law, and the quality of the judiciary in ancient Israel, we must take not Western but Eastern ideas as our standard. Judging from that point of view, it should create no prejudice in our minds if we find on the first glance that all men were not equal before the ancient law of Israel; that for a considerable period, if not during the whole political existence of Israel, there was no very extensive written law; and that arbitrary and corrupt judgment was only too common at all times. For none of these defects would indicate in ancient Israel the same evils as similar defects in nations of our time would indicate. They are rather defects in the process of being overcome, than defects arising from feeble or vitiated life. If there was a constant movement towards the highest state of things, that is all we can demand or expect to find.

Now there does seem to have been that. As has been well pointed out by Dr. Oort,[108] in the tribes which became Israel justice must have been administered by the heads of the various bodies which went to make these up. The household was ruled even in matters of life and death solely by the father; the family, in the wider sense, was judged by its own heads; the tribes by the elders of the tribes, and there probably was no appeal from one tribunal to another. Each tribunal was final in its own domain. It may be, also, that the judicial function was in all these bodies exercised in the lax and timid fashion common among Bedouin tribes to-day.[109] In all cases, too, it is probable that in the pre-Mosaic time the standard of judgment was customary law. Only with this very great modification can Oort's epigrammatic description of the situation—"There was no law, but there were givers of legal decisions"—be accepted. So far as can be ascertained, the customs according to which men were expected to live were perfectly well known, and within certain narrow limits of variation were extraordinarily stable. How stable customary law may be made, even in the midst of a society governed in the main according to written law in its strictest sense, may be seen in the execration which any breach of the Ulster custom of tenant right met with, before that custom was embodied in any statutes. And in antiquity the stringency of custom can hardly be exaggerated. Under it, when thoroughly established, there was, in all the cases covered by it, only this one way of acting for all, both men and women, who were fit for society at all. Any alternative course was probably inconceivable in the tribal stage of the Israelites' existence.

But a change would doubtless be wrought whenever the appointment of a king took place. Then national law would appear, in embryo at least; and at first, until custom had grown up in this region also, it would largely be an expression of the will of the king, and of the royal officers instructed and trained by the king. But it would have free and unchallenged course only when it claimed authority in matters lying outside of the family and tribal jurisdictions. Wherever it attempted to interfere with tribal or family rights, danger to the kingship of the most acute kind would be sure to arise. In all probability, it was disregard of this axiomatic truth which made Solomon's reign so burdensome to the people and tore the kingdom asunder under Rehoboam. Ahab too fell a victim to his disregard of it. Lastly, the introduction of elaborate written codes of law would, if it came as the crown of such a development, depose custom from its supremacy, though it would not abolish it; and would substitute for it as the main element in all judicial matters the written prescription, which is the necessary presupposition of a fully organised judiciary of the modern type, with a regulated and definite power of appeal.

But in the case of ancient Israel there is a distinguishing element which has to be fitted into this ordinary scheme of progression, and that is the Divine revelation to Moses. Taken up at the tribal stage by the Mosaic revelation, the Israelite tribes were touched and welded into coherence, if not quite as a nation, at least as the people of Yahweh, so that during all the distracting days of the Judges they kept up in essentials their social and religious unity.[110] And with the religious union there must have come administrative uniformity to some considerable extent. The jurisdiction of the heads of households, of heads of families, and of the tribal elders would be as little interfered with as possible; but, as we have seen, all customs and rights had to be reviewed from the point of view of the new religion, and appeal to Moses as the prophet of it must have often been unavoidable. Just as his first followers were continually coming to Mohammed, to ask whether this or that ancient custom could be followed by professors of Islam, so there must have been constant appeals to Moses. So long as he lived, therefore, he, and after him Joshua and Moses' fellow-tribesmen the sons of Levi, as being specially zealous for the religion of Yahweh, must have been constantly called in to assist the customary judges; and so the habit of appeal must have grown in Israel long before there was any king. Thus also a common standard of judgment would be established. That standard must necessarily have been the law of Yahweh, *i.e.* the new Yahwistic principles and all that might *prima facie* be deduced from them, together with so much of custom and tradition as had been accepted as compatible with these principles. We have stated the reasons for holding that the Decalogue was Mosaic, and the Book of the Covenant may be taken also to represent what the current law in Mosaic or sub-Mosaic time was held to be. As Oort well says (*loc. cit.*), when we know that the Hittites about the middle of the fourteenth century B.C. concluded a treaty with Rameses II. of Egypt the terms of which were written upon a silver plate, "why may there not also have been written statements regarding the mutual rights and duties of the people of a town, engraved upon stone or metal, and set forth openly for inspection?" What he confines to mere town business and refers to the time of the Judges, we may without risk extend to a general fundamental law like the Decalogue, or even to the Book of the Covenant, and date it in the time of Moses. Writing was so common an accomplishment in Canaan before the Exodus, that such a supposition is not in the least improbable. These written laws formed the crown of the law of Yahweh, and by them all the rest was raised to a higher level and transformed.

As new men, new times, and new difficulties arose, the priest became the special organ of Divine direction. It may be that the priestly Torah was largely the result of the sacred lot; but the questions that were put, and the manner in which they were put, would be decided ultimately by the conception the priest had of the truth about God. The teaching of the Decalogue would therefore be the dominant and formative power in all that was spoken by the priest and for Yahweh. In the disorganised state into which Israel fell during the time of the Judges, when, as Deuteronomy takes for granted, and as 1 Kings iii. 2 and 3 asserts, the legitimate worship of Yahweh was carried on at many centres, the substantial sameness of the tradition as to the history of Israel, in all the varied forms in which we encounter it, is proof sufficient that at each of the great sanctuaries (which were certainly in the hands of Levitical priests) the treasure of ancient knowledge, both in law and history, was carefully and accurately preserved.[111] New decisions would be given, but they came through men penetrated with the high thoughts of God, and of His people's destiny, which Moses had so fruitfully set forth. This was the element in the life of the people which all the higher minds strove to perpetuate, and, being spiritual, it spiritualised and raised all accessory things. Consequently there was, long before the kingship, what was equivalent to a national feeling of the highest kind, and the conception of justice and its administration corresponded to that.

In the Book of the Covenant, which in this matter represents so early a period that there is no mention of "judges," only of Pelilim,[112] *i.e.* arbitrators (Exod. xxi. 22), so that the tribal and family heads can alone have exercised judicial functions, we find the most solemn warnings against any legal perversion of right to gain popularity, against yielding to the vulgar temptation to oppress the poor, or to the subtler and, for generous minds, more insidious temptation, to give an unjust judgment out of pity for the poor. Israel was, moreover, to keep far from bribery, "which blindeth them that have sight, and perverteth righteous causes." In no way was the law to be used for criminal or oppressive purposes. From the very first, therefore, in Israel the higher principles of faith and life set themselves to combat *à outrance* the tendency to unjust judgment, which seems now, at least, quite ineradicable in the East, save among the Bedouin.[113]

A still higher note is struck in the repetition of the law in the Book of Deuteronomy. In chap. i., originally part of a historic introduction to the book proper, we read: "Hear the causes between your brethren, and judge righteously between a man and his brother, and the stranger that is with him. Ye shall not respect persons in judgment; ye shall hear the small and the great alike; ye shall not be afraid of the face of man; for the judgment (*i.e.* the whole judicial process and function) is God's; and the cause that is too hard for you ye shall bring unto me (Moses), and I will hear it." Yes, the judgment is God's. Just as the whole of moral duty towards man was raised by the Decalogue to a new and more intimate relation with God, so here justice, the fundamental necessity of a sound and stable political state, is lifted out of the conflict of mean and selfish motives, in which it must eventually go down, and is set on high as a matter in which the righteous God is supremely concerned. In this, as in all things, Israel was called to a lonely eminence of ideal perfection by the character of the God whom they were bound to serve. Therefore it strikes us with no surprise that justice is insisted upon almost with passion in Deut. xvii. 20: "Justice, justice shalt thou pursue after, that thou mayest live and possess the land which Yahweh thy God giveth thee"; or that it is made one of the conditions of Israel's permanence as a nation. In chap. xxiv. 17 we read, "Thou shalt not wrest the judgment of the stranger, nor of the fatherless; nor take the widow's raiment to pledge"; in xxv. 1 and 2, "If there be a plea between men, ... then they (*i.e.* the judges) shall justify the righteous and condemn the wicked." For any other course of conduct would bring guilt upon the nation in the sight of Yahweh; and how jealously that was guarded against is seen in the sacrifice and ritual imposed for the purification of the people from the guilt of a murder the perpetrator of which was unknown (Deut. xxi. 1-9). Unatoned for and disregarded, such a crime brought disturbance into those relations between Israel and their God upon which their very existence as a nation depended; and the disregard of justice, where wrongs were committed by known persons and were left unpunished, was of course more deadly. So the author of Deuteronomy looked upon it; and the prophets, from the first of them to the last, brand unjust judgment, the perverting the course of legal justice, as the most alarming sign of national decay. The righteous God, with whom there was no respect of persons, could not permanently favour a people whose judges and rulers disregarded righteousness; and when destruction actually came upon this people, it was proclaimed to be God's doing, "because there was no truth nor justice nor knowledge of God in the land."

Nowhere in the world, therefore, has the demand for justice been made more central than here, and nowhere has injustice been more passionately fought against. Nor have the sanctions binding to a pursuit of justice been at any period more nobly or more vividly conceived. In this main point, therefore, Israel's law stands irreproachable—marvellously so, considering its great antiquity. But we have still to inquire whether any really adequate provision was made for the general and inexpensive administration of justice. To take the latter first, law was in old Israel probably *as cheap* as it would be in the primitive East to-day, if bribery were to be stopped. To advise as to the sacred law, to plead for justice according to it, did not then, and does not now in similar circumstances, belong to any special professional class who live by it. The priest could be appealed to freely by all; and the heads of fathers' houses, as well as the tribal heads, were, by the very fact that they were such, bound to give judgment among their people, and to appear for and take responsibility for them when they had a cause with persons beyond the limits of the particular families and tribes. Justice, consequently, was in ordinary circumstances perfectly free to all.

And from a very early time earnest efforts were made to make it equally *accessible.* At first, when the people were in one army or train, before they came to Sinai, an overwhelming burden was laid upon Moses. As the prophet of the new dispensation all difficulties were brought to him. But at Jethro's suggestion, as JE tells us in Exod. xviii. 13 ff., and as Deuteronomy repeats in chap. i. 16, he chose men of each tribe, or took the heads of each tribe, and set them as captains of thousands and hundreds and fifties and tens. Not improbably this was primarily a military organisation, but to these captains was committed also jurisdiction over those under them. In all ordinary cases they judged them and their families in the spirit of Yahwism, as well as commanded them; and in this way, as has already been pointed out, the customary law was revised in accordance with Yahwistic principles. Justice too was brought to every man's door. The only question that suggests itself is, whether these captain-judges were the ordinary family and tribal heads, organised for this purpose by Moses. On the whole this would seem to have been so, and it may well be that Jethro's suggestion had in view the danger of ignoring them, as well as the burden which Moses' sole judgeship laid upon him. But with the advance to the conquest of Canaan a new situation emerged, and the probability is that more and more, as the tribes fell into entire or semi-isolation, the tribal organisation in its natural shape would come to the front again. Deuteronomy, however, tells us little if anything of this. In the main passage regarding this matter (xvii. 8-13), where provision is made for an appeal to a central court, the legislation is entirely for a period much later than Moses. Like the law regarding sacrifice at one altar, the judicial provisions of Deuteronomy seem all to be bound up with the place which Yahweh shall choose, viz. the Solomonic Temple in Jerusalem. We may consequently conclude that the judicial arrangements to which Deuteronomy alludes existed only after the Israelite kingship had been for some time established at Jerusalem. We have no distinct evidence for the existence of a central high court in David's days; and from the story of Absalom's rebellion we should gather that the old, simple Oriental method still prevailed, according to which the king, like the heads of tribes, families, etc., judged every one who came to him, personally, at the gate of the royal city. But Samuel is said in 1 Sam. vii. 16 to have annually gone on circuit to Bethel, Gilgal, and Mizpah. According to the school of Wellhausen, nearly the whole of this chapter is the work of a Deuteronomic writer about the year 600. In that case, of course, it would be difficult to prove that the arrangement attributed to Samuel was not a mere echo of what was done in Josiah's day; though, if the Deuteronomic prescriptions were carried out then, there would be no need for such a system. On the other hand, if Budde and Cornill be right in tracing the chapter back to JE, this habit of going on circuit must have been an ancient one, possibly dating from Samuel's time. That this latter view is the correct one is in a degree confirmed by the statement in viii. 2 that Samuel's sons were installed by him as judges in Israel, at Beersheba. This belongs to E, and it would seem to indicate the beginnings of such a system as Deuteronomy presupposes.

But it is only in the days of Jehoshaphat (873-849 B.C.) that an arrangement like that in Deuteronomy is mentioned. From 2 Chron. xix. 5 ff. we learn that "he set judges in the land throughout all the fenced cities of Judah, city by city. Moreover in Jerusalem did Jehoshaphat set of the Levites and of the priests, and of the heads of the fathers' houses, for the judgment of Yahweh and for controversies." Further, it is stated that Amariah the chief priest was set over the judges in Jerusalem in all Yahweh's matters, *i.e.* in all religious questions, and Zebadiah the son of Ishmael the prince of the house of Judah in all the king's matters, *i.e.* in all secular affairs. Of course few advanced critics will admit that the Books of Chronicles are reliable in such matters. But that judgment is altogether too sweeping, and here we would seem to have a well-authenticated record of what Jehoshaphat actually did.

For it will be observed, that when we take up the various notices in regard to the administration of justice, we have a well-defined progress from Moses to Jehoshaphat. Moses was chief judge and committed ordinary cases to the tribal and family heads who were chosen as military leaders, each judging his own detachment. After passing the Jordan, the whole matter would seem to have fallen back into the hands of the tribal heads, with the occasional help of the heroes who delivered and judged Israel. At the end of this period Samuel, as head of the State, went on circuit, and appointed his sons judges in Beersheba, thus initiating a new system, which, had it been successful, might have superseded the tribal and family heads altogether. But it was a failure, and was not repeated. With the rise of the kingship the courts received further organisation. If the Chronicler can be trusted, Levites to the number of six thousand were appointed to be judges and Shoterim. The number seems excessive; but the appointment of Levites to act as assessors with the tribal and other heads would be a natural expedient for a king like David to have recourse to, if he desired to secure uniformity of judgment, and to bring the courts under his personal influence. The next step would naturally be that which is attributed to Jehoshaphat, and it is precisely that which Deuteronomy points to as being already at work in his time. We have, consequently, more than the late authority of the Chronicler for Jehoshaphat's high court. The probabilities of the case point so strongly to the rise of some such judicial system about that period, that it would require some positive proof, not mere negative suspicion, to lead us to reject the narrative. In any case this must have been the system in Josiah's day, and afterwards. For when Jeremiah was arraigned for prophesying destruction to the Temple and to Jerusalem, the process against him was conducted on similar lines to those laid down in Deuteronomy. The princes judged, the priests (curiously enough along with the false prophets) made the charge, *i.e.* stated that the prophet's conduct was worthy of death, and the princes acquitted. During the Exile it is probable that the "elders" of the people were permitted to judge them in all ordinary cases, but we have no certain proof that this was so. After the return from Babylon, however, the local courts were re-established, probably in the very form in which they appear in the New Testament (Matt. v. 22, x. 17; Mark xiii. 9; Luke xii. 14-58).

Throughout the whole history of Israel, therefore, courts of justice were easily accessible to every man, whether he were rich or poor. No doubt the free, open-air, Eastern manner of administering justice was favoured to that; but from the days of Moses onward we have fairly conclusive proof that the leaders of the people made it their continual care that wherever a wrong was suffered there should be some court to which an appeal for redress could be made.

The justice aimed at in Israel was, therefore, *impartial* and *accessible*. We have still to inquire whether it was *merciful* or cruel in its infliction of punishment. Dr. Oort says it was a hard law in this respect, but one is at a loss to see how that view can be sustained. There is no mention of torture in connection with legal proceedings, either in the history or in the legislation. Nor is there any instance mentioned in which an accused person was imprisoned until he confessed. Indeed imprisonment would not appear to have been a legal punishment in Israel, nor in any antique state. The idea of providing maintenance for those who had offended against the law was one which could never have occurred to any one in antiquity. Prisons are, of course, frequently mentioned in Scripture; but they were used, up to the time of Ezra, only for the safe-keeping of persons charged with crime till they could be brought before the judges. Sometimes, as in the case of the prophets, men were imprisoned to prevent them from stirring up the people; but this procedure was nowhere sanctioned by law. Further, the crimes for which the punishment prescribed in the ancient law was death were few. Idolatry, adultery, unnatural lust, sorcery, and murder or manslaughter, together with striking or cursing parents and kidnapping—these were all. Considering that idolatry and sorcery were high treason in its worst forms, so far as this people was concerned, and that impurity threatened the family in a much more direct and immediate fashion then than it does now, while the people were naturally inclined to it, one must wonder that the list of capital crimes is so short. Contrast this with Blackstone's statement in regard to England (quoted *Ency. Brit.*, iv., p. 589): "Among the variety of actions which men are daily liable to commit, no less than one hundred and sixty have been declared by Act of Parliament to be felonies without benefit of clergy, or, in other words, to be worthy of instant death." It is only in comparatively recent years that the punishment of death has been practically restricted to murder in England. Yet that is almost the case in the ancient Jewish law; for the exceptions are such as would reappear in England if it were more sparsely populated and manners were rougher. In Australia, for example, highway robbery under arms and violence to women are capital crimes, just because the country is sparsely inhabited and the households unprotected. Nor were the modes of death inflicted cruel. Only three—viz. impalement, and burning, and stoning—appear to be so. But it may be believed that in the cases contemplated by the law death in some less painful manner had preceded the two former, as is certainly the case in

Josh. vii. 15 and 25, and in Deut. xxi. 22. As for the latter, it must have been horrible to look upon, but in all probability the criminal's agony was rarely a prolonged one. The other method of execution, by the sword namely, was humane enough. Dr. Oort tells us that mutilations were common; but his proof is only this, that in the treaty between the Hittite king and Rameses II. we read, concerning inhabitants of Egypt who have fled to the land of the Hittites and have been returned, "His mother shall not be put to death; he shall not be punished in his eyes, nor on his mouth, nor on the soles of his feet." The same provision is made for Hittite fugitives. From this evidence of the custom of surrounding peoples, and from the fact that the *jus talionis* is announced in the Scriptures by the familiar formula, "Eye for eye, tooth for tooth, hand for hand, foot for foot," Dr. Oort draws this conclusion. But he appears to forget that the *jus talionis* was common to almost all the peoples of the ancient world, and is referred to in the Pentateuch, not as a new principle, but as a custom coming down from immemorial time. Consequently, though there must once have been a time in which it was carried out in its literal form, that time probably was past when the laws referring to it were written. In Rome, and probably in other lands where this custom existed, it early gave place to the custom of giving and receiving money payments. Most probably this was the case in Israel, at least from the time of the Exodus. For the new religion introduced by Moses was merciful. But these references to the principle of retaliation tell us nothing as to the frequency or otherwise of mutilation as a punishment. No instance of mutilation being inflicted either as a retaliation or as a punishment occurs in the Old Testament, and the probability is that cases were never numerous. Apart from retaliation they are never mentioned; and we may, I think, set it down as one of the distinctive merits of the Israelite law that it never was betrayed into sanctioning the cutting off of hands or feet or ears or noses as general punishment for crime. But so far as the principle of the *lex talionis* was retained, its effect was wholesome. It was a continual reminder that all free Israelites were equals in the sight of Yahweh. And not only so, it enforced as well as asserted equality. Any poor man mutilated by a rich man could demand the infliction of the same wound upon his oppressor. He could reject his excuses, and refuse his money, and bring home to him the truth that they had equal rights and duties.

In this way this seemingly harsh law helped to lay the foundation for our modern conception of humanity, which regards all men as brethren. For the teaching of our Lord, which fulfilled all that the polity and religion of ancient Israel had foreshadowed of good, broke down the walls of partition between Jew and Gentile, and made all men brethren by revealing to them a common Father. It surely is strange and sad that those who specially make liberty, equality, and fraternity their watchwords, have received so false an impression of the religion of both the Old and New Testaments, that they pride themselves on rejecting both. When all is said, the levelling of barriers which the crushing weight of Roman power brought about, and the common methods and elements of thought which the Greek conquests had spread all over the civilised world, would never have made the brotherhood of man the universally accepted doctrine it is. The truths which made it credible came from the revelation given by God to His chosen people, and its final and conclusive impulse was given to it by the lips of Christ.

In face of that cardinal fact it is vain to point out as one of the defects of this law that all men were not equal before it. Women were not equal with men, nor were foreigners nor slaves equal with freeborn Israelites; but the seed of all that later times were to bring was already there. The principles which at the long end of the day have abolished slavery, raised women to the equal position they now occupy, and made peace with foreigners increasingly the desire of all nations, had their first hold upon men given them here. In all these directions the Mosaic law was epoch-making. In the fifth commandment, as well as in the legislation regarding the punishment of a rebellious son, the mother is put upon the same level as the father. However subordinate woman's position in the larger public life might be, within the home she was to be respected. There, in her true domain, she was man's equal, and was acknowledged to have an equal claim to reverence from her children.

In precisely the same way the "stranger" was freed from disability and protected. In the earliest days, when the Israelite community was still being formed, whole groups of strangers were received into it and obtained full rights, as for example the Kenites and Kenizzites. But though this was a promise of what Israel was ultimately to be to the world, the necessities of the situation, the need to keep intact the treasure of higher religion which was committed to this people, compelled the adoption of a more separatist policy. Yet "in no other nation of antiquity were strangers received and treated with such liberality and humanity as in Israel." They were freely afforded the protection of the law; they were, in short, received as "a kind of half-citizens, with definite rights and duties."[114] Further, though the ger was not bound to all the religious practices and rites of the Israelite, yet he was permitted, and in some cases commanded, to take part in their religious worship. If he consented to circumcise all his house he might even share in the Passover feast. All oppression of such an one was also rigorously forbidden, and to a large extent the stranger shared in the benefits conferred by the provision for the poor of the land which the law made compulsory.

Nor was the case otherwise with slaves. Equality there was not, and could not be; but in the provisions for the emancipation of the Israelite slave and the introduction of penalties for undue harshness, it began to be recognised that the slave stood, in some degree at least, on the same level as his master—he too was a man.

Taking it as a whole, therefore, the ancient world will be searched in vain for any legislation equal to this in the "promise and the potency" of its fundamental ideas as to justice. Here, as nowhere else, we can see the radical principles which should dominate in the administration of justice laying hold upon mankind, and that there was a living will and power behind these principles is shown in the steady movement toward something higher which characterised Israelite law. In the pursuit of impartiality, accessibility, and humanity, the teachers of Israel were untiring, and the sanctions by which they surrounded and guarded all that tended to make the administration of justice effective in the high sense were unusually solemn and powerful. The result has been most remarkable. All the ages of civilised men since have been the heirs of Israel in this matter. Roman influence and the influence of the Christian Church have no doubt been powerful, and the manifold exigencies of life have drawn out and made explicit much which was only implicit in the ancient days. But the higher qualities of our modern administration of justice can be traced back step by step to Biblical principles, and the course of development laid bare. When that is done, it is seen that the almost ideal purity and impartiality of the best modern tribunals is the completion of what the Israelite law and methods began. In this one instance at least the great Mosaic principles have come to fruition; and from the security and peace, the contentment and the confidence, with which impartial justice has filled the minds of men, we can estimate how potent to cure the ills of our social and moral state the realisation of the other great Mosaic ideals would be. It should be a source of encouragement to all who look for a time when "the kingdoms of this world shall become the kingdoms of our Lord and of His Christ," that something like the ideal of justice has so far been realised. It has no doubt been a weary time in coming, and it has as yet but a narrow and perhaps precarious footing in the world. But it is here, with its healing and beneficent activity; and in that fact we may well see a pledge that all the rest of the Divinely given ideals for the Kingdom of God will one day be realised also. Such a consummation, however remote it may seem to our human impatience, however devious and winding the paths by which alone it can draw near, will come most surely, and in our approach to the ideal in our judicial system we may well see the firstfruits of a richer and more plentiful harvest.

CHAPTER XXII
LAWS OF PURITY (CHASTITY AND MARRIAGE)

In dealing with the ten commandments it has been already shown that, though these great statements of religious and moral truth were to some extent inadequate as expressions of the highest life, they yet contained the living germs of all that has followed. But we cannot suppose that the reality of Israelite life from the first corresponded with them. They contained much that only the experience and teaching of ages could fully bring to light; therefore we cannot expect that the actual laws in regard to the relations of the sexes and the virtue of chastity should stand upon the same high level as the Decalogue. The former represent the reality, this the ultimate ideal of Israelite law on these subjects. But neither is unimportant in forming an estimate of the value of the revelation given to Israel, and of the moral condition of early Israel itself, nor can either be justly viewed altogether alone. The actual law at any moment in the history of Israel must be regarded as inspired and upborne by the ideal set forth in the ten commandments. But it must, at the same time, be a very incomplete realisation of these, and its various stages will be best regarded as instalments of advance towards that comparative perfection.

In regard to the relations of the sexes and the virtue of purity this must be peculiarly the case. For though chastity has been safeguarded by almost all nations up to a certain low point, it has never been really cherished by any naturalistic system. Nor has it ever been favoured by mere humanism. [115] Consequently there is no point of morals in regard to which man has more conspicuously failed to work out the merely animal impulse from his nature than in this. And yet, for all the higher ends of life, as well as for the prosperity and vigour of mankind, purity in the sexual relations is entirely vital. One great cause of the decay of nations, nay, even of civilisations, has been the abandonment of this virtue. This was the main cause of the destruction of the Canaanites. It may even be said to have been the cause of the wreck of the whole ancient world. We should consequently measure what the Mosaic influence did for purity of life, not by comparing early Israelite laws with what has been accomplished by Christianity, but with the condition of the Semitic peoples surrounding Israel, in and after the Mosaic times.

What that was we know. Their religions, far from discouraging sexual immorality, made it a part of their holiest rites. Both men and women gave themselves up to natural and unnatural lusts, in honour of their gods. To the north, and south, and east, and west of Israel these practices prevailed, and as a natural result the moral fabric of these nations' life fell into utter ruin. In private life adultery, and the still more degrading sin of Sodom were common. The man had a right to indiscriminate divorce and remarriage, and marriage connections now reckoned incestuous, such as those between brother and sister, were entirely approved. In all these points Israel as a nation was without reproach. The higher teaching this people had received in respect to the character of God, and it may be some reminiscence of Egyptian custom, which was in some respects purer than that of the Semitic peoples, raised them to a higher level. Yet in the main the early Israelite view of women was fundamentally the uncivilised one.

But at all periods of Israelite history, even the earliest, women had asserted their personality. In the eye of the law they might be the chattels of their male relatives, but as a fact they were dealt with as persons, with many personal rights. They had no independent position in the community, it is true. They could take no part in a festival so important as the Passover, nor were they free to make vows without the consent of their husbands. In other ways also social restraints were laid upon them. Nevertheless their position in early Israel was much higher than it is in the East to-day, and their liberty was in no wise unreasonably abridged. In David's day women could appear in public to converse with men without scandal.[116] They also took part in religious festivals and processions, giving life to them by beating their timbrels, by singing, and by dancing.[117] They could be present also at all ordinary sacrifices and at sacrificial feasts; and, as we see in the case of Deborah and others, they could occupy a high, almost a supreme, position as prophetesses. In the main, too, the relations between husband and wife were loving and respectful, and in Israel's best days, when the people still remained landed yeomanry, the wife, by her industry within the house, supplemented and completed her husband's labour in the fields. The Israelite woman was consequently a very important person in the community, whatever her status in law might be; and if she had not the full rights which are now granted to her sex in Western and Christian lands, her position was for the times a noble and independent one. That all this was so was largely due to the improvements which Mosaism wrought on the basis of that ancient Semitic custom which we sketched at the beginning of this chapter, and with which it seems natural to suppose the Israelite tribes had also begun.

Bearing these preliminary considerations in mind, we now go on to consider the actual legislation in regard to the relations of the sexes. But here we must once more recall the fact that, in regard to all matters vitally affecting the community, there had always been a custom, and even before written law appears that custom had been adopted and modified in Yahwism by Moses himself. That this was actually the case here is rendered highly probable by the history of legislation in this matter. In the Book of the Covenant there is no mention of sexual sin, save in one passage (Exod. xxii. 16), where the penalty for seduction of a virgin who is not betrothed is that the seducer shall offer a "*mohar*" for her, and marry her without possibility of divorce, if her father consent. If he will not, then the "*mohar*" is forfeited to the father nevertheless, as compensation for the degradation of his daughter. But it is obvious that there must have been laws or customs regulating marriage other than this, for without them there could have been no such crime as is here punished. Obviously, also, there must have been laws or customs of divorce. But of what these laws of marriage and divorce were Exodus gives us no hint. Deuteronomy, the next code, which on the critical hypothesis arose at a much later time as a revision of the Book of the Covenant, contains much more, *i.e.* it draws out of the obscurity of unwritten custom a more extensive series of provisions in regard to purity. The Law of Holiness then adds largely to Deuteronomy, and with it the main points of the law of purity have attained to written expression. But the influence of the higher standard set in the Decalogue also makes itself felt,—not in the law so much as in the historic books and the prophets—and our task now is to trace out first the legal development, then the prophetical, and to show how the whole movement culminated and was crowned in the teaching of Christ.

Beginning then with Deuteronomy, we find that the chastity of women was surrounded by ample safeguards. Religious prostitution was absolutely prohibited (Deut. xxiii. 18). Further, if any violence was done to a woman who had been betrothed, the punishment of the wrong was death; if done to a woman who was not betrothed, the wrong was atoned for by payment of fifty shekels of silver to her father, and by offering marriage without possibility of divorce. If marriage was refused, then the fifty shekels was retained by the father in consideration of the wrong done him. When the woman was a sharer in the guilt the punishment in all cases was death; while pre-nuptial unchastity, when discovered after marriage, was punished, as adultery also was, with the same severity.[118] In women who were free, therefore, purity was demanded in Israel as strenuously as it ever has been anywhere, though in man the only limit to sexual indulgence was the demand, that in seeking it he should not infringe upon the father's property in his daughter, or the husband's in his wife or his betrothed bride.

Admittedly the original underlying motive for this moral severity was a low one, the mere proprietary rights of the father or husband. But it would be a mistake to suppose that purely ethical and religious motives had no place in establishing the customs or enactments which we find in Deuteronomy. With the lapse of time higher motives entwined themselves with the coarse strand of personal proprietary interest, which had originally, though perhaps never alone, been the line of limitation. Gradually there grew up a standard of higher purity; and when Deuteronomy was written, though the original line was still clearly visible, it was justified by appeals to a moral sense which reached far beyond the original motives of the customary law. The continually recurring burden of Deuteronomy in dealing with these matters is that to work "folly in Israel" is a crime for which only the severest punishment can atone. To "extinguish the evil from Israel," and to put away such things as were "abominations to Yahweh their God," are the great reasons on which the writer of Deuteronomy founds the claim for obedience in these cases. Obviously, therefore, by his time, under the teaching of the religion of Yahweh, Israel had risen to a moral height which took account of graver interests than the rights of property in legislating for female purity. The cases included in the law had been determined by considerations of that kind; but the sanctions by which the commands were buttressed had entirely changed their character. The holiness of God and the dignity of man, the consideration of what alone was worthy of a "son of Israel," have taken the place of the coarser sanctions. In this way a possibility of unlimited moral progress was secured, since the cause of purity was indissolubly bound to the general and irresistible advance of religious and moral enlightenment in the chosen people.

Moreover the personality of the woman was acknowledged in the entire acquittal of the betrothed woman who had been exposed to outrage in the country, where her cries could bring no help. In the earliest times most probably the punishment of death would have been inflicted equally in that case, since the husband's property had been deteriorated to such a degree as to make it unworthy of him. But in the Deuteronomic provision quite other things are drawn into the estimate. The moral guilt of the person concerned is now the decisive consideration. The woman has ceased to be a mere chattel, and the full claims of her personality are in the way to be recognised. These were great advances, and for these it is vain to seek for other causes than the persistent upward pressure of the Mosaic religion. The moral superiority of Israel at the time of the conquest over the much more cultured Canaanites, as also over the nomadic tribes to which they were more nearly related, is due, as Stade says, ultimately to their religion; and no reader of the Old Testament, in our time at least, can fail to see that their moral progress in the land they conquered depended entirely upon the same cause. At the Deuteronomic epoch purity had already been placed upon a worthy basis, as a moral achievement of the first importance, and impurity had taken its proper place as a degrading sin. But much still remained to be done before these principles could be extended into all domains of life equally.

How far they had penetrated in early times may perhaps best be seen in the Deuteronomic references to divorce. Before Deuteronomy there is no law of divorce, nor indeed is there any after it. We may perhaps even say that there is in it not so much the statement of a law of divorce, as a reference to custom which the writer wishes to correct or reinforce in one particular respect only. Notwithstanding the Jewish view, therefore, which finds in Deut. xxiv. 1-4 a divorce law, we must adduce the passage as a new and striking proof of what we have all along asserted, that neither Deuteronomy nor any other of the legal codes can be taken as complete statements of what was legally permitted or forbidden in Israel. Behind all of them there is a vast mass of unwritten customary law, and divorce was doubtless always determined by it. That this was the case will be seen at once if the passage we are now concerned with be rightly translated. It runs thus: "When a man taketh a wife and marrieth her, and it shall be (if she find no favour in his eyes, because he hath found in her some unseemly thing) that he writeth her a bill of divorcement, and giveth it into her hand, and sendeth her out of his house, and she go forth out of his house and goeth and becometh the wife of another man, and if the latter husband also hate her, and write her a bill of divorcement, and give it in her hand and send her out of his house, or if the latter husband die who took her to him to wife, then her former husband who sent her away may not take her again to be his wife after that she has permitted herself to be defiled." All the passage provides for, therefore, is that a divorced woman shall not be remarried to the divorcing man after she has been married again, even though she be separated from her second husband by divorce or death. There is consequently no law of divorce here stated. There is merely a reference to a general law or custom by which divorce was permitted for "any unseemly thing," and according to which a chief wife at any rate could be divorced only by a "bill of divorcement," and not by mere word of mouth, as is common in many Eastern lands to-day. Mosaic influence may have procured this last slight increase in rigour, and Deuteronomy certainly adds three other restrictions, viz. that after remarriage a woman cannot be again married to her first husband, and that pre-nuptial wrong done to a woman by her husband, or a false accusation by him after marriage, takes away his right of divorce altogether. But the woman has no right of divorce at all, so firmly fixed throughout all Old

Testament time was the belief in the inferiority of women. On the whole, therefore, divorce in Israel remained, after the law had dealt with it, much on the level to which the tribal customs had brought it. So far as the legislation dealt with it, it tended to restriction; but when all is said it remains true that the Israelite *law* of divorce was in the main much what it would have been had there been no revelation. But the *spirit* of the religion of Yahweh was against laxity in this matter, and this more rigorous feeling finds expression in the evident distaste for the remarriage of a divorced woman which is expressed in Deut. xxiv. 4. Remarriage is not forbidden; but the woman who remarries is spoken of as one who has "let herself be defiled." No such expression could have been used, had not remarriage after divorce been looked upon as something which detracted from perfect feminine purity. The legislator evidently regarded it as the higher way for a divorced woman to remain unmarried so long at least as the divorcing husband lived. If she remained so, the possibility of reunion was always kept open, and the law evidently looked upon the ultimate annulment of the divorce as the course which was most consonant with the ideal of marriage.

It is thus clearly seen how our Lord's statement (Matt. xix. 8)—"Moses because of the hardness of your hearts suffered you to put away your wives, but from the beginning it hath not been so"—is true.

And when we leave the law and come to history and prophecy, we find this view to have been a prevalent one from early times. In one of the earliest connected historical narratives, that of J (Gen. ii. 24), the union of husband and wife is said to be so peculiarly intimate that it makes them one body, so that separation is equivalent to mutilation. And the prophets remain true to this conception of marriage, as the one which fitted best into their deeper and loftier views of morality. From Hosea onwards[119] they represent the indissoluble bond between Yahweh and His people as a marriage relation, founded on free choice and unchangeable love. The possibility of divorce is no doubt often admitted, and the conduct of Israel is represented as justifying that course. But the prophetic message always is that the love of God will never permit Him to put away His people; and the people are often addressed as faithless and faint-hearted, because they yield to the temptation of believing that He has cast them off (Isa. l. 1). Evidently, therefore, the prophetic ideal of marriage was that it should be indissoluble, that it should be founded upon free mutual love, and that such a love should make it impossible for either husband or wife to give the other up, however desperate the errors of the guilty one might have been.

Perhaps the finest expression of this view occurs in Isa. liv., in the exhortation addressed to exiled Israel and beginning "Sing, O barren, thou that didst not bear." There the ideal Israel is urged to lay aside all her fears with this assurance: "For thy Maker is thine husband; Yahweh of Hosts is His name: and thy Redeemer, the Holy One of Israel, the God of the whole earth shall He be called. For Yahweh hath called thee as a woman forsaken and grieved in spirit; how can a wife of youth be rejected? saith thy God." The full meaning of this last touching question has been well brought out by Prof. Cheyne (*Isaiah*, ii., p. 55): "Even many an earthly husband (how much more then Yahweh!) cannot bear to see the misery of his divorced wife, and therefore at length recalls her; and when his wife is one who has been wooed and won in youth, how impossible is it for her to be absolutely dismissed." The rising tide of prophetic feeling on this subject culminates in the pathetic scene depicted by Malachi, who in chap. ii. 12 ff. reproves his people for their cruel and frivolous use of divorce. Drawn away by love of idolatrous women, they had divorced their Hebrew wives; and these in their misery crowded the Temple, covering the altar of Yahweh with "tears and weeping and sobbing," till He could endure it no more. He had been witness of the covenant made between each of these men and the wife of his youth; yet they had broken this Divinely sanctioned bond. He therefore warns them to take heed, "for Yahweh the God of Israel saith, I hate putting away, and him who covers his garment with violence." The Rabbinic interpreters, not being minded to give up the privilege of divorce, have wrested these words into "for Yahweh the God of Israel saith, If he hate her put her away." But, so wrested, the words bring down the whole context in one ruin. They are intelligible only if they denounce divorce, and in this sense they must undoubtedly be taken.

There remains for consideration, however, a marriage which the Deuteronomist permits, which seems to run counter to all the finer feelings and instincts of his later time. It is dealt with in chap. xxv. 5-10, and is notable because it is a clear breach of the definite rule that a man should not marry his deceased brother's wife. But it will be obvious at once that the permission of this marriage stands upon quite a different footing from the prohibition. It is permitted only in a special case for definite ends; and while the sanction of the prohibition is the infliction of childlessness (Lev. xx. 21), the man who refuses to enter upon marriage with his deceased brother's wife is punished only by being put to shame by her before the elders of his city. We have not here, therefore, a law in the strict sense. It is only a recognition of a very ancient custom which is not yet abolished, though evidently public feeling was beginning to make light of the obligation. Its place in the twenty-fifth chapter, away from the marriage laws (which are given in xxi. 10 ff., xxii. 13 ff., and xxiv. 1-4), and among duties of kindness, seems to hint this, and we may consequently take the law as a concession. That the custom was ancient in the time of Deuteronomy may be gathered from the fact that in Hebrew there is a special technical term, *yibbēm*, for entering on such a marriage. The probability is, indeed, that levirate marriage was a pre-Mosaic custom connected with ancestor-worship. It certainly is practised by many other races, *e.g.* the Hindus and Persians, whose religions can be traced to that source. Under that system, it was necessary that the male line of descent should be kept up in order that the ancestral sacrifices might be continued, and to bear the expense of this the property of the brother dying childless was jealously preserved. In India, at present, both purposes are served by adoption, either by the childless man or by the widow. In earlier times, when fatherhood was to a large extent a merely juridical relationship,[120] when, that is to say, it was a common thing for a man to accept as his son any child born of women under his control, whether he were the father or not, the same end was also attained by this marriage.[121] Originating in this way, the practice was carried over into the Israelite social life when it changed its form, and the motives for it were then brought into line with the new and higher religion. The motive of keeping alive the name and memory of the childless man was substituted for that of securing the continuance of his worship; and the purpose of securing the permanence of property, landed property especially, in each household, was substituted for that of supplying means for the sacrifice. Later, the motive connected with the transmission of property possibly became the main one. For, since the levirate marriage came in, according to the strict wording of our passage, whenever a man died without a son, whether he had daughters or not, this marriage would seem to have been an alternative means of keeping the property in the family to that of letting the daughters inherit.[122] But the spirit of the higher religion, as well as a more advanced civilisation, was unfavourable to it. The custom evidently was withering when Deuteronomy was written, though in Judaism it was not disallowed till post-Talmudic times.

The impression, therefore, which the laws and customs regulating the relations of men and women in Israel give to the candid student must be pronounced to be a strangely mixed one. It would probably not be too much to say that it is at first a deeply disappointing one. We have been accustomed to fill all the Old Testament utterances on this subject with the suffused light of Gospel precept and example, till we have lost sight of the lower elements undeniably present in the Old Testament laws and ideas concerning purity. But that is no longer possible. Whether of enmity or of zeal for the truth, these less worthy elements have been dragged forth into the broad light of day, and in that light we are called upon to readjust our thoughts so as to accept and account for them. Evidently at the beginning the Israelite tribes accepted the uncivilised idea of woman. On that as a basis, however, customs and laws regarding chastity, marriage and divorce were adopted, which transcended and passed beyond that fundamental idea. The moral complicity of woman, or her innocence, in cases where her chastity had been attacked, came to be taken into account. Polygamy, though never forbidden, received grievous wounds from prophets and others of the sacred writers; and as marriage with one became more and more the ideal, the higher teachers of the people kept the indissolubleness of marriage before the public mind, till Malachi denounced divorce in Yahweh's name. In regard to the bars to marriage there was little change, probably, from the days of Moses; but the old family rules were reinforced by a deep and delicate regard for even the less palpable affections and relations which grew up in the home.

The final attainment, therefore, was great and worthy enough; but the cruder and less refined ideas, which had been inherited from pre-Mosaic custom, always make themselves felt, and have even dominated some of the laws. They dominated, even more, the practice of the people and the theory of the scribes; so that on the very eve of His coming who was to proclaim decisively the indissolubility of marriage, the great Jewish schools were wrangling whether mere caprice, or some immodesty only, could justify divorce. Nevertheless the Decalogue, with its deep and broad command, culminating in prohibition even of inward evil desire, had always had its own influence. The teachings of the prophets, which breathe passionate hatred of impurity, had taught all men of good-will in Israel that the wrath of God surely burned against it. But the stamp of imperfection was upon Old Testament teaching here as elsewhere. Like the Messianic hope, like the future of Israel, like all Israel's greatest destinies, the promise of a higher life in this respect was darkened by the inconsistencies of general practice; and uncertainty prevailed as to the direction in which men were to look for the harmonious development of the higher potencies which were making their presence felt. It was in them rather than in the law, in the ideals rather than in the practice of the people, that the hidden power was silently doing its regenerating work. The religion of Yahweh in its central content, surrounded all laws and institutions with an atmosphere which challenged and furthered growth of every wholesome kind. The axe and hammer of the legislative builder was rarely heard at work; but in the silence which seems to some so barren, there slowly grew a fabric of moral and spiritual ideas and aspirations, which needed only the coming of Christ to make it the permanent home of all morally earnest souls.

With Him all that the past generations "had willed, or hoped, or dreamed of good" came actually to exist. He made what had been aspiration only the basis of an actual Kingdom of God. As one of its primary moral foundations

He laid down the radical indissolubility of marriage, and made visible to all men the breadth of the law given in the Decalogue by forbidding even wandering desires. In doing this He completely surpassed all Old Testament teaching, and set up a standard which Christian communities as such have held to hitherto, but which from lack of elevation and earnestness they seem inclined in these days to let slip. That such a standard was ever set up was the work of a Divine revelation of a perfectly unique kind, working through long ages of upward movement. Humanity has been dragged upwards to it most unwillingly. Men have found difficulty in living at that height, and nothing is easier than to throw away all the gain of these many centuries. All that is needed is a plunge or two downwards. But if ever these plunges are taken, the long, slow effort upwards will only have to be begun again, if family life is to be firmly established, and purity is to become a permanent possession of men.

CHAPTER XXIII
LAWS OF KINDNESS

With the commands we now have to consider, we leave altogether the region of strict law, and enter entirely upon that of aspiration and of feeling. Kindness, by its very nature, eludes the rude compulsion of law, properly so called. It ceases to be kindness when it loses spontaneity and freedom. Precept, therefore, not law, is the utmost that any lawgiver can give in respect to it; and this is precisely what we have in Deuteronomy, so far as it endeavours to incite men to gentleness, goodness, and courtesy to one another. The author gives his people an ideal of what they ought to be in these respects, and presses it home upon them with the heartfelt earnestness which distinguishes him. That is all; but yet, if we are to do justice to him as a lawgiver, we must consider and estimate the moral value of these precepts; for, properly speaking, they are the flower of his legal principles, and they reveal in detail, and therefore, for the average man, most impressively, the spirit in which his whole legislation was conceived. In the abstract no doubt he had told us that love—love to Yahweh—was to be the fundamental thing, and we have seen how deep and wide-reaching that announcement was. But a review of the precepts which indicate how he conceived that love to God should affect men's relations with men, will give that general principle a definiteness and a concreteness more impressive than a thousand homilies. For the conception that a relation of love is the only fit relation between man and God, could not, if it were sincerely taken up, fail to throw light upon men's true relations to each other. Consequently the great declaration of the sixth chapter was bound to re-echo in the precepts to guide conduct, giving new sanctity and breadth to all man's duty to his fellows.

Of course the risk of great failure was nigh at hand: for men may be intellectually convinced that love is the element in which life ought to be lived, and may proclaim it, who are far from being actually penetrated and filled with love, tested and increased by communion with God. As a result, much talk about love and kindly human duty has fallen with but little impulsive power upon the hearts of men. When, however, it is felt to be the expression of a present experience, such exhortation has power to move men as no other words can do. And the author of Deuteronomy was one of those who had this divinely given secret. In all parts of his book you find his words becoming winged with power, wherever love to God and man is even remotely touched upon. If our hypothesis as to the age in which he lived and wrote be correct, his must have been one of those high and rare natures which are not embittered by persecution or contemptuous neglect. Long before our Lord had spoken His decisive words on our duty to our neighbour, or St. Paul had written his great hymn to love, this man of God had been chosen to feel the truth, and had suffused his book with it, so that the only principle which can be recognised as binding together all his precepts is the central principle of the New Testament. Of course that made his ideal too high for present realisation; but he gained more than he lost; for, from Jeremiah and Josiah downwards through the years, all the noblest of his people responded to him. The splendour of his thought cast reflections upon their minds, and these glowed and shone amid the meaner lights which Pharisaism kindled and cherished, till He came whose right it was to reign. Then Deuteronomy's true rank was seen; for from it Christ took the answers by which He repelled Satan in the temptation, and from it, too, He took that commandment which He called the first and greatest. Of course the humanity of the book had not, in expression at least, the imperial sweep of Christian brotherhood which makes all men equal, so that for it there is neither Jew nor Gentile, neither wise nor unwise, neither male nor female, neither bond nor free. But *all* the chosen people are included in its sympathy; and in this field, without undue interference with private life, the author sets forth by specimen cases how the fraternal feeling should manifest itself in loving, neighbourly kindness.

As these laws or precepts of kindness are not systematically arranged, it will be necessary to group them, and we shall take first those in which it is prescribed that injury to others should be avoided. Of course criminal wrongs are not dealt with here. They have already been forbidden in the strictly legal portions of the book, and penalties have been attached to them. But in the region beyond law, there are many acts in which the difference between a good, and kindly, and sympathetic man, and a morose, and sullen, and unkindly one, can be even more clearly seen. In that region Deuteronomy is unmistakably on the side of sympathy. The poor, the slave, the helpless should, it teaches, be objects of special care to the true son of Israel. They should be treated, it shows, with a generous perception of the peculiar difficulties of their lot; and pressure upon them at these special points where their lot is hard should be abhorrent to every Israelite.

The first in order of the precepts which we are considering (chap. xxii. v. 8)—"When thou buildest a new house, then thou shalt make a railing for thy roof, that thou bring not blood upon thine house, if any man fall from thence"—reveals the fatherly and loving temper which it is the author's delight to attribute to Yahweh. As earthly parents guard their children from accidents and dangers, so Yahweh thinks of possible danger to the lives of His people, and calls for even minute precautions. The habit of sitting and sleeping upon the flat roofs of the houses has always been, and is now, prevalent in the East. Many accidents take place through this habit. In recent years Emin Pasha, who ruled so long at Wadelai, nearly lost his life by one; and here the house-owner is required in Yahweh's name to minimise that danger, "that he bring not blood upon his house." The life of each one of Yahweh's people is precious to Him; therefore it is that He will have them to guard one another. This is the principle which runs through all these precepts. In the sphere of ritual and religion the Deuteronomist does not transcend Old Testament conditions. For him as for others it is the nation which is the unit. But in the region now before us he virtually goes beyond that limitation, and emphasises the care of Yahweh for the individual, just as in the demand for love to God he had already made Israel's relation to their God depend upon each man's personal attitude. The thought that the Divine care was exerted over even "such a set of paltry ill-given animalcules as himself and his nation were," according to Carlyle's phrase, does not stagger him as it staggered Frederick the Great.

In matters like these, the unsophisticated religion of the Old Testament is most helpful to us to-day. We have analysed, and refined, and dimmed all things into abstractions, God and man among the rest. The fearless simplicity of the Old Testament restores us to ourselves, and pours fresh blood into the veins of our religion. No faith in God as the living orderer of all the circumstances of our lives can be too strong or too detailed. The stronger and more definite it becomes, the nearer will it approach the truth. Only one danger can threaten us on that line, the danger of taking all our own plans and desires for the Divinely appointed path for us. But most men will by natural humility be saved from that presumption; and the glad assurance that they are wrapped about with the love of God is perhaps the greatest need of God's people in their many sceptical and unspiritual hours.

We cannot, therefore, be surprised that, in connection with debts and pledges for payment, the same kindness in the Divine commands should be observable. As usury was forbidden in Israel, and precautions against excessive indebtedness were exceedingly elaborate, the possibilities of oppression in connection with debt in Israel were much more limited than in most ancient communities. Nevertheless there was here a region of life in which great wrongs could still be done by a harsh and unscrupulous creditor. In order that the creditor might have some security for what he had lent, it was permitted to receive and give pledges. The precepts regarding these are contained in chap, xxiv., vv. 6, 10 ff. and 17, and express a considerate brotherly spirit, for which it would be hard to find a parallel either in ancient or modern times. The creditor who has taken a poor man's upper garment as a pledge is commanded, both in the Book of the Covenant and in Deuteronomy, to restore the garment to its owner in the evening, that he may sleep in it. In Palestine for much of the year the nights are cold enough, and the poor man has no covering save his ordinary clothes. To deprive him of these, therefore, is to inflict punishment upon him, whereas all that should be aimed at is the creditor's security. This was peculiarly offensive to Israelite feeling, as we see from the mention in Amos ii. 8 of the breach of this prescription as one of the sins for which Yahweh would not turn away Israel's punishment. Further, in no case was a widow's garment to be taken in pledge, nor the handmill used for preparing the daily flour, for that is taking "life" in pledge, as the Deuteronomist says with the feeling for the conditions of the poor man's life which he always shows.

But the crown of all this kindness is found in the beautiful tenth verse: "When thou dost lend thy neighbour any manner of loan, thou shalt not go into his house to fetch his pledge thou shalt stand without, and the man to whom thou dost lend shall bring forth the pledge without unto thee." Not only does Yahweh care for external and physical pain, He sympathises with those deeper wrongs and pains which may hurt a man's feelings. If a pledge to satisfy the lender had to be given, scruples of delicacy on the part of the borrower would appear to the "practical" man, as he would call himself, contemptibly misplaced. If the man's feelings were so very superfine, why did he borrow? But the author of Deuteronomy knew the heart of God better. With the fine tact of a man of God, he knew how even the well-meaning rich man's amused contempt for the poor man's few household treasures, would cut like a whip, and he knew that Yahweh, who was "very pitiful and of tender mercy," would desire no son of Israel to be exposed to it. He knew, too, how human greed might dispose the lender to seize upon the thing of greatest value in the poor house, whether its price was in excess of the loan or not. Finally, he knew how it deteriorates the poor to be dealt with in an unceremonious, tactless way even by the benevolent. And in the name and with the authority of God he forbids it. The poor man's home, the home of the man whom we desire to help especially, is to be sacred. In our dealing with him of all men the finest courtesy is to be brought into play. Just because he needs our help, we are to stand on points of ceremony with him, which we might dispense with in dealing with friends and equals. "Thou shalt stand without," unless he asks thee to enter; and thou shalt show thereby, in a deeper way than any gifts or loans can show, that the fraternal tie is acknowledged and reverenced.

In two other precepts the same delicate regard for the finer feelings finds expression. In the fifth verse it is commanded that "When a man taketh a new wife, he shall not go out in the host, neither shall he be charged with any business: he shall be free at home one year, and shall cheer his wife that he hath taken." The strangeness and loneliness which everywhere make themselves felt as a formidable drawback to a young wife's joy, and which in a polygamous family, where jealousies are bitter, must often have reached the point of being intolerable, are provided for. In chap. xxv. 1-3 again, which deals with the punishment of criminals by beating, it is provided that in no case shall the number of blows exceed forty, and that they shall be given in the presence of the judge. This in itself was a measure of humanity, but the reason given for the direction is greatly more humane. "Forty stripes he may give him," says ver. 3; "he shall not exceed; lest, if he should exceed, and beat him above these with many stripes, then thy brother should seem vile unto thee." Even in the case of the criminal care is to be taken that he be not made an object of contempt. Punishment has gone beyond its true aim when it makes a man seem vile unto his neighbours by attacking his dignity as a man; for that should be inalienable even in a criminal. A man may have all his material wants satisfied, and yet be sorely vexed and injured. God sympathises with these hurts of the soul, and defends His people against them.

After the lovingkindness of these commands, it seems almost needless to say that the smaller social wrongs which men may inflict upon each other are sternly forbidden. Often, the rich from want of thought about the life of the poor carelessly do them wrong. Such a case is that dealt within chap. xxiv. 14 f.: "Thou shalt not oppress an hired servant that is poor and needy, whether he be of thy brethren, or of thy strangers (*gerim*) that are in thy land within thy gates: in his day thou shalt give him his hire, neither shall the sun go down upon it; for he is poor, and setteth his heart upon it: lest he cry against thee unto Yahweh, and it be sin unto thee." The same command is given in Lev. xix. 13, and Dillmann is probably right in regarding this as a Deuteronomic repetition of that, since there the precept forms part of a pentade of commands dealing with similar things, while here it stands alone. From early times, therefore, Yahweh had revealed Himself as considering the poor and the necessities of their position. Further, the poor man or the wayfarer was permitted to satisfy his hunger by taking fruit or grain in his hands as he passed through the fields. No one was to die of starvation if the fields were "yielding meat." Last of all, estrangement between brethren, *i.e.* all Israelites, was not to free them from duties of neighbourly love. If a man find a stray ox or sheep or ass, or a garment or any other lost thing, he is not to leave it where he finds it. He is to restore it to the owner; and if the owner is unknown or too far off, the finder is to keep that which he has found till it is inquired after. Then if he see his brother's, *i.e.* his neighbour's, ass or ox fallen by the way, he must not pass by, but must help the owner to set it on its feet again. That an estranged "brother" was especially in view is shown by the fact that in the parallel passage (Exod. xxiii. 4) "thine enemy's ox" and "the ass of him that hateth thee" are mentioned.

Now, we have called these precepts and provisions the flower and blossom of the Deuteronomic legislation, because they reveal in their greatest perfection that sympathy with the commonest and the innermost cares of men which is the moving impulse of it all. But they reveal more than that. They show that already in those far-off days the secret of God's love to man had been made known. Its universality so far as Israel was concerned, its penetrative sympathy, its quality of regarding no human interest as outside its scope, its superhuman impartiality—all are here. They are not of course present in their full sweep and power, as Christ made them known. Outside of Israel there were the Gentiles, who had a share only in the "uncovenanted mercies" of God; and even among the chosen people there were the slaves and the strangers, who had a comparatively insecure relation to Him. Further, the thought of the self-sacrifice of God, though soon to have its dawning in the later chapters of Isaiah, was not as yet an appreciable element in the Israelite theology. Nevertheless the passages we have been considering throw a light upon social duty, as seen by this inspired servant of God, which puts to shame the state of the Christian mind on these subjects even now.

The great principles underlying right relations between men of different social status are, according to these precepts, courtesy and consideration. Now it is precisely the want of these which lies at the root of the bitterness which is so alarming a symptom of our social state at present. There is not, we are willing to believe, much of intentional, deliberate oppression exercised by the strong upon the weak. The injustice that is done is probably inherent in the present social system, for the character of which no one living is responsible. But one reason why reform comes so slowly, and why patience till it can come dies out among the masses of men, is that the employing classes, and those who have inherited privileges, often convey to those they employ the impression that they are beyond the pale of the courtesies which are recognised as binding between men of the same class. Often without intending it, their manner when they are approached by those they employ, their short and half-aggrieved replies, reveal to the latter that they are regarded much more as parts of the machinery, than as men who might naturally be expected to claim, and who have a right to, the recognition of their rights as men.

Of course there are excuses. There is the long tradition of subordination to arbitrary power, from which none in earlier ages of the world have been free. There is the impatience with which a governing and organising mind listens to grievances which it sees either to be inevitable under the circumstances, or to be compensated by some corresponding privilege, which stands or falls with the thing complained of. And then there is the absence of outlook, which is the foible of the directing mind. It is set to rule and make successful a large and intricate business under given circumstances. The more effective such a mind is for practical purposes, the more thoroughly will it limit itself to working out the problem committed to it. When grievances have to be dealt with which have their root in the present circumstances, and which imply changes more or less radical in his fixed point if they are to be redressed, it is hard for the employer to persuade himself that his employees are not merely crying for the moon. If he think so, he will probably say so; and working men go away from such interviews with the feeling that it is vain to expect from employers any sympathy for their aspirations towards a better social state, which yet they cannot give up without a slur upon their manhood.

But though these are excuses for the attitude we have been describing, there can be no question that the fine and delicate courtesy which Deuteronomy prescribes is indispensable in order to avert class hostility. Courtesy cannot, of course, change our social state, and where it works badly evils that produce friction will remain. But the first condition of a successful solution of our difficulties is, that evil tempers should as far as possible be banished, and for that purpose courtesy even under provocation is the one sovereign remedy. For it means that you convey to your neighbour that you consider him in all essentials your equal. It means, too, that you are willing to recognise his rights and to respect them. Though power may be on your side, and weakness on his, that will only make it more incumbent upon you to show that mere external circumstances cannot impair your reverence for him as man. If that be sincerely felt, it opens a way, otherwise absolutely closed, to mutual confidence and mutual understanding. These once established, light on all parts of the social problem (which, be it remembered, employers and employed must solve together if it is to be solved at all) will break in upon the minds of both classes. In spite of the diversity of their immediate interests, the ultimate interest of all is the same. If contempt and suspicion were excluded, eyes which are now holden would be opened, and a common effort to reach a social state in which all men shall have the opportunity of living lives worthy of men would become possible. If all would learn to treat those of other classes with the courtesy which they constantly show to those of their own, a great step in the right direction would be taken. Men overlook much and forgive much to their fellows when these recognise their equality, and show that they attach importance to having good relations with them.

But much more is to be aimed at than that. The esteem for man as man has great conquests yet to make before even the Deuteronomic courtesy becomes common. But if these nobler manners are to come in, then the motives suggested by Deuteronomy will have to be made effective for our day. What these were it is not difficult to see. They all had their source in the author's own relations and the relations of his people to God. Each of his brethren of the chosen people was a friend of Yahweh. There was no difference between Israelite men before Him. He had brought them all, the poor and the weak, as well as the rich and the strong, out of the house of bondage; He had guided them all through the wilderness, and had appointed each household a place in His land where full communion with Him was to be had. He had thought many thoughts about them, had given them laws and statutes dictated by loving insight, so as to fill their life with the consciousness that Yahweh loved them, condescended to them, and even allowed Himself to be made to serve by their sins. Whatever else they might be, they were friends of God, and had a right to respect on that ground. And for us who are Christians all these motives have been intensified and raised to a higher power. It is not lawful for us to call any man common or unclean. It is not lawful to overwhelm and bear down the minds of others by sheer energy and power. Those "for whom Christ died" are not to be dealt with save on the worthy plane of moral and spiritual conviction. That is the law of Christ; and so long as it is broken in our labour troubles by contemptuous refusal of conference when it can be granted without compromising principle, or by slighting references to labour leaders and a refusal to meet them, when leaders of another class would be courteously met, so long will the bitterness which inevitably springs up trouble us.

It is not, however, to be supposed that only the rich can sin in this respect. The labour organisations are becoming in many places, the stronger,[123] and so far they have learned the law of courtesy no better than their opponents. Opprobrious epithets and injurious suspicions and accusations are the stock-in-trade of some who lead the labour cause. That is as unworthy in them as it would be in others; it is not only a crime, but a blunder.

But the practice of courtesy does not end with itself. It opens the way for that consideration of the circumstances of the poor which we have found so conspicuous in Deuteronomy. As we have seen, Yahweh's precepts contemplate with the nicest care the unavoidable necessities of the poor man's life. So He stirs us to endeavour to realise the conditions of our poorer brethren, and by doing so to avoid the blunders which well-meaning people make by assuming that the conditions of their own life are the norm. There are vast varieties of circumstance in the world; and from lack of consideration those more favourably situated excite envies and hatreds the bitterness of which they cannot conceive, by simply taking it for granted that every one has the same opportunities for recreation, the same possibilities of rest. To realise clearly what life and death mean to the toiling millions of men; to see that matters which are small to those who live the materially larger and freer life of the class above them are of vital moment to the poor; to consider and allow for all such things in their dealings with them,—this is the teaching of Deuteronomy. Hence the command to pay the labourer his wages in the same day. The heart of man responds when this note is struck. In nothing is the story of Gautama the Buddha more true to the best instincts of humanity than in this, that it represents him as making his great renunciation through coming into intimate contact with the pain and misery of ordinary life.[124] That gave him insight, and insight wrought sympathy, and sympathy transformed him from being a petty prince of Northern India into the consoler and helper of millions in all Eastern lands. Even hopeless pessimism, when born of sympathy, has an immense consoling power. Much more should the inextinguishable hope given by Christ, combined as it is with the same sympathetic insight, console men and uplift them.

But the sixteenth verse of chap. xxiii. reminds us that in that ancient Deuteronomic world there were sad limitations to these lofty sympathies and hopes. If intensively Deuteronomy almost reaches the Gospel, extensively it shows the whole difference between Judaism at its best and Christianity. Below the world of free-born members of the Israelite community, to whom the precepts we have hitherto been considering alone apply, there was the class of slaves, who in many respects lay beyond the region of the finer charities. The origin of slavery we need not discuss. It was a quite universal feature in all ancient communities, and was doubtless a step upwards from the custom of destroying all prisoners taken in war. Among the Hebrews it had always been customary; but in historic times it was not among them the all-important matter it was in Greek and Roman polity. Had it been so, it would have been impossible to discuss the economic ideals of Israel without taking this social feature into consideration first. But slaves were comparatively few in Israel, and the slave trade can never have been extensive, since no slave markets are mentioned in the Old Testament. Moreover the social state of the country made owners of slaves share in the slaves' work, and that of itself prevented the growth of the worst abuses. But the most powerful element in making the lot of the slave tolerable was undoubtedly the just and pitiful character of the Israelite religion.

The fundamental position with regard to him was, however, the common one: he was the property of his master. He could be sold, pledged, given away as a present, and inherited, and could even be sold to foreigners. But a female slave, if taken as a subordinate wife, could not be sold, but only freed if she ceased to occupy that position. Exclusive of the Canaanites, subject to forced labour, and the Nethinim, the servants of the Sanctuary, who occupied much the same place as the *servi publici* in Rome, there were two classes of slaves, non-Israelites and Israelites. The ways in which a non-Israelite slave could come into Israelite hands were just what they were elsewhere. They might be prisoners of war, they might be purchased from travelling merchants, they might voluntarily have sold themselves from poverty in a strange land, or might have been sold for debt, and finally they might be children born of slaves. Their lot was of course the hardest. Yet even they were not so entirely unprotected by the law as slaves were among Greeks and Romans. They were recognised as men, having certain general human rights. The master had no right to kill; and if he maimed his slave he had to give him his freedom, according to the oldest law (Exod. xvi. 20 f.). The law regarding the killing of a slave has often been quoted as singularly harsh, especially that clause which says that if a slave when fatally smitten lives for some days after the blow, his death shall not be avenged, "for he is his (the master's) money." But it ought, notwithstanding the harshness of the expression, to be judged quite otherwise. The fact that death was not immediate was taken to indicate that death was not intended, and consequently the loss of the slave was thought a sufficient punishment. But the prohibition of the deliberate murder of a slave was a humane provision which could not be paralleled in the Græco-Roman world. Moreover these laws would not seem to have been widely called into action. The humane spirit became so general in Israel that slaves were generally well treated. In Prov. xxix. 21 over-indulgence to a slave is deprecated, as if it were a common error; and during the whole history there is no mention of evils resulting from cruel treatment of slaves, much less any record of servile insurrection. Nor is there very frequent mention even of runaway slaves. On the other hand, we read of slaves who were stewards of their masters' houses; others probably were entrusted with the charge of the education of children.

In Deuteronomy we find, as we should expect, that the movement towards humanity in dealing with slaves is greatly furthered. In chap. xxi. 10 ff. the hardship of a woman's lot when she was taken captive in war is mitigated with sympathetic insight. To modern women of the Western world the lot of such an one seems so dreadful that no mitigation of it can make any difference. The current teaching among even religious men is that rather than submit to it a woman is justified in suicide. But in antiquity the personality of woman was undeveloped, the chances of life constantly passed her from one master to another, and things intolerable now were tolerable then. Making even these allowances, however, if we look at the law of the Old Testament as being in all its provisions and *ab initio* Divine, it seems impossible to praise it. A law which graciously permitted a captive woman to mourn for her people for a month, and only then allowed her captor to marry her, but if he wished afterwards to get rid of her provided that he should not sell her, but should let her go whither she would, cannot be said to be in itself compassionate. But, if the customary law of the Israelite tribes, restrained and purified by the higher spirit, be regarded as the basis of Old Testament legislation, then the leaven of religion and humanity can be seen working nobly, and in a manner worthy of revelation, even in such cases as these. Long after the Christian era we see what the ordinary fate of a captive woman was, in the conduct of Khalid the "sword of the Lord," one of the first great Mohammedan soldiers. When he had captured Malik ibn Noweira, who had resisted Islam, along with his wife, he gave orders which led to Malik's death, and the same night he married his widow.[125] Shortly afterwards, at the battle of Yemama, he demanded the daughter of his captive Mojda, and married her, as the Caliph wrote in reproof, "whilst the ground beneath the nuptial couch was yet moistened with the blood of twelve hundred." Horrors like these Deuteronomy forbids. The frenzied moments of a captive's first grief are respected, and some tenderness is shown to woman in a world where her lot at its best had always in it possibilities which cannot now be even thought of with equanimity. The same steady pressure to a nobler form of life is likewise seen in the Deuteronomic law dealing with the case of a foreign slave who had taken refuge in Israel (Deut. xxiii. 15 f.). In the words, "Thou shalt not deliver unto his master the slave which is escaped from his master unto thee; he shall dwell with thee, in the midst of thee, in the place which he shall choose within one of thy gates, where it liketh him best; thou shalt not oppress him," we have, thus early, the same legislation which it is the peculiar boast of England to have introduced into the modern world. "Slaves cannot breathe in England," and the moment they touch British soil in any part of the world they are free. This was the case with the land of Israel according to the Deuteronomic conception of what it ought to be.

But the highest points of privilege come to the non-Israelite slave in a way which disturbs the modern conscience, for they came by means of compulsion in religion. In contrast to the day labourer and the "Toshab" or sojourner, the slave *must* be of his master's religion. For a heathen, however, that was not a difficulty. His gods were gods of his land; and when he left his land and was carried into a foreign country, he had no scruple about worshipping the god of the new land. A typical case of this is found in the narrative 2 Kings xvii., where the immigrants whom the king of Assyria had settled in Samaria after Israel had been carried captive besought him to send some one to teach them how to worship Yahweh. This adoption of the master's religion secured equality of slave and free to a degree which could not otherwise have been attained, and brought the slaves fully within the humanity of the Hebrew law. It gave them the Sabbath (chap. v. 14). It gave a full share in all the religious festivals and a part in the sacrificial feasts (Deut. xii. 12 and xvi. 11, 14). Such slaves were, in fact, fully adopted into the family of God, and became brethren, poorer and more unfortunate, but still brethren of their masters. They had indeed no claim to freedom, as Israelite slaves had; they were slaves in perpetuity. But their slavery was of a kind that did not degrade them beneath the condition of man.

With regard to Israelite slaves the beneficence of the law was naturally still greater. The fullest statement in regard to them is found, not in Deuteronomy, but in Lev. xxv. 39-46; but in the main we may suppose that in its larger outlines the distinction between Israelite and non-Israelite slaves there insisted on was always acknowledged. They were not to be thrust down into the lowest depth of slavery, and they were not to be set to the lowest kinds of labour, rather to that which hired labourers were wont to do, because they were of the children of Israel, of the nation whom Yahweh had brought out of the house of bondage. Further, they had a right to emancipation every seventh year, that is to say, whenever they had served six full years they could claim freedom in the seventh. Their original property was meant to be restored to them in the Sabbatic year, and so their degradation could last only for a very limited time. In Exod. xxi. 2 ff. we find the original provisions concerning the Israelite slave. Deuteronomy simply took these up, and modified them in certain respects. It extends all that Exodus says of the slave to the female slave also, and, in its care for and understanding of the difficulties of the poor, enacts that a slave when set free shall receive a fresh start in life from the cattle, the barn, and the winepress of the former owner. But this anticipation of discharged prisoners' aid societies was too high a demand upon a faithless generation. Even Jeremiah could not get it carried out; and the probability is that none but the most spiritually minded of the Jews ever regarded it as binding law.

The love which love of Yahweh inspired spread still more widely. It took in not only the poor and the slave, but it took account also of the lower animals. It has been often made a reproach to Christianity that it makes no such appeal on behalf of the lower creation as Buddhism does. But that reproach (like the kindred one brought by J. S. Mill, that in comparison with the Qur'an the New Testament is defective in not pressing civil duty) is tenable only if the New Testament be absolutely severed from the Old. Taken as the completion of the moral and religious development begun in Israel, Christianity takes up into itself all the experience, and all the teaching by example, which the Old Testament contains. It does not repeat it, because to the first Christians the Old Testament was the Divinely inspired guide. It was at first their whole Bible, and to take the New Testament by itself as an independent product is to mutilate both the Old and the New. When the Old Testament, therefore, enjoins kindness to animals we may set down all that it prescribes to the credit of Christianity. So much, at least, the latter must be held to teach; and if we consider the spirit as well as the letter of this law, there is no exaggeration in saying that it covers all the ground. Here, as in the case of slaves and the poor, the fundamental reason for kindness is relation to God. In the Yahwist's narrative in Gen. ii. all creatures are formed by God, and God Himself shows kindness to them. Indeed in passages like Psalm xxxvi. 7, as Cheyne well remarks, there is an implication "that morally speaking there is no complete break of continuity in the scale of sentient life," and that, as is seen by passages like Jer. xxi. 6, and Isa. iv. 11, the mild domesticated animals "are in fact regarded as a part of the human community." In the Decalogue the animals that labour with and for man have their share in the Sabbath rest, and the produce of the fields during the Sabbatic year (Exod. xxiii. 11; Lev. xxv. 7) is to be for them as well as for the poor. That they were mere machines of flesh and blood, to be driven till they were worn out, and were then to be cast aside, seems never to have occurred to the Israelite mind. These helpful creatures had made a covenant with man, and had a share in the consideration which the sons of Israel were taught to have for one another. In reaching that attainment Israel had reached the only effective ground for dealing with animals, as Cheyne says, "without inhumanity and without sentimentalism." The individual prescriptions of Deuteronomy emphasise and bring down these principles into the practical life. It is probable that the precept not to seethe a kid in its mother's milk (Deut. xiv. 21) was, in part at least, a law of kindness, founded upon a reverential feeling for the parental relationship even in this lower sphere. The command in Deut. xxii. 6 is certainly so. We read there: "If a bird's nest chance to be before thee in the way, in any tree or on the ground, with young ones or eggs, and the dam sitting upon the young, or upon the eggs, thou shalt not take the dam with the young; thou shalt in any wise let the dam go, but the young thou mayest take unto thyself; that it may be well with thee, and that thou mayest prolong thy days." Evidently the ground of sympathy here is the existence and the sacredness of the parental relationship. The mother bird is sacred as a mother; and length of days is promised to those who regard the sanctity of motherhood in this sphere, as it is promised to those who observe the fifth commandment of the Decalogue. Thus intimately the lower creation is drawn into the human sphere.

The only other precepts under this head are that a fallen animal is always to be lifted (Deut. xxii. 4), and the ox is not to be muzzled when it is treading out the corn (Deut. xxv. 4). These were ordinary prescriptions of humanity, but they too rest upon the sympathetic identification of the sufferings and wants of all sentient beings with those of mankind. It may be objected, however, that St. Paul denies that the last precept really was due to pity for the oxen. In 1 Cor. ix. 9, referring to it, he says, "Is it for the oxen that God careth, or saith He it altogether for our sake? Yea, for our sake it was written." But there is no real contradiction here. It is quite impossible that a devout Jew like St. Paul did not believe that God's "tender mercies are over all His works" (Psalm cxlv. 9). He would have been false to all his training had he not accepted that as a fundamental axiom. His apparent denial does not refer at all to the historic fact that the precept *was* given because of God's care for oxen. It only signifies that, when taken in its highest sense, it was meant to form character in *men*. St. Paul argues, as Alford says, "that not the oxen, but those for whom the law was given, were its objects. Every duty of *humanity* has for its ultimate ground, not the mere welfare of the animal concerned, but its welfare in that system of which man is the head, and therefore man's welfare." In fact St. Paul understood the Old Testament as we have seen it demands to be understood, and places the duty of kindness to animals in its right relation to man.

In all relations, therefore, Deuteronomy insists that life's main principle shall be love illumined by sympathy. Beginning with God and giving man's unquiet heart a firm anchorage there, it commands that all creatures about us shall be embraced in the same sympathising tenderness. It forbids us to look upon any of them as mere instruments for our use, for all of them have ends of their own in the loving thought of God. God is for it the great unifying, harmonising power in the world, and from a right conception of Him all right living flows. If the New Testament asks with wonder how a man who loves not his brother whom he hath seen can love God whom he hath not seen, the Old Testament teaches with equal emphasis the complementary truth that he who loves not God whom he hath not seen will never love as he ought his brother whom he hath seen. For to it Yahweh is the first and last word; and all the growth in kindness, gentleness, consideration, and goodness which can be traced in the revelation given to Israel, has its source in a conception of the Divine character which from the first was spiritual, and was moreover unique in the world.

CHAPTER XXIV
MOSES' FAREWELL SPEECHES

Deut. iv. 1-40, xxvii.-xxx

With the twenty-sixth chapter the entirely homogeneous central portion of the Book of Deuteronomy ends, and it concludes it most worthily. It prescribes two ceremonies which are meant to give solemn expression to the feeling of thankfulness which the love of God, manifested in so many laws and precepts, covering the commonest details of life, should have made the predominant feeling. The first is the utterance of what we have called the "liturgy of gratitude" at the time of the feast of firstfruits; and the second is the solemn dedication of the third year's tithe to the poor and the fatherless, and the disclaimer of any misuse of it. Further notice of either after what has already been said in reference to them would be superfluous. The closing verses (16-19) of the chapter are a solemn reminder that all these transactions with God had bound the people to Yahweh in a covenant. "Thou hast avouched Yahweh this day to be thy God" and, "Yahweh hath avouched thee this day to be a peculiar people (*'am segūllāh*) unto Himself." By this they were bound to keep Yahweh's statutes and judgments, and do them with all their heart and with all their soul, while He, on His part, undertakes on these terms to set them "high above all nations which He hath made in praise, and in name, and in honour," and to make them a holy people unto Himself.

But the original Deuteronomy as read to King Josiah cannot have ended with chapter xxvi., for the thing that awed him most was the threat of evil and desolation which were to follow the non-observance of this covenant. Now though there are indications of such dangers in the first twenty-six chapters of Deuteronomy, yet threats are not, so far, a prominent part of this book. The book as read must consequently have contained some additional chapters, which, in part at least, must have contained threats. Now this is what we have in our Biblical Deuteronomy. But in chapters xxvii. and xxviii. there are reduplications which can hardly have formed part of the original author's work. An examination of these has led every one who admits composite authorship in the Pentateuch to see that from chapter xxvii.

onwards the original work has been broken up and dovetailed again with the works of JE and P; so that component parts of the first four books of the Hexateuch appear along with elements which the author of Deuteronomy has supplied. We have, in fact, before us, from this point, the work of the editor who fitted Deuteronomy into the framework of the Pentateuch; and it is of importance, from an expository point of view even, to endeavour to restore Deuteronomy to its original form, and to follow out the traces of it that are left.

As we have said, we must look for the threats and promises which undoubtedly formed part of it. These are contained in chapters xxvii. and xxviii. But a careful reader will feel at once that chapter xxvii. disturbs the connection, and that xxviii. should follow xxvi. In chapter xxvii., vv. 9 and 10 alone seem necessary to give a transition to chapter xxviii.; and if all the rest were omitted we should have exactly what the narrative in Kings would lead us to expect, a coherent, natural sequence of blessings and curses, which should follow faithfulness to the covenant, or unfaithfulness. The rest of chapter xxvii. is not consistent either with itself or with Josh. viii. 30, where the accomplishment of that which is commanded here is recorded. In vv. 1-3 Moses and the elders command the people to set up great stones and plaister them with plaister and write upon them all the words of this law, on the day when they shall pass over Jordan, that they may go in unto the land. In ver. 4 it is said that these stones are to be set up in Mount Ebal, and there an altar of unhewn stones is to be built, and sacrifices offered, "and thou shalt write upon the stones very plainly." From the position of this last clause and the mention of Mount Ebal, the course of events would be quite different from that which vv. 1-3 suggest. The stones were, according to the verses 4 ff., to be set up in Mount Ebal; out of these an altar of unhewn stones was to be built; and on them the law was to be inscribed, and this is what Joshua says was done. But if we take all the verses, 1-8, together, we can reconcile them only by the hypothesis that the stones were set up as soon as Jordan was crossed, plaistered, and inscribed with the law; that afterwards they were removed to Mount Ebal and built into an altar "of unhewn stone," upon which sacrifices were offered. But that surely is in the highest degree improbable; and since we know that in other cases two narratives have been combined in the sacred text, that would seem the most probable solution here. Verses 4-8 will in that case be a later insertion, probably from J. In the same connection vv. 15-26 contain a list of crimes which are visited with a curse and no blessings; this cannot be the proclamation of blessing and cursing which is here required. Further, this list must be by a different author, for it affixes curses to some crimes which are not mentioned in Deuteronomy, and omits such sins as idolatry, which are continually mentioned there. This section must consequently have been inserted here by some later hand. It must probably have been later even than the time of the writer of Josh. viii. 33 ff., since the arrangement as reported there differs from what is prescribed here. Moreover, as there is nothing new in these sections, and all they say is repeated substantially in chapter xxviii., we may give our attention wholly to chapter xxviii. 1-68, as being the original proclamation of blessing and curse.

But other entanglements follow. Chapters xxix. and xxx. manifestly contained an adieu on the part of Moses, who turns finally to the people with an affecting and solemn speech of farewell. That appears in chapters xxix. and xxx. But for many reasons it is impossible to believe that these chapters as they stand are the original speech of Deuteronomy.[126] The language is in large part different, and there are references to the Book of the Law as being already written out (chap. xxix. 19 f. 26, and chap. xxx. 10). It is probably therefore an editor's rewriting of the original speech, and from the fact that "it contains many points of contact with Jeremiah in thoughts and words," it is probably to be dated in the Exile. But there is another noticeable thing in connection with it. It has a remarkable resemblance in these and other respects to chapter iv. 1-40. That passage can hardly have originally followed chapters i.-iii., if as is most probable these were at first an historic introduction to Deuteronomy. The hortative character of iv. 1-40 shows that it must have been placed where it is by a reviser. But the language, though not altogether that of Deuteronomy, is like it, and the thought is also Deuteronomic. Probably the passage must have been transferred from some other part of Deuteronomy and adapted by the editor. A clue to its true place may perhaps be found in ver. 8, where "all this law" is spoken of as if it were already given, and in ver. 5, where we read, "Behold, I have taught you statutes and judgments." These passages imply that the law of Deuteronomy had been given, and in that case chapter iv. must belong to a closing speech. We probably shall not be in error, therefore, in thinking that chapters iv. 1-40 and xxix. and xxx. are all founded on an original farewell speech which stood in Deuteronomy after the blessing and the curse.

But it may be asked, if that be so, why did an editor make these changes? The answer is to be found in two passages in chapters xxxi. and xxxii. which cannot be harmonised as they stand. In xxxi. 19 we are told that Yahweh commanded Moses to write "this song" and teach it to the children of Israel, "that this song may be a witness for Me against the children of Israel," and ver. 22, "So Moses wrote this song." But in vv. 28 f. we read that "Moses said, Assemble unto me all the elders of the tribes and your officers, that I may speak these words in their ears, and call heaven and earth to witness against them." Obviously "these words" are different from "this song," and are meant for a different purpose. The same ambiguity occurs at the end

of the song in vv. 44 ff., where we first read of Moses ending "this song,"
and in the next verse we read, "And Moses made an end of speaking all
these words to all Israel." Now what has become of *these words*? In all
probability they were the substance of chapters iv. and xxix. and xxx., and
were separated and amplified, because the editor who fitted Deuteronomy
into the Pentateuch took over the song in chapter xxxii., as well as those
passages of xxxi. and xxxii. that speak of this song, from JE. He accepted
them as a fitting conclusion for the career of Moses, and transferred the
original speech, which we suppose to have been the last great utterance of
the original Deuteronomy, putting the main part of it immediately before
the song, but taking parts out of it to form a hortatory ending (such as the
other Moses' speeches have) to that first one which he had formed out of
the historic introduction. This may seem a very complicated process and an
unlikely one; but after the foundation had been built by Dillmann, Westphal
has elaborated the whole matter with such luminous force that it seems
hardly possible to doubt that the facts can be accounted for only in this way.
By piecing together iv., xxx., and xxxi. he produces a speech so thoroughly
coherent and consistent that the mere reading of it becomes the most cogent
proof of the substantial truth of his argument.[127]

An analysis of it will show this, (1) There is the introduction; up till now
the people have understood neither the commands nor the love of Yahweh
(xxix. 1-9). (2) There is the explanation of the Covenant (xxix. 10-15); (3) A
command to observe the Covenant (iv. 1, 2); (4) Warning against individual
transgression, which will be punished by the destruction of the rebel (xxix.
16-21, iv. 3, 4); (5) Warning against collective transgression, which will be
punished by the ruin of the people (iv. 5-26). The author, from this point
regarding the transgression as an accomplished fact, announces: (6) The
dispersion and exile of the people (iv. 27, 28); (7) The impression produced
on future generations by the horror of this dispersion (xxix. 22-28); (8) The
conversion of the exiles to God (iv. 30, 31); (9) Their return to the land of
their fathers xxx. (1-10). (10) In conclusion, it is stated that the power of
Yahweh to sustain the faith of His people and to save them is guaranteed by
the past (iv. 32-40); and there is no reason therefore that the people should
shrink from obeying the commandment prescribed to them. It is a matter of
will. Life and death are before them; let them choose (xxx. 11-20).

The analysis of the remaining chapters is not difficult. Chapter xxxi., vv.
14-23 and 30, form the introduction to the song, chapter xxxii., vv. 1-43, just
as ver. 44 is the conclusion of it. Both introduction and song are extracted
probably from J and E. Verses 48-52 are after P. Then follows the blessing of
Moses, chapter xxxiii. Finally, chapter xxxiv. contains an account of Moses'
death and a final eulogy of him, in which all the sources JE, P, and D have

been called into requisition. The threefold cord which runs through the other books of the Pentateuch was untwisted to receive Deuteronomy, and has been re-twisted so as to bind the Pentateuch into one coherent whole. That is the result of the microscopic examination which the text as it stands has undergone, and we may pretty certainly accept it as correct. But we should not lose sight of the fact that, as the book is now arranged, it has a notable coherence of its own, and the impression of unity which it conveys is in itself a result of great literary skill. Not only has the editor combined Deuteronomy into the other narratives most successfully, but he has done so not only without falsifying, but so as to confirm and enhance the impression which the original book was meant to convey.

We turn now to the substance of the two speeches—the proclamation of the blessing and the curse, and the great farewell address. As we have seen, the first is contained in chapter xxviii. If any evidence were now needed that this chapter was written later than the Mosaic time, it might be found in the space given to the curses, and the much heavier emphasis laid upon them than upon the blessings. Not that Moses might not have prophetically foretold Israel's disregard of warnings. But if the heights to which Israel was actually to rise had been before the author's mind as still future, instead of being wrapped in the mists of the past, he could not but have dwelt more equally upon both sides of the picture. Whatever supernatural gifts a prophet might have, he was still and in all things a man. He was subject to moods like others, and the determination of these depended upon his surroundings. He was not kept by the power of God beyond the shadows which the clouds in his sky might cast; and we may safely say that if the curses which are to follow disobedience are elaborated and dwelt upon much more than the blessings which are to reward obedience, it is because the author lived at a time of unfaithfulness and revolt. Obviously his contemporaries were going far in the evil way, and he warns them with intense and eager earnestness against the dangers they are so recklessly incurring.

But after all we have seen of the spirituality of the Deuteronomic teaching, and its insistence upon love as the true bond between men and God and the true motive to all right action, it is perhaps disappointing to some to find how entirely these promises and threats have their centre in the material world. Probably nowhere else will the truth of Bacon's famous saying that "Prosperity is the blessing of the Old Testament" be more conspicuously seen than here. If Israel be faithful she is promised productivity, riches, success in war. Even when it is promised that she shall be established by Yahweh as a holy people unto Himself, the meaning seems to be that the people shall be separated from others by these earthly favours, rather than that they shall have the moral and spiritual qualities which the word "holy" now connotes. Other nations shall fear Israel because of the Divine favour. Israel shall be raised above them all. If it become unfaithful, on the other hand, it is to be visited with pestilence, consumption, fever, inflammation, sword, blasting, mildew. The earth is to be iron beneath them, and the heaven above them brass. Instead of rain they are to have dust; they are to be visited with more than Egyptian plagues. Their minds are to refuse to serve them; they are to be defeated in war; their country is to be overrun by marauders; their wives and children, their cattle and their crops, are to fall into the enemy's hands. Locusts and all known pests are to fall upon their fields; and they themselves are to be carried away captive, after having endured the worst horrors of siege, and been compelled by hunger to devour their own children. And in exile they shall be an astonishment, a proverb, and a by-word, and shall be ruled by oppressive aliens. Worst of all, they shall there lose hope in God and "shall serve other gods, even wood and stone." Their lives shall hang in doubt before them. In the morning they shall say, "Would God it were evening," and at even they shall say, "Would God it were morning." All the deliverance Yahweh had wrought for them by bringing them out of Egypt would be undone, and once more they should go back into Egyptian bondage.

All that is materialistic enough; but there is no need to make apology for Deuteronomy, nevertheless. The prophet has taught the higher law; he has rooted all human duty, both to God and man, in love to God, and now he tries to enlist man's natural fear and hope as allies of his highest principle. How justifiable that is we have already seen in Chapter XII., pp. 231 ff.

But a more serious question is raised when it is asked, does Nature, in definite sober truth, lend itself, in the manner implied throughout this chapter, to the support of religious and moral fidelity? At a time when imaginative literature is largely devoting itself to an angry or querulous denial of any righteous force working for the unfortunate and the faithful,[128] there can be no question what the popular answer to such a question would be. But from the ranks of literature itself we may summon testimony on the other side. Mr. Hall Caine, in his address at the Edinburgh Philosophical Institution, maintains in a wider and more general way the essence of the Deuteronomic thesis when he says, "I count him the greatest genius who touches the magnetic and Divine chord in humanity which is always waiting to vibrate to the sublime hope of recompense; I count him the greatest man who teaches men that the world is ruled in righteousness." And his justification of that position is too admirable not to be quoted: "Life is made up of a multitude of fragments, a sea of many currents, often coming into collision and throwing up breakers. We look around and see wrong-doing victorious, and right-doing in the dust; the evil man growing rich and dying in his bed, the good man becoming poor and dying in the street; and our hearts sink and we say, What is God doing after all in this world of His children? But our days are few, our view is limited, we cannot watch the event long enough to see the end which Providence sees." "It is the very province of imaginative genius," he goes on to say, "to see that which the common mind cannot see, to offer to it at least suggestions of how these triumphs of unrighteousness may be accounted for in accordance with the law that righteousness rules in the world." We would go further. It is one of the main purposes of inspiration to go beyond even imaginative genius, to point out in history not only how right may perhaps ultimately triumph, but how it has been in reality and must be victorious. For it will not do to shut off the world of material things from the working of this great and universal law. Owing to the narrow fanaticism of science, modern men have become sceptical, not only of miracle, but even of the fundamental truth that righteousness is profitable for the life that now is, that in following righteousness men are co-operating with the deepest law of the universe. But it remains a truth for all that. It is written deep in the heart of man; and in more wavering lines perhaps, but still most legibly, it is written on the face of things. With the limitations of his time and place, this is what the Deuteronomist preaches. Doubtless he has not faced, as Job does, the whole of the problem; still less has he attained to the final insight exhibited in the New Testament, that temporal gifts may be curses in disguise, that the highest region of recompense is in the eternal life, in the domain of things which are invisible but eternal. He does not yet *know*, though he has perhaps a presentiment of it, that being completely stripped of all earthly good may be the path to the highest victory—the victory which makes men more than conquerors through Christ. Nevertheless he is, making these allowances, right, and the moderns are wrong. In many ways obedience to spiritual inspirations does bring worldly prosperity. The absence of moral and spiritual faithfulness does affect even the fruitfulness of the soil, the fecundity of animals, the prevalence of disease, the stability of ordered life and success in war. This was visible to the ancient world generally in a dim way; but by the inspired men of the Old Covenant it was clearly seen, for they were enlightened for the very purpose of seeing the hand of God where others saw it not. But they never thought of tracing out the chain of intermediate causes by which such results were connected with men's spiritual state. They saw the facts, they recognised the truth, and they threw themselves back at once upon the will of God as the sufficient explanation.

We, on the other hand, have been so diligent in tracing out the immediately preceding links of natural causation that, for the most part, we have been fatigued before we reached God. We consequently have lost view of Him; and it is wholesome for us to be brought sharply into contact with the ancient Oriental mind as we are here, in order that we may be forced to go the whole way back to Him. For the fact is that much of that very process of decay and destruction from moral causes is going on before us in countries like Turkey and Morocco, where social righteousness is all but unknown, and private morality is low. A truly modern mind scorns the idea that the fertility of the soil can be affected by immorality. Yet there is the whole of Mesopotamia to show that misgovernment can make a garden into a desert. Where teeming populations once covered the country with fruitful gardens and luxurious cities, there is now in the lands of the Tigris and Euphrates a few handfuls of people, and all the fertility of the country has disappeared. Irrigation channels which made all things live have been choked up and have been gradually filled with drifting sand, and one of the most populous and fertile countries of the world has become a desert. In Palestine the same thing may be seen. Under Turkish domination the character of the soil has been entirely changed. In many places where in ancient days the hills were terraced to the top the sweeping rains have had their way, and the very soil has been carried off, leaving only rocks to blister in the pitiless sun. Even in the less likely sphere of animal fecundity modern science shows that peace and good government and righteous order are causes of extraordinary power. And the movements which are going on around us at this day in the elevation and depression of nations and races have a visible connection with fidelity or lack of fidelity to known principles of order and justice. This can be said without concealing how scanty and partial in most cases such attainments are. Prevailing principles can be discerned in the providence which rules the world. And these are of such a kind that the connection which obedience to the highest known rules of life has with fertility, success and prosperity, is constant and intimate. It is, too, far wider reaching than at first sight would seem possible. To this extent, even modern knowledge justifies these blessings and curses of Deuteronomy.

But it may be asked, Is this all the Old Testament means by such threats and promises? Does it recognise any even self-imposed limitations to the direct action of Divine power? Most probably it does not. Though always keeping clear of Pantheism, the Old Testament is so filled and possessed by the Divine Presence that all second causes are ignored, and the action of God upon nature was conceived, as it could not fail to be, on the analogy of a workman using tools. Now that the methods of Divine action in nature have been studied in the light of science, they have been found to be more fixed and regular than was supposed. The extent of their operation, too, has been found to be immeasurably wider, and the purposes which have to be cared for at every moment are now seen to be infinitely various. As a result, human thought has fallen back discouraged, and takes refuge more and more in a conception of nature which practically deifies it, or at least entirely separates it from any intimate relation to the will of God. It is even denied that there is any purpose in the world at all, or any goal, and to chance or fate all the vicissitudes of life and the mechanical changes of nature are attributed. But though we must recognise, as the Old Testament does not, that ordinary Divine action flows out in perfectly well-defined channels, and is so stable in its movement that results in the sphere of physical nature may be predicted with certainty; and though we see, as was not seen in ancient days, that even God does not always approach His ends by direct and short-cut paths,—these considerations only make the Old Testament view more inspiring and more healthful for us. We may gather from it the inference that if the fertility of a land, the frequency of disease, and success in war are so powerfully affected by the moral and spiritual quality of a people, it is very likely that in subtler and less palpable ways the same influences produce similar effects, even in regions where they cannot be traced. If so, whatever allowance may be required for the inevitable simplicity of Old Testament conceptions on this subject, however much we miss the limitations we have learned to regard as necessary, the Deuteronomic view as to the effects of moral and spiritual declension upon the material fortunes of a people is much nearer the truth than our timorous and hesitating half-belief. To find these effects emphasised and affirmed as they are here, therefore, acts as a much needed tonic in our spiritual life. Coming too from a man who possessed, if ever man did, Divinely inspired insight into the process of the world and the ideal of human life, these promises and warnings bring God near. They dissipate the mists which obscure the workings of God's Providence, and keep before us aspects of truth which it is the present tendency of thought to ignore too much. They declare in accents which carry conviction that, even in material things, the Lord reigneth; and for that the world has reason to be supremely glad.

Certainly Christians now know that prosperity in material things is by no means God's best gift. That great principle must be held to firmly, as well as the legitimacy of the vivid hopes and fears of Old Testament times regarding the material rewards of right-doing. In many ways the new principle must overrule and modify for us those hopes and fears. But with this limitation we are justified in occupying the Deuteronomic standpoint and in repeating the Deuteronomic warnings. For to its very core the world is God's; and those who find His working everywhere are those whose eyes have been opened to the inmost truth of things.

With regard to the farewell speech contained in chapters xxix. and xxx. and the related parts of chapter iv. and chapter xxxi. there is not much to be said. Taken as a whole, it develops the promises and threats of the previous chapters, and repeats again with affectionate hortatory purpose much of the history. But there is not a great deal that is new; most of the underlying principles of the address have been already dealt with. Taken according to the reconstruction of the speech and its reinsertion in its original framework, the course of things would seem to have been this. After the threats and promises had been concluded, Moses, carrying on the injunction of iii. 28, addressed (chapter xxxii. 8) all the people and appointed Joshua to be his successor; then he wrote out "this law," and produced it before the priests and elders of the people, with the instruction that at the end of every seven years, at the feast of release, in the feast of tabernacles, it should be read before all Israel, men, women, and children (chapter xxxi., w. 9-13). Then he gave the book to the Levites, that they might "lay it up" by the side of the Ark of the Covenant of Yahweh their God, that it might be there for a witness against them when they became unfaithful, as he foresaw they would. He next summons all Israel to him, and delivers the farewell address contained in chapters iv., xxix., and xxx., an outline of which has already been given (p. 438), according to Westphal's recombination. This would seem to indicate that Moses himself inaugurated the custom of reading the law and giving instruction to all the people, which he prescribed for the feast of tabernacles in the year of release. After the law had been given he addressed the whole people in this farewell speech.

But though on the whole there is no need for detailed exposition here, there are one or two things which ought to be noticed, things which express the spirit of Deuteronomy so directly and so sincerely that they can be identified as forming part of the original Deuteronomic speech. One of these is unquestionably xxx. 11-20. At the end of the farewell address a return is made to the core of the whole Deuteronomic teaching: "Thou shalt love Yahweh thy God with all thy heart, and with all thy soul, and with all thy might." This was announced with unique emphasis at the beginning; it has lain behind all the special commands which have been insisted upon since; and now it emerges again into view as the conclusion of the whole matter. For beyond doubt this, and not the whole series of legal precepts, is what is meant by "this commandment" in verse 11. Both before it, in the sixth and tenth verses, and after it, in the sixteenth and twentieth verses, this precept is repeated and insisted on as the Divine command. Had the individual commands or the whole mass of them together been meant, the phrase used would have been different. It would have been that in ver. 10, where they are called "His commandments and His statutes which are written in this book of the law," or something analogous. No, it is the central command of love to God, without which all external obedience is vain, which is the theme of this last great paragraph; and a clear perception of this will carry us through both the obscurities of it, and the difficulties of St. Paul's application of it in the Romans.

Of this then the author of Deuteronomy says: "It is not too hard for thee, neither is it far off. It is not in heaven, that thou shouldest say, Who shall go up for us to heaven, and bring it unto us, and make us to hear it, that we may do it? Neither is it beyond the sea, that thou shouldest say, Who shall go over the sea for us, and bring it unto us, and make us to hear it, that we may do it? But the word is very nigh unto thee, in thy mouth, and in thy heart, that thou mayest do it." That is to say, there is no mystery or difficulty about this commandment of love. Neither have you to go to the uttermost parts of the sea to hear it, nor need you search into the mysteries of heaven. It has been brought near to you by all the mercy and forgiveness and kindness of Yahweh; it has been made known to you now by my mouth, even in its pettiest applications. But that is not all; it is graven on your own heart, which leaps up in glad response to this demand, and in answer to the manifestation of God's love for you. It is really the fundamental principle of your own nature that is appealed to. You should clearly feel that life in the love of God and man is the only fit life for you who are made in the image of God. If you do, then the fulfilment of all the Divine precepts will be easy, and your lives will lighten more and more unto the perfect day.

Now, for an Oriental of the pre-Christian era such teaching is most marvellous. How marvellous it is Christians perhaps find it difficult to see. In point of fact, many have denied that Old Testament teaching ever had this character. Misled by the doctrines of Islam, the great Semitic religion of to-day, many assert that the religion of ancient Israel called upon men to submit to mere power in submitting to God. But the appeal of our text to the heart of man shows that this is an error. No such appeal has ever been made to Mohammedans. Their state of mind in regard to God is represented by the remark of a recent traveller in Persia. Speaking of the Persian Babis, who may be described roughly as an heretical sect whose minds have been formed by Mohammedanism, he says: "They seemed to have no conception of absolute good, or absolute truth; to them good was merely what God chose to ordain, and truth what He chose to reveal, so that they could not understand how any one could attempt to test the truth of a religion by an ethical and moral standard."[129] Now that is precisely the opposite of the Deuteronomic attitude. Israel is encouraged and incited to right action by having it pointed out that not only experience, not only Divinely given statutes and judgments, but the very nature of man itself guarantees the truth of this supreme law of love. The law laid upon men is nothing strange to, or incongruous with, their own better selves. It is the very thing which their hearts have cried out for; when it is proclaimed the higher nature in man recognises it and bows before it. It is not received because of fear, nor is it bowed before because it is backed by power which can smite men to the dust. No; even in its ruins human nature is nobler than that; and Deuteronomy everywhere teaches with burning conviction that God is too ethical and spiritual in nature to accept the submission of a slave.

This reading of our passage is plainly that which St. Paul takes in Rom. x. 5 and 6. He perceives, what so many fail to do, that the spirit and scope of the Deuteronomic teaching are different from that of the purely legal sections of the Pentateuch. Paul therefore quotes the Pentateuch as having already made the distinction between works and faith which he wishes to emphasise, and as having distinctly given preference to the latter. Leviticus, keeps men at the level of the worker for wages, while Deuteronomy in this passage, by making love to God the essence of all true observance of the law, raises them almost to the level of sons. And just as in those ancient days the highest manifestations of God had not to be laboured for and sought by impotent strivings, but had plainly been made known to them and had found an echo in their hearts, so now the highest revelation had been brought near to men in Christ, and had found a similar response. They did not need to seek it in heaven, for it had been brought to earth in the Incarnation. They did not need to descend into the abyss, for all that was needed had been brought thence by Christ at His resurrection. And in the New Testament as in the Old, the simplicity of the entrance into true relations with God is emphasised. Love and faith are the fundamental conditions. From them obedience will naturally issue, since "to faith all things are possible, and to love all things are easy."

CHAPTER XXV
THE SONG AND BLESSING OF MOSES

(A). The Song of Moses
Deut. xxxii

Critics have debated the date, authorship, and history of this song. For the present purpose it is sufficient, perhaps, to refer to the statement on these points in the note below.[130]

But in discussing the meaning and contents of the song the differences referred to cause no difficulties. On any supposition the time and circumstances, whether assumed as present, or actually and really present to the prophet's mind, can clearly be identified as not earlier than those of the Syrian wars. Accepted as dealing with that time, this poem takes its place among the Psalms of that period. Its subject is a very common one in Scripture: the goodness of Yahweh to His people, and their unfaithfulness to Him; His grief at their rebellion; His punishment of them by heathen oppressors; and His turning in love to them, along with His destruction of the nations who had prematurely triumphed over the people of God. Practically this is the burden of all the prophecies, as indeed it may be said to be the burden of the whole Book of Deuteronomy itself. Here it is stated and elaborated with great poetic skill; but in the main, the essential thought, there is little that has not already been elucidated.

As regards form the poem is among the finest specimens of Hebrew literary art which the Old Testament contains. Every verse contains at least two parallel clauses of three words or word-complexes each, and the parallelism in the great majority of instances is of the "Synonymous" kind; that is to say, "the second line enforces the thought of the first by repeating, and as it were *echoing* it in a varied form."[131] But into this as a foundation there is wrought a great deal of pleasing variation. The two-clause verses are varied by single instances or couplets or triplets of four-clause verses; while in two cases, at the emphatic end of sections, in vv. 14 and 39, the rare five-clause verse is found. Further, the synonymous parallelism is relieved by occasional appearances of the "synthetic" parallelism, in which "the second line contains neither a repetition nor a contrast to the thought of the first, but in different ways supplements and completes it,"[132] *e.g.* vv. 8, 19, and 27.

The contents of the song are in every way worthy of the origin assigned to it, and higher praise than that it is impossible to conceive. Beginning with a fine exordium calling upon heaven and earth to give ear, the inspired poet expresses the hope that his teaching may fall with refreshing and fertilising power upon the hearts of men, for he is about to proclaim the name of Yahweh, to whom all greatness is to be ascribed. In vv. 4 ff. the character and dealings of Yahweh are set over against those of the people:—

> "The Rock! His deeds are perfect,
> For all His ways are judgment;
> A God of faithfulness and without falsity,
> Just and upright is He."

They, on the contrary, were perverse and crooked; and, acting corruptly, they requited all Yahweh's benefits with rebellion. To win them from that perverseness, he calls upon his people to look back upon the whole course of God's dealings with them. Even before Israel had appeared among the nations, Yahweh had taken thought for His people. When He assigned their lands to the various nations of the world He had always before Him the provision that must be made for the children of Israel, and had left a space for them from which none but Yahweh could ever drive them out. For He had the same need of and delight in His people as the nations had in the lands assigned to them, the lot of their inheritance. And not only had He thus prepared a place for Israel from the beginning, but He had led him through the wilderness, through "the waste, the howling desert."

> "He compassed him about, He cared for him,
> He kept him as the apple of His eye."

To depict the Divine care worthily, he ventures upon a simile of a specially tender kind, rare in the Old Testament, but to which our Lord's comparison of His own brooding affection for Jerusalem to that of a "hen gathering her chickens under her wing" is parallel.

> "As an eagle stirs up her nest,
> Flutters above her young;
> He, Yahweh, spread abroad His wings, He took him,
> He bore him upon His pinions."

All the hardship and the toil were of God's appointment to drive His beloved people upwards and onwards. Whatever they might think or believe now, it was Yahweh alone, without companion or ally, who had done this for them, borne them up through it, and had bestowed upon them all the luxury of the goodly land once promised to their fathers. Even from the rocks He had given them honey, and the rocky soil had produced the olive tree. They had, too, all the luxuries of a pastoral people in abundance, and the wheat and foaming wine which were the finest products of agriculture.

In every way their God had blessed them. They had all the prosperity which a complete fulfilment of the will of God could have brought, but the result of it all was unfaithfulness and rejection of Him. Jeshurun, the upright people, as the sacred singer in bitter irony calls Israel, waxed fat and wanton. Instead of being drawn to God by His benefits, they had been puffed up with conceit concerning their own power and discernment. Full of these, they had mingled idolatrous rites with their worship of Yahweh. He had suffered them to reap the results of their own unfaithfulness in defeat at the hands of their foes.

Instead of seeking the cause of their ill-success in themselves, they had found it in the weakness of their God. All the victories Yahweh had given them over foes whose strength they had feared were forgotten, and they "despised the Rock of their salvation." They had adopted new and upstart deities whom their fathers had never heard of, who as they had come up in a day might disappear in a day, and neglected the Rock who begat them.

Yahweh on His part saw all this, and scorned His people and their doings. In a vivid imaginative picture the poet represents Him as resolving to hide His face from them, to see what their end would be. Without the shining of God's countenance there could be but one issue for a people who were so faithless and perverse. He will recompense them for their doings.

> "They made Me jealous with a no-God,
> They vexed Me with their vain idols,
> And I will make them jealous with a no-people,
> With a foolish nation will I vex them."

For the fire of Divine wrath is kindled against them. It burns in Yahweh with an all-consuming power, and fills the universe even to the lowest depths of Sheol. Upon this sinful people it is about to burst forth; Yahweh will exhaust all His arrows upon them. By famine and drought; by disease and the rage of wild beasts, and of "the crawlers of the dust"; by giving them up to their enemies, and by overwhelming them with terror. He will destroy this people, "the young man and the virgin, the suckling and the man of grey hairs" alike. Nothing could save them, save Yahweh's respect for His own name.

> "I had said, I shall blow them away,
> I shall make their memory to cease from among men:
> Were it not that I feared vexation from the enemy,
> Lest their adversaries should misdeem,

Lest they should say, *Our* hand is exalted,
And Yahweh hath not done all this."

Nothing but that stood between them and utter destruction, for as a nation they had no capacity for receiving and profiting by instruction. If they had been wise they would have known that there was but a step between them and death; they would have seen that their deeds had separated them from Yahweh, and could have but one issue. Their frequent and shameful defeats should have taught them that, for

"How could one chase a thousand,
And two put to flight ten thousand,
Were it not that their Rock had sold them,
And that Yahweh had delivered them up?"

There was no possible explanation of Israel's defeats but this; for neither in the gods of the heathen nor in the heathen nations themselves was there anything to account for them. Their gods were not comparable to the Rock of Israel; even Israel's enemies knew as much as that. Israel might forget and doubt Yahweh's power, but those who had been smitten before Him in Israel's happier days knew that He was above all their gods. Nor was the explanation to be sought in the heathen nations themselves. For they were not vines of Yahweh's planting, but shoots from the vine of Sodom, tainted by the soil of Gomorrah. They were, perhaps, in race, of the old Canaanite stock; in any case they were morally and spiritually related to them, and their acts were such as brought death and destruction with them. In themselves, consequently, they could not have been strong enough to discomfit the people of God as they were doing, nor could they have been helped to that by any favour of His. Only the determination of Yahweh to chastise His people could explain Israel's unhappy fate in war.

But Yahweh's purpose was only to chastise. He was in no way finally forgetful of His chosen, nor of the ineradicable evil of their enemies' nature. The inner character of men and things is always present to Him, and their deeds are laid up with Him as that which must be dealt with, for it is one of the glories of Deity to sweep evil away and to restore anything that has good at its heart. Recompense is God's great function in the world, and evil, however strong it may be, and however long it may triumph, must one day be dealt with by Him. It is laid up and sealed

"Against the day of vengeance and of recompense,
Against the time when their foot shall slip;
For the day of their calamity is at hand,
And hastening are the things prepared for them."

Without that, justice could never be done to the people of God; and justice should be done to them when they had been brought to the verge of extinction, when, according to the antique Hebrew phrase, there "was none fettered or set free," none left under or over age. Then when all but the worst had come, Yahweh would demand, "Where are their gods, with whom they took refuge, and who have eaten the fat of their sacrifices, and drunk the wine of their drink offerings?" He will challenge them to arise and help in this last disastrous state of their votaries.

But there will be no response, and it will be made clear beyond all doubting that Yahweh alone is God. He will declare Himself, saying:—

> "See now that I, I, am He,
> And there is no god with Me:
> *I* kill, and *I* make alive;
> I wound, and I heal:
> And there is none that delivereth out of My hand."

In that great day of Yahweh's manifested glory He will stand forth in the fulness of avenging power. Before the universe He will pledge Himself by the most solemn oath to bring down the pride of His enemies. In a death-dealing judgment, such as is seen only when the evil elements in the world have brought about a mere carnival of wickedness, and only universal death can cleanse, He will recompense upon evil-doers the evil they have wrought, and to a renovated world bring peace. There are few finer or more impressive imaginative passages in Scripture than this:—

> "For I lift up My hand to heaven,
> And say, (As) I live for ever,
> If I whet My gleaming sword,
> And My hand take hold on judgment,
> I will take vengeance upon Mine enemies,
> And I will recompense them that hate Me.
> I will make Mine arrows drunk with blood,
> And My sword shall devour flesh,
> With the blood of the slain and the captives,
> From the chief of the leaders of the enemy."

With this great vision of judgment the poet leaves his people. For them the first necessity evidently was that they should be assured that Yahweh reigned, that evil could not ultimately prosper. With their whole horizon dominated and illumined by this tremendous figure of the ever living and avenging God, their faith in the moral government of the world and in the ultimate deliverance of their nation would be restored.

The poem closes with a stanza in which the seer and singer calls upon the nations to rejoice because of Yahweh's people. The deliverance worked for them will be so great and so memorable that even the heathen who see it must rejoice. They will see His justice and His faithfulness, and will gain new confidence in the stability and the moral character of the forces which rule the world.

(B) The Blessing of Moses
Deut. xxxiii

Besides the farewell speeches and the farewell song, we have in this chapter yet another closing utterance attributed to Moses. Here, as in the case of the song, we relegate critical matters to the note below.[133]

We must notice in the first place the remarkable difference in tone and outlook between the blessing and the song of Moses. In the latter evil-doing and approaching judgment are the burden; here the outward and inward condition of Israel leaves little to be desired. Satisfaction is breathed in every line, for both temporally and spiritually the state of the people is almost ideally happy. Nowhere is there a shadow; even on the horizon there is scarcely a cloud. Now even an optimist would need a background of actual prosperity to draw such a picture of idyllic happiness for any nation, and we may therefore conclude that the poem has in view one of the few halcyon periods of Israel, before social wrongs had ruined the yeomen farmers, or war and conquest had corrupted the powerful. The nation is as yet faithful to Yahweh, and possesses in peace the land which He had given them to inherit.

The central part of the poem is of course the ten blessings promised to the various tribes, but these are preceded by an introduction (vv. 2-5), in which the formation of the people is traced to Yahweh's revelation of Himself and His coming forth as their King. They are followed also by a concluding section (vv. 26-29), in which the God of Jeshurun is declared to be incomparable, and His people are depicted as supremely happy under His protecting care. The language is in parts obscure, and though the general scope is always plain, yet there are verses the meaning of which can only be conjectured. This is especially the case in the introduction. Of the five lines of ver. 2, the fourth and fifth as they stand are hardly intelligible; the fifth indeed is not intelligible at all. In ver. 3 again, while the first and second clauses are fairly clear, the third and fourth are as they stand untranslatable. But the general signification of the introductory verses (2-5) is that the Divine revelation of Himself which Yahweh bestowed upon His people as He came with them from Sinai, Paran, and Seir through the wilderness, and the establishment of the covenant which made Yahweh Israel's King, together with the bestowal of an inheritance upon them, is the foundation and beginning of that happiness which is to be described. It is all traced back to the "dawning" of God upon them, His "shining out" upon them from Sinai, and Seir, and Paran. These are named simply as the most prominent points in that region whence the people came out into Canaan, and where the great revelation had been bestowed. God had risen like the sun and had shed forth light upon them there, so that they walked no more in darkness. The sight of God was, on this view, the great and fundamental fact in the history of the chosen people. They, like all who have seen that great sight, were henceforth separate from others, with different duties and obligations, with hopes and desires and joys unknown to all beside. And the ground of this condescension on the part of God was His love for His people. He loved them, and the saints among them were upheld by Him. By Moses He gave them a law, which was to hold from generation to generation; and He had crowned His gifts to them by becoming their King when the heads of the people entered into covenant with Him.

Then follow the blessings, beginning with good wishes for Reuben as the firstborn. But the tribe is not highly favoured. It is however less severely dealt with than in Jacob's blessing. There instability and obscurity are foretold of it. Here it would seem as if the fortunes of the tribe were at the lowest ebb, and a wish is expressed that it may not be suffered to die out. From the earliest times the tribe of Reuben seems to have been tending to decay. At the first census taken under Moses the number of Reubenites capable of bearing arms was 46,500 men (Numb. i. 21), at the second 43,730 (Numb. xxvi. 7). Both passages are from P, and consequently this decadence of the tribe must have been present to that author's mind. In David's day they had still possession of part of their heritage, but even then their best estate was past. They had allowed many Moabites to remain in the territory they conquered. These most certainly caused trouble and gained the upper hand in places, until before the days of Mesa, king of Moab, as we learn from his inscription,[134] a great part of the cities formerly Reubenite were in Moabite or Gadite hands. In Isaiah xv. and xvi. again, Heshbon and Elealeh, cities still Reubenite in Mesa's day, appear as Moabite, so that the bulk of the territory assigned to the tribe must have been lost.[135] This record confirms the view that the blessing was written between Rehoboam and Jehoshaphat, and throws light upon our verse:—

"May Reuben live, and not die,
So that his men be few."

The blessing of Judah follows, but in contrast with the great destiny foretold for this tribe in Jacob's blessing what is here said is strangely short and unenthusiastic:—

> "Hear, O Yahweh, Judah's voice,
> And bring him to his people;
> With his hands has he striven for it (his people);
> And a help against his enemies be thou."

Some whose opinions we are bound to respect, as Oettli, think this refers merely to Judah's being appointed to lead the van of the invasion, as in Judges i. 1 and xx. 8. In that case we should have to conceive that on some occasion Judah was absent leading the conquest, and got into dangerous circumstances, which are here referred to. But it would seem that any such temporary danger could hardly have a place here. In all the other blessings permanent conditions only are regarded; and the sole historical fact we really know that would explain this reference is the division of the kingdom. But, it may be said, all critics agree that the author of the blessing is a Northern Israelite: now we cannot suppose a Northern man to speak in this way of Judah, for it was the ten tribes that revolted from the house of David, not Judah from them. We must remember, however, that though that is how Scripture, which in this matter represents the Southern view, regards the matter, the Northern Israelites could look at the separation from another standpoint. To those even who were favourable to the Davidic house, and regretted the folly of Rehoboam, it might seem that Judah had first broken away from the kingdom as united under Saul; and the revolt under Jeroboam would appear to be only a resumption of the older state of things, from which Judah had again separated itself. What circumstance can be referred to in the request to hear Judah's voice cannot now be ascertained; but it is not at all unlikely that some indication of a wish for reunion, perhaps expressed in some public prayer, may have been given in the first period of the separation. The rest of the verse would fit this hypothesis as well as it fits the other, and I think with the light we at present have we must hold the reference to be as suggested.

With the eighth verse the blessing of Levi (one of the two most heartfelt and sympathetic) begins. In it Yahweh is addressed thus:—

> "Thy Urim and thy Thummim be to the men (*i.e.* tribe) of
> thy devoted one (*i.e.* Moses or Aaron),
> Whom thou didst prove at Massah,
> With whom thou didst strive at the waters of Meribah."

In the last lines the relative pronoun is ambiguous, as it may refer either to "men," for which in Hebrew we have the collective singular '*ish*, or to "thy devoted one." The last is the more probable; but in either case there is a superficial discrepancy here between the historical books and this statement. In Exod. xvii. 1-7, as well as in Deuteronomy itself, it is the people who strove with Moses and proved or tempted Yahweh. On this account some would have us believe that a different account of the events at Massah and Meribah was in this writer's mind. But that is the result of a mere itch for discovering discrepancies. It lies in the very nature of the case that there should be another side to it. The beginning was with the people; but just as the wandering in the wilderness is said to have been meant by God to prove Israel, so this insubordination of the people was meant to prove Moses or Aaron, and their failure to stand the proof made Yahweh strive with them. The verse, then, founds Levi's claim to possess the chief oracle and to instruct Israel first of all upon their connection with Moses or Aaron, or both, since they had been exceptionally tried and had proved their devotion. The next verse, then, goes on to found it also on the faithfulness of the Levites, when they were called upon by Moses (Exod. xxxii. 26-29) to punish the people for their worship of the golden calf. In vv. 27 and 29 of that chapter we find the same phrases,

> 9 "Who (*i.e.* the tribe) said unto his father and to his
> mother,
> I have not seen him;
> Who recognised not his brother, and would know nought
> of his son;
> For they kept Thy commandment,
> And kept guard over Thy covenant."

Being such—

> 10 "Let them teach Jacob Thy judgments,
> And Israel Thy Torah;
> Let them put incense in Thy nostrils,
> And whole burnt-offerings upon Thine altars."

Here we have the whole priestly duties assigned to the Levites. They are to perform judicial functions; to give Torah, or instruction, by means of the Urim and Thummim and otherwise; to offer incense in the Holy Place, and sacrifices in the court of the Temple. As early as this, therefore (on any supposition we need regard, long before Deuteronomy), we find the Levites fully established as the priestly tribe. Before the earliest writing prophets this was so—a fact of the greatest importance for the history of Israelite religion. The remaining verse beseeches Yahweh to accept the work of Levi's hands, and to smite down his enemies. Evidently when this was written special enmity was being shown to this tribe; and, as has been said already, the religious proceedings of Jeroboam I. would be sufficient to call forth such a cry to Yahweh.

In ver. 12 the tribe of Benjamin is dealt with, and it is depicted as specially blessed by the Divine favour and the Divine presence. Yahweh covers him all the day long, and dwells between his shoulders. There can hardly be a doubt that the reference is to the situation of the Temple at Jerusalem, on the hill of Zion, towards the loftier boundary of Benjamin's territory.

Verses 13-17 contain the blessing of Joseph, *i.e.* of the two tribes Ephraim and Manasseh.

> 13 "Blessed of Yahweh be his land
> By the precious things of heaven from above,
> By the deep which crouches beneath;
>
> 14 "By the precious things of the sun,
> And the precious things of the moons;
>
> 15 "And by the (precious things of the) tops of the ancient mountains
> And by the precious things of the everlasting hills;
>
> 16 "And by the precious things of the earth and its fulness.
> And may the good-will of Him that dwelt in the bush
> Come upon Joseph's head,
> And upon the top of the head of the crowned among his brethren.
>
> 17 "May the firstborn of his ox be glorious;
> And the horns thereof like the horns of the wild-ox;
> With them may he gore the peoples, even all the earth's ends together.
> These (*i.e.* thus blessed) are the myriads of Ephraim,
> And these the thousands of Manasseh."

Supreme fertility is to be his, and the favour of Yahweh is to rest upon him as the kingly tribe in Israel. The curious phrase at the beginning of the seventeenth verse has been supposed to be a reference to some individual, Joshua, Jeroboam II., or to the Ephraimite kings as a whole. But the subject of the blessing is the Josephite tribes, and there seems to be no good reason why the reference should be changed here. It cannot, therefore, refer to less than a whole tribe, and as according to Gen. xlviii. 14 Ephraim received the blessing of the firstborn, it must be Ephraim which is Joseph's firstborn ox.

This view is confirmed by the last clause of the verse, in which the myriads of Ephraim are spoken of, and only the thousands of Manasseh. Obviously this must refer to times like those of Omri, when the Israelite kingship was in its first youthful energy, and was extending conquest on every hand.

The benedictions which remain are addressed to Zebulun, Issachar, Gad, Dan, Naphtali, and Asher. They need little comment beyond close translation.

18 "And of Zebulun he said,
Rejoice, Zebulun, in thy going out;
And, Issachar, in thy tents.

19 "They shall call the peoples unto the mountain;
They shall offer sacrifices of righteousness:
For they shall suck the abundance of the seas,
And the hidden treasures of the sand."

The territory of Zebulun stretched from the Sea of Galilee to the Mediterranean, probably quite down to the sea near Akko, in any case near enough to give it an active share in the sea traffic. Issachar, whose tribal land was the plain of Esdraelon, also shares in it; but the contrast between "thy going out" and "thy tents" implies that Zebulun took the more active part in the traffic. The reference in verse 19, clauses *a* and *b*, is obscure. As the Septuagint reads "they shall destroy" instead of "unto the mountain," the text may be corrupt. It may perhaps be an allusion to the sacrificial feasts at inaugurated fairs to which surrounding peoples were called, as Stade suggests.

20 "And of Gad he said,
Blessed be the enlarger of Gad:
He dwelleth as a lioness,
And teareth the arm, yea, the crown of the head.

21 "And he looked out the first part for himself,
Because there a (tribal) ruler's portion lay ready;
And he came with the heads of the people,
He executed the justice of Yahweh,
And His judgments in company with Israel."

At this time Gad was in possession of a wide territory, and was famed for courage and success in war. His foresight in choosing the first of the conquered land as a worthy tribal portion is praised, and his faithfulness in carrying out his bargain to accompany the nation in its attack on the west Jordan land.

22 "And of Dan he said,
Dan is a lion's whelp,
Leaping forth from Bashan."

This does not mean that Dan's territory was Bashan, but only that his attack was as fierce and unexpected as that of a lion leaping forth from the crevices and caves of the rocks in Bashan.

23 "And of Naphtali he said,
O Naphtali, sated with favour,
And full of the blessing of Yahweh:
Possess thou the sea and the south."

The soil in the territory of Naphtali was specially fruitful, in the region of Huleh and on the shore of the Sea of Gennesaret. These are the sea and the hot south part which the tribe is called upon to take as a possession, and because of which the favour of Yahweh and His blessing specially rested upon it.

24 "And of Asher he said,
Blessed above children be Asher;
May he be the favoured of his brethren,
And dip his feet in oil.

25 "Iron and brass (be) thy bars;
And as thy days (so may) thy strength (be)."

The last line is extremely doubtful. The word translated "thy strength" is really not known, and that meaning probably implies another reading; "thy bars" in the previous line is also doubtful. The reference to oil probably implies that the olive tree was specially fruitful, in the country inhabited by Asher, but why he should be specially favoured of his brethren can now hardly be conjectured.

In the concluding verses we have an exaltation of Israel's God and of His people. Speaking out of the time when Israel had driven out its enemies and was in full and undisturbed possession of its heritage (ver. 28), the poet declares to Jeshurun how incomparable God is. He rides upon the heaven to bring help to them, and He comes in the clouds with majesty. The God of old time is Israel's refuge or dwelling, covering him from above, and beneath, i.e. on the earth. His everlasting arms bear His people up in their weariness, and shelter them there against all foes. He has proved this by thrusting out before them, and by commanding them to destroy, their enemies.

28 "And so Israel came to dwell in safety,
The fountain of Jacob alone,

In a land of corn and wine;
Yea, His heavens drop down dew.

29 "Happy art thou, O Israel:
Who is like unto thee?
A people saved by Yahweh,
The shield of thy help
And the sword of thy majesty!
Thine enemies shall feign friendship to thee;
And thou shalt tread upon their high places."

CHAPTER XXVI
MOSES' CHARACTER AND DEATH

It has been often said, and it has even become a principle of the critical school, that the historical notices in the earlier documents of the Old Testament represent nothing but the ideas current at the time when they were written. Whether they depict an Abraham, a Jacob, or a Moses, all they really tell us is the kind of character which at such times was held to be heroic. In this way the value of the historic parts of Deuteronomy have been called in question, and we have been told that all we can gather from them about Moses is the kind of character which the pious, in the age of Manasseh, would feel justified in attributing to their great religious hero. But it is manifestly unfair to estimate the statements of men who write in good faith, as if they were only projecting their own desires and prejudices upon a past which is absolutely dark. It may be true that such writers might be unwilling to narrate stories concerning the great men of the past which were inconsistent with the esteem in which they were held; but it is much more certain that their narratives will represent the tradition and the current knowledge of their time regarding the heroes of their race. Unless this be true, no reliance could be placed upon anything but absolutely contemporary documents; even these would be open to suspicion, if the human mind were so lawless as to have no scruple in filling up all gaps in its knowledge by imaginations. We must protest, therefore, against the notion that what J and E and D tell us concerning the life and character of Moses must be discounted in any effort we make to represent to ourselves the life and thought of that great leader of Israel. They tell us much more than what was thought fitting for a leader of the people in the ninth and eighth and seventh centuries B.C. They tell us what was *believed* in those times about Moses; and much of what was believed about him must have rested upon good authority, upon entirely reliable tradition, or upon previous written narratives concerning him.

Up till recently it was held, by men as eminent even as Reuss, that writing was unknown in the days of Moses, and that for long afterwards oral tradition alone could be a source of knowledge of the past. But recent discoveries have shown that this is an entire mistake. Long before Moses writing was a common accomplishment in Canaan; and it seems almost ridiculous to suppose that the man who left his mark so indelibly upon this nation should have been ignorant of an art with which every master of a village or two was thoroughly conversant. Moreover the fact that the same root (k-t-b) occurs in every Semitic tongue with the meaning "to write," would seem to indicate that before their separation from one another the art of writing was known to all the Semitic tribes. The new facts enormously strengthen that probability, and make the arguments advanced by those who hold the opposite view look even absurd. But if writing were known and practised in Moses' day in Canaan, it would be marvellous if many of the great events of the early days had not been recorded. It would be still more marvellous if the comparatively late writings, which alone we have at our disposal had not embodied and absorbed much older documents.

But for still another reason the critical dictum must be held to be false. Applied in other fields and in regard to other times, this same principle would deprive us of almost every character which has been considered the glory of humanity. Zarathustra and Buddha have alike been sacrificed to this prejudice, and there are men living who say that we know so little about our Lord Jesus Christ that it is doubtful whether He ever existed. A method which produces such results *must* be false. The great source of progress and reform has always been some man possessed by an idea or a principle. Even in our own days, when the press and the facilities for communication have given general tendencies a power to realise themselves which they never had in the world's history before, great men are the moving factors in all great changes. In earlier ages this was still more the case. It is an utterly unjustifiable scepticism which makes men contradict the grateful recollection of mankind, in regard to those who have raised and comforted humanity. Through all obscurities and confusions we can reach that Indian Prince for whom the sight of human misery embittered his own brilliant and enjoyable life. We refuse to give up Zarathustra, though his story is more obscure and entangled than that of almost any other great leader of mankind. Especially in a history like that of Israel, which purports to have been guided in a special manner by revelations of the will of God, the individual man filled with God's spirit is quite indispensable. Even if mythical elements in the story could be proved, that would not shake our faith in the existence of Moses; for as Steinthal, who holds the very "advanced" opinion that solar myths have strayed into the history of Moses, wisely says, it is quite as possible to distinguish between the mythical and the historical Moses as it is to distinguish between the historical Charlemagne and the mythical. Because of the general reliability of tradition regarding great men therefore, and because also of the proofs we have that writing was common before

Moses' day, we need not burden ourselves with the assumption or the fear that the Deuteronomic character of Moses may be unreliable.

But in endeavouring to set forth this conception of the character of Moses, we cannot confine ourselves to what appears in this book. It is generally acknowledged that the author had at least the Yahwist and the Elohist documents in their entirety before him, and regarded them with respect, not to say reverence. Consequently we must believe that he accepted what they said of Moses as true. The only document in the Pentateuch that he may not have known in any shape was the Priest Codex, but that makes no attempt to depict the inner or outer life of Moses. All the personal life and colour in the Biblical narrative belongs to the other sources. For a personal estimate, therefore, we lose little by excluding P. Only one other cause of suspicion in regard to the historical parts of Deuteronomy *could* arise. If it, comparatively modern as it is, contained much that was new, if it revealed aspects of character for which no authority was quoted, and of which there was no trace in the earlier narratives, there might be reasonable doubt whether these new details were the product of imagination. But there is very little more in Deuteronomy than there is in the historical parts of the other books, though the older narratives are repeated with a vivid and insistive pathos which almost seems to make them new.

Combining then what the Deuteronomist himself says with what the Yahwist and Elohist documents contain, we find that the claim usually made for Moses, that he was the founder of an entirely new religion, is not sustained. Again and again it is asserted that Yahweh had been the God of their fathers, of Abraham, Isaac, and Jacob—so that Moses was simply the renewer of a higher faith which for a time had been corrupted. Some have even asserted that there had been all down the ages to Moses the memory of a primeval revelation. But if there ever was such a thing, we learn from Josh. xxiv. 2, a verse acknowledged to be from the Elohist, that that "fair beginning of a time" had been entirely eclipsed, for Terah, the father of Abraham, had served other gods beyond the flood. Abraham, therefore, rather than Moses, is regarded as the founder of the religion of Yahweh. Whether the word Yahweh (Exod. vi. 3) was known or not makes little difference, for all our four authorities teach that Moses' work was the revival of faith in that which Abraham, Isaac, and Jacob had believed. But the bulk of the people would appear to have been ignorant regarding the God of their fathers; and probably the conception which Deuteronomy shares with J and E is that in Moses' day Yahweh was the special God of a small circle, perhaps of the tribe of Levi, among whom a more spiritual conception of God than was common among their countrymen had either been retained, or had arisen anew. Probably then we ought to conceive the circumstances of Moses' early life somewhat in this way. A number of Semitic tribes, more or less nearly related to each other and to Edom and Moab, had settled in Egypt as semi-agricultural nomads. At first they were tolerated; but they were now being worn down and oppressed by forced labour of the most brutal sort. Either a tribe or a clan among them had the germs of a purer conception of God, and in this tribe or clan Moses, the deliverer of his people, was born. Providentially he escaped the death which awaited all Israelite boys in those days, and grew up in the camp of the enemies of his people. By this means he received all the culture that the best of the oppressors had, while the tie to Israel was neither obscured nor weakened in his mind. At the court of Pharaoh he could not fail to acquire some notions of state-craft, and he must have seen that the first step towards anything great for his people must be their union and consolidation. But his earliest effort on their behalf showed that he had not really considered and weighed the magnitude of his task. Killing an Egyptian oppressor might conceivably have served as a signal for revolt. But in point of fact it frustrated any plans Moses might have had for the good of his people, and drove him into the wilderness. Here the germs of various thoughts which education and experience of life had deposited in his mind had time to develop and grow. According to the narrative, it was only at the end of his long sojourn in Midian that he had direct revelation from God. But amid the wide and awful solitudes of that wilderness land, as General Gordon said of himself in the kindred solitudes of the Soudan, he learned himself and God. Whatever deposits of higher faith he had received from his family, no doubt the long, silent broodings inseparable from a shepherd's life had increased and vivified it. Every possible aspect of it must have been reckoned with, all its consequences explored; and his great and solitary soul, we may be sure, had many a time let down soundings into the deeps which were, as yet, dark to him. And then—for it is to souls that have yearned after Him in the travail of intellectual and spiritual longing that God gives His great and splendid revelations—Yahweh revealed Himself in the flame of the bush, and gave him the final assurance and the first impulse for his life's work. It is a touch of reality in the narrative which can hardly be mistaken, that it represents Moses as shrinking from the responsibility which his call must lay upon him. Behind the few and simple objections in the narrative, we must picture to ourselves a whole world of thoughts and feelings into which the call of God had brought tumult and confusion. One would need to be a dry-as-dust pedant not to see here, as in the case of Isaiah's call, the triumphant issue of a long conflict and the decisive moment of a victory over self, which had had already many stages of defeat and only partial success. It is perennially true to human nature and to the Divine dealings with human nature, that help from on high comes to establish and touch to finer issues that which the true man has striven for with all his powers.

Enlightened and assured by this great revelation of God, Moses left the quiet of the desert to undertake an extraordinarily difficult task. He had to weld jealous tribes into a nation; he had to rouse men whose courage had been broken by slavery and cruelty to undertake a dangerous revolt; and he had to prepare for the march of a whole population, burdened with invalids and infants, the feeble and the old, through a country which even to-day tries all but the strongest. These things had to be done; and the mere fact that they were accomplished would be inexplicable, without the domination of a great personality inspired by great ideas of a religious kind. For, in antiquity, the only bond able to hold incongruous elements together in one nationality was religion. With the people whom Moses had to lead the necessity would be the same, or even greater. But the political work which must have preceded any common action likewise demanded a great personality. Though no doubt a common misery might silence jealousies and make men eager to listen to any promises of deliverance, yet many troublesome negotiations must have been carried through successfully before these sentences could have been written with truth: "And Moses and Aaron went and gathered together all the elders of the children of Israel, and the people believed, and bowed their heads and worshipped."

Many conjectures have been hazarded as to what the centre of Moses' message at this time really was. Some, like Stade, bring it down to this, that Yahweh was the God of Israel. Others add to this somewhat meagre statement another equally meagre, that Israel was the people of Yahweh. But unless the character of Yahweh had been previously expounded to the people, there seems little in these two declarations to excite any enthusiasm or to kindle faith. The mere fact of inducing the tribes to put all other gods aside is insufficient to account for any of the results that followed, if to Moses Yahweh had remained simply a tribal God, of the same type as the gods of the Canaanites. On the other hand, if he had risen to the conception of God as a spirit, of Yahweh as the only living God, as the inspirer and defender of moral life, or even if he had made any large approach to these conceptions, it is easy to understand how the hearts of the mass of the people were stirred and filled, even though things so high were not, by the generality, thoroughly understood or long retained. But the hearts of all the chosen, the spiritually elect, would be moved by them as the leaves are moved by the wind. These, with Moses at their head, formed a nucleus which bore the people on through all their trials and dangers, and gradually leavened the mass to some extent with the same spirit.

Even after this had been accomplished, the main work remained to be done. We cannot agree indeed with many writers who seem to think that the whole life of the Israelite people was started anew by Moses. That would involve that every regulation for the most trivial detail of ordinary life was directly revealed, and that Moses made a *tabula rasa* of their minds, rubbing out all previous laws and customs, and writing a God-given constitution in their place. Obviously, that could hardly be; but still a task very different, yet almost as difficult, remained for Moses after his first success. His final aim was to make a virtually new nation out of the Hebrew tribes; and their whole constitution and habits had, consequently, to be revised from the new religious standpoint. He and the nation alike had inherited a past, and it was no part of his mission to delete that. Reforms, to be stable, must have a root in the habits and thoughts of the people whom they concern. Moses would, consequently, uproot nothing that could be spared; he would plant nothing anew which was already flourishing, and was compatible with the new and dominant ideas he had introduced. A great mass of the laws and customs of the Hebrews must have been good, and suitable to the stage of moral advancement they had reached before Moses came to them. Any measure of civilised life involves so much as that. Another great mass, while lying outside of the religious sphere, must have been at least compatible with Yahwism. All laws and customs coming under these two categories, Moses would naturally adopt as part of the legislation of the new nation, and would stamp them with his approval as being in accord with the religion of Yahweh. They would thus acquire the same authority as if they were entirely new, given for the first time by the Divinely inspired lawgiver.

But besides these two classes of laws and customs there must have been a number which were so bound up with the lower religion that they could not be adopted. They would either be obstructive of the new ideas, or they would be positively hostile to them; for on any supposition heathenism of various sorts was largely mingled with the religion of the Israelite people before their deliverance, and even after it. To sift these out, and to replace them by others more in accord with the will of Yahweh as now revealed, must have been the chief work of the lawgiver. In that more or less protracted period before Israel came to Sinai, during which Moses burdened himself with judging the people personally, he must have been doing this work. His reflections in the wilderness had doubtless prepared him for it. In a mind like his, the fruitful principles received by the inspiration of the Almighty could not be merely passively held. Like St. Paul in his Arabian sojourn, we must believe that Moses in Midian would work out the results of these principles in many directions; and when he led Israel forth, he must have been clearly conscious of changes that were indispensable. But it needed close every-day contact with the life of the people to bring out all the incompatibilities which he would have to remove. Every day unexpected complications would arise; and the people at any rate, if Moses himself be supposed to be raised by his inspiration above the needs of experience, would be able to receive the instruction they needed only in concrete examples, here a little and there a little. When they came to "seek Yahweh" in any matter which perplexed them, Moses gave them Yahweh's mind on the subject; and each decision tended to purify and render innocuous to their higher life some department of public or private affairs. Every day at that early time must have been a day of instruction how to apply the principles of the higher faith just revived. The better minds among the chiefs were thereby trained to an appreciation of the new point of view; and when Jethro suggested that the burden of this work should be divided, quite a sufficient number were found prepared to carry it on. After this it must have gone on with tenfold speed, and we may believe that when Sinai was reached the preliminaries on the human side to the great revelation had been thoroughly elaborated. The Divine presence had been with Moses day by day, judging, deciding, inspiring in all their individual concerns as well as in their common affairs. But that would only bring out more clearly the extent of the reformation that remained to be wrought; doubtless too it had revealed the dulness of heart in regard to the Divine which has always characterised the mass of men. The need for a more complete revelation, a more extended and detailed legislation on the new basis, must have been greatly felt. In the great scene at Sinai, a scene so strange and awe-inspiring that to the latest days of Israel the memory of it thrilled every Israelite heart and exalted every Israelite imagination, this need was adequately met.

In connection with it Moses rose to new heights of intimacy with the Divine. What he had already done was ratified, and in the Decalogue the great lines of moral and social life were marked out for the people. But the most remarkable thing to us, in the narrative of the circle of events which made the mountain of the law for ever memorable, is the sublimity attributed to the character of Moses. From the day when he smote the Egyptian, at every glimpse we have of him we find him always advancing in power of character. The shepherd of Midian is nobler, less self-assertive, more overawed by communion with God, than the son of Pharaoh's daughter, noble as he was. Again, the religious reformer, the popular leader, who needs the very insistence of God to make him lead, who speaks for God with such courageous majesty, who teaches, inspires, and manages a turbulent nation with such conspicuous patience, self-repression, and success, is greatly more impressive than the Moses of Midianite days. But it is here, at Sinai, that his rank among the leaders of men is fixed for ever. To the people of that time God was above all things terrible; and when they came to the mount and found that "there were thunders and lightnings and a thick cloud upon the mount, and the voice of the trumpet exceeding loud," they could only tremble. Their very fear made it impossible for them to understand what God desired to reveal concerning Himself. But in Moses love had cast out fear. Even to him, doubtless, the darkness was terrible, because it expressed only too well the mystery which enwrapped the end of the Divine purposes of which he alone had seen the beginnings; even his mind must have been clouded thick with doubts as to whither Yahweh was leading him and his people; yet he went boldly forth to seek God, venturing all upon that errand.

In previous perplexities the narrative represents Moses as calling instantly upon Yahweh; but now, when experience had taught him the formidable nature of his task, when difficulties had increased upon him, when his perplexities of all kinds must have been simply overwhelming, he heard the voice of Yahweh calling him to Himself. Straightway he went into solitary communion with Him; and when he passed with satisfied heart from that communion, he brought with him those immortal words of the Decalogue which, amid all changes since, have been acknowledged to be the true foundation for moral and spiritual life. He brought too a commission authorising him to give laws and judgments to his people in accord with what he had heard and seen on the mount. However we are to understand the details of the narrative therefore, its meaning is that at this time, and under these circumstances, Moses attained his maximum of inspiration as a seer or prophet, and from that time onward stood in a more intimate relation to God than any of the prophets and saints of Israel who came after him. He had found God; and from where he stood with God he saw the paths of religious and political progress plainly marked out.

Henceforth he was competent to guide the nation he had made as he had not yet been, and with his power to help them his eagerness to do so grew. Twice during this great crisis of his life the people broke away into evil, and national death was threatened. But with passionate supplications for their pardon he threw himself down between God and them. At precisely the moment when his communion with God was most complete, he rose to the loving recklessness of desiring that if they were to be destroyed he might perish with them. Strangely enough, though the author of Deuteronomy had this before him, he does not mention it. It cannot have struck even him as the crowning point of Moses' career, as it does us. Even in his day the fitness, nay, the necessity, of this self-sacrificing spirit as the fruit of deeper knowledge of God, was not yet felt; much less could it have been felt in the days of the earlier historians. There must, therefore, be reliable information here as to what Moses actually did. Such love as this was not part of the Israelite ideal at the time of our narrative, and from nothing but knowledge of the fact could it have been attributed to Moses. We may rank this enthusiasm of love, therefore, as a reliable trait in his character. But if it be so, how far must he in his highest moments have transcended his contemporaries, and even the best of his successors, in knowledge of the inmost nature of God! His thought was so far above them that it remained fruitless for many centuries. Jeremiah's life and death first prepared the way for its appreciation, but only in the character of the Servant of Yahweh in Second Isaiah is it surpassed. Now if in this deepest part of true religion Moses possessed such exceptional spiritual insight, it is vain to attempt to show that his conception of God was so low, and his aim for man so limited, as modern theorists suppose. The truth must lie rather with those who, like Dr. A. B. Davidson,[136] see in him "a profoundly reverential ancient mind with thoughts of God so broad that mankind has added little to them. Nothing in the way of sublimity of view would be incongruous with such a character, while nothing could be more grotesque than to shut it up within the limits of the gross conceptions of the mass of the people. He was their guiding star, not their fellow, in all that concerned God, and his religious conceptions were by a whole heaven removed from theirs. The entire tragedy of his life just consisted in this, that he had to strive with a turbulent and gainsaying people, had to bear with them and train them, had to be content with scarcely perceptible advances, where his strenuous guidance and his patient love should have kindled them to *run* in the way of God's commandments. But though their progress was lamentably slow, he gave them an impulse they were never to lose. Under the inspiration of the Almighty he so fixed their fundamental ideas about God that they never henceforth could get free of his spiritual company. In all their progress afterwards they felt the impress of his mind, moulding and shaping them even when they knew it not, and through them he started in the world that redemptive work of God which manifested its highest power in Jesus Christ."

From this point onward the idea of Moses that Deuteronomy gives us is that of a great popular leader, meeting with extraordinary calmness all the crises of government, and guiding his people with unwavering steadfastness. Without power, except that which his relation to God and the choice of the people gave him, without any official title, he simply dominated the Israelites as long as he lived. And the secret of his success is plainly told us in the narrative. He would not move a single step without Divine guidance (Exod. xxxiii. 12): "And Moses said unto the Lord, See, Thou sayest unto me, Bring up this people: but Thou hast not let me know whom Thou wilt send with me." (Ver. 14) "And He said, Must I go in person with thee and bring thee to thy place of rest? And Moses said, If Thou dost not go with us in person, then rather lead us not away hence." That can only mean that he laid aside self-will, that he put away personal sensitiveness, that he had learned to feel himself unsafe when vanity or self-regard asserted themselves in his decisions, that he sought continually that detachment of view which absolute devotion to the Highest always gives. It means also that he knew how dark and dull his own vision was, that clouds and darkness would always be about him, and that it would be impossible for him to choose his path, unless he knew what the Divine plan for his people was. And all that is narrated of him afterward shows that his prayer was granted. His patience under trial has been handed down to us as a marvel. Though his brother and sister rebelled against him, he won them again entirely to himself. Though a faction among the people rose against his authority under Dathan and Abiram, his power was not even shaken. Amid all the perversity and childish fickleness of Israel he kept them true to their choice of the desert, "that great and terrible wilderness," as against Egypt with the flesh-pots. He kept alive their faith in the promise of Yahweh to give them a land flowing with milk and honey, and what was more and greater than that, their faith in Him as their Redeemer. By his intercourse with Yahweh he was upheld from falling away from his own ideals, as so many leaders of nations have done, or from despairing of them.

The complaints and perversities of the people did however force him into sin; and perhaps we may take it that the outbreak of petulance when he smote the rock was only one instance of some general decay of character on that side, or perhaps one should rather say, of some general falling away from the self-restraint which had distinguished him. It seems strange that this one failure should have been punished in him, by exclusion from the land he had so steadfastly believed in, the land which most of those who actually entered it would never have seen but for him. And it is pathetic to find him among that great company of martyrs for the public good, those who in order to serve their people have neglected their own characters. Under the stress of public work and the pressure of the stupidity and greed of those whom they have sought to guide, many leaders of men have been tempted, and have yielded to the temptation, to forget the demands of their better nature. But whatever their services to the world, such unfaithfulness does not pass unpunished. They have to bear the penalty, whosoever they be; and Moses was no more an exception than Cromwell or Savonarola was, to mention only some of the nobler examples. He had been courageous when others had faltered. He had been pre-eminently just; for in founding the judicial system of Israel he had guarded alike against the tyranny of the great and against unjust favour to the small. He had laid a firm hand upon the education of youth, determined that the best inheritance of their people, the knowledge of the laws of Yahweh and of His providences, should not be lost to them. He had cleared their religion in principle of all that was unworthy of Yahweh, and he had by resolute valour, and by uncompromising sternness to enemies, brought his great task to a successful issue. But the reward of it all, the entrance into the land he had virtually won for his people, was denied to him. It is one of the laws of the Divine government of the world, that with those to whom God specially draws near He is more rigorous than with others. Amos clearly saw and proclaimed this principle (Amos iii. 2). "Hear this word that Yahweh hath spoken against you, children of Israel," he says; "You only have I known of all the families of the earth: *therefore* I will visit upon you all your iniquities." The pathetic picture of the aged lawgiver, judge, and prophet, beseeching God in vain that he might share in the joy which was freely bestowed upon so many less known and less worthy than he, pushes home that strenuous teaching. For his sin he died with his last earnest wish unfulfilled, and it was sadly longing eyes that death's finger touched. We remember also that, so far as we can judge, he had no certain hope of a future life other than the shadowy existence of Hades. "Though he slay me yet will I trust him" had a much more tragic meaning for Old Testament saints than it can ever have for us, for whom Christ has brought life and immortality to light. Yet, with a so much heavier burden, and with so much less of gracious support, they played their high part. That solitary figure on the mountain-top, about to die with the fulfilment of his passionate last wish denied him by his God, must shame us into silence when we fret because our hopes have perished. All those nations which have had that figure on their horizon have been permanently enriched in nature by it. In a thousand ways it has shot forth instructions; but, above all, it has made men worthy in their own eyes; for it has been a continuous reminder that God can and ought to be served unfalteringly, even when the reward we wish is denied us, and when every other consolation is dim.

But the question may now arise, Is not this character of Moses which the author of Deuteronomy partly had before him and partly helped to elaborate, too exalted to be reliable? Can we suppose that a man in Moses' day and circumstances could actually have entertained such thoughts, and have possessed such a character as we have been depicting? In essentials it would appear to be quite possible. Putting aside all distracting questions about details, and remembering that it is a mere superstition to suppose that the wants and appliances of civilisation are necessary to loftiness of character and depth of thought, where is there anything in the situation of Moses which should make this view of him incredible? No doubt there was a rudeness in his surroundings which must necessarily have affected his nature; and the forms of his thinking in that early, though by no means primitive, time must have differed greatly from ours. Moreover, as an instrument for scientific inquiry and for the verification of facts, the human mind must have been greatly less effective then than it is to-day. But none of these things have much influence upon a man's capacity to receive a new and inspiring revelation as to God. Otherwise no child could be a Christian. As regards the rudeness of his surroundings, we must not consciously or unconsciously degrade him to the level of a modern Bedouin. Among the host he led, some doubtless were at that level; but the bulk of Israel must have been above it; and Moses himself, from his circumstances and his natural endowment, must have stood side by side with the most cultured men of his time. Whatever ignorance or error in science he may have been capable of, and however rude, according to our ideas, his manner of life, there was nothing in these to shut him out from spiritual truth. That which Prof. Henry Morley has finally said of Dante[137] must have been true, *mutatis mutandis*, of a man like Moses. "Dante's knowledge is the knowledge of his time," but "if spiritual truth only came from right and perfect knowledge, this would have been a world of dead souls from the first to now, for future centuries in looking back at us will wonder at the little faulty knowledge that we think so much. But let the *known* be what it may, the true soul rises from it to a sense of the Divine mysteries of wisdom and love. Dante's knowledge may be full of ignorance, and so is ours. But he fills it as he can with the spirit of God." In the East this is even more conspicuously true, even to this day. What an Israelite under similar conditions might be is seen in the prophet Amos. His external condition was of the poorest—a gatherer of sycamore fruit must have been poor even for the East—yet he knew accurately the history, not only of his own people, but of the surrounding nations, and brooded on the purpose of God in regard to his own people and the world, till he became a fit recipient of prophetic inspirations. But indeed the whole history of Christianity is a demonstration of this truth. From the first days, when "not many mighty, not many noble were being called," when it was specially the message to listening slaves, the religion of Christ has had its greatest triumphs among the "poor of the world, rich in faith," but in nothing else. These have not only believed it, but they have lived it, and amid the meanest and rudest surroundings, with the most limited outlook, have built up characters often of even resplendent virtue. Whatever primitiveness we may fairly ascribe, therefore, to the life and surroundings of Moses, that is no reason why we should think it incredible that he had received lofty spiritual truth from God. If he did such things for Israel as we have seen, if, as almost all admit, he actually made a nation, and planted the seeds of a religion of which Christianity is the natural complement and crown, then the view that he had a greatly higher idea of God than those about him is not only credible but necessary. If his teaching concerning Yahweh had amounted only to this, that He was the only God Israel was to worship, and that they were to be solely His people, then on such a basis nothing more than the ordinary heathen civilisations of the Semitic people could have been built. But if he had the thought of God which is embodied in the Decalogue, that could bring with it everything in the character of Moses that seems too high for those early days. The knowledge of God as a spiritual and moral being could not fail to moralise and spiritualise the man. The lofty conception of human duty, the submission to the will of God, the passionate love for his nation which made personal loss nothing to Moses, may well have been evoked by the great truth which formed his prophetic revelation.

But the narrative itself, considered merely as a history, is of such a nature as to give confidence that it rests upon some record of an actual life. Ideal sketches of great men (setting aside the products of modern fictive art) are much more uniform and superficially coherent than this character of Moses. The purpose of the writer either to exalt or to decry carries all before it, and we get from such a source pictures of character so consistent that they cannot possibly be true. Here, however, we have nothing of that kind. Rashnesses and weaknesses are narrated, and even Moses' good qualities are manifested in unexpected ways in response to unexpected evils in the people. The mere fact, also, that his grave was unknown is indicative of truth. Though it would be absurd to say that wherever we have the graves of great men pointed out, there we have a mythical story, it is nevertheless true that in the case of every name or character which has come largely under the influence of the myth-making spirit, the grave has been made much of. The Arabian imagination here seems to be typical of the Semitic imagination; and in all Moslem lands the graves of the prophets and saints of the Old Testament are pointed out with great reverence, even, or perhaps we should say especially, if they be eighty feet long. Though a well-authenticated tomb of Moses, therefore, would have been a proof of his real existence and life among men, the absence of any is a stronger proof of the sobriety and truth of the narrative. That with the goal in sight, and with his great work about to come to fruition, he should have turned away into the solitude of the mountains to die, is so very unlikely to occur to the mind of the writer of an ideal life of an ideal leader, that only some tradition of this as a fact can account for it. The unexpectedness of such an end to a hero's career is the strongest evidence of its truth.

The result of all the indications is that the story of Moses, as the author of Deuteronomy knew it, rests upon authentic information handed down somehow, probably in written documents, from the earliest time. Apart from the question of inspiration, therefore, we may rest upon it as reliable in all essentials. Only in him, and the revelation he received, have we an adequate cause for the great upheaval of religious feeling which shaped and characterised all the after-history of Israel.

FOOTNOTES:

[1] Driver, *Introduction*, 5th Ed., p. 84.

[2] Cf. Deut. i. 1-5, iv. 41-43, iv. 44, v. 1, xxvii. 1, 9-11, xxix. 1, xxxi. 1-30.

[3] Cf. Deut. i. 1, 5, iv. 41, 46, 47, 49.

[4] iii. 20, 25, and xi. 30.

[5] Cf. *Pentateuch Kritische Studien* in Luthardt's *Zeitschrift*, 1880.

[6] It is scarcely necessary to remind readers that, from the point of view of the critics, J signifies one of the constituent documents of the Pentateuch which uses the name Yahweh for God. Its date is about 850 B.C. E is that document which uses the name Elohim, and may be dated about the same period as J. D is the author of Deuteronomy, who wrote, it is supposed, in the reign of Manasseh, perhaps about 670 B.C. P is the Priestly document, which Dillmann dates before Deuteronomy, but which most critics think was brought substantially into its present shape by Ezra. The portions of the Pentateuch assigned to these various documents will be found in Driver's *Introduction*.

[7] Driver, *Introduction*, p. 76.

[8] Josh. xxiv. 30.

[9] *Introduction*, p. 117.

[10] Cf. for the passages on which this statement is founded Driver's *Introduction*, p. 80, and note in small print.

[11] Dillmann, *Exodus and Leviticus*, p. 199.

[12] Josh. iii. 14-17 and *passim*.

[13] Driver, *Introduction*, p. 145; Oettli, *Deuteronomy*, p. 7; Kuenen, *H.K.O.*, p. 113.

[14] See further in exposition of chapter xvii; xviii.

[15] *Ezekiel*, Introduction, p. liv. f.

[16] *Additional Answer to the Libel*, p. 80.

[17] Cf. Driver, art. "Deuteronomy," Smith's *Dictionary*, p. 770.

[18] *Pentateuch Kritische Studien*, X.

[19] *Answer to the Form of Libel*, p. 34. Note: where Arnold and Masson's *Life of Milton* are referred to.

[20] Art. "Deuteronomy," Smith's *Bible Dict.*, pp. 769 ff.

[21] *Answer*, pp. 41 f.

[22] See this brought out in detail in Robertson Smith, *Old Testament in Jewish Church*, p. 431.

[23] Wellhausen, *Prolegomena*, p. 439.

[24] *Ency. Brit.*, vol. xx., p. 670.

[25] Granting that the commandment did not exist, one asks, *What* was it in Yahwism which determined the Jerusalem Sanctuary to be imageless?

[26] iii. 14.

[27] Exod. xxi. 7.

[28] Numb. xxx. 6.

[29] Deut. xxi. 8.

[30] Kalisch, *Exodus*, p. 364:—yet taught in all Victorian State schools under the vicious system at present admitted.

[31] *Journal Anthropological Institute*, May 1884, p. 28.

[32] See Page Renouf, *Hibbert Lectures*.

[33] Browning's *Poetical Works*, vol. vi., p. 69.

[34] Cf. Schultz, *Alttestamentliche Theologie*, p. 92.

[35] Browning, "James Lee's Wife," VII.

[36] Augustine's *Confessions*, p. 64.

[37] Lev. xix. 18, 34.

[38] *Geschichte des Alterthums*, p. 249.

[39] *Religion of the Semites*, p. 330.

[40] Cf. Wiedemann, *Religion der alten Aegypter*, p. 3.

[41] Wiedemann, p. 1, 35.

[42] Cf. Meyer, p. 71.

[43] *Egypt under the Pharaohs*, Brodick's edition p. 423.

[44] Meyer, p. 117.

[45] Sayce, *Babylonian Literature*, p. 36. Both poems here referred to are pre-Assyrian, being found as translations in the library of Assurbanipal. But Assyrian religion made no progress; it seems to have remained always dependent on Babylonian, even in details.

[46] Meyer, p. 178. Cf. however Sayce, *The Higher Criticism and the Monuments*, p. 114. Sayce maintains that the Assyrian epic attributes the flood to the moral guilt of men. But that is by no means proved, for it is more than doubtful whether sin to the Assyrian was not always mainly a ceremonial matter.

[47] Browning's Poems, "The Boy and the Angel."

[48] *Theol., Ethik* i., p. 515.

[49] *Doctrine of Sin*, vol. i., p. 114.

[50] *Jewish Quarterly Review*, October 1888, p. 55, where Professor Schechter finds himself compelled to discuss the question whether a man may be a good Jew and yet deny the existence of God.

[51] For an illustration of the way in which land-hunger and the rush to satisfy it operates on men, see the account of "The Invasion of Oklahoma" (a territory lately thrown open to occupation in the United States), *Spectator*, April 27th, 1889.

[52] *The Caliphate*, by Sir William Muir, p. 185.

[53] *Central and Eastern Arabia*, vol. i., p. 373.

[54] This shows how precarious the fundamental principle of much new criticism is. The non-observance of rites laid down as Divine commands, and the appearance of ancient superstitions such as the worship of the dead at any period, are held sufficient in the history of Israel to prove that monotheism did not then exist, and that ancestor-worship was then the prevailing cult. If applied to Islam that principle would lead to utterly false conclusions. Is there any reason for thinking that it may not give similar results when applied to the history of Israel?

[55] Driver, *Notes on Hebrew Text of the Books of Samuel*, p. 101, note.

[56] Cf. Dillmann, *Exodus and Leviticus*, p. 634.

[57] Mozley's *Lectures on the Old Testament*, p. 102.

[58] Driver, *Notes on the Hebrew Text of the Books of Samuel*, p. 101.

[59] Riehm, *Old Testament Theology*, p. 98.

[60] *The Social Movements of the Age*, by Professor Pearson, Melbourne Church Congress, 1882.

[61] Vide Church's *Spenser*, p. 16.

[62] *Memoirs of Colonel Hutchinson*, by his wife.

[63] *History of Rome*, vol. iv., Part II., p. 467.

[64] *Contemporary Review*, August 1893 p. 293.

[65] *"Heures d'Histoire."*

[66] Cf. Lange, *Geschichte des Materialismus*, vol. ii., pp. 510, 528.

[67] Chap. x. 12.

[68] *Old Testament in Jewish Church*, 2nd edition, p. 308.

[69] *Cathedral Sermons*, p. 26.

[70] Ritschl's *Rechtfertigung und Versöhnung*, vol. ii., pp. 311 ff.

[71] Cf. Riehm, *Old Testament Theology*, p. 25.

[72] Wellhausen, *History*, p. 420.

[73] Luke xiv. 26.

[74] *Ency. Brit.*, vol. xxi., p. 138.

[75] Tupper, *Our Indian Protectorate*, p. 248.

[76] *Commentary on Pentateuch*, vol. i., p. 448.

[77] *The Old Testament in the Jewish Church*, p. 366.

[78] *Religion of the Semites*, p. 304.

[79] *Ibid.*, p. 306.

[80] Smith's *Dictionary of the Bible*, vol. iii. p. 1589.

[81] Dillmann, *Deuteronomy*, p. 483.

[82] This, of course, does not show that P must have been known to D, but it proves that as regards material P and D have drawn from the same source, and that older documents, or customs at least, underlie both.

[83] Tupper, *Our Indian Protectorate*, pp. 248, 249.

[84] *Ibid.*, p. 321.

[85] Kuenen, *H. K. O.*, Eerste Deel, p. 113.

[86] The same conclusion must be come to in connection with the sanitary duties of the priesthood as laid down, or rather as alluded to, in Deut. xxiv. 8, 9. This implies that the Levitical priests had special duties in connection with such matters, duties which, if not precisely the same as those laid down in the Law of Leprosy (Lev. xiii., xiv.), must have nearly resembled them. Semi-medical skill must have been necessary for

the satisfactory discharge of these duties, and we must suppose that the priests who discharged them were selected from the tribe of Levi on some principle either of special proved knowledge and fitness, or on the ground of hereditary devotion to such work.

[87] *History of Israel*, p. 145.

[88] Cf. also Muirhead, article "Roman Law," in *Ency. Brit.*, vol. xx. p. 669, 2nd col., and Ramsay, *Church in Roman Empire*, p. 190.

[89] Rägelsbach, *Homerische Theologie*, p. 198.

[90] Exod. xxiv. 5.

[91] Exod. xxxiii. 11.

[92] Cf. Kittel's *Geschichte der Hebräer*, II., p. 63.

[93] Cf. Exod. xxxii. 15-20.

[94] Only two in any one law; Lev. xviii. 21, xix. 26, 31, xx. 6, 27.

[95] *Lehrbuch der Alt-Testamentlichen Religion's Geschichte*, pp. 169 ff.

[96] *Prophecy and History in Relation to the Messiah*, p. 150.

[97] Cf. Numb. xxvi. 53-55 from P and Josh. xvii. 14 ff. from JE.

[98] The questions connected with the jubilee year are numerous and intricate, and it may be for ever impossible, from lack of data, to decide at what period in Israelite history it originated, or whether it was ever actually observed; but it undoubtedly expressed the spirit of the Israelite legislation and customary law at all times. It is the natural culmination of tendencies and ideas which were always present. That it is not mentioned in Deuteronomy at all is surprising, if it had been previously to Manasseh's day embodied either in custom or in law; yet, on the other hand, there are references in Ezekiel and other exilic books which are almost unintelligible except on the supposition that the jubilee year was a perfectly well-known institution (cf. Jer. xxxiv. 8 ff.; Ezek. vii. 12 f.; Ezek. xlvi. 16 ff.; Isa. lxi. 1 ff.). It is referred to in a merely allusive way, which implies that every hearer or reader of the prophetic warnings would know at once the full scope and meaning of the reference. Now, had the jubilee year been unknown before the Exile, had it been introduced by the author of Lev. xxv. just before Ezekiel, no such assumption could have been made. It would, therefore, seem necessary to suppose that the ordinance for a jubilee year must have existed in pre-exilic time; for, strange as Deuteronomy's silence in regard to it is, the *argumentum e silentio* cannot weigh against indications of a positive kind, were they even fainter than those we have in regard to this matter.

[99] Cf. Kübel, *Die sociale und wirthschaftliche Gesetzgebung des Alten Testaments* p. 47.

[100] *Prophets of Israel*, p. 88.

[101] Cf. Jer. xxxiv. 8 ff.

[102] Cf. Amos ii. 6 ff.

[103] Neh. v. 1 seq.

[104] *Contemp. Rev.*, 1880, April, p. 681.

[105] *Essays on Political Economy*, p. 201.

[106] Wallace, *Land Nationalisation*, p. 16.

[107] See *ante*, p. 304.

[108] Cf. *Oud-Israël Rechtswezen*, pp. 10 ff.

[109] Cf. Doughty, *Arabia Deserta*, vol. i., p. 249.

[110] Cf. Nowack, *Die sozialen Probleme in Israel*, p. 5.

[111] Oort, *Oud-Israël Rechtswezen*, p. 14.

[112] A probable parallel to these may be found in the non-official arbiters mentioned by Doughty, *Arabia Deserta*, vol. i. pp. 145 and 502-3.

[113] Doughty, vol. i., p. 249.

[114] Riehm, *Handwörterbuch*, Baethgen, vol. i., p. 463.

[115] Cf. Renan, *Philosophic Dialogues*, iii. p. 26: "La nature a intérêt à ce que la femme soit chaste et à ce que l'homme ne le soit pas trop. De là un ensemble d'opinions qui couvre d'infamie la femme non chaste, et frappe presque de ridicule l'homme chaste. Et l'opinion quand elle est profonde, obstinée, c'est la nature même."

[116] Cf. 1 Sam. xxv. 18 ff; 2 Sam. xiv. 1 ff.

[117] Cf. Exod. xv. and 1 Sam. xviii. 6 f.

[118] Chap. xxii. 13-18.

[119] Hosea ii. 19.

[120] *The Primitive Family*, Starcke, p. 141.

[121] Indeed in India it was not only the widow of the childless man who might bear him a son whose real father was a near relation, but his childless wife also.—Maine, *Early Law*, p. 102.

[122] That the latter course may in some cases have been unpopular with the sonless man's nearest kin is clear, since under it the inheritance

must be divided, and it might pass to remoter connections, though not beyond the tribe. The nearer relations would, therefore, probably prefer that their brother's property should be kept intact and be transmitted with his name, and this ancient custom, sanctioned and modified by Mosaism, would give them that choice.

[123] Especially in some of the Southern Colonies in one of which this exposition is written.

[124] *Buddhism*, by T. W. Rhys Davids, p. 29.

[125] Sir W. Muir, *Caliphate*, pp. 26 and 33.

[126] Cf. Dillmann, *Deuteronomy*, pp. 178 ff.

[127] Le *Deuteronome* (Toulouse, 1891), pp. 62-75. The order in which he disposes of the verses is as follows: Deut. xxxi. 24-29, xxix. 1-15, iv. 1, 2, xxix. 16-21, iv. 3-30, xxix. 22-28, iv. 30, 31, xxx. 1-10, iv. 32-40, xxx. 11-20, xxxii. 45-47. If before this we place xxxi. 1-13, we shall probably have the original sequence fully restored.

[128] Cf. Recent fiction, *e.g. The African Farm, Tess of the D'Urbevilles, The Heavenly Twins*.

[129] *A Year Among the Persians*, E. G. Browne, p. 406.

[130] The song is described, in the narrative framework, as delivered through Moses to the children of Israel. On the other hand, internal evidence points to a date after the establishment of the monarchy—when the days of Moses and the events of the wilderness were old, when the fruits of the land were gifts of God in present use, and when ingratitude and rebellion had become conspicuous, so that judgment was impending. Either, then, Moses took his stand, in the spirit, at a point of time long subsequent to his own death, adapted the song to its circumstances, and spoke not to his own generation but to one much later; or a later prophet must be the writer. The objection to the former view is supported by arguments drawn from various features in the language and the allusions of the song, which are asserted to be indicative of the later origin. On the detail of these we cannot dwell. But the most interesting part of the argument is the position that the transference of the prophetic consciousness to a remote future period, in order to give hope and guidance to a generation not the prophet's own, is too improbable to be admitted.

Such a process is now generally regarded as not impossible indeed, but unheard of in the history of prophecy. The examination of the prophets of the Old Testament has convinced students that the prophet's vision starts from his own time, and is primarily for the comfort and warning of his contemporaries. His words may have a more remote reference, but must have the nearer one. Hence Isa. xl.-lxvi. is now ascribed to a prophet or prophets of the Exile. The principle is really the same as that which determines the authorship of Deut. xxxiv. 5-12. No one now holds the view of some Jews, that Moses by the spirit of prophecy wrote this himself. Yet if Moses could in a poem address his people as sinning and suffering through rebellions induced by their prosperity in Canaan, which they had not entered when he died, one might as well believe him to describe his own decease. In both cases we have to suppose the mind of Moses transported to a period when he had been removed by death, that he might look back upon and speak of events which when he wrote were still future. Now in both cases a reason is lacking. Every one accepts the view that since Joshua or Eleazar was there to write the account of Moses' death, it is unlikely the lawgiver should have been inspired to write it himself. Just so, since Yahweh inspired new prophets at every crisis of His people's history, it seems unlikely that the spirit of Moses should be transferred to, and made at home in, the circumstances of a distant generation, in order to deliver to it a message which could have been made known by a prophet to whom the time was present. Neither Kamphausen nor Oettli nor Dillmann nor the English expositors who accept the non-Mosaic authorship of the song have any doubt as to the supernatural character of prophecy. They found upon observations as to the manner of Old Testament prophecy, which ought to regulate interpretation.

According to critical views the ascription to Moses of the reception and delivery of this song was taken by the Deuteronomist from JE. Kautzsch supposes that an editor to whom the song was known as passing under the name of Moses may have inserted it. Dillmann suggests grounds for believing that several prayers and poems ascribed to Moses (including Psalm xc.) were in circulation in prophetic circles in the Northern Kingdom, and that this one of them was inserted here as its appropriate place. The case would be parallel to the ascription of various later Psalms to David. Compare also the discussions as to the song of Hannah, 1 Sam. ii.

The view that a mistake as to the Mosaic authorship, for which the writers of JE were not responsible, was handed on in perfect good faith, is compatible with the doctrine of inspiration as held by representatives of the orthodox Evangelical school in Germany, and by the newer Evangelicals in England. Cf. Oettli, *Deuteronomy*, p. 22, and Sanday's *Bampton Lecture*.

[131] Cf. Driver's *Introduction*, 5th edition, p. 340.

[132] Cf. Driver, *cit. loc.*

[133] The blessing of Moses was certainly not written by the author of Deuteronomy: the vocabulary and the style are different from his. Nor

probably was the poem inserted here by him, but rather by the final editor of the Pentateuch who is believed to have brought these closing chapters into their present shape (cf. Chap. XXIV.). The authority on which he relied may have been E.

As to the authorship of the blessing, Volck and Keil ascribe it to Moses. The great majority of recent students regard it, at all events in its present form, as post-Mosaic, on grounds drawn from features in the poem, and from the principles of prophetic exegesis referred to in the note (p. 452). Opinions differ much as to the date to be assigned, varying from the time of David to that of Jeroboam II. The general assumption is that the blessing is the work of a Northern Israelite; and the feeling for the tribes of Levi and Judah which it embodies is the chief indication on which a conjecture can be hazarded. That would agree with a date later than Solomon and not later than Jehoshaphat—a period when many in the Northern Kingdom still looked with reverence to the sanctuary at Jerusalem, and when the Northern Levites still resented the intrusion by Jeroboam of a mixed multitude into the priesthood.

As to form, and partly as to contents, the blessing of Moses is modelled on the blessing of Jacob (Gen. xlix). One conspicuous difference is the introduction into that before us of a prose heading before most of the sections, analogous to the headings which appear in Arabic poetry (as the *Hamasa*) before each quatrain or longer poem. There is no ground for treating these as later insertions, nor for separating other portions, as some have proposed, as later than the main composition.

[134] Dillmann, *Deuteronomy*, p. 420.

[135] Baethgen's Riehm, *Handwörterbuch*, p. 1321.

[136] "Moses' God," *British Weekly*, February 2, 1893.

[137] *Convito of Dante*, Morley's *Universal Library*, Introduction, pp. 6 ff.